HUMANISTIC PSYCHOLOGY: A SOURCE BOOK

Edited by
I. David Welch
George A. Tate
Fred Richards

Ю Prometheus Books
1203 Kensington Avenue
Buffalo, New York 14215

Published by Prometheus Books
1203 Kensington Avenue, Buffalo, New York 14215

Library of Congress Catalog Card Number 77-90497
ISBN 0-87975-103-7   Cloth

Printed in the United States of America

This book is dedicated to

Arthur W. Combs
Sidney M. Jourard
Earl C. Kelley
Abraham H. Maslow
Carl R. Rogers

Pioneers of modern humanistic psychology

CONTENTS

Education

SECTION IV.   PHYSICAL ENVIRONMENT 281

Ecology

Science

Medicine, Dying and Death

SECTION V.   POLITICAL/ECONOMIC SYSTEMS 389

Business, Industry and Management

Politics and Government

FOREWORD

In the fall of 1951, when Abraham Maslow and I came together to form the psychology department of the then Brandeis University in Waltham, Massachusetts, we sought to re-expand psychology to its original and wider dimensions and concerns. We decided to call our emphasis "general psychology," one acknowledging the whole range of human experience and expression previously recognized and explored by early psychologists such as Wilhelm Wundt and William James. This larger view of psychology remained the dominant theme at Brandeis for almost two decades while we continued our work there. During this time, a few other programs around the country began to move in the same direction as Brandeis. It was also at this time that the term "humanistic psychology" was coined to describe this increasing concern of psychologists with all aspects of what it means to be human.

In the forties and fifties, many psychologists in academic institutions around the country viewed the early beginnings of humanistic or Third Force psychology as a radical departure from mainstream or traditional psychology. Few recognized that humanistic psychology was a "conservative" but creative thrust to re-emphasize the traditional or original concern of psychology with the whole person. With the exception of the so-called applied areas of psychology, psychology's domain had shrunk to eliminate almost any area of concern which could not be worked out with laboratory rats or harmless experiments on college sophomores. This narrow view of the field led Kurt Goldstein to call it "a psychology of desperate rats." Maslow, commenting on the psychology of the forties and fifties, was moved to ask, "but where is love, decency, values, honesty, truth, or integrity?"

A recent review of one hundred years of experimental work with memory of nonsense syllables suggests that much research produced little of worth. The review concludes that we now know a lot more about nonsense syllables than we previously knew, but little more about memory. Indeed, memory was lacking in those psychologists who, coming to view the human being as a simple mechanism or as an animal, behaved as if unaware of psychology's original focus on personal experience and social phenomena. They seemed more preoccupied with nonsense than human problems. The nonsense and human irrelevance evident in the vast bulk of experimental efforts prompted Maslow to remark, "What isn't worth doing isn't worth doing well."

Yet the bulk of academic work and study in psychology ignored Maslow's insight. Rat studies virtually replaced comparative concerns calling for a wide variety of animal subjects. Such studies, of course, were cheaper. Most academics paid for the early research out of their own pockets, or out of the pay of their professors. Who, for example, could afford ten dogs or monkeys during the Depression, the war years and the early post-war years? The domain of psychology became the Skinner box, the T-maze, or the straight runway. Certainly, this was an economical, practical, and manageable way for academics to practice psychology. Unfortunately, as more and more psychologists would come to recognize, such a psychology had little to do with (or to contribute to) human beings.

It was probably the cultural climate created by the Depression and war and its attendant anxieties that caused psychology to shrink to the narrow concerns of academia. As previously suggested, the easy, if not relevant, research on rats and students gave a pseudojustification to such concerns. Published research piled up in the easy, if non-relevant, areas and actually increased the academic power of those willing to do it over the few who preferred the more painstaking results of complex, long-term research. (At the University of Michigan it took two years to conduct a good experiment on large maze learning with seasoned animals, while at Indiana University or Yale a few weeks sufficed for T-maze or Skinner box techniques.)

The crypto-Marxist results of such research re-established a truism of reward and possible punishment but ignored "values" or the creative learning implicit in large maze problems. This cheapened research won the day for publications, prestige and positions in psychology during the hard-pressed thirties and forties. Further, many of those left in academia during the war and the cold war aftermath continued to justify themselves by such pseudoaccountability. In academic departments where they dominated, they tried to deny a voice to other considerations and concerns by censorship. Today, nationally and even professionally, these psychologists are a minority—though one still holding power by dogmatic methods, intolerance, and a refusal to change in order to deal with the critical problems facing humankind.

The experience at Brandeis University is a case in point. The changes undertaken by Maslow and myself in the department of psychology at Brandeis were not disguised efforts to ignore or abandon the more traditional offerings of academic psychology. Ironically, the effort to provide such courses resulted in the eventual elimination of the humanistic emphasis. Maslow, myself, and others, attempting to cover as much of psychology as possible, took in large numbers of people from varied fields. The very first were experimental in the best sense, even exploratory and field-oriented (empirical). As these persons went on to high-paying positions elsewhere, their replacements felt less inclined to explore, were more laboratory and test-oriented. The latter soon outnumbered the founders. And, while we saw the value of their research, they could not or would not reciprocate. As their demands for exactitude influenced the graduate students more and more, few students, indeed none, were willing to risk the more complex, more relevant issues. In Maslow's last years no student would risk working with him in view of the narrowness of their concerns and the probable evaluations of the rest of the faculty. Maslow went on leave and moved to Palo Alto in 1968. The following year I journeyed to West Georgia College to join Myron Arons and others in creating a new program in humanistic psychology.

Though the minority of psychologists I described above still prevails in most departments of psychology, an increasing number of psychologists, particularly over the past few decades, has continued to move psychology in more person-centered directions. The consequences of this re-focus on the person has sparked an explosion in psychology of concerns that, in the beginning, were more accurately or sensitively addressed by fiction, theater and film than by "official" psychology. The individual as active participant rather than passive object—whether as student or as subject in experimental research—emerged to such an extent that even those most familiar with techniques like hypnosis, for example, considered the vast accumulation of so-called scientific data virtually worthless, since it had been so tainted by suggestion from the experimenter and the student's or paid subject's desire to please. The subjects in experimental research, more often treated in the past as objects, began to emerge as persons.

It followed that if any research was a cooperative effort of subject and researcher, research needed to move in the direction of phenomenology, existentialism, and oriental complexity. Sidney Jourard spoke for many psychologists when he said that more and more it was evident that experimental research, if it were to contribute significantly to our understanding of human beings, had to be grounded in dialogue between experimenter and subject. Anne C. Richards, as did others, called for a re-examination of past theoretical assumptions, a re-appraisal of experimental designs, and a search for more adequate approaches to understanding human behavior. Humanistic theory and practice, she wrote, could provide valuable and viable alternatives to psychologists seeking a non-mechanistic approach to conducting research.

Consequently a growing number of psychologists came to agree that the former emphasis of nineteenth-century, direct mechanical manipulation was at best naïve and probably fallacious as well. Research at its best was a "slice of life" rather than a scientific enterprise to be kept pure and uncontaminated in the laboratory setting. In education, psychotherapy, and psychological research, a new paradigm or model was coming into focus. More and more this new paradigm was being described as holistic, humanistic, perceptual or phenomenological—as person-centered.

One of the major achievements of Maslow's and/or humanistic psychology of the fifties and sixties was also the focus upon the "healthy personality" to describe the optimal end of human development or growth. What many believed to be urgently needed in this century was a new image of the person, a new conception of what human beings can become. Over the years humanistic psychologists have variously described this human potential as increased personal adequacy, self-actualization, the fully-functioning person, the transparent self. While their descriptions have varied, they have sought an understanding of human nature going beyond the limitations of the image of man contained in the psychoanalytical and behavioristic psychologies.

Maslow's early work on the self-actualizing personality had disclosed the strength of holding relatively positive values in comparison to the deficiency of the want/need orientation of the average person. In an attempt to formulate a theory of human motivation for the individual as an integrated or organized whole, Maslow proposed a hierarchy of basic needs. The hierarchy of basic needs—physiological needs, safety needs, the needs for belongingness and love, esteem needs and the need for self-actualization—can be viewed as a pyramid with the more basic needs forming the large base and the higher needs emerging at the top. The peak experience was the culmination. Seen by Maslow as experiences of awe, self-sufficiency, playfulness and wonder, peak experiences are those moments in which life is experienced as full of meaning and purpose.

In his later years, Maslow began to explore a whole new list of needs related to self-actualization which he described as growth or Being needs in contrast to deficiency needs. In the self-actualizing personality, the so-called deficiency needs were seen to give way more and more to positive Being-values. As they were satisfied, the basic needs became relatively inactive or functionally absent as forces of motivation. Thus, the need for self-actualization became more active and capable of fulfillment as the basic needs were met. The self-actualizing personality became increasingly motivated by such higher needs as the needs for truth, goodness and beauty. This meta-motivation, as Maslow termed it, found its best expression in those self-actualizing persons who, more than most, could be described as spontaneous, natural and free. Such persons were motivated by a movement toward wholeness, completion, simplicity, honesty and justice.

During the last years of his life Maslow defined normalcy in terms of these Being-values and cognitions, an almost neo-Kantian emphasis on experience in and of itself. That is, each experience stood on its own feet; the mountains are mountains and the trees are trees, as D. T. Suzuki loved to phrase it. To the harried householder, it was "one thing after another"; to the naturalist it was the immense variety that was nature. Maslow's "peak" became a range, a way of being in the world, a plateau that included, it seemed to him, the so-called basic needs as simply some among the many needs of whole human beings. Such a conception of motivation made more comprehensible those persons who, while sacrificing so much of the basic comforts of life, had held on to their creative visions, findings and insights. It is equally significant when we attempt to understand and experience this process of self-actualization in a world now faced with a scarcity rather than an abundance of many resources.

Many academic psychologists viewed such theorizing as an irresponsible deviation from the hard-nosed, tough-minded approach of what they considered valid psychological inquiry. Outside the walls of Academe, however, many saw in Maslow's conception of human motivation a description of the desired outcomes of education and psychotherapy. As Frank Goble was to point out, Maslow's "theory of human motivation can be applied to almost every aspect of individual or social life." The larger view of human nature in humanistic psychology paralleled, to varying degrees, the new image of the person motivating other revolutionary movements such as the civil rights movement, the black revolution, women's liberation, the sexual revolution and so on. In each case, an expanded view of the rights and potentials of human beings urged them on. Similarly, the emergence of the new image of the person prompted many to explore and question what kind of society or community might best promote the health and well-being of its members. Medicine, economics, politics, marriage—these human institutions and many more were re-perceived in terms of this new understanding of the healthy, self-actualizing person.

Back in 1963 James Bugental recognized the impact that humanistic psychology was having upon not only the field of psychology but the culture at large. In an address, he told his audience that "a major breakthrough is occuring right now in psychology. . . . I think we are on the verge of a new era in man's concern about man which may—if allowed to run its course—produce as profound changes in the human condition as those we have seen the physical sciences bring about in the past century." Humanistic psychology, emerging as a protest against the limited perspectives of mainstream psychology, was becoming, as Carl Rogers said it must, a positive force seeking to "discover constructive resolutions for some terribly perplexing problems." Further, many departments of psychology, perhaps hundreds, are learning to respond to the pressure of both students and employers to educate persons adequately for the task of living creative, effective lives in a world bearing little resemblance to the mechanistic model of reality espoused by mainstream academic psychology. Presently these departments, teachers and students of psychology are having to face the challenge of choosing between a narrow understanding of the field of psychology, or one that will contribute to humankind's capacity to survive this century. Thus these departments are recognizing the need to include as part of their offerings courses in humanistic psychology, particularly those in which the humanistic perspective is applied to the problems and crises of our time.

Humanistic Psychology: A Source Book is designed for such courses. A significant contribution of this volume is the humanistic perspective it brings to an understanding of the revolutionary changes taking place not only in psychology but in health care, marriage, social organization, economics, politics, and many other areas as well. This humanistic focus is of great importance to students in psychology who desire to apply their knowledge and understanding to solving human or people-oriented problems. The volume is important also to those who struggle to find meaning and personal direction within our cultural malaise. While it is an excellent book for both graduate and undergraduate courses in psychology, it could contribute as well to courses in sociology, political science, education, and other disciplines. Finally, it is a valuable text for persons in the helping professions—teachers, counselors, ministers, nurses and others who recognize they are working with persons rather than objects or things.

The editors of this volume bring to the task a variety of experiences and qualifications. All, personally and professionally, have been involved for many years in the humanist movement.

David Welch has written widely in the areas of humanistic psychology and education. A member of the Department of Psychology, Counseling and Guidance at the University of Northern Colorado, Dr. Welch is a past president of the Colorado chapter of the Association for Humanistic Psychology, a charter member of the Association for Humanistic Education and on the editorial staff of its journal, and a founder and core faculty member of the Council for Humanistic Learning and Research, an interdisciplinary, innovative program in higher education at the University of Northern Colorado.

George Tate had worked in the field of mental health for twenty years before joining the Department of Psychology, Counseling and Guidance at the University of Northern Colorado. A past director of the Malcolm X Center for Mental Health in Denver, Colorado, he continues to explore the use of radical modalities for conducting psychotherapy with oppressed/minority persons. Dr. Tate is also the first and still one of the few psychologists to have addressed humanistic psychology to the experience and concerns of black persons in America.

Fred Richards, with a background in psychology, literature, religion, and education, has contributed to psychology's search for a new image of human potential and to the possible impact this new image may or can have upon education, counseling and social/political change. A past member of the Department of Psychology at West Georgia College, one of the few departments offering a graduate program in humanistic psychology, Dr. Richards is presently director of the Foundation for Person-Centered Projects and Research in Carrollton, Georgia.

These are times of great change and crises, what the Chinese wisely saw as times of both opportunity and danger. Humanistic psychology is grounded in the belief that humankind has the potential to respond effectively to such crises, that human beings have the capacity to live with integrity and dignity in the face of danger and to grasp the opportunity to create a more human world. It is imperative that we do so. It is urgent that psychology, as a science of persons, become a positive and relevant part of our response to this great challenge. This book is an expression of such a response.

James B. Klee

PREFACE

This is a book that tries to capture the influences that humanistic psychology has had on many fields of endeavor. It is a book that goes back to some of the early writings in the humanistic psychology movement, gives some perspective on those early years, and moves into the present with some of the most up-to-date writing in developing areas of concern for people.

It came about because the three of us became increasingly aware that our field, psychology, was only one of many in which humanistic ideas and concerns were finding a place. But, the problem was that the writings were scattered throughout the literature and required a search. Much of it could be lost, except to the most dedicated reader. Most of us, because we are specialists of one sort or another, do not venture into the unknown fields of other specialities. If one is a psychologist, for example, the medical literature or the political science literature is often not of much interest. The problem is that a movement as large as the humanistic movement is not confined to a single discipline. What we in psychology were considering as a psychological movement has in fact turned out to be more widespread. The German word *Zeitgeist* means something like, "the times we live in." The times we live in are becoming increasingly concerned with human questions. The human questions touch every one of us no matter what our discipline is. The service we have performed for you is to search the literature for you so that in a single place you may become quickly aware of the impact the humanistic position is having on many facets of life. If you share the humanistic point of view and feel that you are alone, then do not despair. There are many who share similar concerns.

This book is a sampler. It is not meant to present all of the ideas of the humanistic movement, nor is it meant to present all of the ideas in a particular discipline. It has holes in it as well. Sections such as Education and Medicine could in themselves provide enough material for a book, rather than a section to catalog the new developments in their respective fields. This is not an apology. It is a teaser. If you are excited by any of the readings in this book, then recognize that there is more. We invite you to search it out.

No book comes into print through the efforts of two or three people alone. In this case, we are indebted to the authors whose writings we have used and to the journals which have allowed us to reprint the material. These journals are cited individually on the first page of each article. Paul Kurtz, Elizabeth King, Lee Nisbet, and Barbara Bergstrom of Prometheus Books have been considerate and conscientious throughout the process, and have become colleagues through the mail and telephone.

This book gives you the gift of the thoughts and feelings of many dedicated people. As the editors, we invite you to profit from them—to learn and to grow.

I. D. W.
G. A. T.
F. R.

SECTION I
THE EMERGENCE OF
HUMANISTIC
PSYCHOLOGY

THE HUMANIST PERSPECTIVE

James B. Klee

At the moment the humanist banner might best be thought of as an umbrella under which many dissatisfied spirits have found refuge. It has not as yet developed one specific slogan or stance. On the positive side its multipleness may be its primary virtue but not one exclusive to it. The multicolored Buddhist banner might best serve as an example. (I hope it never becomes as exclusive as some of its antecedents.) It ranges in depth from the profundity of a Rollo May, Henry Murray, or A. H. Maslow to the latest public titillations of the groupie. Like most growing edges humanistic psychology contains more individuals each doing his thing than people doing a specific program on which all members agree. Yet some methodological trends are now discernible among at least a plurality of its members. It has two journals under its auspices, one the official *Journal of Humanistic Psychology,* the other, *The Journal of Transpersonal Psychology.* Both were founded by Anthony Sutich without whose efforts many of us would still be just unhappy "loners." It has some fringe allies such as *Trans-action. Manas* has done a great deal to give stature to the intellectual aspects of the movement and moral support to its members.

As for its leaders one thinks more of the Titans of the Greek pantheon than of either of the later gods or the more Christian hierarchy of angels under a single monarch, "the Lawd." Indeed I am tempted to cast my net so wide as to cover a number of individuals who might not dream of classifying themselves as psychologists (much less humanistic ones) yet who have had a great effect upon the lives of many of the recognized leaders. One might even say that humanistic psychology has received its impetus and inspiration more from developments outside of psychology than from within.

SOURCE: Presented to discussion group members concerned with: Perspectives on the Subject Matter of Psychology, Division 24, American Psychological Association, Miami Beach, Florida, September 6, 1970.

3

Part of its romantic adventuring comes not only from its partial rejection both of and by "official" psychology but also from its welcome and new opportunity outside psychology, in those areas of human endeavor heretofore neglected by the "official line" if indeed psychology can be so characterized. The recent election of A. H. Maslow, one of our Titans, as president of the American Psychological Association, reflects the strong support he received from social psychology, education and the more progressive aspects of the business community, in addition to that furnished by those "straight" souls who admire his published researches in the areas of Personality and Comparative Social Psychology. Yet I do not think of humanistic psychology as an *applied* science. Indeed the word *applied* misses the primary effort that characterizes most of its participants.

I. First let me try to describe some of the living strands that have woven themselves together to form the movement. Perhaps first and foremost was a growing concern with the individual's place in the scheme of things as seen by psychologists at the end of World War II. The "hurry up and wait" characteristic of much postwar or wartime research was a function of problems which had to be solved or to which psychologists felt they could make a contribution. Often goals were fixed by the needs of the war or the financial and material limitations of the laboratories. Only means or instruments were potentially variable.

Man became largely an object of research. Even in the rat world the "Snark had become a Boojum" according to Frank Beach and was more a validation device than a living animal in its own right. The white rat disappeared as a participant and became only a part of the computer circuit. Animals, from a breeding house and often newly obtained fresh from American Railway Express platforms, were starved to three quarters or two thirds of their body weight to insure adequate "motivation." When it is remembered that these rats were two to three months old, "teen-agers" in the human time scale, at the onset of the experimentation (to have waited longer would have increased laboratory costs), it is no wonder Kurt Goldstein, another of our Titans, could characterize our efforts as the "psychology of desperate rats." It was very desperate indeed. We were as inhumane in our animal experiments as the Nazis. We used no humans but the urgency of the Depression, war, and postwar years made frightful treatment of subhumans plausible beyond its shabby subhuman-ness. (I know, I did it too.)

Kurt Goldstein's emphasis on self-actualization as characteristic even of his brain-damaged patients did much to help break us loose. That a brain-injured man did his best despite the injury, that he pulled what remained together for a new organization of behavior, that he could be seen as not *just* a victim of damaged brain mechanics was Goldstein's contribution. Carl Rogers, another Titan, also recognized the participation of the individual in the therapeutic process to a degree that went far beyond the beginning recognition given by psychoanalysis. Rogers had studied Otto Rank via the social work school of Jessie Taft at Pennsylvania. Rank emphasized the creative role of the individual to a degree far beyond the victimized individual Freud had described. Rank's observations that "most people are not even neurotic yet," and that beyond neurosis lay creativity helped emphasize the individual's creative role. Maslow was similarly responsive to Alfred Adler's "individual psychology" with its emphasis on the participant individual. Similarly Horney, Sullivan, and Fromm saw the individual as more responsive to the social milieu. Hence the growth of ego psychology among the New York and Washington groups of neo-Freudians.

Although slower to appear, Jung's shadow also began to grow on the American scene, not within academic psychology directly, but through the efforts of those who would study mythology and especially man's participation in its creation. Jung had the courage to accept most of man's symbolic creations as more than just symptoms of underlying illness. Indeed he helped in the restoration of man's greatest achievements, his art, religion, and science, to the creative edge of man's development. But few psychologists accepted Jung until the last decade. Instead he came in from the wings via Ernest Cassirer's magnificent study of symbolization and the more recent efforts of Northrop Frye and Joseph Campbell. Henry Murray is another original. Although to a degree focused in the popular interpretations more on diagnostic procedures, nevertheless the breadth of his interests encouraged many of his students towards more imaginative interpretations of man and his participant place in the scheme of things. Here his confessed "polytheism" is and was most important in the continuity of James's pluralism so basic to humanistic psychology. Allport here helped too. His notion of participation inspired one of Robert Ardrey's finest novels, *World's Beginning*, a book that got to many of us after the Titans.

A. L. Kroeber, Clyde Kluckhohn, Margaret Mead and Ruth Benedict also are part of the picture, especially insofar as they helped many of us in our timid need to be objective by giving us human behavior in forms sufficiently strange that we could continue to be timidly "objective." Behavior as described by the anthropologist was not as embarrassing to face as the everyday behavior around us. Few of us had, or even have now, sufficient detached perspective to see what is before our eyes. But Mead could talk about human behavior as could Kroeber and some of the other anthropologists, and a psychological anthropology more loving and accepting of man, more descriptive than analytic, began to emerge. (I still count Leslie White's anthropology courses which I audited at Michigan as valuable as any psychology course I ever had.) These are great people and like great people they never demeaned their "people" to the mechanical robots many of us have passed off as a description of man.

Other extrapsychological contributions came from existentialism and phenomenology. Although basically inherent in the work of Kurt Lewin and Kurt Koffka, the *phenomenological* reduction or "bracketing" of the subject-object dichotomy (Koffka's behavioral world or Lewin's field) helped break through the exaggerated emphasis on the subject-object differentiation. To suddenly not have that separating block but to have "participation" (mystique or otherwise) made it possible to break through that Lockean hangup in a way that went beyond even sensation, perception, or what is euphemistically called today "cognition."

The rigid subject-object separation had grown out of learning theory despite J. R. Kantor's efforts and dominated much of our epistemological thinking. Even B. F. Skinner's emphasis on the *selectivity* of operant conditioning rather than some "accumulative" Locke-like theory of learning failed to break this set for most psychologists. Reinforcement is too often seen as an external event only. But once over the subject-object differentiation we could once again talk to people about their experiences and at their level without feeling we were talking down to them. Other people regained a degree of equality in participation and were liberated from the expertise to which the profession had begun to pretend, sometimes without a shred of humor. We could not take notes on *their* problems (often our own) as participant observers without pretending to an objectivity and disinterest beyond human capacity.

Another strand was the reappearance of oriental philosophy on our doorstep. According to Walter Van Meter Ames much of the more secular forms of Confucianism, Buddhism, especially *Zen*, and Taoism had interested and influenced those early humanists, Emerson, Thoreau, and later William James and John Dewey. (Perhaps James is of true *God* status in our pantheon. He did it all with sheer common sense before he abandoned our "dirty little science.") But the newer form of orientalia fleshed out phenomenology with its very human presentations of fable and folklore and especially wisdom literature.

The Titans here for the younger members of our fraternity were D. T. Suzuki, J. Krishnamurti and Alan Watts. All were without status either in Buddhism, Hinduism or the academic community respectively. Yet each stimulated an awareness essentially experiential in nature that went far beyond the intellectual *purists* in either camp. Many others have since followed. Fromm's seminars in Cuernavaca did much to bring Suzuki to the psychologists' attention and Maslow similarly used him in his values symposium in Cambridge. Yet Watts, via the persuasive quality of his clear style, sold Zen and Taoism in a way that is almost miraculous. The sheer intrinsic clarity in his writing just made certain aspects of oriental philosophy really sing. The late Father Thomas Merton and R. H. Blythe, Christmas Humphreys and Archie Bahm all helped. They were more "respectable." But Watts broke the ice, thawed our frozen aesthetic sensibilities and released our reactions to the message. Indeed for many of us Watts made it our medium.

Other writers and thinkers made the new outlook even more appropriate. Paul Tillich's and Martin Buber's existential emphasis made much of the new materials and ways more livable, not only by direct contributions to understanding such unfashionable terms as being, faith, courage, and I-thou I-it distinctions but also by setting a frame of reference that made participation part of the whole and the individual's hopes more than just a level of aspiration.

All the foregoing groups, psychologists only in the more meaningful sense of the word, brought us together and reminded us of man's participant place in the world of nature not just as a collection of responses, conditioned or stimulated, and sensations, emotions, and cognitions. Meaning became less a dirty word. Man was of nature but man's formulations of nature as he saw it were also accepted as man's contributions for which he was responsible. And not responsible just for the accuracy of his calculated significant differences or controls, man was completely enmeshed as a part of the ecological totality. Few individuals have seen the ecological consequences of man's behavior as early as many of those mentioned above. Lewis Mumford, George R. Stewart, Marston Bates, Rachael Carson, Buckminster Fuller, Rene Dubos, and Loren Eiseley all penetrated the consciousness of the meaningfully concerned psychologist as part of his professional efforts, not just as affecting his "extracurricular" life as an individual.

The emphasis on this interaction, of course, was especially intensified in the social encounter. The encounter group and/or marathon are rapidly becoming in consequence the brand label of humanistic psychology and are bringing to it some of the aspects of a social movement. Our trade mark like the couch, the Skinner box, the ink blot, or the I.Q., will undoubtedly be the encounter group. Indeed some of the lesser but more enthusiastic members of the movement are, as in Gresham's law, in fair danger of driving out the Titans themselves in their single-minded discipleship. The AHP barely weathered the "groupies" in Washington in 1969.

I am painfully aware of the single-mindedness of the groupie in his enthusiasm to "actualize himself" into a "permanent peak experience." The drug cult, pot, and LSD certainly contributed its share to the seeking of pleasure or thrill to the exclusion of all else. Yet the encounter movement had very respectable beginnings in Lewin's group dynamics, Bronfenbrenner's social creativity projects, N. R. F. Maier's and others' emphasis on role playing in leadership training, and the sensitivity T-groups of the National Training Laboratories. These we hoped would unlock the protocol-frozen business and community encounters and confrontations so that more reasonable forms of interaction could develop. A recent paper by Argyris suggests that the actual efficaciousness of the procedure is beginning to wane, much as psychoanalysis had begun to mark time in its effectiveness. At least the early years of accelerating progress have peaked out and we now seem to be on a bit of a plateau.

In psychoanalysis, however, the enthusiasts continued to flourish and in their enthusiasm made psychoanalytic concepts the central concern of the cocktail hour, the tea party and the lover's tryst. So the encounter group has begun to furnish the social contact that bridge furnished before it was replaced by color television. To the degree it is a fad it will pass. Already Esalen has discontinued the week-end encounters of the suburban thrill seekers. If substantial and beneficial, something will remain of the "meaningful relations" it develops. Somehow I believe the work of Sid Jourard, Abe Maslow, to name but two, or Gardner Murphy who belongs to almost all factions will survive any nonsense that encounter groupings produce in their enthusiastic naïveté. Here only time will tell. And that sense of time brings us to the final and I believe the most important point in the development of humanistic psychology.

II. I believe it was the relation to time both as the concept and as the flow of history itself that gave humanistic psychology its prime reason for being. The straight psychologies in my experience had and have adopted the spatial-mechanical time of their stop watches and other timing devices. With the many exceptions such a broad generalization must make in all fairness to many individuals such as B. F. Skinner and his "cumulative record" we have as psychologists aimed more at the repetitive than the fact of the historical uniqueness of each moment of *time's arrow*. Some recognition in the clinical sense of the ideographic of Gordon Allport, of Robert White's "Lives in Progress" and many others has occurred. Some of this has a cyclical aspect to it as in Freud and Erikson. Yet one also senses a basic repeatableness in the cyclic emphasis especially in Freud not unlike that *intended* by the clock or calendar. This cyclic aspect is certainly used that way by the unthinking and unwary. The phases despite an "all at once" emergence in Freud's anthropology seem to have always been. Of course, Erikson's two historical ventures concerning Luther and Gandhi are more in the time-flow sense. There have been many names used to communicate this flowing sense of time in recent years. We could call it history, karma, destiny, duration (Bergson), "time's arrow." This flow concept is distinguishable from the repetitive (by definition) sense of past, present, and future.

Perhaps the problem may be best exemplified by the performing musician who drops a note yet carries on or who improvises his way through a miscue. In a sense he "fakes" it until he gets on the track again. Much music—jazz, the Indian raga, the incompletely written out classical music prior to but including Mozart—set a situation where the very essence of the performance was the improvisation. One could look at this as merely "time out" from the written piece, yet the primary thing was the *going on*, the continuity of the performance to which the "time out" was the written piece. The musician did not stop for corrections and start it all over again. He continued to play if necessary around the gap or lapse. What's more, much music did and still does provide for improvised performance. Each performance is a new adventure. When medicine is practiced as an *art* the doctor also must continuously improvise, "perform." Too many of us often feel only shame or guilt to go through a class hour that way little realizing that to the student, we are then at our best—for them.

What I am trying to say is that humanistic psychology began to develop where individuals could not wait for sufficient rehearsal to become letter-perfect before acting. It faced up to the important things of life, even if in but a rough-hewn way. It grew where research caused endless "time outs" while awaiting the really statistically significant valid answer. Waiting is appropriate where the problem faced is mainly a non-pressing but recurrent one. No one can totally live that way and very few people, even in the most traditional societies, ever actually did. In these traditional societies, the myth of a trickster, Pan, coyote, or Cupid developed to explain change. Our *re*search models with few exceptions, emphasized primarily the *re*peatable if only on the "wait till next time" basis of the Dodger fans of legend.

Humanistic psychology is more "deadline" conscious. It works at the creative edge of business or mental health. I do not mean it has a new way of obtaining highly *reliable* and *validated* data. Rather it *seeks* ways of meeting *now*-type problems of which there are always more than it can begin to handle. Many of its chief practitioners are consequently to be found on the fringe of the more enterprising and new business consulting concerns and social agencies. Rogers is now at the Western Institute for the Behavioral Sciences at La Jolla, which is primarily a consulting concern. Before his death Maslow had abandoned Brandeis and joined the McLaughlin Foundation. Indeed there are very few academic institutions which make any pretense of offering a program in the field. Somehow everything humanistic psychology stands for antagonizes the more research-oriented tried and true academic mentalities at least in the field of psychology.

Surprisingly, it is education which has seen some new hope in the field, this despite former emphasis on *re*petition and *re*producibility as its primary technique. Perhaps the growing unrest of student and teacher alike in the postwar years has much to do with this freer attitude now developing in educational circles. Of the three academic psychology programs now recognized at this writing as humanistic in nature, one at West Georgia College, Carrollton, Georgia, is in the division of education; the second, at United States International University, is leadership (business-social agency) oriented. Only the third at Sonoma State, California, is primarily in what was once a conventional psychology department. Most of the other programs, although growing, such as at Georgia State University, the University of Florida, West Florida University, and the University of Northern Colorado are hard-won partial programs built around a few outstanding individuals. They exist almost by virtue of the personal charisma and power of those individuals. The former partial program at Brandeis virtually collapsed when Maslow left. A similar project in the Brandeis sociology department has been under a continual attack that even threatened "investigations" into the department, especially by other members of the various social science departments, for what was deemed unscientific and unscholarly. By not conforming to the promise of seemingly endless repetitions characteristic of so much academic research, humanistic psychology seems very much an illegitimate enterprise.

In my own experience, the contracts of individuals, even with the best academic credentials, excellent teaching abilities, and of more than usual student interest, are passed over unrenewed while that of some "safe" researcher is extended as that of promising and sound "respondent." All of this *re*search is of course being carried on through riot, fire, war, and destruction. One of the strongest reactions by psychologists to a building seizure by blacks at Brandeis University involving among other facilities some auxiliary psychology laboratories was that "research was being interrupted." These were historically and perhaps are important repetitive problems in psychology. But they interest an increasingly smaller segment of one dimension out of the thirty odd divisions of the American Psychological Association.

I am not saying research should wait until the students get happy again; nor should psychologists all be more socially aware. Yet the student problem is a new and growing one, and to get rid of the one new teacher most in contact with the students suggests a very peculiar set of values on the part of the "straight" majority of our psychology department. In terms of John Flannagan's critical incidence technique, I cannot think of a more vivid demonstration of what the students term "irrelevance" in higher education. Nor am I saying the students are right, either. But both together make a problem which the academic attitude somehow is failing to meet *now* whatever its history. It becomes increasingly clear that despite the Indochina war and the opportunities for student-faculty rapprochement the academy is not holding its own with its rigid research-bound, department-dominated "baronies" in its dealings with student problems. And that is what I mean by history or *karma*. Psychology is thus committed to double problem areas, those relating to the repeatable "verities" and secondly those relating to the ongoing life we are going to be leading. In the former we try for permanence as if eternally repetitive. In the latter we "let go," repeatedly "die," "let it be" as we flow along. To the former we say: "Don't just stand there do something, here it comes again." To the latter: "Don't just do something, stand there" and flow with it: both attitudes are necessary. Only wisdom and courage can help us recognize which we choose when.

Perhaps the individual with the most comprehensive grasp of the whole humanistic problem is Arnold Toynbee. Toynbee in his *Study of History* starts not with *stimulus* and response but *challenge* and response. He sees people participating in the formulation of their problems, some responding wisely, others not. He sees people if not aware beginning to imitate and repeat themselves, instead of meeting the ever new challenges of the flow of history. Yet he never completely despairs of repetition because that too is a challenge to be met. His is not a cyclic theory of eternal return as has characterized traditional societies. Nor is it a shallow utopian or progressive theory. He senses the difficulties in the way of avoiding unnecessary repetitions. Like Vico, Spengler, Hegel, and more recently, Ortega, the problems are raised so that we may deal with them more relevantly. *How* must always be answered in the *now*.

Humanistic psychology offers no answers, and indeed few if any methods. It asks for no exclusiveness. Exclusiveness is one of the virtues of tradition or method-oriented societies. Humanistic psychology is human because it recognizes the double problem of knowledge. It must deal with the "knowledge about" of the academy. It must also face the "knowing" in the *now* (as in the biblical "he knew her"), what we "know" or are this very minute. Its sympathies are at least for the moment more with that of *presence,* of now and the existential awareness of the potential "nothingness of nextness," of "time's arrow," of *karma*.

Perhaps as we tire we join the groupies in organized emotional irrelevance. (The encounter does give the ivory tower or the vacation cruise or resort the appearance of vitality.) But until that tiredness grips us perhaps we can keep abreast of the now of history. History certainly is not going to wait for us to get all the research data in. And in view of the cultural explosion, who frankly reads more than a smidgen of it any more? Yes, I know you read all you can; but that's the problem. You can't read it *all* any more. And of course your students, even your graduate students, can't begin to catch up. Since 1900 alone, we have created more knowledge, well information anyway, than existed for all of man's history until 1900. More scientists are now alive than have died ever. So that is the challenge. To meet it we are going to have to awake to our humanness. We are too limited to *only* keep on the safe tried and true way. We are often going to have "to fake it," to improvise. But we have both the capacity for—largely unused—and the interest in the adventure that lies now before us. Perhaps a line from Stanley Kramer's production of *Home of the Brave* would help here: "Coward take my coward's hand."

THE THIRD FORCE IN PSYCHOLOGY

J. F. T. Bugental

I remember years ago climbing a mountain, endlessly following the trail through forest, through rocky channels. Each point was interesting and had its own beauty, but all sense of where on the path I was in relation to the peak gradually faded as the altitude pulled at my lungs and the demands of each new stretch of hiking pulled at my muscles and mind. Then suddenly—startlingly—I emerged above the timber line on a narrow shoulder and saw ahead of me the summit, and all around the vista spread out for miles. The sense of discovery restored perspective, was as breathtaking as were the altitude and the view. It is an experience such as this that I want to describe to you now.

Much has been happening in our field in the postwar years: the establishment of our new professional life, the battles for legal recognition, the concerns with new topics such as habit strength, ideal image, gestalt therapy, games theory, human factors engineering, and so on. Yet many of us have cried alarm that our concerns are still trivial, that the sciences of man are so badly outdistanced by the sciences of things that the very race of man is in jeopardy. We have hoped for and sought a "breakthrough."

What I recognized quite simply was this: a major breakthrough is occurring right now in psychology. Like many another such major change process—the end of feudalism, the introduction of electricity, the beginnings of the laboratory method in psychology—its presence and potentialities are difficult to recognize for us who are so deep among the trees of daily concerns. Yet I am convinced that the parallels I cite are not vainglorious. I think we are on the verge of a new era in man's concern about man which may—if allowed to run its course—produce as pro-

SOURCE: J. F. T. Bugental, "The Third Force in Psychology," *Journal of Humanistic Psychology*, Spring, 1964. Reprinted by permission.

13

found changes in the human condition as those we have seen the physical sciences bring about in the past century.

Now I don't mean to tease you unduly by delaying specification of the breakthrough I have in mind. However, I do need to say a few words to prepare you to grasp my meaning. I don't want too many of you to say "Oh, that!" and turn away. You see, I think that we are prisoners of our own involvement with our work. It would be much easier for us to appreciate the report of a breakthrough in historical scholarship or in space physics than in our own familiar domain. Yet I imagine historians and physicists would have the same difficulties in their own provinces. So listen, if you can and will, with the perspective of psychology's whole development in the past 100 years.

Psychology is at last becoming the study of man. Psychology is recognizing that man, as man, has eluded our segmental approaches, our attempts to deal with part-functions, and is beginning to face up to the task of recognizing that no amount of additional findings about parts will ever yield an appreciation or understanding of man in the world.

Now, I'm pretty sure that a majority of you are saying the equivalent of "Oh, that!" I know I would be. Stay with me a bit, and I'll try to show you that this is no small thing I'm trying to depict.

Recall your undergraduate course in the history of psychology: Wundt, Titchner, Watson, Hull; psychophysics, mental elements, conditioned response, factor analysis, habit strength; Stanford-Binet, Kohs Blocks, Porteus Mazes, Wechsler, Iowa Tests.

All along we had had this implicit assumption at foundation: Discover the basic components and from these we can synthesize the whole person. Concurrently, we have rigorously disciplined ourselves to avoid the subjective and the poetic.

Listen to Clark Hull (1943), a near saint of pre-breakthrough psychology (p. 27):

> A device much employed by the author has proved itself to be a far more effective prophylaxis. This is to regard, from time to time, the behaving organism as a completely self-maintaining robot, constructed of materials as unlike ourselves as may be.

Contrast this with the following:

> A man can understand astronomy only by being an astronomer; he can understand entomology only by being an entomologist (or, perhaps, an insect); but he can understand a great deal of anthropology merely by being a man. He is himself the animal which he studies. Hence arises the fact which strikes the eye everywhere in the records of ethnology and folk-lore—the fact that the same frigid and detached spirit which leads to success in the study of astronomy or

botany leads to disaster in the study of mythology or human origins. (G. K. Chesterton, *Science and the Savages*, 1909; quoted in Cantril and Bumstead, 1960, p. 12.)

Or this:

. . . a poem, a painting, or a prayer should be regarded as a psychological datum just as much as the establishment of a sensory threshold in the laboratory or the measurement of an I.Q.

The last quotation is from Cantril and Bumstead's exciting book *Reflections on the Human Venture* (1960), itself an evidence of the change process I am trying to characterize. Other books that are part of this wave have come from Rogers (1961), Maslow (1962), May (1961), Bühler (1962), Cohen (1962), and so on.

Another way of describing what is happening is to say that two great human traditions are converging, and from their convergence we may expect a tremendous outpouring of new awareness about ourselves in our world. One such tradition is that of science; the other is the humanities. It is as though we are suddenly made heirs to a tremendous storehouse of data which has been but little utilized scientifically before or—to use a different analogy—as though a whole new hemisphere of our globe had been discovered by some new Columbus. Certainly much exploration and development must be done, but at last we are reaching its shores.

There is another evidence—a kind of validation—of the significance of the breakthrough I am trying to depict. An ancient and vast body of human experience has for centuries been accumulating in the Eastern countries. Our Western contacts with this have been chiefly to treat it as a curiosity, as pagan error to be destroyed, or as material for ignorant distortion in melodramas. Now we are beginning to appreciate the tremendous amount of wisdom and insight which has been achieved along routes quite different than those we have traveled. Zen and Taoism and other Oriental cultural traditions have much to say to us, much that we can begin to hear now that our separate ways have drawn close in the evolution of men's thoughts about man (Fingarette, 1963; Watts, 1961).

As an aside let me point out that there is tremendous encouragement for the hope of some achievement of an eventual citizenship of humanity in this start on a genuine dialogue between these two great heritages of man's thought, the Oriental and the Occidental.

You will have observed, I am optimistic about our field. Certainly there are still dangers, but I think psychology—or perhaps I should say, humanity—has proven itself hardier than once seemed to me to be the case. I mean by this last to say that I believe the renewed psychology of which I speak is but a phase of an evolutionary process which is arising as a survival response to the biology-threatening forces of nuclear destruction. Just as in a single organism, invasion by disease evokes a counter process of antibody production in defense, so do I think it is with the total evolutionary process.

BASIC POSTULATES AND ORIENTATION OF HUMANISTIC PSYCHOLOGY*

Humanistic psychology is an emerging orientation to the study of man (Bugental, 1963; Cantril, 1955; Maslow, 1956; Rogers, 1963). Sometimes referred to as "the third force" in psychology, the humanistic orientation endeavors to go beyond the points of view of behaviorism or psychoanalysis, the two most dominant perspectives presently discernible within the broad area of psychology. Humanistic psychology generally does not see itself as competitive with the other two orientations; rather, it attempts to supplement their observations and to introduce further perspectives and insights.

To date it has been hard to designate just what is meant by humanistic psychology, since it is a movement with diverse spokesmen and widely ranging contents and perspectives. The *Journal of Humanistic Psychology,* founded in 1961, has brought together a wide spectrum of papers and a distinguished, though diverse, editorial panel, and it is only through inspection of such publications and of the views of the editorial panel that an implicit definition of the field may be arrived at. Similarly, the Association for Humanistic Psychology (Sutich, 1962) has found it necessary to use a catalogue type of description of just what it is the Association seeks to represent:

> Humanistic Psychology may be defined as the third main branch of the general field of psychology (the two already in existence being the psychoanalytic and the behaviorist) and as such, is primarily concerned with those human capacities and potentialities that have little or no systematic place, either in positivist or behaviorist theory or in classical psychoanalytic theory: e.g., love, creativity, self, growth, organism, basic need-gratification, self-actualization, higher values, being, becoming, spontaneity, play, humor, affection, naturalness, warmth, ego-transcendence, objectivity, autonomy, responsibility, meaning, fair-play, transcendental experience, psychological health, and related concepts. This approach can also be

*Appreciation is expressed to my colleagues in a Psychological Service Associates seminar which discussed an earlier version of this list: Drs. A. A. Lasko, T. C. Greening, and G. V. Haigh; also to Dr. S. L. Zelen, who took part in this discussion.

characterized by the writings of Allport, Angyal, Asch, Bühler, Fromm, Goldstein, Horney, Maslow, May, Moustakas, Rogers, Wertheimer, etc., as well as by certain aspects of the writings of Jung, Adler, and the psychoanalytic ego-psychologists, existential and phenomenological psychologists.

The present paper will make a beginning on an affirmative statement of the nature of the humanistic orientation in psychology. We will undertake to do this by setting forth five postulates of humanistic psychology which may represent common elements in the perspectives of most writers identifying with this field. We will also attempt to make some defining statements about the humanistic orientation in psychology. These defining statements will be of the nature of process descriptions as opposed to the substantive or content descriptions provided by our postulates. In setting forth these postulates and these characteristics of the humanistic orientation, the writer is well aware of the very tentative nature of these statements. We are only now beginning really to discover the commonalities in the diverse spokesmen in the humanistic perspective. It is probable and highly desirable that the list of postulates that follows be criticised, revised, and supplemented many times.

FIVE BASIC POSTULATES FOR HUMANISTIC PSYCHOLOGY

Man, as man, supercedes the sum of his parts

When we speak of "man" in humanistic psychology, we do so with the intent of characterizing a person rather than an "organism." Humanistic psychology is concerned with man at his most human or, to say it differently, with that which most distinguishes man as a unique species.

Our first postulate states the keystone position that man must be recognized as something other than an additive product of various part-functions. Although part-function knowledge is important scientific knowledge, it is not the knowledge of man as man, but knowledge of the functioning of parts of an organism.

Man has his being in a human context

We postulate second that the unique nature of man is expressed through his always being in relationship with his fellows. Humanistic psychology is always concerned with man in his interpersonal potential. This is not to say that humanistic psychology may not deal with such issues as man's aloneness, but it will be evident that even in so designating it "aloneness," we are speaking of man in his human context. The psychology of part-functions is a psychology which ignores this relatedness (actual or potential) of the human experience.

Man is aware

A central fact of human experience is that man is aware. Awareness is postulated to be continuous and at many levels. By so viewing it, we recognize that all aspects of his experience are not equally available to man, but that, whatever the degree of consciousness, awareness is an essential part of man's being. The continuous nature of awareness is deemed essential to an understanding of human experience. Man does not move from discrete episode to discrete episode, a fact overlooked by experiments of the behavioristic orientation when they treat their subjects as though they had no prior awareness before coming into the experimental situation. Our postulation also provides for unconsciousness as a level of awareness in which there is not direct apprehension, but in which awareness is nevertheless present though denied. This is not the same as the Freudian concept of the unconscious, but it is probably more valid within the humanistic orientation.

Man has choice

There is no desire here to resume the hoary debate regarding free will versus determinism. Phenomenologically, choice is a given of experience. When man is aware, he is aware that his choices make a difference in the flow of his awareness, that he is not a bystander but a participant in experience. From this fact flows man's potential to transcend his creatureliness (Fromm, 1959). Also from this postulation we derive man's capability of change.

Man is intentional

In his experience, man demonstrates his intent. This does not mean "striving," but it does mean orientation. Man intends through having purpose, through valuing, and through creating and recognizing meaning. Man's intentionality is the basis on which he builds his identity, and it distinguishes him from other species.

The characteristics of man's intentionality need to be specified. Man intends both conservation and change. Mechanistic views of man frequently deal only with drive-reduction and homeostatic conceptions. Humanistic psychology recognizes that man seeks rest but concurrently seeks variety and disequilibrium. Thus we may say that man intends multiplely, complexly, and even paradoxically.

THE ORIENTATION OF HUMANISTIC PSYCHOLOGY

In the following statements we will specify some of the characteristics of the humanistic orientation in psychology, trying to articulate and identify those characteristics which are distinguishing of this point of view.

Humanistic psychology cares about man

Humanistic psychology disavows the sort of scientific detachment pretended to or achieved at great cost by other orientations. Humanistic psychology recognizes that man cannot help but be invested in his study of his own condition. Accepting this as a given, humanistic psychology is founded on man's concern about man and is an expression of that concern.

Humanistic psychology values meaning more than procedure

Although humanistic psychology must find its own methods and must validate those methods as providing dependable knowledge about the human condition, humanistic psychology would be untrue to itself were it to become preoccupied with methodology to the loss of concern with meaningful issues in the human condition.

Humanistic psychology looks for human rather than nonhuman validations

It seems to be a basic tenet of the humanistic position that only that validation which is borne out by human experience can ultimately be counted upon. Humanistic psychology does not disavow the use of statistical methods or of experimental tests. However, it does insist that these are but means and that the ultimate criterion must be that of human experience.

Humanistic psychology accepts the relativism of all knowledge

Humanistic psychology postulates a universe of infinite possibility. Thus it recognizes that all knowledge is relative and subject to change. This tenet does much to free humanistic psychology to use the imaginative and creative potential of its orientation.

Humanistic psychology relies heavily upon the phenomenological orientation

What has been said above about the importance of meaning and about human validation will have indicated the centrality of the phenomenological orientation to the humanistic approach. This is not to deny the merits of other orientations but to insist that the ultimate focus of our concern is in the experience of the human being.

Humanistic psychology does not deny the contributions of other views, but tries to supplement them and give them a setting within a broader conception of the human experience

Let me make a few concluding remarks. I have tried to give one man's view of what I think is a tremendously exciting development in our field of psychology. If I see it correctly, we are leaving the state of preoccupation with part-functions and getting back to what psychology seemed to us to mean when we first entered the field. We are returning to what psychology still seems to mean to the average, intelligent layman—that is, the functioning and experience of a whole human being. I have chosen to make my statements in somewhat dogmatic fashion, hoping that this will prove stimulating to your thinking and observation. I am sure I am not right in all details; I sincerely hope that I do correctly assess the general trend.

This is a bare initial statement for our third force in psychology. We will need much thought, much imagination, much discussion and argument, much creativity—in short, much of being human to bring our perspective to the place it must have as an affirmation of man's respect for man.

REFERENCES

Bugental, J. F. T., Humanistic Psychology: A New Break-Through, *American Psychologist*, Vol. 18 (1963), pp. 563-567.

Buhler, Charlotte. *Values in Psychotherapy*. New York: Free Press of Glencoe, 1962.

Cantril, H. Toward a Humanistic Psychology, *Etc.*, Vol. 12 (1955), pp. 278-298.

_____, and Bumstead, C. H. *Reflections on the Human Venture*. New York: New York University Press, 1960.

Cohen, J. *Humanistic Psychology*. New York: Collier, 1962.

Fingarette, H. *The Self in Transformation*. New York: Basic Books, 1963.

Fromm, E. Value, Psychology, and Human Existence, in A. H. Maslow (ed.), *New Knowledge in Human Values*. New York: Harper, 1959, pp. 151-164.

Hull, C. L. *Principles of Behavior*. New York: Appleton-Century, 1943, p. 27.

Maslow, A. H. Toward a Humanistic Psychology, *Etc.*, Vol. 13 (1956), pp. 10-22.

_____. *Toward a Psychology of Being.* Princeton, N.J.: Van Nostrand, 1962.

May, R. *Existential Psychology.* New York: Random House, 1961.

Rogers, C. R. *On Becoming a Person.* Boston: Houghton Mifflin, 1961.

_____. Toward a Science of the Person, *Journal of Humanistic Psychology,* Vol. 3 (1963), No. 2.

Sutich, A. American Association for Humanistic Psychology: Progress Report. Palo Alto, California, November 1, 1962; mimeographed.

Watts, A. *Psychotherapy East and West.* New York: Pantheon, 1961.

HUMANISTIC THEORY: THE THIRD REVOLUTION IN PSYCHOLOGY

Floyd W. Matson

The oft-used term "humanistic psychology" has the appearance of what semanticists call a "redundant tautology." After all, psychology is the science of mind, is it not? And is not mind the property of human beings? And is not all psychology then humanistic?

The answer to all of the questions is, in a word, no. Psychology is the study of more than mind, and of less than mind. It is the science of behavior, much of which is "mindless." Nor is the behavior studied by psychologists only that of humans; much of it, perhaps most, is that of animals. And where it is human behavior that is being studied, it is very often physiological rather than psychical. It would not be stretching the truth too far to observe that much of what goes on in psychology is not "psychological" at all. And that brings us to the reason for the third revolution—the renaissance of humanism in psychology.

Humanistic psychology tries to tell it not like it is, but like it ought to be. It seeks to bring psychology back to its source, to the *psyche*, where it all began and where it finally culminates. But there is more to it than that. Humanistic psychology is not just the study of "human being"; it is a commitment to human becoming.

It was a humanistic philosopher, Kurt Riezler, who said that "science begins with respect for the subject matter." Unfortunately that is not the view of all scientists, whether in the hard sciences of nature or in the softer sciences of man and mind. It is almost, as it seems to me, a defining characteristic of behaviorist psychology that it begins with *dis*respect for the subject matter, and therefore leads straightaway to what Norbert Wiener (a pretty hard scientist himself) called the "inhuman use of human beings." At any rate, I know of no greater disrespect for the

SOURCE: Floyd Matson, "Humanistic Theory: The Third Revolution in Psychology." This article first appeared in *The Humanist*, March/April 1971 and is reprinted by permission.

human subject than to treat him as an object—unless it is to demean that object further by fragmenting it into drives, traits, reflexes, and other mechanical hardware. But that is the procedure of behaviorism, if not of all experimental psychology; it is a procedure openly admitted, indeed triumphantly proclaimed, in the name of Science and Truth, of Objectivity and Rigor, and of all else that is holy in these precincts. And it leads in a straight line out of the ivory tower into the brave new world of Walden Two.

Everyone remembers, I am sure, that curious utopian novel, *Walden Two*, written more than 20 years ago by the preeminent behaviorist of our generation, B. F. Skinner. His book presented such a stark scenario of behavioral engineering and mind manipulation, such a "conditional" surrender of autonomy and freedom on the part of its docile characters, that many readers at the time mistakenly supposed it to be a clever put-on, a satirical prophecy of the nightmare shape of things to come if ever a free society should relax its vigilant defense of the values of liberty and responsibility—especially the liberty and responsibility of choice.

But that was what Skinner's novel openly defied and disparaged; the Elysian community it projected was a sort of crystal palace (or womb with a view) within which perfect peace and security might abide forever—tranquility without trauma, pleasure without pain, attainment without struggle—and all at the trivial price of the freedom to make choices, the right (as it were) to blunder. The key to the kingdom of Walden Two was operant conditioning; by this magical technique, applied to all residents from birth, the "Hamlet syndrome" (the anxiety of choice) was efficiently removed. Like that wonderful Mrs. Prothro in Dylan Thomas's Christmas story, who "said the right thing always," so the creatures of Skinner's novel were conditioned to make the right choices automatically. It was instant certitude, at the price of all volition. Like Pavlov's dogs, Skinner's people made only conditioned responses to the stimulus of their master's voice.

Let us recognize that such a homeostatic paradise, like the classless society and the heavenly city, has great seductive appeal for many, especially in an age of anxiety and a time of troubles. It appeals particularly to those with a low tolerance for ambiguity and a high rage for order. I believe it was Thomas Huxley who was so fearful of chance and choice as to declare that if he were offered a world of absolute security and certainty, at the price of surrendering his personal freedom, he would close instantly with the bargain. Unlike his grandson, Aldous, whose own futuristic novel made just the opposite point, the elder Huxley would surely have enjoyed the still life on Skinner's Walden Pond.

Let me recall now a different disposition, both existential and humanistic. It is Dostoevsky's underground man, struggling to be heard by the Establishment above. "After all," he says,

I do not really insist on suffering or on prosperity either. I insist on my *caprice,* and its being guaranteed to me when necessary. Suffering would be out of place in vaudevilles, for instance; I know that. In the crystal palace it is even unthinkable; suffering means doubt, means negation, and what would be the good of a crystal palace if there could be any doubt about it? . . . You believe in a crystal edifice that can never be destroyed; that is, an edifice at which one would neither be able to stick out one's tongue nor thumb one's nose on the sly. And perhaps I am afraid of this edifice just because it is of crystal and can never be destroyed and that one could not even put one's tongue out at it even on the sly. (*The Short Novels of Dostoevsky,* Dial Press, New York, 1945, p. 152)

Now *there,* as Sarte might say, is an existentialism that is a humanism.

There have been, as I believe, three distinct conceptual revolutions in psychology during the course of the present century. The first, that of behaviorism, struck with the force of a revelation around 1913 and shook the foundations of academic psychology for a generation. Behaviorism arose in reaction to the excessive preoccupation of 19th-century psychology with consciousness, and with introspection as a way of getting at the data of conscious mental activity. The behaviorists reacted with a vengeance. They threw out not only consciousness, but all the resources of the mind. The mind, to them, was the ghost in the machine, and they did not believe in ghosts. The founding father of the movement, John B. Watson, declared in an early proclamation, a kind of behaviorist manifesto, that the behaviorist began "by sweeping aside all medieval conceptions. He dropped from his scientific vocabulary all subjective terms such as sensation, perception, image, desire, purpose, and even thinking and emotion as they were subjectively defined" (*Behaviorism* [1924], University of Chicago Press, Chicago, 1958, pp. 5-6).

Overt behavior, that which could be seen and measured, was all that counted. And all that was needed to explain it was the simple and classical formula of stimulus-response—with one added refinement, that of the conditioned reflex. It was this concept of conditioning, borrowed from the Russian laboratories of Pavlov and Bechterev, that gave the real revolutionary impetus to Watson's behaviorist movement. Conditioning was power; it was control. This was no merely objective psychology, for all its scientific claims; it was an applied psychology—and what it was applied to, or rather against, was man. "The interest of the behaviorist," said Watson, "is more than the interest of a spectator; he wants to control man's reactions as physical scientists want to control and manipulate other natural phenomena" (Ibid., p. 11). Just as man was simply "an assembled organic machine ready to run," so the behaviorist was no pure scientist but an engineer unable to keep from tinkering with the machinery. Pointing out that such sciences as chemistry and biology were gaining control over their subject matter, Watson inquired, "Can psychology ever get control? Can I make someone who is not afraid of snakes, afraid of them, and how?" The answer was clear: And how!

"In short," said Watson, "the cry of the behaviorist is, 'Give me the baby and my world to bring it up in and I'll make it crawl and walk; I'll make it climb and use its hands in constructing buildings of stone or wood; I'll make it a thief, a gunman, or a dope fiend.' The possibility of shaping in any direction is almost endless" (*The Ways of Behaviorism*, Harper, New York, 1926, p. 35).

That should be enough to suggest the general character (and authoritarian personality) of behaviorist psychology, the first of the three psychological revolutions that have taken place in our century. The second revolution was, of course, that of Freud. It is noteworthy that psychoanalysis and behaviorism made their appearance at roughly the same time, give or take a decade, and that both of them emerged in reaction against the accent on consciousness in traditional psychology. Apart from these coincidences, however, there was little in common between these two movements, and there was a great deal that put them at opposite poles.

Whereas behaviorism placed all its stress upon the external environment (that is, upon stimuli from the outer world) as the controlling factor in behavior, psychoanalysis placed its emphasis upon the internal environment (upon stimuli from within, in the form of drives and instincts). For Freud, man was very much a creature of instinct—and in particular of two primary instincts, those of life and death *(Eros* and *Thanatos)*. These two instincts were in conflict not only with each other but with the world, with culture. Society was based, said Freud, on renunciation of the instincts via the mechanism of repression. But the instincts did not give up without a struggle. In fact, they never gave up; they could not be vanquished, only temporarily blocked. Life, then, was a constant alternation between frustration and aggression. Neither for the individual person nor for the culture was there a permanent solution or "happy ending"; there were only compromises, expedients, working adjustments. The price of civilization, indeed, was mass neurosis—the result of the necessary suppression of the natural instincts of man. But if that seems bad, the alternative was worse; whenever the repressive forces are for a moment relaxed, declared Freud, "we see man as a savage beast to whom the thought of sparing his own kind is alien" (*Civilization and Its Discontents*, Hogarth, London, 1930, p. 86).

Perhaps the most interesting, not to say frightening, concept advanced by Freud was that of *Thanatos,* the aggression or death instinct, which he regarded as an innate and irresistible drive toward the destruction of oneself and others. What is especially significant about this bleak concept of man's aggressive nature is the "comeback" it has been making in recent years after a long period of almost total eclipse. The current revival of the shadow side of Freud, the pessimistic musings of his later years, does not tell us so much about Freud as it does about the temper of our own time. I shall return to this point.

The main point I want to make immediately about the psychoanalytic movement, in its Freudian form, is that it presents a picture of man as very much the "victim-spectator," as Gordon Allport has put it, of blind forces working through him. For all its differences with behaviorism, Freudian theory agrees in the fundamental image of man as a stimulus-response machine, although the stimuli that work their will upon the human being come from within rather than from without. Freud's determinism was not environmental, like Watson's, but psychogenetic; nevertheless, it was a determinism, and it left little room for spontaneity, creativity, rationality, or responsibility. The declared faith in conscious reason that underlay Freudian therapy (rather more than Freudian theory) did not prevent his insistently minimizing the role of reason as an actual or potential determinant of personality and conduct—nor, on the other hand, from maximizing the thrust of irrational forces that press their claims both from "below" (the id) and from "above" (the superego). In Freud's topographical map of the mind, the ego, itself only partially conscious, never achieves full autonomy but functions as a kind of buffer state between the rival powers of instinct and introjected culture, between animal nature and social nurture.

I have been deliberately hard on Freud in these remarks in order to emphasize those aspects of his theory and therapy that, by virtue of their pessimism and determinism, have called out over the years the critical and creative response that (for want of a better term) we may call "humanistic psychology." This new psychology, the third revolution, represents a reaction against *both* behaviorism and orthodox psychoanalysis; it is for that reason that humanistic psychology has been called the "third force." But perhaps the first thing to say about it is that, unlike the two movements of thought that precede and oppose it, humanistic psychology is not a single body of theory but a collection or convergence of a number of lines and schools of thought. If it owes nothing to behaviorism, it does owe much to psychoanalysis, although less perhaps to Freud himself than to the considerable number of Freudian heretics and deviationists, beginning with his own associates of the original Vienna Circle and culminating in the so-called neo-Freudians (anti-Freudians really) of the second generation.

For despite the many differences among them, those who broke away one by one from the side of Freud shared a number of crucial insights and commitments. Adler, Jung, Rank, Stekel, Ferenczi—all these early associates found themselves unable to accept Freud's theory of instinctual determinism (specifically, his libido theory) and his tendency to find the source of all difficulty and motivation in the remote past. These deviationists began to place equal or greater emphasis upon the present (that is, upon the here and now, the "presence" of the patient) and also upon the future (that is, upon the pull of aspiration and purpose, the goal or life-plan of the individual). What this implied was a greater reliance upon the consciousness of the person in analysis or therapy: a new respect for his powers of will and of reason, his capacity to choose and to understand.

In Adler's work, this emphasis took the form of virtually converting the psychoanalytic therapy session into a dialogue or conversation on the conscious level—which of course enraged Freud, who thought that Adler had betrayed the basic postulate of unconscious motivation. In Jung's work, the new approach took the form of emphasizing what he called the "prospective factor," the pull of purpose as opposed to the push of instinct (and in particular the push of erotic instinct); it also took the form, in Jung's later years, of increasing stress upon understanding the other, whether neurotic patient or normal individual, in his unique identity. This involved a kind of intuitive and sympathetic understanding, which Jung distinguished from scientific knowledge and which led him finally to advocate abandoning the textbooks altogether in any venture into helping or healing. In the case of Otto Rank, another of the heretics of the original Freudian circle, the deviation took the form of an emphasis upon the existential will of the person, that is, upon his capacity for self-direction and self-control.

The common denominator in these various lines of theory and therapy was, I believe, *respect for the person,* recognition of the other not as a case, or an object, or a field of forces, or a bundle of instincts, but as himself. In terms of theory, it meant respect for his powers of creativity and responsibility; in terms of therapy, it meant respect for his values, his intentions, and, above all, his peculiar identity.

This recognition of *man-in-person,* as opposed to *man-in-general,* goes to the heart of the difference between humanistic psychology, in any of its forms or schools, and scientific psychologies such as behaviorism. Not only in psychoanalysis, but in other fields as well, increasing numbers of students have found themselves drawn to the unsettling conclusion that the definitive features of a human being cannot be made out at all from a "psychological distance," but can be brought into focus only by understanding (literally, by "standing under") the unique perspective of the individual himself.

This emphasis upon the human person, upon the individual in his wholeness and uniqueness, is a central feature of the "psychology of humanism." But there is an important corollary without which this personalistic emphasis would be inadequate and distorted. That corollary is the recognition, to use a phrase of Rank, that "the self needs the other." This recognition is variously expressed: For the neo-Freudians, it points to the importance of relationship in the growth of personality; for the existentialists, it leads to emphasis on the themes of dialogue, encounter, meeting, intersubjectivity, and so on.

While this recognition is broadly shared by humanistic psychotherapists, analysts, personality theorists, perceptual psychologists and others, perhaps the most impressive and systematic development of the idea has been provided by existential thinkers, both in psychology and philosophy. There is a striking similarity in the formulation of this self-other relationship by various existentialists. Martin Buber's philosophy of dialogue, centering around the I-Thou relation, is probably the most influential and possibly the most profound. Among other fruitful effects, it has given rise to a "psychology of meeting" that finds its paradigm in the therapeutic encounter. The significance of Buber's general concept has been well described by Will Herberg:

> The term I-Thou points to a relation of person to person, of subject to subject, a relation of reciprocity involving "meeting" or "encounter," while the term I-It points to a relation of person to thing, of subject to object, involving some form of utilization, domination, or control, even if it is only so-called "objective" knowing. The I-Thou relation, which Buber usually designated as "relation" par excellence, is one in which one can enter only with the whole of his being, as a genuine person. (*The Writings of Martin Buber*, Meridian Books, New York, 1956, p. 14.)

It follows that the relationship of therapy in its ideal development represents an authentic encounter "on the sharp edge of existence" between two human beings, one seeking and the other helping. This mutual recognition, which is never immediate but only a possibility to be achieved, cuts through the conventional defenses and postures of both partners to permit each to reach out as a person to the other as a person. What is demanded of the doctor in particular, says Buber, is that he "himself step forth out of his protected professional superiority into the elementary situation between one who asks and one who is asked" (Maurice Friedman, *Martin Buber: The Life of Dialogue*, Harper Torchbooks, New York, 1960, p. 190).

Apart from its uses by existential psychologists and psychoanalysts—such as Ludwig Binswanger, Viktor Frankl, Rollo May, and others—Buber's immensely fertile concept of I-Thou "meeting" finds parallels and reverberations in the work of other existential philosophers, especially those commonly referred to as the religious existentialists or existential theologians. For Gabriel Marcel, who came independently to the formula of I-and-Thou, the sense of genuine encounter is conveyed by the term "intersubjectivity," implying an authentic communication on the order of communion. "The fact is," writes Marcel, "that we can understand ourselves by starting from the other, or from others, and only by starting from them; . . . it is only in this perspective that a legitimate love of self can be conceived" (*The Mystery of Being*, Gateway, Chicago, 1960, Volume II, p. 9). This insight, quite similar to Fromm's concept of productive love and self-realization, implies a reciprocity of knowing in which what "I am" as well as what "Thou art" is made known only through the mutual experience of what "We are." Each communicant recognizes himself in the other.

In Paul Tillich's "therapeutic theology," this general appreciation of the enlightening role of engagement or meeting is applied directly to psychotherapy, which is regarded as the "community of healing." In common with other existentialists, Tillich believes that the personal troubles represented by neurosis stem fundamentally from failures in relationships with others, thereby resulting in self-alienation from any genuine contact with the world. The central therapeutic problem thus becomes one of "acceptance" or, more precisely, of successive stages of acceptance culminating in acceptance of oneself and of the world of others.

In this new kind of therapeutic encounter—and here is another humanistic tenet—there are no silent partners. The existential therapist (which is to say, the humanistic therapist) is no longer the blank screen or "mute catalyzer" that he was in Freud's day, but rather is a participant with the whole of his being. He participates not only for the purpose of helping, but even more basically for the purpose of knowing or understanding. "You must participate in a self," according to Tillich, "in order to know what it is. By participation you change it" (*The Courage to Be*, Yale University Press, New Haven, 1959 p. 124). The inference is that the kind of knowledge essential to psychology and psychotherapy is to be gained not by detached observation but by participant-observation (to use Harry Stack Sullivan's phrase). It may be possible, through detachment, to gain knowledge that is "useful"; but only through participation is it possible to gain the knowledge that is *helpful*.

In any adequate account of the sources and forces that have nourished the movement of humanistic psychology (which this brief sketch does not pretend to be), much more would have to be said in acknowledgment of the contributions of individual theorists and therapists. Fortunately, there are a number of comprehensive surveys available; among them, James Bugental's *Challenges of Humanistic Psychology*, Anthony Sutich and Miles Vich's *Readings in Humanistic Psychology*, and my own *The Broken Image* (especially Chapters 6 and 7). But even the present essay cannot avoid mention of at least a few of the movers and shakers behind the third revolution, notably: Abraham Maslow, who more than any other deserves to be recognized as the "spiritual father" of the humanistic movement in psychology; Gordon Allport, the great American personalist and heir to the mantle of William James; Rollo May, who introduced the existential approach to American psychology and has developed it creatively; Carl Rogers, whose therapeutic mandate of "unconditional regard" for the client resembles Tillich's philosophy of ultimate concern; Erich Fromm, the most influential of the neo-Freudians, who has long since moved from psychoanalysis to the higher ground of social philosophy and cultural criticism; Henry A. Murray, inspired teacher and exemplar of humanism; Charlotte Buhler, who has made us all aware of how important personal goal-values and the whole course of human life are to psychological understanding.

In conclusion—if I may be excused the puff of vanity—I wish to suggest something of the activist potential of humanistic psychology by repeating a few paragraphs from a talk I gave before the annual conference of the Association for Humanistic Psychology:

I'd like to propose one line of commitment, and of protest, that we might well undertake as humanistic psychologists. That course is, following Jefferson, to swear undying opposition to all forms of tyranny over the mind of man. I propose that we commit ourselves to the defense of psychological liberty. For I believe that quite possibly the greatest threat to freedom in the world today (and tomorrow) is the threat to freedom of the mind—which is, at bottom, the power to choose.

That freedom is threatened now on all sides. It is threatened by what Herbert Marcuse has called the "one-dimensional society," which seeks to reduce the categories of thought and discourse to a kind of consensual endorsement of the directives of an aggressive and acquisitive culture. It is threatened by the technology of mass society, mass culture and mass communication, which manufactures (pace Marshall McLuhan) a marshmallow world of plastic pleasures in which the bland lead the bland endlessly into the sea of tranquility.

Freedom of the mind is also threatened by the biological revolution and its psychological corollaries—not only by the familiar cuckoo's nest of lobotomies and shock treatments, over which no one can fly, but by the imminent breakthroughs in "genetic surgery" and kindred interventions that promise to make feasible the rewiring and reprogramming of the brain mechanism.

Perhaps most critically of all, our psychological liberty is threatened by failure of nerve: by our inability to live up to and live out the democratic dogma, which rests upon faith in the capacity of the ordinary human being to lead his own life, to go his own way and to grow his own way, to be himself and to know himself and to become more himself. This failure of nerve is rampant in the field of education; it is a kind of occupational disease of social work, where the aided person becomes a client who is treated as a patient who is diagnosed as incurable. And it is a pervasive feature of the landscape of academic psychology and behavioral science in so many saddening ways that it would take a book (which I have already written) to enumerate them all.

But let me mention just one of the ways in which this failure of nerve manifests itself in the study of man. The old reactionary doctrine of Original Sin, of innate depravity, has lately been enjoying a very popular and large-scale revival. It takes the form of the hypothesis of aggression as a fixed instinctual endowment of man—a genetic taint in the blood, as it were, a dark stain in the double helix of each of us. The alleged discovery or rediscovery of this killer instinct is being hailed in the book clubs and popular journals as if it were the ultimate benediction, the final good news of man's redemption. How are we to account for the popularity of this darkly pessimistic thesis? How account for the best-seller status of Lorenz's *On Aggression,* Ardrey's *Territorial Imperative* and *African Genesis,* and Desmond Morris's *Naked Ape*?

I believe the answer is clear: mass failure of nerve. Nothing could be better calculated to get us off the uncomfortable hook of personal responsibility, of self-control and self-determination, than this doctrine of our innate aggressive propensities. That's why we fight; that's why we hate; that's why we cannot love one another or ourselves. People are no damn good—and there's an end of it.

Well, I do not believe that humanistic psychologists will accept that cop-out. I propose therefore that we place the full weight of our movement, the whole third force of it, against this and all other threats to the freedom of the mind and the autonomy of the person. Let us become the active conscience of the psychological fraternity, searching out and exposing—and condemning—each and every dehumanizing, depersonalizing and demoralizing force that would move us further down the road to the Brave New World and the technocratic society—that social laboratory of the behaviorist's dreams and the humanist's nightmares.

For down that road lies not just the end of psychological freedom, but the death of humanity.

NOTES ON BEING-PSYCHOLOGY

Abraham H. Maslow

DEFINITION OF BEING-PSYCHOLOGY BY ITS SUBJECT MATTER, PROBLEMS, JURISDICTIONS (COULD ALSO BE CALLED ONTO PSYCHOLOGY, TRANSCENDENTAL PSYCHOLOGY, PSYCHOLOGY OF PERFECTION, PSYCHOLOGY OF ENDS)

1. Deals with ends (rather than with means or instruments); with end-states, end-experiences (intrinsic satisfactions and enjoyments); with persons insofar as they are ends-in-themselves (sacred, unique, noncomparable, equally valuable with every other person rather than as instruments or means-to-ends; techniques of making means into ends, of transforming means-activities into end-activities. Deals with objects per se, as they are in their own nature, not insofar as they are self-validating, intrinsically valid, inherently valuable, per se valuable, needing no justification. Here-now states in which the present is experienced fully, per se (as end in itself) and not as repetition of past or prelude to future.

    2. Deals with states of *finis* and of *telos;* i.e., of completion, finality, ending, totality, consummation, finishing (states in which nothing is lacking, nothing more is needed or wanted, no improvement is possible). States of pure happiness, joy, bliss, rapture, ecstasy, fulfillment, realization, states of hopes fulfilled, of problems solved, of wishes granted, of needs gratified, of goals attained, of dreams realized. Already being there; having arrived rather than striving to get there. Peak experiences. States of pure success (transient disappearance of all negation).

    2a. Unhappy, tragic states of completion and finality, insofar as they yield B-cognition. States of failure, despair, of collapse of defenses, acute failure of value system, acute confrontation with real guilt, can *force* perception of truth and reality in some instances where there is enough strength and courage.

    3. States felt to be, perceived to be perfect. Concepts of perfection. Ideals, models, limits, exemplars, abstract definitions. The human being

SOURCE: A. H. Maslow, "Notes on Being Psychology," Fall 1962. Reprinted by permission.

insofar as he potentially is, or can be conceived to be perfect, ideal, model, authentic, fully human, paradigmatic, godlike, exemplary, or insofar as he has potentialities and vectors in these directions (i.e., man as he *might* be, *could* be, or potentially *is* under best conditions; the ideal limits of human development, to which he approaches, but never attains permanently). His Destiny, Fate. These ideal human potentialities extrapolated out from the ideal far goals of psychotherapy, education, family training, end-product of growth, self development, etc. (See, "Operations that Define B-Values.") (See also, "Movement Toward Health and Away from Illness" for Extrapolation forward of sub-aspects of health toward the limit or ideal.) Deals with Definition of Core and with defining characteristics of the human being; his nature; his "intrinsic core" or "inner core"; his essence, his presently existing potentialities; his *sine qua non*s (instincts, constitution, biological nature, inherent, intrinsic human nature). This makes possible definition (quantitatively) of "full humanness" *or* "degree of humanness" *or* "degree of human diminution." Philosophical Anthropology in European sense. (Differentiate *"sine qua non,"* defining characteristics (which define the concept "humanness"), *from* the exemplar (model, Platonic idea, ideal possibility, perfect idea, hero, template, die). Former is the minimum; latter is the maximum. Latter is pure, static Being which the former tries to Become. Former has very low entrance requirements to the class, e.g., human is featherless biped. Also membership is all-or-none, in *or* out.

4. States of desirelessness, purposelessness, of lack of D-need, of being unmotivated, non-coping, non-striving, of enjoying rewards, of having been satisfied. Profit taking. (Able, therefore, "to leave one's interests, wishes and aims entirely out of sight; thus of entirely renouncing one's own personality for a time, so as to remain pure knowing subject . . . with clear vision of the world."—Schopenhauer).

4a. States of fearlessness; anxiety-free states. Courage. Unhampered, freely-flowing, uninhibited, unchecked human nature.

5. Metamotivation (dynamics of action when all the D-needs, lacks, wants, have been satisfied). Growth-motivation (?) "Unmotivated" behavior. Expression. Spontaneity.

5a. States and processes of pure (primary and/or integrated) creativeness. Pure here-now activity ("freedom" from past or future insofar as this is possible). Improvisation. Pure fitting of person and situation (problem) to each other, moving toward person-situation fusion as an ideal limit.

6. Descriptive, empirical, clinically or personologically or psychometrically described states of fulfillment of the promise (or destiny, vocation, fate, call) of the self; (self-actualization, maturity, the fully evolved person, psychological health, authenticity, attainment of "real self," individuation, the creative personality, identity, real-izing or actual-izing of potentiality).

7. Cognition of Being (B-Cog.) Transactions with extra-psychic reality which are centered upon the nature of that reality rather than upon the nature of, or interests of, the cognizing self. Penetration to the essence of things or persons. Perspicuity. Conditions under which it occurs. Peak experiences. Nadir-experiences. B-Cog. before death. B-cog. under acute psychotic regression. Therapeutic insights as B-Cog. Fear and evasion of B-Cog; dangers of B-Cog.

   a. Nature of the percept in B-Cognition. Nature of reality as *described* and as *ideally extrapolated* under B-Cognition, i.e. under "best" conditions. Reality conceived to be independent of the perceiver. Reality unabstracted.
   b. Nature of the perceiver in B-Cognition, Veridical because detached, desireless, unselfish, disinterested, Taoistic, fearless, herenow, (see Innocent Perceiving), receptive, humble (not arrogant), without thought of profit, etc. Ourselves as most effficient perceivers of reality.

8. Transcending time and space. States in which they are forgotten (absorption, focal attention, fascination, peak-experiences, Nadir-experiences), irrelevant or hampering or harmful. Cosmos, people, objects, experiences seen insofar as they are timeless, eternal, spaceless, universal, absolute, ideal.

9. The sacred; sublime, ontic, spiritual, transcendent, eternal, infinite, holy, absolute; states of awe; of worship, oblation, etc. "Religious" states insofar as they are naturalistic. Everyday world, objects, people seen under the aspect of eternity. Unitive Life. Unitive consciousness. States of fusion of temporal and eternal, of local and universal, of relative and absolute.

10. States of innocence, (using child or animal as paradigm). (See B-Cognition) (using mature, wise, self-actualizing as paradigm). Innocent perceiving (ideally no discrimination of important and unimportant; everything equally probable; everything equally interesting; less differentiation of figure and ground; only rudimentary structuring and differentiation of environment; less means-ends differentiation as everything tends to be equally valuable in itself; no future, no prognosis, no foreboding, therefore no surprises, apprehensions, disappointments, expectations, predictions, anxieties, rehearsals, preparations, or worries, one thing is as likely to happen as another; non-interfering-receptiveness; acceptance of whatever happens; little choosing, preferring, selecting, discriminating; little discrimination of relevance from irrelevance; little abstraction; wonder.) Innocent behaving (spontaneity, expressiveness, impulsiveness, no fear, controls or inhibitions; no guile, no ulterior motives; honesty; fearlessness; purposeless; unplanned, unpremeditated, unrehearsed; humble (not arrogant); no impatience (when future unknown); no impulse to improve world, or reconstruct it; (Innocence

overlaps with B-Cognition very much; perhaps they will turn out to be identical in the future).

11. States tending toward ultimate holism, i.e., the whole cosmos, all of reality, seen in a unitary way; insofar as everything is everything else as well, insofar as anything is related to everything; insofar as all of reality is a single thing which we perceive from various angles. Bucke's cosmic consciousness. Fascinated perception of a portion of the world as if it were the whole world. Techniques of seeing something as if it were all there was, e.g., in art and photography, cropping, magnification, blowing up, etc. (which cut off object from all its relations, context, imbeddedness, etc., and permit it to be seen in itself, absolutely, freshly.) Seeing *all* its characteristics rather than abstracting in terms of usefulness, danger, convenience, etc. (The Being of an object is the whole object; abstracting necessarily sees it from the point of view of means and takes it out of the realm of the *per se*).

Transcending of separateness, discreteness, mutual exclusiveness, and of law of excluded middle.

12. The observed or extrapolated characteristics (or Values) of Being. The B-realm. The Unitive Consciousness.

13. All states in which dichotomies (polarities, opposites, contradictories) are resolved (transcended, combined, fused, integrated), e.g., selfishness and unselfishness, reason and emotion, impulse and control, trust and will, conscious and unconscious, opposed or antagonistic interests, happiness and sadness, tears and laughter, tragic and comic, Appollonian and Dionysian, romantic and classical, etc. All integrating processes which transform oppositions into synergies, e.g., love, art, reason, humor, etc.

14. All synergic states (in world, society, person, nature, self, etc.). States in which selfishness becomes the same as unselfishness (when by pursuing "selfish ends" I *must* benefit everyone else; and when by being altruistic, I benefit myself, i.e., when the dichotomy is resolved and transcended). States of society when virtue pays, i.e., when it is rewarded extrinsically as well as intrinsically; when it doesn't cost too much to be virtuous, or intelligent, or perspicuous, or beautiful or honest, etc. All states which foster and encourage the B-values to be actualized. States in which it is easy to be good. States which discourage resentment, counter-values and counter-morality, (hatred and fear of excellence, truth, goodness, beauty, etc.). All states which increase the correlation between the true, the good, the beautiful, etc., and move them toward their ideal unity with each other.

15. States in which the Human Predicament (Existential Dilemma) is transiently solved, integrated, transcended, or forgotten, e.g., peak-experience, B-humor and laughter, the "happy ending," triumph of B-justice, the "good death," B-love, B-art, B-tragedy or comedy, all integrative moments, acts and perceptions, etc.

COLLATION OF THE VARIOUS WAYS IN WHICH THE WORD "BEING" HAS BEEN USED IN "TOWARD A PSYCHOLOGY OF BEING"[1]

1. It has been used to refer to the whole cosmos, to everything that exists, to all of reality. In peak-experiences, in states of fascination, of focal attention, attention can narrow down to a single object or person which is then reacted to "as if" it were the whole of Being, i.e., the whole of reality. This implies that it is all holistically interrelated. The only complete and whole thing there is is the whole Cosmos. Anything short of that is partial, incomplete, shorn away from intrinsic ties and relations for the sake of momentary, practical convenience. It refers also to Cosmic Consciousness. Also implies hierarchical-integration rather than dichotomizing.

2. It refers to the "inner core," the biological nature of the individual—his basic needs, capacities, preferences; his irreducible nature; the "real self" (Horney); his inherent, essential, intrinsic nature. Identity. Since "inner core" is both species-wide (every baby has the need to be loved) and individual (only Mozart was perfectly Mozartian) the phrase can mean either "being fully human" and/or "being perfectly idiosyncratic."

3. Being can mean "expressing one's nature," rather than coping, striving, straining, willing, controlling, interfering, commanding, (in the sense that a cat is being a cat, as contrasted with the sense in which a female impersonator is being a female, or a stingy person "tries" to be generous). It refers to effortless spontaneity (as an intelligent person expresses intelligence, as a baby is babyish) which permits the deepest, innermost nature to be seen in behavior. Since spontaneity is difficult, most people can be called the "human impersonators," i.e., they are "trying" to be what they think is human, rather than just being what they are. It therefore also implies honesty, nakedness, self-disclosure. Most of the psychologists who have used it, include (covertly) the hidden, not-yet-sufficiently-examined assumption that a neurosis is *not* part of the deepest nature, the inner core, or the real Being of the person, but is rather a more superficial layer of the personality which conceals or distorts the *real self*, i.e., neurosis is a defense against real Being, against one's deep, biological nature. "Trying" to be may not be as good as "being" (expressing), but it is also better than not trying, i.e., hopelessness, not coping, giving up.

4. The Being of any person, animal or thing can mean its "suchness" or its "isness," its raw, concrete nature, its being whatever it phenomenologically and sensuously is, its own particular experiential quality, e.g., the redness of the red, the felinity of the cat, the Renoirishness of a Renoir, the particular, peculiar, like-nothing-else sound of the oboe, the unique, idiographic pattern of qualities that now "means"

Uriah Heep, Don Quixote or Abraham Lincoln. Obviously there is no question here of validation, justification, explanation, or meaning. The answer to the question "Why?" is "It just *is* so. This is what it is. It is so because it is so." In this sense, Being is pointless and has no excuse or reason for existing: it just *does* exist.

5. Being can refer to the concept "human being," "horse," etc. Such a concept has defining characteristics, includes and excludes from membership within it by specific operations. For human psychology this has limitation because any person can be seen *either* as a member, or example of, the concept or class "human being," *or* as the sole member of the unique class "Addison J. Sims."

Also, we can use the class concept in two extremely different ways, minimum or maximum. The class can be defined minimally so that practically no one is excluded, e.g., human beings are featherless bipeds. This gives us no basis for grading quality or for discriminating among human beings in any way. One is either a member of the class or not a member of the class, either in or out. No other status is possible.

Or else the class can be defined by its perfect exemplars (models, heroes, ideal possibilities, Platonic ideas, extrapolations out to ideal limits and possibilities). Hundreds of defining characteristics of perfect humanness could then be listed and degrees of humanness can then be quantitatively determined by the number of defining characteristics fulfilled (R. Hartman). This usage has many advantages, but its abstract and static quality must be kept in mind. There is a profound difference between describing carefully the best actual human beings I can get (self-actualizing people), none of whom are perfect, and on the other hand, describing the ideal, the perfect, the conceptually pure concept of the exemplar, constructed by extrapolating out ahead from the descriptive data on actual, imperfect people. The concept "self-actualizing people" describes not the people but the ideal limit to which they approach. This should make no difficulty. We are used to blueprints and diagrams of "the" steam engine, or automobile, which are certainly never confused with, e.g., a photograph of my automobile or your steam engine.

Such a conceptual definition gives the possibility also of distinguishing the essential from the peripheral, (accidental, superficial, nonessential). It gives criteria for discriminating the real from the not-real, the true from the false, the necessary from the dispensable or expendable, the eternal and permanent from the passing, the unchanging from the changeable.

6. Being can mean the "end" of developing, growing and becoming. It refers to the end-product or limit, or goal, or *telos* of becoming rather than to its process, as in the following sentence: "In this way, the psychologies of being and of becoming can be reconciled, and the child, simply being himself, can yet move forward and grow." This sounds very

much like Aristotle's "final cause," or the telos, the final product, the sense in which the acorn now has within its nature, the oak tree which it will become. (This is tricky because it is our tendency to anthropomorphize and say that the acorn is "trying" to grow up. It is not. It is simply "being" an infant. In the same way that Darwin could not use the word "trying" to explain evolution, so also must we avoid this usage. We must explain his growth forward toward his limit as an epiphenomenon of his being, as "blind" by-products of contemporary mechanisms, and processes).

REFERENCES

[1]Toward a Psychology of Being, Van Nostrand, 1962.

SOME QUESTIONS AND CHALLENGES FACING A HUMANISTIC PSYCHOLOGY

Carl R. Rogers

I believe there is no doubt that Humanistic Psychology is part of a developing trend. I feel sure that a concern with, and a belief in, the subjective human being as an active agent in his own life, and in life in general, is to be a growing part of the wave of the future. I feel that my past record indicates that I have a fairly good intuition as to the next developments in psychology and this intuition informs me that the humanistic emphasis is a coming trend. I feel quite certain that it is one manifestation of a developing direction in our whole culture.

The important question for us is whether we will be able to meet the challenges posed by such a trend. Will we be adequate and worthy representatives of a direction which will, I am sure, be evident in art and literature, in education, and in science? Here I am somewhat less sure.

I have to face the possibility that perhaps this orientation is only a protest group of temporary value. It certainly serves a useful function to deplore the sterility of most present-day psychological science, to oppose a completely S-R psychology, to resist the way in which man is treated as an object in present-day behavioral science, to protest against the view of man as completely mechanical, and to disavow the view that the world is a clock already wound up and running its completely determined course. These protests need to be made. We are part of a growing body of belief which stresses that man is more than is encompassed in these views. But if deploring and resisting is all that we do, then we are only a temporary protestant group soon to be superseded.

If we are to be more viable, then we must make positive contributions—must discover constructive resolutions for some terribly perplexing problems. I would like to talk of some of the challenges which I see

SOURCE: Carl R. Rogers, "Some Questions and Challenges Facing a Humanistic Psychology," *Journal of Humanistic Psychology*, Spring 1965. Reprinted by permission.

Informal remarks addressed to a meeting of the American Association for Humanistic Psychology, Los Angeles, September 3, 1964.

facing us. Perhaps in this audience there are individuals, especially perhaps some younger individuals, who may make significant contributions in the coming years to the answering of these challenges.

Here, then, are some of the basic questions I see, questions which we will either meet and help to resolve, or fail to meet and hence die out as a significant force in psychology.

1. Can we develop an adequate concept of psychology as a discipline? Will it be a discipline like physics? Physics has gone from one discovery to another, from the law of the lever to atomic fission and fusion to the structure of the nucleus of the atom. Each of its discoveries has been characterized by the discernment of invariant lawful order in relationships. It has been true of physics that the order which has been so discerned generalizes into areas initially undreamed of. Thus, this is a discipline in which new discoveries give order to vast areas of natural events. Is psychology this kind of a science? Or is psychology, as Michael Scriven has suggested, a science such as geography or oceanography? Since in my new home I look down upon the Scripps Institute of Oceanography, I will choose that as an example of a science quite different from physics. Oceanography keeps exploring new areas, coming up with new findings, adding a great deal of useful information. There is no doubt that its findings may change our economics and our way of life. It is not, however, a science which is likely to have a breakthrough because its discoveries and findings have limited generalization. Perhaps this is the kind of science which psychology will be.

In any event, we need a great deal more thoughtful and sound thinking as to the basic conceptual picture of our discipline.

2. The second challenge is as to whether we can develop a science which is humanistic. Can we develop an adequate philosophy of science and an adequate methodology of science which will truly add to verified knowledge and at the same time truly recognize the place of the subjective human being? We are not fond of a mechanistically oriented, hardheaded empiricism. But what will we put in its place? An existential mysticism will not, in my judgment, be good enough. Private subjective opinion will not be good enough. What is to be our way of knowing, of adding to knowledge? Will we be able to combine a logical positivism with some more human view? Will we develop some new formulation of what it means to add to knowledge? This is an area in which I am deeply interested and in which I hope to work.

To me this seems like a vital area of concern and one in which psychologists are weak at the present time. Perhaps in this audience or in this convention there may be some brilliant young thinker who will see his way through to a new way of meeting this challenge. It is all very well to be opposed to the atomistic scientific approach which characterizes most of psychology. It is all very well to be opposed to the shaping up of human behavior as being the ultimate goal of psychological science. But it is simply not enough, in my estimation, to settle comfortably back into the principle that since we appreciate the mysterious and the unique in man we are, therefore, somehow superior. William James wrestled with this issue long ago and said of these two extremes—both an atomistic empiricism and a subjective mysticism—"they are but spiritual chloroform." I heartily agree with his view. What will we contribute that will avoid these extremes? Will we incorporate the methods of phenomenology? Will we discover generally new modes of knowing upon which we can build? I am not certain. I am only sure that if we are to exist in a scientific world of DNA and RNA molecules, a world of microbiology, of electronic stimulation of the brain, of chemical analyses of psychological states, we must develop a mode of knowing which has *promise*.

3. A closely related issue on which I will dwell only briefly is this: can we develop humanistic scientists who are capable of the dedication, the commitment, the creative thinking, the bold theories and hypotheses, the toughness of thinking in regard to problems and paradoxes which the "hard" sciences have developed? This is our challenge and it is still an unanswered question. But the answer given by time will determine whether we are a flash in the cultural pan or whether we are a continuing flame which will illuminate modern life.

4. Still another challenge has to do with our views of education. Can we develop a philosophy of education and methods of education which are consistent with our concerns with the human being? Can we effectively put such a philosophy and such methods to work?

What is a view of education which humanistic psychologists could buy, could approve of? How would this new psychology facilitate learning? We have little love for teaching machines as a complete view of education, nor do we believe that the shaping up of behavioral responses to meet preconceived goals is a sufficient picture of teaching and learning. Very well, what do we put in place of these alternatives? First, what is our overall view or philosophy of education, and, second, what are the methods we would employ?

When I look at what has been achieved thus far in this field I find I am not only skeptical, I am somewhat discouraged. We *talk* a good protesting game but can we *do* anything new—*behave* in new ways, *think* in new terms? It is too early to know but the signs thus far would make no one unduly optimistic.

5. Can we develop approaches to interpersonal relationships which are actually more effective than those now in use or those prescribed by a hard-nosed American psychology? This is another challenge of an essentially practical sort.

If our interest in the unique human being is real, if we value spontaneity and creativity and expressiveness, are we able to facilitate the kind of interpersonal relationships in which these qualities are released? This, it seems to me, is one of the real tests of our position.

Here there are exciting developments all over the country. The intensive group experience is coming to be used more and more widely—with delinquents, with business executives, in Synanon, with educators, even at times with psychologists. I know that some individuals in this organization are playing an important part in this development. I hope that the organization as a whole will aid in meeting this challenge. Again, I trust it is clear that what I am saying is that protest is not enough, promise is not enough; we will have to be able to *deliver* in ways the common man can understand and in ways that the culture can assimilate and use if we are to grow and become important.

6. Still another challenge which I see is of a much more general nature. Will we be able to make a significant contribution to a philosophy of life? There is no doubt that sub-groups in our American culture, much of the Japanese culture, and many of the cultural groups in Europe no longer have a viable philosophy of life, a meaningful way by which to live. Existentialism is endeavoring to provide this. It has both strengths and weaknesses. Groups such as the Association for Humanistic Psychology and the new APA Divisions of Philosophical Psychology and Humanistic Psychology should be concerned with the philosophy of life which will be suitable for tomorrow. Do we have the individuals who will be able to contribute to it? I sincerely hope so.

What will this newer philosophy of life be? I certainly cannot answer this question but I would guess that it will have a certain existential flavor—man choosing himself, man the architect of himself. It will stress the value of the individual. It will, I think, center itself in the individual as the evaluating agent. These are, of course, only my opinions. I am very well aware of the strong counter-forces in the world which see the individual as existing only to serve the group, the corporation, or the state.

I believe that this newer philosophy will have a process quality, not a static quality. We will recognize that the *value* of living is in the *process* of living, not in some static goal to be reached. I have a dim recognition of what this process view would mean in many fields. It would make a difference in the questions asked. Instead of asking, "Have you learned fractions or biology or mathematics?" the question might be, "What is there in the process of these learnings which you find valuable?" Instead of the question, "Have you achieved a happy marriage?" it might be, "What is the process of your marriage? Are its process qualities viable, satisfying, growth promoting?" Instead of the question, "What is the goal for our country?" it might be, "Are we pleased with the process characteristics of our country at this time?" Instead of the question, "What are the absolute values and absolute truths in which we find security?" there might be the question, "Can we find security in being involved in the forward-moving process of change?"

Let me illustrate a bit of what I mean by this process quality. The true scientist does not find security in the knowledge which has been accumulated, because he knows that any day that knowledge may be contradicted by some new finding. His security lies in the scientific *method,* a *process* of arriving at approximations to the truth. I believe that in this same sense we must learn to live in a process mode. To me, it seems that our culture and our civilization will probably perish unless we can achieve this. In a world which is changing at an incredible rate in knowledge and technology we can find security only in a knowable process, not in knowable certainties. That at least is my judgment.

SUMMARY

I hope that the questions I have raised will stimulate discussion. Let me review briefly the issues or problems which I have raised.

1. What kind of a discipline are we? Do we resemble physics? Oceanography? Religion? Or?

2. What is to be the nature of our science and what are the methods of that science to be? Or more deeply, how do we contribute effectively to knowing?

3. Can we develop tough, dedicated, persistent, humanistic scientists?

4. How do we plan to contribute to the process of learning? What is education? What is a suitable philosophy of education? What do we propose as the methods of education?

5. Do we have the skills actually to promote more effective and creative interpersonal relationships?

6. What is to be our view as to what makes life worth living? What is the philosophy of life and living which we will contribute to our culture? Will it have an existential flavor? Will it be a philosophy of process? Or?

In conclusion, I would just like to say that in my judgment Humanistic Psychology will never go down in history for what it is *against.* The important question is, what are we *for*? I am sure we cannot answer this question today or in any official statement, but over the coming years this is where we will stand or fall. If we are for views which the culture finds valuable and freeing and life-giving, then we will survive and will deserve to survive. If we cannot meet these various challenges then we are just an interesting, protesting, splinter group. Time will tell which we are.

I should like to make a final confession. When I am speaking to outsiders I present Humanistic Psychology as a glowing hope for the future. But within the bosom of our family I have been trying to say that we have no reason whatsoever for feeling complacent as we look toward the future.

SECTION II
HUMAN RIGHTS

Human Rights. Two beautiful words put together. Both are abused, and perhaps they are more abused than they are honored. In this section it is our intention to honor them and present the views of others who have tried to preserve the dignity of Human Rights.

The concerns of minorities in this nation and in all the nations of the world have been and remain the concern of all humanity. To demean the lowliest in power, money or status is to demean the entire human condition. What is lacking from our section on minority concerns is any discussion of Mexican-Americans/Chicanos/Hispanos/ the people of La Raza and of Native Americans. In point of fact, we could not find writings from the humanistic position that were concerned with these ethnic minorities. That is a sore lack, and it points to a direction that the humanistic movement, humanistic psychology in particular, will have to take if it is to endure. A major concern of the humanistic psychologists is that their work does not touch the life of poor and disenfranchised people, and that the humanistic movement runs the danger of being a luxury of middle- and upper-middle income individuals. Certainly, as this book demonstrates, that does not have to be the case. Nevertheless, sensitive and dedicated members of minorities who are either presently a part of the professions or becoming a part of them need to become aware of the important parallels between the concerns represented in this book, the humanistic position and their own insistence on their individual and group human rights.

Similar concerns can be voiced for the women who have suffered a kind of second-class citizenship in our nation. Women have been a vital

47

part of the humanistic position and continue to hold leadership positions in organizations representative of the humanistic movement. The most notable of these organizations might be the American Humanist Association and the Association for Humanistic Psychology. It is our view, and the view of the authors in the section devoted to the psychology of women, that while many problems remain for women in our society they, as a group, have a future which promises to bring equality of males and females.

What may not have such an optimistic future, and what has plagued humankind throughout recorded history and into the present, is the problem of our sexuality. While it is not new to wonder aloud or in writing about the human sexual condition or to recommend a more "healthy" attitude toward sex, neither is it possible to simply allow our human dilemma over sex to continue undebated. Our human sexuality is a part of our being and while our rights to our sexuality, our use of it and the manner in which we use it are open to many different religious, philosophical, ethical, moral and cultural interpretations, the humanistic point of view is one which tries to remind us that sex is a human right which can be enjoyed lustily, totally and lovingly. The humanistic view invites us to give individuals as much freedom of choice in their sexual preferences as is possible while respecting the dignity and worth of all persons in our sexual activities. Certainly, humanists do not want to be read as advocates of demeaning and insulting sexual practices such as sado-masochism or other cruelties. But, we do invite the readers to consider how harsh the controls on human sexual activity have been in the past, and continue to be in the present, and to decide whether we wish to continue to maintain an oppressive and harmful individual and societal attitude toward human sexuality.

The last section of Human Rights deals with Humanistic Psychotherapy. Perhaps, it is in this area of concern that the humanistic position has had the most impact. As is sometimes the case, a speciality that was evolved as a help to humankind came to be as repressive and as dogmatic as the oppression and intolerance it was meant to relieve. Psychotherapy, and its conception of the nature of human nature, badly needed a revolution. The Humanistic Psychotherapies brought a fresh new point of view to the field of psychotherapy, and with it a belief that psychological health was a right of all humans; that often the person with a problem was in the best position to provide solutions for the problem; that health could be a matter of individual actualization rather than adjustment to cultural norms; and finally that the therapist and the client were partners in an agreement that could lead to the personal growth of both. They were not master and slave, boss and employee, superior and subordinate but, rather, they could be two people grappling together over the problem of being a human being.

A. SEX

THE DEPERSONALIZATION OF SEX

Viktor E. Frankl

When we speak and think about love, we should remember that it is a specifically human phenomenon. We must see to it that it is preserved in its humanness, rather than treated in a reductionistic way. Reductionism is a pseudoscientific procedure which takes human phenomena and either reduces them to, or deduces them from subhuman phenomena. Love, for example, is frequently interpreted in a reductionistic way as a mere sublimation of sexual drives and instincts which man shares with all the other animals. Such an interpretation blocks a true understanding of the various human phenomena.

In fact, love is one aspect of a more encompassing human phenomenon which I have come to call *self-trancendence*.[1] By this term I wish to denote that being human always relates to and is directed toward something other than itself. Man is not, as some current motivation theories would like to make us believe, basically concerned with gratifying needs and satisfying drives and instincts, and by so doing, maintaining, or restoring, homeostasis, i.e., the inner equilibrium, a state without tensions. By virtue of *the self-transcendent quality of the human reality* man is basically concerned with reaching out beyond himself, be it toward a meaning which he wants to fulfill, or toward another human being whom he wants to lovingly encounter. In other words, self-transcendence manifests itself either by one's serving a cause, or loving another person.

Loving encounter, however, precludes considering, and using, another human being merely as a means to an end. It precludes, for example, using a person as a mere tool to reduce the tensions aroused and created by libidinal, or aggressive, drives and instincts. This would amount to some sort of masturbation, and in fact, many of our sexually neurotic patients actually speak of their own way of treating their partners in terms of "masturbating on them." Such an attitude toward one's partner, however, is a distortion of human sex.

SOURCE: Viktor E. Frankl, "The Depersonalization of Sex." Reprinted from *Synthesis, The Realization of the Self,* Copyright © 1974. The Synthesis Press, Redwood City, California.

This is due to the fact that *human sex is always more than mere sex,* and it is more than mere sex precisely to the extent to which it serves and functions as *the physical expression of something meta-sexual,* namely, the physical expression of love. And only to the extent to which sex carries out this function of an embodiment, an incarnation, of love—only to this extent is it also climaxing in a really rewarding experience. Thus, Maslow was justified when he once pointed out that those people who cannot love, never get the same thrill out of sex as those people who can love. And among those factors which contributed most to enhancing potency and orgasm the highest ranking, according to 20,000 readers of an American psychological magazine who had answered a pertinent questionnaire, was romanticism, that is to say, something that comes close to love.

Of course, it is not quite accurate to say that only human sex is more than mere sex. As Irenaeus Eibl-Eibesfeldt[2] has evidenced, in some vertebrates sexual behavior serves group cohesion, and this is particularly the case in primates that live in groups; thus, in certain apes sexual intercourse sometimes exclusively serves a social purpose. In humans, Eibl-Eibesfeldt states, there is no doubt that sexual intercourse not only serves the propagation of the species but also the monogamous relation between the partners.

But while love is a human phenomenon by its very nature, the humanness of sex is only the result of a developmental process—it is the product of progressive maturation.[3] Let us start with Sigmund Freud's differentiation between the *goal* of drives and instincts over against their *object:* one might say that the goal of sex is the reduction of sexual tensions whereas its object is the sexual partner. But as I see it, this only holds for neurotic sexuality. Only a neurotic individual is out first and foremost to get rid of his sperma, be it by masturbation, or by using the partner as a means to the same end. To the mature person the partner is no "object" at all; the mature person, rather, sees in him another *subject,* another *human being,* seeing him in his very *humanness;* and if he really loves him, he even sees in him another *person* which means that he sees in him his very *uniqueness*—and it is only love that enables a person to seize hold of another person in that very uniqueness which constitutes the personhood of a human being.[4]

Promiscuity is, by definition, the very opposite of a monogamous relation. An individual who indulges in promiscuity need not care for the uniqueness of a partner and therefore cannot love him. Since only that sex which is embedded in love can be really rewarding and satisfactory, the quality of the sexual life of such an individual is poor. Small wonder, then, that he tries to compensate for this lack of quality by the quantity of sexual activity. This, in turn, requires an ever more multiplied and increasing stimulation as is provided, for example, by pornography.

From this, one might understand that we are in no way justified in glorifying such mass phenomena as promiscuity and pornography by considering them as something progressive; they are rather regressive; after all, they are symptoms of a retardation that must have taken place in one's sexual maturation.

We should not forget that the myth of sex-just-for-fun's-sake (rather than letting sex become the physical expression of something meta-sexual) as something progressive is sold and spread by people who know that this is good business. What intrigues me is the fact that the young generation not only buys the myth, but also the hypocrisy behind it. In an age such as ours in which hypocrisy in sexual matters is so much frowned upon, it is strange to see that the hypocrisy of those who propagate a certain *freedom from censorship* remains unnoticed. Is it so hard to recognize that their real concern is *unlimited freedom to make money?*[5]

But there cannot be successful business unless there is a substantial need that is met by this business. And in fact, we are witnessing, within our present culture, what one might call an *inflation of sex.* We can only understand this phenomenon against a comprehensive background. Today, we are confronted with an ever increasing number of clients who complain of a feeling of meaninglessness and emptiness, of an inner void, of the *existential vacuum*[6] as I am used to calling it. This is due to the following two facts: In contrast to an animal, man is not told by drives and instincts what he must do; and in contrast to man in former times, he is no longer told by traditions and values what he should do. In our day, he sometimes no longer knows what he really wishes to do.

It is precisely this existential vacuum into which the sexual libido is hypertrophying. And it is precisely this hypertrophy that brings about the inflation of sex. As any kind of inflation, e.g., that on the monetary market, sexual inflation is associated with de-valuation. And sex is de-valuated inasmuch as it is dehumanized. Thus, we observe the present trend to living a sexual life which is not integrated into one's personal life, but rather lived out for the sake of pleasure. The *depersonalization of sex* is understandable once we diagnose it as a symptom of what I call *existential frustration:* the frustration of man's search for meaning.[7]

So much for causes; but what about the effects? The more one's search for meaning is frustrated, the more such an individual embarks on what since the American Declaration of Independence has been termed the "pursuit of happiness." In the final analysis, the pursuit is intended to serve the purpose of intoxication and stupefaction. But, alas, it is the very pursuit of happiness that dooms it to failure. *Happiness cannot be pursued because it must ensue,* and it can ensue only as a result of living out one's self-transcendence, one's dedication and devotion to a cause to be served, or another person to be loved.

Nowhere else is this general truth more perceptible than in the field of sexual happiness. *The more we make it an aim, the more we miss it.* The more a male client tries to demonstrate his potency, the more he is likely to become impotent; and the more a female client tries to demonstrate to herself that she is capable of fully experiencing orgasm, the more liable she is to be caught in frigidity. And most of the cases of sexual neurosis I have met in my many decades of practice as a psychiatrist can easily be traced back to this state of affairs.

Accordingly, an attempt to cure such cases has to start with removing that demand quality which the sexual neurotic usually ascribes and attributes to sexual achievement. I have elaborated on the technique by which such a treatment can be implemented, in a paper published in the *International Journal of Sexology* in 1952.[8] What I want to state here, however, is the fact that our present culture which, due to the motivation outlined above, idolizes sexual achievement, further adds to the demand quality experienced by the sexual neurotic, and thus further contributes to his neurosis. The use of the Pill, by allowing the female partners to be more demanding and spontaneous, has unwittingly encouraged the trend. American authors observe that the women's liberation movement, by having freed women of old taboos and inhibitions, has had as one result that even college girls have become ever more demanding of their sexual satisfaction, demanding it from college boys. The paradoxical result has been a new set of problems variously called "college impotence" or "the new impotence."[9]

The Victorian sexual taboos and inhibitions are going, and to the extent that real freedom is gained, a step forward has been taken. But, freedom threatens to degenerate into mere license and arbitrariness, unless it is lived in terms of responsibleness. And that is why I do not tire of recommending that the Statue of Liberty on the East Coast be supplemented by a Statue of Responsibility on the West Coast.

REFERENCES

1. VIKTOR E. FRANKL: *Psychotherapy and Existentialism,* Washington Square Press, New York, 1967.
2. IRENAEUS EIBL-EIBESFELDT: *Frankfurther Allgemeine Zeitung,* February 28, 1970.
3. VIKTOR E. FRANKL: *The Doctor and the Soul,* Vintage Books, New York, 1973.
4. _____: *Man's Search for Meaning,* Pocket Books, New York, 1963.
5. _____: "Encounter: The Concept and Its Vulgarization," *The Journal of the American Academy of Psychoanalysis,* 1, 1973, p. 73.

6. _____: "The Feeling of Meaninglessness: A Challenge to Psychotherapy," *The American Journal of Psychoanalysis*, 32, 1972, p. 85.
7. _____: *The Will to Meaning*, New American Library, New York, 1969.
8. _____: "The Pleasure Principle and Sexual Neurosis," *The International Journal of Sexology*, 5, 1952, p. 128.
9. GEORGE L. GINSBERG, WILLIAM A. FROSCH AND THEODOR SHAPIRO: "The New Impotence," *Arch. Gen. Psychiat.*, 26, 1972, p. 218. Konrad Lorenz has shown that it is not only in humans that the demand quality or—for that matter—sexual aggressiveness on the part of the female partner can result in impotence for the male; this also happens in animals. There is a species of fish whose females habitually swim "coquettishly" away from the males who seek mating. However, Lorenz succeeded in training a female to do the very opposite—to forcefully approach the male. The latter's reaction? Just what we would have suspected to be shown by a college boy: a complete incapacity to carry out sexual intercourse!

THE MALE SEXUAL CYCLE

Warren Mintz

In analyzing the male sexual cycle, Masters and Johnson divide the experience into four identifiable stages: excitement, plateau, orgasm, and refraction. This essay is mainly focused on the stage of plateau, with some reference, toward the end, to refraction.

Briefly described: *excitement* is the stage in which the male becomes sexually aroused; *plateau* is the sustaining of the excitement; *orgasm* is the release; and *refraction* is a time of quiescence, after which excitement may once again be experienced.

The stages flow into one another and may be viewed as parts of a single process. In spite of this holistic recognition, I find myself putting excitement and orgasm into one category and plateau and refraction into another.

If the focus of sexuality were on procreation, the two key phases would be excitement (the response to stimuli) and orgasm (the deposition of semen in the female); the sustaining of the sex act and what happens after become of secondary concern. Here, the priorities are reversed. Those parts of sex least concerned with conception are of most concern here. In my opinion, the stages of plateau and refraction reflect the most "human" dimensions of sexuality.

PLATEAU

Some of the most frantic, depressing, and self-destructive information in the field of sexuality deals with the sensations of the plateau. Briefly stated, the information recognizes that unless a man does something to redirect the process it is possible to go from excitement to orgasm in a matter of seconds with only a momentary pause, if any, at the stage of plateau.

Two basic strategies, neither of them good, have thus far been developed to deal with the situation. Each will be mentioned here and developed further on. The first recognizes that sustaining the sensations of

SOURCE: Warren Mintz, "The Male Sexual Cycle." This article first appeared in *The Humanist*, September/October 1976, and is reprinted by permission.

the plateau is difficult and focuses on the development of sufficient social power to define and basically avoid the problem. The result of this strategy has largely been to deprive females of knowledge of their own sexuality so that a standard could not emerge that would force men to feel inadequate. The second is more considerate of women but less considerate of men. Techniques were developed to enable men to decrease excitement so that it could be experienced in more manageable levels. Both of these self-defeating strategies will be analyzed, and a new, more promising orientation will be offered in their place.

Is female sexuality a threat that has been controlled by men for their own protection? Such is the thesis of a book called *The Nature and Evolution of Female Sexuality*, by Dr. Mary Jane Sherfey (New York: Vintage Books, 1973). Drawing heavily on the work of Masters and Johnson, Sherfey calls attention to the highly developed sex drive and capacity of female primates. Human females, she argues, would act like other female primates given a chance. But the consequences of such uncontrolled sexual behavior would cause havoc in the predictable relationships required of a well-structured kinship system, especially since the development of private property, which requires that a legitimate heir be produced. In Sherfey's view, the control and domination of female sexuality by men was one of the central conditions necessary for the development of society as we know it.

On the assumption that she is correct, in what position does this leave the male? He is bonded to a female who has a sexual capacity far in excess of his own. A capacity that, if expressed, could leave him with a sense of inadequacy and hatred. I suspect that a great deal of human history can be understood as men protecting themselves by keeping women dependent and pregnant, by convincing women that sex is a male thing, and by threatening to abandon any woman who might confront his feelings of inadequacy.

If this was all there was to the analysis, it would be bad enough. One would be forced to deal with situations in which more than half of the human population has been kept dependent and isolated and in denial of a basic human need. But it gets worse. Somewhere there emerged an ethic that rewarded those men who could sustain the sex act for a long time. In the language of this piece, the goal for many became to stay on the plateau for as long as possible. Given the nature of the devices used to achieve this goal, I find it hard to believe that the changes were oriented toward increased pleasure. The things that men did to stay on the plateau were essentially self-destructive. The key strategies became a sense of noninvolvement with the woman and a mutilation of physical and emotional sensations.

In *Sexual Politics* (Garden City, N.Y.: Doubleday, 1970), Kate Millett portrayed male power based on the hatred and fear of women. She begins the book by quoting a section from *Sexus,* by Henry Miller, in which Val (Miller himself) is with a woman called Irma. Millett describes in careful detail the degradation of Irma. In my opinion, she focused on the wrong aspects of their relationship. Val did degrade Irma. He could do this because he was largely indifferent to her as a person. Irma was very beautiful. The men she met became infatuated with her. Not so for Val, and in this distance lay his power. She wanted him to care; and the more she wanted, the more distance he felt.

But there are more aspects to Miller than the one portrayed. In *Tropic of Capricorn* (London: John Calder, 1964), he is with a woman who has him very excited, and his behavior is quite different:

> Whenever I felt in danger of going off I would stop moving and think—think for example of where I would like to spend my vacation, if I got one, or think of the shirts lying in the bureau drawer, or the patch in the bedroom carpet just at the foot of the bed . . . I didn't dare to think what she might be thinking or I'd have come immediately. Sometimes I skirted dangerously close to it, but the saving trick was always Monica and the corpse at the Grand Central Station. The thought of that, the humorousness of it, I mean, acted like a cold douche. . . .

No more distance, no more indifference, no more the luxury of control that comes from not caring. He wants to stay inside the woman, and in order to do it he must deaden his feelings.

This is not an unusual strategy. There are men who think of the most nonsexual things imaginable while having sex. There are some who do arithmetic. There are some who come to bed with a pin, and when the excitement becomes too much they secretly jab themselves, in hopes that concentration on the pain will shift the focus of their feelings and bring down their level of excitement. There are men who tell the woman not to move and not to show any emotion, in hopes of keeping the input of excitement down to a manageable level: mutilation—physical and mental mutilation—of both the man and the woman.

I know a man who has a friend who told him that he and his wife have an excellent sex life and have sustained it for over thirty years. The man's "trick" is to take a shower before having sex and before leaving the shower to rub adhesive cream for dental plates on his penis. It seems that this cream has anesthetic properties, for deadening sensitive gums, that also works to deaden the sensations of the sensitive penis. There is presently a multi-million-dollar business in products such as Detain and Prolong that partially anesthetize the penis. I have even heard that cocaine on the penis deadens the sensations.

Personally, I am in favor of these products in the absence of alternatives. Anything that increases a person's confidence can be parlayed into a self-fulfilling prophecy that can lead to increased pleasure. The focus of this essay, however, is on an increased sense of self and its capacity for pleasure, without the artificial aids of alcohol, drugs, or "pain killers."

Wouldn't it be nice if there were some simple formula that, if followed, would solve the problem? I remember once meeting a man who said that he had a great sex life. I asked him for the secret, and he told me that I would have to discover it for myself. I asked him for a clue, and he said, "The sphincter muscle." When I got home I asked my wife what she knew about the sphincter muscle. She told me that the sphincter muscle keeps the rectum closed between trips to the bathroom. I learned that there are no easy formulas no matter how "tight-assed" I was willing to become.

Maybe the man is right, that each of us has to discover our own process and that what works for one may be irrelevant to another. I don't know. What I would like to do is to share some aspects of my process even as it is now unfolding. Not all of it relates to sex, except insofar as sex is a situation that can involve the total person. The "streams" that feed the process often find their source far removed from the bedroom.

In terms of sexuality, anxiety is real and is based on situations that are so important that they become dangerous. What seems to be true, however, is that the situations become even more dangerous, unless some means are developed to deal with the anxiety. I have argued that for a man the fear of not being able to sustain the excitement of sex has thus far led to two socially destructive solutions. First, women have been kept from knowledge of their sexual capacity, in hopes that without standards of comparison any level of performance will have to be acceptable. Why else the premium on virgins and the social stigma that has been attached to "bad" (read "experienced") women? Second, men have mutilated themselves both mentally and physically in the attempt to avoid the anxiety of excitement and the fear of failure—falling. The dilemma of the man becomes: can he enjoy the intensity of the feeling of sexual excitement or must the feelings be approached with a sense of control and/or dread in the face of what Sherfey describes as potential female insatiability?

The situation can be appreciated for what it is, and the anxiety/danger can be faced rather than avoided or denied. A person can learn to function at a more efficient peak. I think that the process lies in the direction "not worrying about oneself so much," and what follows are some guidelines to the path.

It seems to me that men have a vested interest in the liberation of women, in spite of the fact that the women will become more independent and perhaps more critical and demanding. From the male point of view, the drawbacks will be more than compensated for by having another active human being who is also responsible for sharing and bringing energy into the relationship.

I remember teaching a class on human sexuality during which the topic of contraception came up. One of the men said that he didn't like using a condom because it required that he stop what he was doing in order to put it on. The class and I questioned what might lie under such an opinion and arrived at the conclusion that the man felt responsible for keeping the woman stimulated and that he couldn't do this and put on the condom at the same time. In delving deeper, we uncovered an additional dimension. The young man believed that the woman really didn't want to have sex, that she felt what she was doing was "wrong," and that if she had time to think she would reconsider and leave the situation. What he was afraid of was that the thirty seconds it took to put on the condom might cost him his chance at sex.

I asked him whether he could accept the fact that the woman knew perfectly well what was happening and that she wanted to share the situation, that she was not about to run away. I asked him whether he would consider including her in the experience by giving her the condom to put on for him. He shook his head no.

What a "trip" we men have laid on ourselves. We view it as our responsibility to lead the woman through the sex act. We touch, we stimulate, we get on top, and we assume that the woman will be the receiver. We don't consider or won't allow the process to be shared. The increasing rate of male impotency is testimony enough to the anguish of this burden.

One of the prices we have paid for this imbalance is that many men don't know what it feels like to be touched. The major focus of our sensation becomes the penis, because that is the first part of the male to receive stimulation. Excitement of sensations focused only on the penis can be overwhelming.

We have the capacity to feel sensation in all parts of our body. During sex we can feel the experience in places other than our penis. An active, participating female can share with us the dimensions of this exploration. For a start, there is George Downing's The Massage Book (New York: Random House, 1970). People who share the experiences offered in this book learn what it feels like to be touched all over, to take and to give pleasure. What a relief to share an experience with someone who takes responsibility for bringing energy and excitement into the situation. It opens up a situation different from "combat in the erogenous zone." It opens up the possibility that a man may experience the plateau with greater pleasure rather than with denial. A new sharing that is not personally or interpersonally destructive becomes possible.

In all that follows, the basic assumption is that the responsibility for the sexual act will be shared between the man and the woman. It is important to restate this assumption because it might be possible to view what is to follow as a further contribution to potentially destructive strategies of interaction. I say this because I'm about to shift the focus from the couple to the man himself. It must be understood from the outset that what goes on between two people is shared and that it is the responsibility of each to bring to the other the "gift" of the relationship.

With this caveat, I would like to call attention to the fact that there is a limit on the extent to which an interpersonal experience can be shared. I believe that one of the key elements of pleasure on the plateau becomes a man's feeling of his own sexuality.

I'm going to introduce a concept that I think is of fundamental importance. It is called "grounding." As it is being used here, grounding means a base of reference and security that a person can turn to for orientation. In the sex act, some of this grounding can come from the other person, especially if the relationship is good. What is to be probed now are the sources of grounding that lie within the control of the individual himself. Here we will deal with two dimensions: the control of the physical environment so that it feeds back to the person a sense of orientation and security and a process of self-awareness by which a person can expand knowledge of himself as a more complete human being.

I remember reading *Total Orgasm*, by Jack Rosenberg (New York: Random House, 1973), which contained a sentence that struck me as self-evidently true. Rosenberg was talking about water beds and he was responding to the general feeling that sex is better on a water bed. He disagreed and phrased his position by arguing that it is hard to get a feeling of grounding on a water bed. At the time I read this we had had a water bed for about three years. I knew that there was something about it that made me uncomfortable, and Rosenberg's sentence helped to crystallize my thinking. The water bed moved. I did not get the feeling of substance underneath that fed back a sense of security and support. My knees, for example, did not feel solid and I could not turn to sensations in my feet as a source of predictable reference. I was never sure what the effect of shifting my weight would be on the rest of my body. This uncertainty was a source of anxiety and discomfort. I feel much more grounded on the hard mattress that we bought as a replacement.

The same need for predictable support can be said of other aspects of the surrounding environment, like color, sound, taste, and smell—things that give not only pleasure through contact but also a sense of security and reference. I am not sure how important these external supports have to be once a person has more deeply internalized a sense of grounding. But during a time of transition, when other aspects of the situation may be shaky, anything that feeds back a feeling of positive orientation has value. I would suggest that a man think about the place in which he will make love and surround himself with references that give him support. He should also recognize that the woman has similar needs and may have a desire to surround herself with things that give her a sense of orientation and pleasure. Happily, it is also possible for both to get pleasure from the same sources.

More difficult to confront is the idea of finding grounding through internal reference. Men have been taught from an early age to be competitive, to be strong, and to achieve in situations in which others have a vested interest in their failure. None of these are likely to be sources that can be turned to for personal grounding. In addition, we live in a world in which many of the basic social institutions, are being changed or challenged. We lean on such things as education, family structure, male-female relationships, the economy, the church, our political institutions, and our national role in world affairs, only to find them shifting under our pressing need, like the water bed. Some of these movements have the possibility of helping to build a better society, but all of these changes are unsettling. Where in the midst of this unrest can a man find a sense of personal grounding?

I think it begins with the acceptance of ourselves as persons. This means the recognition that we are made up of a mixture of aspects, of which some make us proud and other make us ashamed. We must learn to live with the things that make us vulnerable or we will be like the hypochondriac who fears illness so much that he lives with it all the time. We must get free of unrealistic standards that make almost all achievements seem commonplace and all men mediocre. I would not readily allow my achievements to be denied so that someone else can add points to his score by subtracting from my own. This is especially true in the area of sex, where people lie and make points by impressing others with tales of sexual prowess. By internalizing such unrealistic standards, we are all inferior—even the person telling the story, who believes it enough to wish it were true. Men can learn a lesson from women's consciousness-raising groups and begin to share real experiences in which we can locate ourselves as real human beings.

In addition to coming to terms with oneself as a person, it is also possible to learn to expand our capacity for experiences that include pleasure. The direction of this path has already been indicated in the mention of massage and learning to feel sensations all over the body. But there are other things that I am learning that other cultures seem to have known for thousands of years. One of these is the importance of getting in touch with the properties of breathing. In *Zen in the Art of Archery* (New York: Pantheon, 1953), Eugen Herrigel was unable to shoot the bow until he learned to breathe properly. Breath is a source of self-controlled energy. One can get grounding from the processes of breathing. It is no accident that women preparing for natural childbirth are taught how to breathe.

REFRACTION

Refraction begins following ejaculation. It is a time in which sexual energy is spent and the male has a reduced capacity to respond to sexual stimuli. It is a time of quiescence during which the male is vulnerable.

The more I deal with the subject of sexuality the more interested I become in the stage of refraction. I was recently asked to organize a workshop in male sexuality at a conference sponsored by the National Organization for Women. Along with the request came a copy of an article written by a husband and wife who were going to give the keynote address. In essence, the article argues for a more permissive attitude toward sexual intimacy. Sexual intercourse should not be put into a special category but rather should become a generally accepted part of interpersonal relationships. I knew that I was having difficulty accepting the argument and decided to organize a workshop around my response.

I went for a walk and, as I did, I followed my response to some of its deeper roots. I love my wife, and the idea of her being sexually intimate with someone else causes me pain. I used thoughts of her to probe my response. How open could I be about our relationship and where was I especially vulnerable?

I thought of films that I have seen about rodents copulating and recalled scenes of guinea pigs milling around until a male mounted a female, gave a few vigorous thrusts, got down, and walked away. Excitement and orgasm; something like Erica Jong's "zipless fuck." I am not comfortable with even this amount of openness, but I do recognize that while the interchange may be highly charged it doesn't seem especially intimate.

I followed my thoughts to the stage of plateau and refraction and found that these made me more uncomfortable. To experience the pleasure of the plateau, each must have a deeper, more intimate knowledge of the other. This is no longer a meeting of personal needs but a blending and sharing of one person's needs with another's.

When I thought of the refractory stage, my discomfort reached its most acute level. I sensed that of all the aspects of sexual openness the sharing of the refractory experience would be the most difficult for me to accept.

I probed my own experience and came to the conclusion that I am probably never as defenseless and as vulnerable as I am following orgasm. I think this is true of men in general. Some ask women, "Did you come?" not for the purpose of being told what good lovers they are, but to find out whether the woman is satisfied and whether it is safe to relax into vulnerability. Some can't handle the feelings of defensiveness and immediately light up a cigarette and use the smoke for a cover, or go to sleep, or watch television, or get out of bed, and some even go so far as to leave the woman.

Some, however, are able to stay with this open, vulnerable self and share it. It is a time in which the basic human relationship becomes the source of interpersonal energy. There is no longer a high level of excitement to mask the feelings.

I find that it is most difficult for me to be open concerning the deep touch that is possible following an orgasm. The idea of the person I love sharing with another the time of his greatest openness and vulnerability causes me pain. It is this experience, which can happen during the refractory stage, that places sexual intimacy, for me, into a category separate from other forms of social intercourse.

I think a man must feel good enough about his basic sense of worth to share with the woman his feelings of vulnerability. It is a time in which defenses are down and emotional antennas are out testing the situation. It is a time in which "stroking" is greatly appreciated and criticism is blown out of all proportion. An angry woman can collect her "dues" during such a time. A loving woman can experience depths in the man that cannot be touched when the normal defenses are in place. I think the feelings of the refractory period are the clearest indicants of the nature of the interpersonal relationship. It is a time of sharing, if there is anything to be shared.

CONCLUSION

This essay has focused on the plateau and refractory stages of the male sexual cycle, the two stages least necessary in procreation. I stated that in my opinion these stages reflect the most "human" distinctions of sexuality. To experience them as pleasure, the person involved will have to establish sufficient grounding to trust not only the other person but himself. What is required is sufficient confidence to deal with anxiety and to relax inhibiting controls. The process, as it has been presented, is not easy and offers no formulas. It holds forth the promise of pleasure and well-being for those who are willing to let go of the older, self-defeating strategies and take the risk of establishing a new base. If the future lies in the direction of the development of a more complete human being, it is impossible to imagine such a person deprived of the pleasure of his full sensual and sexual abilities.

WHY BOTHER WITH GAY RIGHTS?

Brian McNaught

Hypocrites, stated Matthew Henry, "do the devil's drudgery in Christ's livery."

"Patriotism," insisted Samuel Johnson, "is the last refuge of a scoundrel."

Once again, misuse of the hyphenated proper noun *God-and-Country* has been employed to express fear and hatred and has succeeded in undermining basic human rights. Immediately prior to the June 7, 1977, defeat of a civil-rights ordinance for homosexuals in Dade County, Florida, Anita Bryant Green, spokesperson for the Florida Citrus Commission and Save Our Children from Homosexuality, Inc., told her followers: "[I dare to speak out] as a mother—as an American—as a Christian. I urgently need you to join with me and my family in a national crusade against this attack on God and His laws. It's really God's battle, not mine!"

According to most national press reports, many of the 202,319 Dade County residents who voted to repeal the Human Rights Ordinance saw the issue as a religious question. While much of our media intelligentsia found Ms. Bryant comical, she succeeded in convincing her public that gay civil rights were anti-God and anti-American, playing upon their fear that Miami would become "Sodom by the Sea."

There was little education disseminated in the Florida fight. Save Our Children perpetuated every known myth about homosexuals and created a couple of new ones. Homosexuals, insisted Ms. Bryant, are condemned by God. They seek to wear women's clothing, if they are men. They are sexually interested in children. Even those who aren't should not be allowed to be around children, who might be persuaded to become gay because of the influence of the positive role model. Homosexual acts, she said, are hideous because men eat each other's sperm, which is the essence of life. The Dade County ordinance would promote bestiality. Cali-

SOURCE: Brian McNaught, "Why Bother with Gay Rights?" This article first appeared in *The Humanist*, September/October 1977, and is reprinted by permission.

fornians, she concluded, suffered a major drought because of God's wrath over that state's protection of gay civil rights. Ms. Bryant, who announced that many of her friends were homosexuals, insisted there would be no problem if gays would only stay in the closet.

If arguments for or against civil rights must be based upon the Bible, homosexuals should have nothing to fear. While the traditional position has been that selections of the Old and New Testaments (Genesis 19, Leviticus 18, Paul's letters to Romans, Corinthians, and Timothy) indicate God's abhorrence of homosexuality, a growing number of Scripture scholars from every major Christian denomination are now insisting those passages have been taken out of context and actually have nothing to do with what we know as "constitutional homosexuality." These arguments have been most recently supported by the controversial report on human sexuality by the Catholic Theological Society's Committee on Sexuality.

Wearing the clothing of the opposite gender is known as transvestism, which according to every available study is generally engaged in by heterosexuals. Ms. Bryant televised film clips from a San Francisco Gay Pride parade, in which several persons in "drag" participated. While there are certainly a number of gay men who parade in dresses, the number is small and their participation is more tolerated than encouraged.

Pederasts, or those persons who are sexually interested in children, again generally come from the heterosexual community. Police records indicate that the majority of such crimes involve fathers with their young daughters. Dr. Mary Calderone, director of the Sex Information and Educational Council of the U.S., writes: "The statistics are that it's heterosexuals who do most of the raping and seducing."

Nevertheless, Save Our Children frightened voters with their "reminder" that an Orange County high-school band instructor was recently charged with ten counts of sexual relations with boys under eighteen years of age. They also could have recalled the twenty-seven young boys murdered in Houston by thirty-three-year-old bachelor Dean Allen Corll; and had time been on their side, the current charges against Los Angeles homosexuals Patrick Kearney and David Hill for killing forty men, the largest mass murder in this country's history.

This scare tactic prompts several questions. Does anyone presume that gay men and women are not as upset by seduction and murder as nongay persons? Why does the sexual orientation of a homosexual murderer or seducer make headlines when a case involving a heterosexual is never portrayed as a "straight" murder? Did Jack the Ripper, the Boston Strangler, the Dallas sniper, or Richard Speck represent the sickness of all heterosexuals? Despite the statistics that heterosexuals are more prone to rape and seduce, wouldn't it be absurd to characterize all heterosexuals as rapers and seducers of children and therefore unfit for teaching positions?

Furthermore, what kind of society provides victims for this country's Dean Corlls and Patrick Kearneys? Corll's victims were gay runaways who were rejected by their families. Kearney and Hill preyed upon individuals who were forced onto the street to find sexual liaisons. Who saved these children?

Ms. Bryant's insistence that even homosexuals who weren't interested in children should not be allowed to teach because impressionable youth might "become" gay through the influence of a positive role model was answered by both Dr. Calderone and Russell Baker in the *New York Times.*

"It is now generally accepted that homosexuality and heterosexuality both are determined or programmed in the very early childhood years by as yet unidentifiable events," Calderone wrote in a June 15 letter to the editor. "Thus no one can *choose* to be either heterosexual or homosexual, neither of which state depends upon sexual acts but is specifically a state of being. Furthermore, no one who was programmed by five years of age to be heterosexual can be seduced to become homosexual, any more than the reverse. Think of the efforts that have been made through the ages by heterosexuals to seduce homosexuals. It doesn't work either way."

Russell Baker insists he would now be a spinster if teachers directed future role. In his June 26 *New York Times Magazine* column, Baker indicated he had spinster teachers until high school, at which time there were only men at the blackboard teaching all male students. "I had at least two homosexual teachers in that school. They didn't tell us they were, but we all knew it. I learned to jeer about them when they were out of earshot and to laugh about 'queers,' but I learned it from my 'role models' in the schoolyard and not from them. ... One of them was largely responsible for encouraging a classmate to pursue a form of art at which he is now one of the world's best practitioners, besides being a family man."

In discussing homosexual lovemaking, the former Miss Oklahoma not only threw medical science back to the time when we believed that sperm was life in itself and the womb only a receptacle, but also suggested that *all* homosexuals engage in the *same* forms of sexual expression. Furthermore, there was the implication that *only* homosexuals were covered by sodomy laws. Surveys among the gay population clearly indicate that there is no one thing everyone engages in, be it anal intercourse, fellatio, or even kissing.

Ignoring the comment about the California drought, Save Our Children's desire to have homosexuals stay in the closet is perhaps the most troublesome attitude of even rational and sympathetic observers. "Your mother and I don't broadcast what we do in the bedroom," my father once said, "Why must you?" Because, I replied, "you are not oppressed for what you do or don't do in the bedroom."

Battling myths and generalizations of "sick and sinful" labels by the psychiatric and religious professionals, homosexual women and men are incredibly concerned about public image and the mental health that results from self-acceptance and public acceptance.

"Coming out" as homosexual to self, to loved ones, and to working associates not only eliminates the need to dodge questions, dinner invitations, and anti-gay humor, but also enables the individual to produce more effectively and love more genuinely. An article in the Washington *Law Quarterly* by Irving Kovarsky entitled "Fair Employment for the Homosexual" states: "Thus the homosexual employee who is aware of his employer's policy toward homosexuals lives in fear, knowing that he will lose his job and will be unable to find other employment if discovered. A reasonable assumption is that the 'closet' homosexual performs less efficiently because of inner torment . . . The employer, maximizing profit, should be interested in the mental well-being of the unknown (and known) homosexual employee."

For many persons, the Dade County vote was a test of "I'm OK, you're OK." More than a question of civil rights, it was a battle for public- and self-acceptance. The eleven o'clock news on June 7 was felt by homosexuals across the world to be saying: "We're OK, you stink."

Gays in Dade County likened Anita Bryant to Adolph Hitler. Several columnists criticized that rhetoric as a sensationalized appeal to Miami Jews. But how sensationalized was it? Germany was wrought with unemployment, a "swinging" upper class, crime, and discontent. Hitler was seen as a harmless fool whose following was large enough to ensure him a place in the public eye, but too small to be seen as a threat. Gay rights had attracted the attention of a variety of noted scholars and personalities. Legislation pended in the Reichstag to repeal a repressive Paragraph 175. Once Hitler's bandwagon began to roll, he expanded his purist preaching and, with the consent of what was imagined to be the majority, began actualizing his dreams by burning books and enacting laws that limited the freedom of those persons outside his vision. Two hundred twenty thousand homosexuals were herded into concentration camps, forced to wear the pink triangle, and exterminated.

Anita Bryant arrived on the scene during a similar climate, made more dangerous by what pollster George Gallup refers to as "a profound religious revival." Six out of ten persons today, he reports, see "born-again Christians" as "devout, God-fearing persons." Having already established a Pat Boone reputation for wholesomeness by her role as spokesperson for America's favorite breakfast drink, the former Miss

America runner-up and mother of four entered the gay-rights struggle with the announcement that God had singled her out to fight His fight. When confronted with scientific studies that challenged her position, Ms. Bryant would either quote Leviticus 18 or break into a rousing rendition of the "Battle Hymn of the Republic."

Once the sweet taste of victory was anticipated, Anita expanded her saccharine rhetoric and God's crusade to include husbands and wives who engage in fellatio and/or cunnilingus. Save Our Children also announced the intention to carry their campaign across the country with special emphasis placed on the defeat of H.R. 2998, a bill currently before the House of Representatives that would amend the Civil Rights Act to include sexual orientation as grounds upon which no one can be arbitrarily discriminated against.

Ms. Bryant failed in her attempt to drive gay men and women back into the closet. According to *Time* magazine, the 350,000 homosexuals who marched during Gay Pride Week in late June composed the largest single street demonstration since the antiwar rallies of the 1960s. She did succeed in Dade County, however, in eliminating protections for homosexuals against discrimination in housing, employment, and public accommodations. She also succeeded, though I know it wasn't her intent, in escalating violence against homosexuals. Bumper stickers in Florida proclaimed "Kill a Queer for Christ!" Since June 7, there have been a rash of gay-victim murders. In San Francisco, a man was stabbed by four men who proclaimed, "This one's from Anita."

Murder and defeat of civil rights under the banner of God-and-Country should be a familiar scenario to Americans who have studied the struggle for human rights in this country. The Bible and the "Battle Hymn of the Republic" have been used as a one-two punch against Jews, atheists, blacks, women, sex educators, and those who advocate separation of church and state. This dynamic duo was even immortalized in the film *Inherit the Wind,* in which antievolutionist Matthew Brady (William Jennings Bryan) announced he was more concerned with the "Rock of Ages" than he was with the age of rocks, and his followers paraded through town with Bible, flag, and familiar choruses of that old faithful "Battle Hymn," promising to hang the Darwinian schoolteacher from the old apple tree.

What makes the current scene most threatening to the entire American population is the possible meaning of Anita Bryant's "normal majority" and her Dade Country victory chant, "Enough, enough, enough!"

Gay political activists have identified a strange coalition at work against homosexual civil rights. Prior to Save Our Children, the Roman Catholic Church has been seen as the principal foe. With the emergence of popular media figure Anita Bryant, other groups have begun to stick their heads out of the quagmire and identify themselves as anti-gay. These include the John Birch Society, the Ku Klux Klan, Catholics United for the Faith, and the Right-to-Lifers.

In Boston, the Right to Life group took a break from their Saturday-morning rosary recital in front of abortion clinics to send hundreds of telegrams to state senators admonishing them to vote no on legislation that would prohibit discrimination against gays in public employment. One state senator, who affirmed his membership in the John Birch Society, participated in a television debate and lauded Anita Bryant by parroting every argument she presented in Dade County.

In response to this new gathering of forces, the national leaders of the gay-civil-rights movement have arranged meetings with representatives of other civil-rights organizations in an attempt to build supporting coalitions.

Dade County has set the gay-civil-rights movement back. In addition to the escalation of violence, there is now an increase in police witch-hunts, intimidation, and fear and an increased possibility of blackmail. How strange it is to remember the argument against having homosexuals in government employment. It was reasoned that closeted homosexuals were easy prey for blackmailers who might seek important information. The openly gay person, who has nothing to fear from blackmailers, is now told to go back into the closet.

In addition, if the public could be convinced that impressionable children can be converted, the next step will be screening literature and textbooks, and censorship of television programs that depict "happy, healthy homosexuals."

But what of other human-rights issues? If there is a new coalition among superreligious and superpatriot groups, opposition to gay civil rights is not their only common denominator. "Enough, enough, enough" by the "normal majority" means campaigns against sex education in schools, busing, contraceptives for teen-agers, legalization of marijuana, the ERA, affirmative action for minorities, death with dignity, and abortion and campaigns for capital punishment, media censorship, and prayer in schools.

There was a time when civil libertarians could look to the Supreme Court for protection of constitutional rights. No longer, according to critics who suggest that the Nixon-packed court has abdicated its role to what appears to be majority rule as defined by Congress. The House and the Senate have rarely been known to tackle unpopular legislation. Even our "born-again" president has declined full affirmation of gay civil rights. While he has invited gay representatives into the White House and has said that laws should not punish homosexuals, he has refused to comment on whether or not homosexuals should be allowed to teach, indicating he "didn't want to get involved."

If the Gallup poll is correct, majority rule could be by Christian fundamentalists who, for the sake of our own good, will legislate life to comply with what they think is the essence of Scripture and Americana.

Observed C.S. Lewis: "Of all tyrannies, a tyranny exercised for the good of its victims may be the most oppressive. It may be better to live under robber barons than under omnipotent moral busybodies. The robber baron's cruelty may sometimes sleep, his cupidity may at some point be satiated; but those who torment us for our own good will torment us without end, for they do so with the approval of their own conscience."

His truth is marching on. . . .

B. PSYCHOLOGY OF WOMEN

FEMINISM AND HUMANISM

Dorothy D. Nevill

Social movements and social change have as their impetus a sense of dissatisfaction with the current situation, whatever condition exists at the moment. The left out, the disadvantaged, the passed-over, the disenfranchised, if left in that condition long enough, begin to want to move, to grow, to expand, to claim for themselves that part of the world that has been denied to them. Such changes can occur through orderly evolution or through violent revolution. The force of the method is dependent in some degree on the amount of festering frustration that has accumulated over time.

Violent revolution results in the blood baths of the French Revolution and the riots of Watts. Orderly evolution results in gradual, peaceful change of the social system spurred on by the efforts of those involved. Regardless of the nature of the protest, any social movement must contain the whole gamut of political activity in order to accomplish its purpose. Those who press for change must be united philosophically, but be diverse in tactic. There must be the active force, radical if you will, pressing publicly with at least some hint of violence, for immediate change. There must be the active, though establishment-oriented, element working with the existing culture to consolidate and implement the changes that are desired. In between must be all shades of active, dedicated members. Without the efforts of the "street brigades" the work of the more conservative appears weak and ineffectual. Without the efforts of the "bridge builders" the violent often splinter from society and have only themselves to listen to, or if powerful enough, lunge and lurch, almost accidentally, into war and catastrophe.

We are living through one of the most far-reaching evolutionary periods in our civilization. Women and men have begun to look at long sacrosanct sexual stereotypes and to question their continued necessity. "Why must our potentiality be limited in terms of our sexuality?" "Why cannot the opportunity of experiencing wholeness be extended to each

SOURCE: Dorothy D. Nevill, "Feminism and Humanism." This article first appeared in *Humanistic Psychology: New Frontiers*. New York: Gardner Press, Inc., 1977, pp. 101-108. Reprinted by permission of the author and the publisher.

one of us?" "Why are laws allowed which limit and regulate us because we are one sex or another?" "Why do we place value judgements on activities because they are engaged in predominantly by one sex?"

Questions such as these are only possible because of an unprecedented situation. For the first time in our history, the biology of the female reproductive system is clear and can with a high degree of probability be predicted and controlled. Never before in our history has this simple fact been true. Parents can choose whether or not to have children. Children can be born into a world where each one is loved and desired. Compulsory pregnancy can be an incident of the past. Women can enter into the fullness of life with the freedom to choose the manner in which they wish to participate.

Such has not always been true. In the past women have been accorded a more limited, more protected status than men because of biological necessity. Women become pregnant. During this time their bodies are not as lithe and capable as at other times. In an earlier age, without adequate means of refrigeration or pasteurization, the safest food for newborns was mother's milk. Extended lactation increased a woman's dependency. Women were in an almost continual state of bearing or caring for children. It was not from a vacuum that adages such as "barefoot and pregnant" and "a tooth for every child" arose. The vast majority of women, with only a few exceptions of the unusually wealthy or talented, agreed to accept a lesser role in the non-life-productive world, what we have called "man's world." With the establishment of a different status for women it was inevitable that abuses crept into the system so that women have been, at times, regarded as inferior, incapable, fit only for "women's work."

But now, the situation has changed, the cycle has been broken. Women, like men, can choose, to some extent, their destiny. It is hard to envision the far-reaching implications of this change in our lifestyle. For the first time we are consciously deciding on appropriate sex role patterns. What will be the implications for family constellations, childrearing patterns, economic dependency, patriarchal religion, and other central parts of our lives? Our lives are already undergoing the inevitable changes. If one were to list the 100 most influential people of the past century in the United States, the name of Margaret Sanger would probably not appear on a single list. But this woman, who almost single-handedly brought birth control to this country, who got together the monied individuals and the interested scientists in order to develop the "pill," probably has had as significant an impact on our style of living as any other individual that we could name.

A new social movement has arisen to guide the evolutionary change, one would hope, in a loving fashion: called pejoratively by its detractors as "women's lib," known to its intimates as "feminism." Unfortunately the image conjured up in most people's minds by the term feminism is that engendered by the national media, which publicizes the more radical, activist branch of the movement: the fictitious and legendary, bra-burning, lesbian man-haters. Perhaps women like this do exist. But the movement is far more than the press implies. All women are far more united philosophically than the media assumes. The movement embraces degrees of activism differing along the political spectrum from the Association of University Women to the Redstockings. But, the degree of politicism is not the pertinent dimension. What is important is the philosophy that unites feminists of all persuasions, an underlying feminist philosophy which is akin to the basic tenets of humanism, of self-actualization, of the whole human potential movement.

But, I am getting ahead of myself. Let us ask the beginning question first. What is a feminist? We cannot accept popular definitions of feminism, either from a national press attempting to sell their products or from polemic writers who spew hate and division. It is best to go to actual source itself for the data, to the women themselves. What is a feminist?

"a woman who is really aware of womanhood"

"a woman who is aware of her right to everything in life that everyone else has a right to"

"not just a member of a group"

"a woman's claim to happiness and property and money and freedom and independence, all of the things that a person might wish to strive for"

"active, not necessarily an activist"

"a man or a woman or a child that attempts to see people not in relation to their sex but as individuals"

"a broadening of sensitivity, perception, feeling, caring, sharing, all the catchwords of our time, to include everybody"

"recognized in our society as equals"

"growing, loving, caring"

"becoming the best that one can"

"utilizing one's talents to the fullest, regardless of sex"

"being able to choose from the whole gamut of human emotions and experiences, not being arbitrarily limited to only half of life, just because one is female or male."

The theme that is repeated over and over again in these definitions is that of growth, of self-fulfillment, of becoming a truly complete person. The emphasis is on the positive expansion of the individual. It is my contention that the kind of person a feminist desires to become is analogous to that described by Landsman as "beautiful and noble" or by Rogers as "fully-functioning" or by Maslow as "self-actualized."

How can this be? How can the focal point of the feminist movement and humanistic psychology be the same? To answer this question we need to carefully look at the implications of sex stereotyping.

A characteristic common to all cultures is the division of tasks according to sex. The extent and rigidity of the assigning varies widely. In some instances it is determined primarily by biological characteristics. Women are expected to bear children and men to perform a greater share of the tasks involving muscular strength. In other instances the workload pertains to far more than that dictated by physical differences and permeates every aspect of living. Either sex might be required to eat only certain foods, to dress differently, or to engage in specific occupations. For example, men might sow a crop, while women tend and harvest it. Not only can the extent of task assignment vary, but also the rigidity with which it must be followed. The reaction to violation of sex role mores in a society can include severe punishment, ostracism, reprimand, condescension, amused tolerance, or relative indifference. Generally societies in which sex stereotyping permeates many areas of life tend to expect rigid adherence to those standards. Those societies that allocate fewer tasks based on sex tend to allow somewhat more flexibility in behavior. There are no societies to my knowledge that assign tasks based only on genital differences.

Occurring alongside the assignment of tasks by sex is the expectation of certain behaviors by females and males. It is as if the whole continuum of human responses has been divided up and allocated partially to each sex. The commonly held stereotype of femininity in our culture includes the following characteristics: talkative, tactful, gentle, religious, neat, quiet, dependent, illogical, and emotional. Men, in contrast, are expected to be aggressive, independent, objective, dominant, active, logical, adventurous, ambitious, and self-confident. There is much in the literature to suggest a general consensus as to the stereotypes and appropriate behavior for each sex. Groups as diverse as clinical psychologists and undergraduate students, when asked to describe socially competent men or women, agree on the divergent characteristics of each sex (Broverman, Broverman, Clarkson, Rosenkrantz, & Vogel, 1970).

Now you and I know that these stereotypes do not hold fast in everyday life. We all know plenty of talkative men or ambitious women. There is far more overlap in acceptable behavior by the two sexes than the stereotype literature would have us believe. In most instances greater within-sex differences are found than between-sex differences.

Why, then, has research in the past emphasized the presence of clearly delineated and relatively rigid categories? The answer lies in our reliance on traditional research methods both in conceptualization and in methodology. In general, psychological research has assumed an "either-or" philosophy, that is, either one is dependent or independent, passive or aggressive, logical or illogical, and so forth. Only rarely is the whole continuum of the human personality taken into consideration. In short, we have tended to look at a multidimensional world through bipolar glasses. This limited and rigid view of the human personality was partly the result of inadequate statistical techniques and partly the result of petty thinking. The effects of this philosophy have been far ranging, but we are talking now specifically about sex stereotyping. Here we have a ready-made bipolar situation: female and male. Experiments have been designed to highlight the differences between the sexes, rather than to focus on the individual. Undergraduate students have been given forced-choice questions ("Is basket-weaving more feminine or masculine?"); have been asked to list behaviors, attitudes, and personality characteristics that they felt differentiated between men and women; and have been required to define their ideal woman or man. The result has been two sets of characteristics that comprise the definitions of femaleness and maleness. If researchers went looking for stereotypes, they were bound to find them. Fortunately, methods and viewpoints change, and the current researcher is obligated to look at familiar situations from a new perspective. Bem (1974), for example, has proposed an alternative to the traditional view of sex stereotyping which has heretofore treated masculinity and femininity as mutually exclusive categories on a bipolar continuum. The Bem sex-role inventory treats femininity and masculinity as independent, unipolar scales, allowing the derivation of a third score, androgeny, which measures the differential endorsement of masculine and feminine traits by the same individual.

What is needed, then, is a fresh look at an old situation. In their own ways both the feminist and the humanistic psychologist are attempting to do this. Both emphasize the expansive growth of the individual toward wholeness, that is, toward encompassing the whole spectrum of human potentialities. For a woman growth might mean uncovering the more aggressive, independent part of her nature. For a man growth might mean discovering tenderness and gentleness in himself in quantities that he had not been able to acknowledge before.

It is the ability to see the complexity of our nature that defines us as fully human: the ability to see ourselves in vastly different lights, as free and slave, as object and subject, as submissive and dominant, as lovable and unlovable. The existence and acknowledgement of such polarities in an individual's life are the source for a rich variety of productivity and fulfillment. However, complexities can lead to tension and conflict. Choices are inevitable, but it is in the complexity and tension that the human consciousness can fully develop. In the past we have tried to avoid this situation by clinging to one pole or another: men to a cluster of traits labeled masculine and women to a cluster of traits labeled feminine. The truly complete individual is one who can courageously live with the tension generated by complexity, who chooses the creativity and fulfillment that is possible there.

Rollo May (1967) distinguishes between two types of anxiety: neurotic and normal. Neurotic anxiety is destructive and constricting. It prevents people from realizing their full potential, from enjoying life to the fullest, from recognizing their own worth. It causes the person to become less human and to become apathetic. Normal anxiety, which results from recognizing and accepting the complexities of life, enables people to accomplish what they want. It mobilizes forces and helps meet threatening situations. Instead of being constricting, it is expanding. Instead of desensitizing a person, it enables one to see the real world, to make decisions, and to commit oneself to a way of life.

Anxiety, then, is not to be avoided. It is a necessary and important condition of life. As Kierkegaard has said, "Anxiety is the dizziness of freedom." To dare, to challenge, to live is anxiety-provoking. But not to venture is to lose one's essential humanness; to lose the capacity to act, to relate, to become enraptured; to lose the chance to become complete individuals by embracing all of life with all of its complexities.

The whole person realizes that to live a full life one must recognize one's total being and with that total being to engage in real encounters, to reach out to other individuals in love and compassion. Such a life involves risks, but it is creatively enriching.

The whole person accepts and relishes the richness of life. That person is not frightened by complexity, but thrives on it. That person values life to the fullest. "Not life, but the good life is to be valued." (Aristotle)

The feminist, whether female or male, strives to become this creative, courageous person. The humanistic psychologist holds it as a model for all of us. For different reasons, perhaps, and using different techniques, the two philosophies grow toward a common goal.

REFERENCES

Bem, S. L. The measurement of psychological androgyny. *Journal of Consulting and Clinical Psychology*, 1974, *42*, 155-162.

Broverman, I. K., Broverman, D. M., Clarkson, F. E., Rosenkrantz, P. S., & Vogel, S. R. Sex-role stereotypes and clinical judgements of mental health. *Journal of Consulting and Clinical Psychology*, 1970, *34*, 1-7.

May, R. *Psychology and the Human Dilemma*. Princeton, N.J.: Van Nostrand, 1967.

A HIGHER VIEW OF THE MAN-WOMAN PROBLEM

Roberto Assagioli
Claude Servan-Schreiber

The first time that I saw Roberto Assagioli, was about two years ago, at his home, in Florence, in the old house where a large part of his life has unfolded. He showed us into his office, cluttered with books and papers to such a point that he had to move a pile over so that my husband and I could be seated.

For a long moment we looked at each other, all three of us, without speaking. Assagioli smiling, his eyes, astonishingly vital within a face lined by great age, moving over us, going from one to the other. Was he submitting us to an examination? It was instead the opposite. He was allowing us to discover him leisurely, to establish a connection with him, without us even realizing this was happening. It was a climate of communication where words find their place later, while something like a current was developing between us. His face was shining with an extraordinary, radiant inner joy, such as I have never encountered in an octogenarian, and rarely in men much younger. This message of joy, perceived immediately, communicated immediately, is the finest memory which I keep of the numerous meetings which we later had with him. "All is possible and accessible *to you:* joy, serenity, I offer them to you as a gift."

I did not expect to find in Roberto Assagioli the echo of my own concern in a particular, specific area: the psychology of women within a world in which their roles, their functions, leads them to undergo first a conditioning, then an oppression which often they do not yet recognize. In the eyes of the feminist that I am, the father of psychosynthesis has therefore an additional merit: an amazing capacity to adapt to changing attitudes, which comes to him from his will to understand others and from his love of scientific truth, even if different from past beliefs. On the subject of women, he had in the past been limited; and he knows it and

SOURCE: Roberto Assagioli and Claude Servan-Schreiber, "A Higher View of the Man-Woman Problem." Reprinted from *Synthesis: The Realization of the Self.* Copyright © 1974 The Synthesis Press, Redwood City, California.

frankly admits it. He had been influenced by cultural prejudices denoting as "feminine nature" that which is largely the product of a social system. But later he freed himself, in this respect, from the weight of his up-bringing, his environment, his age. He quickly became interested in the new existential research into the nature of women which is our liberation movement. At his age, and for an Italian, this is a double achievement! Especially if one judges according to his conclusions.

There is not, and there cannot be a general psychosynthesis of women or, for that matter, for men. There is only, for each individual, of either sex, a personal, unique journey, toward the development of all his emotional, mental and spiritual faculties. "The human being," he said, "today is no longer defined by any of his roles. I believe in the primacy of the human being not conditioned by his sex." Can there be a more beautiful message? Here, more fully, is what he said to me on the subject:

ASSAGIOLI:

We cannot accurately speak of women and men *in general*. Each one of us is a human being before being 'man' or 'woman.' And each one of us, man or woman, has roles and functions to fulfill, individually, inter-indivi-dually and socially. Here is where the differences begin. These are most emphatically not *differences in value, only differences in function*. The human being is never defined by any of these roles. Women, as human beings, can accept or not accept traditional feminine roles. It is not nec-essary that a woman accept the role of wife or of mother. She can choose another vocation. It is not a 'must,' a necessity. It is a free choice.

Woman therefore is right in demanding that she be treated as a hu-man being and not as a 'mere woman,' as simply a woman and only that. She is right for refusing to be identified with a certain image of woman. She is a living being, with all the dignity and the potential of a whole human being. All attitudes which limit the possibilities of woman are mistaken. Women have the right to demand respect and parity with men. And the same, of course, is true for men.

Each of us can equally choose to play different roles. For instance, a woman can decide to play the role of spouse or of mother, or both. She can carry on a creative, social or business activity. She can choose one role, or she can alternate several of them, perhaps during the same day, perhaps over longer periods of time. This is the free choice of a human being. I believe in the primacy of the human being unconditioned by his or her sex.

The differences between men and women are clearly found reflected in our environment—in the family and in society—and it is here that we must work to eliminate their unfair and harmful crystallization into rigid stereotypes and prejudices.

But it is important to realize that these differences exist also *within* our psyche, in the depths of our unconscious, and, just as much, in the collective unconscious of humanity, where they appear through some of the most powerful archetypes. So there are universal masculine and feminine principles, which manifest themselves in quite diverse ways through different individuals. In other words, while masculine and feminine principles do exist in the universe, different people experience them and describe them in different ways—as is equally the case with beauty, truth, harmony, goodness, justice or any of the other universal principles.

The point is not to try to define what these principles are, but to distinguish, in our consciousness and in our relations with others, 'masculine' and 'feminine' from 'man' and 'woman.' We need to recognize that *both* the masculine and feminine principles exist in their own rights, and that they are present—although in unique forms and different proportions—in *every* man and in *every* woman.

Within each human being is a percentage of psychological masculinity and a percentage of psychological femininity, completely independent of the sex of the individual. Each person is a unique combination of these energies. When we look at women *on the whole,* we find that they are more attuned to the feminine principle, have greater access to it and have a higher percentage of it in their psychological make-up. Of course this is a generality. People are unique. Some men are psychologically more feminine than many women, for instance.

Take the example of the French novelist George Sand (the pen name of Madame Dudevant) and Chopin. They were lovers, and he, physically, had the 'man' role and she the 'woman' role. But psychologically he was feminine and she was masculine. She dressed like a man, wrote in a vigorous style—and smoked cigars! In her personality, masculinity predominated, while Chopin was imaginative, sensitive.

There is therefore a difference between physical sex and psychological characteristics. Over the years, I have met many who feared—or even believed—themselves to be homosexuals just because they did not recognize this distinction.

Only by accepting both the masculine and feminine principles, bringing them together, and harmonizing them within ourselves, will we be able to transcend the conditioning of our roles, and to express the whole range of our latent potential.

As this is true for the individual, so is it true for society. From the social standpoint, there is a great need in present society for the expression of the feminine principle. Society needs women to contribute the higher aspects of their femininity—altruistic love, compassion, the sense of and respect for life—with which they are usually more familiar and which they can often express with greater facility than men. It is therefore desirable for women to be involved in social and political life. If they so choose, they can do this while they continue to play traditional feminine roles in the family, or they can give themselves completely over to activities such as social service, renouncing the traditional family roles. They have the full right to do it. Society must respect and appreciate their valuable contribution.

The fact that a woman may dedicate herself much of the time to certain roles must not prevent her from considering herself equal to men. It is not at all a question of superiority or inferiority. Masculine and feminine psychological characteristics, even though dissimilar, are of the same value. This is a statement of fact.

Women are right to protest and to rise against the long-standing prejudicial attitudes of society. But in the protest one can lose perspective. One can be destructive and not constructive. Psychologically and historically, conflicts and exaggerations can be understood. The ideal would be for them to remain within boundaries that are constructive as well as just.

For example, some women go to the opposite extreme of current social stereotypes. Rather than balancing and integrating their feminine energies with their masculine energies, they may virtually deny the feminine in themselves. A woman may reject traditional feminine roles in order to prove to men that she can play masculine roles. Here exists the danger of the masculinization of women. Ironically, this attitude can proceed from the unconscious evaluation of the masculine principle and masculine roles as inherently superior to the feminine. But there is no such inherent superiority. What is needed is an honoring and valuing of the feminine principle, and the ways and roles through which this energy can be expressed by both men and women. Masculine roles are neither better nor worse than feminine roles. They are both needed and are of equal value.

A controversial question is whether the fact that women frequently have certain functions better developed and men others is the product of nature, or of education, or of social pressure. In my opinion all three factors are present, in different proportions, in each individual.

While this is an important *social* problem, fortunately, from the *individual's* standpoint it can be largely sidestepped. He or she need only consider how he or she is *right now*, and how he or she *can improve*.

For example, if a woman has had fewer opportunities or incentives to express her ideas, her thoughts, it does not seem to me to be necessary to spend much time and energy to search to understand why, who is responsible for this, and so forth. Quite simply, if this function is insufficiently developed, *she can develop it.* And the same is true for a man who has not developed his feelings, or his intuition. (Needless to say, there are men who need to develop their intellect, and women who need to get in

touch with their feelings and cultivate their intuition.) The point is to recognize the strong qualities and the deficiencies in each person—which are
not 'faults' but qualitative, relative deficiencies—and to bring them into
a condition of harmony and balance. This is what I call a psychologically
and spiritually practical approach.

Let us come now to the couple. A couple founded on a basis of fundamental equality, respect, reciprocal appreciation as human beings, can
work out the psychosynthesis of their particular couple together. Each
one can work on his own psychosynthesis, and each one can also collaborate in the psychosynthesis of the other, helping the other to achieve
his own psychosynthesis by helping him strengthen his less developed
functions. Then once they have done this to a certain point, they can
truly act as a couple by combining and complementing their qualities and
functions in all situations: in their marriage, their role as parents, and in
their social activities.

For each function to be developed training is needed—often including specific exercises. The process is analogous to the training of
muscles: if one wants to play a certain sport, he finds someone who is
competent, gets trained and afterwards continues to train himself. If a
man recognizes that his emotional and imaginative sides have been neglected, he can cultivate them. If a woman finds that her mind is not as active as she would like, she can train it. One has to 'cultivate one's garden'
by planting different flowers. A woman or a man can do it alone, but it is
often more effective, much easier and more enjoyable to do it together as
two people.

When we come to particular problems, many difficulties may
emerge, and in each specific case we can apply a therapy. I speak of 'therapy' here in the broadest sense of the word, because none of us is one
hundred per cent healthy in the higher psychosynthetic sense. In difficult
situations a benevolent and wise therapist or counselor can be of great assistance: someone impartial, kindly, comprehensive, who helps the two
members of the couple to become more aware, who explains the situation,
who indicates possible solutions and helps to choose the means to attain
them.

For each couple the situation is different. Each human being is
unique. Thus unique multiplied by unique gives unique squared; this is a
fundamental principle of psychosynthesis. Each case is unique, each
situation is unique. Each couple is unique. Each family is unique. We
need to focus on the unique existential problem of a certain situation,
rather than on generalities, and afterwards to choose techniques which
are most adequate for resolving the problems of that particular case.
This eliminates the fictitious, inauthentic problems. It may be called the
psychoanalytical phase: the discovery of the obstacles to constructive
work. And the obstacles are for the most part those which we spoke

about before: erroneous attitudes of men and of women. I believe therefore in the equality of value, and in the differentiation of functions *up to a certain point.* Collaboration, integration on a base of equality.

In education, the child needs a maternal environment and a paternal environment. Much harm is done in education when the paternal influence is missing. But if for some reason there is no father, the woman can take the paternal role also. It is difficult, but she can do it, if she wants to. And the same for the man: if the woman is not there, the father can take on the maternal role also. We can perform any role that life requires of us or that we decide to play. The same is true for work. In a large variety of situations, there is always in the human being the latent possibility to do anything within reasonable limits, to choose freely, to deliver himself from social pressures, prejudices, obstacles in order to reach his higher goals.

We are now in a period of crisis and profound changes. I believe that woman is evolving perhaps more rapidly than man. For him, the task is to discover the real human being beneath masculine limitations—to be not only a 'masculine-man,' but a *human being,* who plays masculine roles—and if he chooses, feminine ones. We know that historically there were matriarchal civilizations and patriarchal civilizations; the ideal would be a new synthetic civilization, that is neither patriarchal or matriarchal, but one that is psychosynthetic, that is to say, a civilization in which the highest and best qualities of each are manifested.

This would be something new. In all historical civilizations and cultures there has been a preponderance of one or the other element. But in this new civilization and the emerging global culture, for the first time humanity is sufficiently developed to make a planetary, global pattern, incorporating the very best of all men and women. I think that this planetary psychosynthesis, this psychosynthesis of humanity is possible and needed. Each particular problem will then have its frame of reference in the greater whole, and conflict can be replaced by harmonious integration and cooperation. All of this is within our reach—for not only is it very beautiful—it is very *human.*

AN OVERVIEW OF FEMALE SEXUALITY

Susan Dickes Hubbard

Have you noticed that, although endless attention is given to female beauty in our country, there are very few women who feel beautiful? A clinical observation I've made as a feminist therapist is that women tend to focus much more heavily on what they regard as their physical flaws than on their physical assets. Generally, deviations from the standard American pin-up or fashion model are perceived as flaws. In addition, a woman is more likely to evaluate her body from a cosmetic viewpoint than from a standpoint of physical conditioning and health, and forms her relationship with it accordingly. Even when a woman approves of her own looks, likely as not she is in a state of anxiety about how long this will last or is punishing herself for some subtle deviation from her notion of the physically perfect woman. She may also envy those whose body types are entirely different (though not necessarily better) than her own. All this is just one aspect of the tendency in our country for people to be dissatisfied with who they are and what they are doing and to turn to external models as vehicles to find happiness. Yet this physical aspect of alienation from the self has profound effects on the sexuality of women.

In their book *Human Sexual Inadequacy* (Boston: Little, Brown, 1970), Masters and Johnson talk about the "spectator role," which is a state of emotional detachment from the sexual events in which one is participating. This state of mind causes a person to be self-conscious, self-critical and self-absorbed, rather than truly involved with one's partner. Such an emotional stance also interferes with a person's capacity to experience the range of feelings that could be forthcoming in a sexual situation. For women, the spectator role often takes the form of incessant, distracting questions, such as: "Am I really attractive enough?" The spectator role in regard to physical appearance is a norm for American women, and this readily leads to insecurity and detachment in sexual situations. This insecurity is reinforced by the mass media. One glance at a

SOURCE: Susan Dickes Hubbard, "An Overview of Female Sexuality." This article first appeared in *The Humanist*, November/December 1976, and is reprinted by permission of the author.

89

magazine rack in any supermarket will reveal articles and ads for women concerning weight reduction, how to look young and sexy, and how to behave in ways that will begin or maintain a relationship with an elusive male who must be fooled or wooed.

One form of fooling men is to fake orgasm. The main reason women do this is to escape the anxiety created by the real nature of the sexual situation between their partners and themselves. The woman may feel her man needs her climax in order to feel adequate himself and may assume that his ego is too fragile to work patiently with her toward this end. Or she may fear that there is something wrong with her own capacity to respond; and rather than try to learn what kinds of things really please her, she gives up and fakes it. Faking orgasm is something like making sure one's makeup is perfect while in the shower. It is a display intended to make an impression on someone else, and has to do with a woman's desire to appear beautiful, sexy, desirable, and so on. Unfortunately, it is the kind of behavior that makes real orgasm less likely to occur, because it stands in the way of genuine communication about what feels good and what doesn't feel good. The real female person is hiding and absent in the very situation that can be the most intimate of human experiences.

As a feminist therapist, I would encourage a woman to give up this kind of pretense, or at the very least to examine the price she pays in genuine intimacy and in growth potential within the relationship. By faking orgasm, she is in effect saying, "I am not okay the way I really am, and I don't believe anything can change for me." She is also saying covertly to her partner, "I don't trust you either to accept me as I am or to be secure enough in your own sexuality to work with me for changes." It is my opinion and belief that people who care for each other can profitably take the risk of being honest with each other sexually, even when this causes temporary upset and conflict. If the price they choose to pay to continue a relationship is lies and self-denial, then there are issues involving identity and self-esteem that need to be worked out.

Just as I would support honesty in sex as a way out of the spectator role, I also support women experiencing their bodies from the inside out—to see, hear, smell, taste, feel, and move. These things have more to do with the reality of being a human being than a cosmetic appraisal of how one looks to others. Increased comfort and self-confidence are a natural result of a deeper look at one's physical existence.

Lately, there have been endless articles on female sexuality and orgasm. This new openness and wealth of information has some beneficial effects for people, but it is important to notice the liabilities too. Implicit in many of these articles are new performance demands, with new behavioral and emotional standards for people to measure themselves against. Such book titles as *Any Woman Can* (written by a man), the glorification of the multiple orgasm and elaborate notions of what a truly "liberated woman" should be like, create a new series of shoulds to plague the populace. One person's liberation is another's servitude, and people need room to discover what suits their individual personalities, sexually and otherwise.

Feminist therapy, from my point of view, is not a therapy with pre-set goals about how women should function sexually. Whether a woman finds herself drawn to heterosexual relationships, bisexual or lesbian relationships, or whether she chooses to be celibate, it is the role of the therapist to help her explore the feelings, ideas, and experiences that have the most meaning and congruence for her. It is hoped that the therapist will have the skill to help her client assess and work through the intrapsychic blocks that are interfering with her ability to create for herself the kind of life she wants. The therapist has the responsibility to respect and support the client's right to come to her own conclusions, even when these are different from the therapist's value orientation. Feminists have rightly criticized traditional psychiatrists for prodding angry women to adjust to the status quo of a male-dominated family life. Let us not be guilty of the same kind of coercion. If we assess mental health by whether or not our clients emerge as feminists like ourselves, if we perceive sexual well-being only in instances where a woman is very active and experimental, we are different in content but not in process from the kinds of coercion we deplore. Sexual liberation and women's liberation at its best involves the freedom of the individual to choose what fits.

Of course, there is nothing new about arbitrary external standards for male and female behavior. It has been expected for the last century or so that a young man would "sow some wild oats" before settling down, yet premarital sexual experience for women was regarded as indecent, immoral, and deserving of a "lost reputation." Although there have been some changes, these attitudes are far from dead in our country. Now, in addition to past behavioral expectations, there exists a new set of value judgments to contend with. Women and men these days experience anxiety and embarrassment about a *lack* of sexual experience or appetite. I recall seeing a female freshman at the University of Colorado who had come for an appointment at the psychiatric clinic because she was still a virgin and had not yet been in a situation where she had wanted to have sexual intercourse. Most of her friends claimed to have had affairs already, and she presumed there was something wrong with her because she was different.

In that phrase, "something wrong with her because she was different," lies the crux of the cultural contribution to people's identity and self-definition problems. To be different from everyone else is a major component of being an individual. To enjoy and experience one's own unique sexuality one needs to be sensitive and responsive to personal preferences. But here lies a chasm of fear and ignorance for most women. To have a clear personal preference is to stand alone, to take a risk of being refused or ridiculed, and to say, "I am different from you." This is dangerous territory. Women are eager to please and tend to be more dependent on external approval and validation than men. It is only very recently that our society has shown much acceptance of curiosity about the fact that women are sexual beings too. This has been followed by a wealth of directives about how to be sexual. No wonder many women feel paralyzed, inadequate, and confused. Further psychological pressure exists to the extent that a woman accepts the traditional view of the "feminine woman," the pliant, gracious recipient of male passion. Another inhibiting factor is that many men are threatened by a sexually aware and assertive female.

Despite all these obstacles, women are exploring, discovering, and defining their sexuality for themselves more and more. Books such as *For Yourself,* by Lonnie Garfield Barbach (New York: Doubleday, 1975) are appearing on the market. The title of Barbach's book is a good indicator of its orientation. She stresses the woman's right to please herself and reports the feelings and experiences of numerous women in detail. Orgasm is acknowledged and dealt with as important, but the treatment of the word "orgasmic" on the book jacket is significant. (The full title is *For Yourself—the fulfillment of female sexuality: a guide to orgasmic response*). Only the words *For Yourself* are capitalized. The person remains more important than the physiological event and more important than any specific, predetermined goals. Much of the book deals with the value of masturbation for preorgasmic women.

I have found that it is helpful to recommend books like this one to clients. It can also be useful to do some selective sharing of one's own experience as a female in our culture. There is reassurance for a client in knowing that her therapist also has had struggles as a woman and yet has a basic faith in growth and change. Some personal sharing affirms the egalitarian ethic that is a part of feminist therapy. The therapist can serve as a role model for the client by demonstrating her own comfort with herself and her sexuality and can implicitly convey the message that she does not see herself as superior to her client. Yet the therapist must use care and discretion not to burden clients with personal information that would interfere with the client's freedom to work on her own issues. It is also constructive to convey general information about the difficulty women have in achieving sexual and personal identity in our culture, so that the client can understand her own problems in some kind of meaningful social context. If a woman ceases to regard herself as a lone eccentric in a well-adjusted world, her self-image begins to improve immediately.

One form of sexual difficulty I've observed is the phenomenon of two people treating each other like an assembly of erogenous zones. Because they've read descriptions of what areas should be stimulated and how, they adopt a clinical, depersonalized attitude about making love with a partner. Push that button and pull that lever and surely sexual bliss will result. Women tend to describe that dynamic as feeling "worked on," and often there is considerable guilt and confusion about not feeling excited because, after all, "he's doing everything he possibly can." Naturally, the men involved in such interactions feel bewildered, frustrated, and inadequate.

The ingredient missing between the partners during their encounter is the expression of genuine feeling. At that moment, the relationship has ceased to flow because the two personalities involved are treating each other as male and female objects. Even if both people have an orgasm, the experience can feel hollow and lonely. This raises the question of the connection between sex and power, or sex and security. The number of human needs that affect or masquerade as sexual desire are tremendous. For women, the wish to be perceived as sexually attractive is often rooted in a desire to have power over men. The feeling goes something like this: If he wants me sexually, then I really affect him, and therefore I'm important. The issue here is one of low self-esteem and a sense of powerlessness, a common problem for minority groups and women in the United States. This desire for power through sex is not simply a neurotic problem that women carry. It reflects the reality that there have been very few areas of living that have been open to women where they could experience their power, competency, importance, and so on. Security has come largely through a liaison with a man, and a kind of pseudo-identity as well. Sexual intercourse can symbolize that liaison, and so, even if a woman experiences no real sexual desire herself, and even dislikes sexual activity, she may emotionally require that her man continue to be strongly attracted to her.

Every woman and man has a personal power of her or his own. It is the job of the therapist to help a person contact and integrate that power, and as this begins to happen, the craving for external validation becomes less consuming. The feminist therapist encourages her client to find identity and approval inside, by working through in therapy the past pains and disappointments that have interfered with her valuing herself. Then she no longer sees *herself* as a pain and a disappointment, but simply as someone who has experienced those feelings. Gradually, sex can become less burdened by these emotional side issues. Sex as an expression of genuine closeness and mutuality is a rich experience and may take any shape or form that two people create. It may be a joyous, passionate "quickie" or several languorous hours in bed. It may or may not include sexual intercourse or orgasm. Good communication and supportive mutual understanding are crucial, as well as a comfortable acceptance that things need not go well every time a couple gets together.

Another theme I've noticed in my clinical practice with women is the secret fear of being a lesbian. The fact of being involved with men, pleasurably or unpleasurably, does little to dispel that fear. Women quite commonly feel attracted to other women, physically as well as emotionally, yet very few feel truly comfortable with this, or are aware that others have similar feelings. They assume that theirs is a deviant reaction and overestimate its significance and intensity. Also, they fail to distinguish the kind of attraction they are feeling. Visual appreciation is not identical with a desire to touch, which in turn is not the same as a desire for sex. Because it is feared or denied, the attraction can seem larger and more confusing than it need be. The fear of lesbianism, therefore, introduces a measure of anxiety into friendships between women. People in general in our culture have been reserved about displays of physical affection between adults, perhaps because they read in sexual significance even where none is really felt or intended.

In *Women and Madness* (New York: Doubleday, 1972), Phyllis Chesler explores the issue of lesbianism in a sensitive and thoughtful way. She neither dismisses it as a pathological condition nor holds it up as a compulsory end for truly liberated women. Instead, she explores the feelings and ideas that go into a woman's choice of lesbianism in a culture that is very punitive toward such a choice. Lesbianism is a major and controversial issue, worthy of books and papers in its own right. In this brief overall look at female sexuality, I am not going to attempt to probe this subject. I will instead mention it, and say that I think lesbianism needs to be seen, understood, and acknowledged, rather than "diagnosed" and thereby dismissed.

Both sexes grow up in the United States with the notion that women are sexier to look at than men are. Boys and girls alike are exposed primarily to male sexual concepts; so, not surprisingly, that is what they assimilate. The mass media have a profound effect on people's notions about what is erotic, and these media are controlled almost entirely by men. In films, books, magazines, and television, women are always sexually on display. Even magazines that are intended for a female audience are full of photographs of women in various stages of undress. I can't recall an issue of *Cosmopolitan* magazine that didn't have pictured on the cover a young woman with acres of cleavage. Female audiences react on a number of levels: there are feelings of competition, identification, jealousy, or sexual arousal.

Recently, there have been increased efforts on the part of women to define their sexuality for themselves. This is just one dimension of the burgeoning women's movement. Books written by women, for women, and about women are becoming more common. There is a new trend in the movies to present heroines who are not classically beautiful, either in face or form, as sexually and personally attractive nevertheless. Television and radio shows about one aspect or another of the female experience are offered from time to time. Even the fashion industry has had to take into account that some of us have an interest in comfort and self-acceptance, and it is producing casual clothes that do not require either girdles, ironing, or dry cleaning. In consciousness-raising groups all over the country, women are sharing feelings and perceptions and are discovering vital information about themselves. Women are beginning to infiltrate the male bastions of power—government, industry, banks, the media—but thus far it is indeed only a beginning. How far we get, and how rapidly, remains to be seen.

Let me give a qualitative example of the changes that have occurred over the past ten years or so for a woman with a sexual problem. In the past, there were fewer options for dealing with problems. Women could talk with their gynecologists, who had experience about anatomical realities but not necessarily any understanding of, or comfort with, sexuality itself. A woman might have found her way to a male psychiatrist, who would do his best to help her unravel the neurotic causes of her "frigidity" in the context of a paternalistic doctor-patient relationship. Today, this paternalism and intrapsychic focus is being challenged by some psychiatrists and by nonmedical therapists as well. Certainly, an inability to experience orgasm can have roots in a neurotic conflict that needs resolution. But sexual inhibition in women must be seen in the repressive social context within which it occurs. Today, a woman can seek out an all-female, preorgasmic group. In an atmosphere of mutual support and caring, the participants share feelings, experiences, suggestions, and specific anatomical information in order to allow the occurrence of orgasm, a natural physical event. Masturbation techniques are spelled out in detail, and masturbation is seen as a pleasurable, healthy experience in its own right. There is a clear recognition that there is no difference between "vaginal" and "clitoral" orgasms, and no value judgments are made of which are the "best" ways to become sexually excited.

Overall, the field of female sexuality and female identity is being taken on more and more by the real experts—females; and as women become more secure and comfortable in the knowledge of who they are, everyone will benefit. In my opinion, it is a sign of vitality and health that there are female groups in disagreement with each other about the true nature of womanhood. People are by nature varied, and for clashes to occur bespeaks a measure of freedom within and without.

C. ETHNIC MINORITY CONCERNS

HUMANISTIC PSYCHOLOGY AND BLACK PSYCHOLOGY: A STUDY OF PARALLELS

George A. Tate

Roderick W. Pugh (1972), in *Psychology and the Black Experience*, describes Black psychology as a vital expression of the Black Revolution "born out of the American black man's will to survive, his will to overcome the effects of radical oppression, and his will to achieve self-actualization." As a protest against those cultural forces which inhibit the self-actualization of the black person, Black psychology seeks to shape and articulate a more positive image of the black man, one enhancing rather than diminishing his basic dignity and worth.

Likewise, in *Toward a Psychology of Being*, Abraham Maslow (1968) describes Humanistic psychology as a "revolution in the truest sense of the word," one reaching beyond the more limited contributions of the psychoanalytic and behavioristic psychologies. Radically transforming man's image of himself, it "seeks to perceive and form an image of man grounded in present reality but also expressing the deepest and fullest realization of man's capacity to become more rather than less human" (Richards and Richards, 1973).

Emerging as parallel voices of dissent and expressing a new direction and focus in the study of human behavior, Humanistic psychology and Black psychology have prompted us to raise serious questions about the validity and relevance of the more traditional approaches to understanding man. Humanistic psychology questions the short sightedness and exclusiveness of an academic psychology which has often diminished and distorted man's essential humanness. Confronting the traditional or establishment psychologies which function too often as a political extension of an oppressive socio-economic system, Black psychology debates the assumed infallibility of such psychologies with their white middle-class frame of reference.

Both Humanistic psychology and Black psychology have emerged out of a marginal existence. Humanistic psychologists have been viewed

---

SOURCE: Reprinted by permission of the author.

as *less than* psychologists and have, at times, been exiled to the periphery of establishment psychology. Originally identified as a new movement or Third Force, it is often ignored or considered unscientific by more traditional psychologists. Similarly, Black psychologists, the objects of a racial oppression which has inhibited the self-actualization of black people in America for 300 years, have been viewed as *less than* human and have been exiled to the periphery of establishment personhood. As Ellison (1947) describes it, the Black psychologist is invalidated by a white racism that denies his full emergence as a person.

> I am an invisible person. No I am not a spook like those who haunted Edgar Allan Poe; nor am I one of your Hollywood movie ectoplasms. I am a man of substance, of flesh and bone, fiber and liquids—and I might even be said to possess a mind. I am invisible, understand, simply because people refuse to see me.

This failure to perceive clearly or take seriously the Black psychologist as a person similarly expresses itself, at times, in an almost automatic discounting of black ability. Hence, Black psychology is a movement of the Third World, the insistence on the part of the oppressed that they define and determine their own destiny. Insisting there are insights and understanding about human existence other than merely those of establishment psychology, it challenges and threatens those who identify completely with the more entrenched and traditional positions in psychology, those who embrace rigidly values and perceptions that dehumanize the black person and are now obsolete and even suicidal in the modern world.

In addition to the general parallels listed above, I will briefly call attention to three specific parallels between Humanistic psychology and Black psychology.

A MISTRUST OF TRADITIONAL PSYCHOLOGY

First, both share and express a mistrust of the prevailing perceptions of man implicit in the psychoanalytic and behavioristic psychologies. Humanistic psychology views the more traditional psychologies as too limited and inadequate, as closed systems with a basically anti-humanistic (diminishing, dehumanizing, distorting) orientation. It believes that academic psychology cannot always be trusted to take the human factor into account. Establishment psychology is perceived as too often neglecting or denying that which makes man human: his values, attitudes, feelings, aspirations, beliefs, etc. Furthermore, Humanistic psychologists often hold that establishment psychology is very unwilling to relinquish its power, that it is too jealous of its status and prestige and, locked into its "system-confirming role," too preoccupied with reaping the rewards of the system. To illustrate, note how tenaciously establishment psychology clings to its insistence that it has the sole authority to answer the questions, "Who is a psychologist?" or "What is mental illness?"

Waldman (1971) questions the limited and inadequate understanding of mental illness prevailing in establishment psychology and his challenge is similar to that of many Humanistic psychologists. Waldman believes that the phenomenon called "mental illness" must be understood in terms of the micro-social environment, in terms of one's life situation and the "events of the social order." Viewing such phenomena only within a biological-medical framework is inadequate and often misleading. They must be understood within a socio-political, ethico-moral or humanistic context as well. Such an orientation would allow us to understand mental illness as a response to social forces which dehumanize and diminish the person. Waldman insists we must focus our concern on the forces of oppression and alienation that reduce man from a person to a thing. Mental illness becomes, then, a manifestation of how these social forces make of one a thing rather than a person freed to grow and develop in terms of his own unique potential.

Black psychology's agreement with Humanistic psychology is clear here. It too sees establishment psychology as a rather closed system with dehumanizing or anti-black orientation. It believes that the more traditional psychologies cannot be trusted to take into account the concrete realities of the black experience. Many black psychologists and psychiatrists call attention to this fact. Grier and Cobbs (1968) discuss a "healthy paranoia" among blacks which is often seen by more traditional psychologists as a sign of mental illness or personal inadequacy. White (1970) calls attention to how traditional psychological theories ignore the life styles common to the black culture. Poussaint (1969) points to the inadequacy of those traditional frames of reference when they are employed to theorize about self-hatred and self-destructiveness among blacks. Poussaint agrees that blacks have feelings of self-hatred. However, he adds that the black person confronts a system which seeks to castrate him and render him abjectly compliant while, at the same time, making him pay heavily for expressing his rage when protesting such emasculation. Thus, the black person's appropriate rage is repressed and suppressed, and always at a great cost to his own personal development and growth.

It follows that Black psychology views the more traditional psychologies as confirming, rather than confronting, a system which has been and continues to be oppressive to the black person. It considers its task one of evaluating past psychological theories in light of their socio-historical, socio-cultural contexts and of clarifying and shaping an image of the black man that is grounded in the realities of the black experience. This two-fold task is discussed elsewhere (Tate, 1972) as the total discounting of traditional theories about the black person *(demythologization)* and the substitution of new theories in their place *(re-mythologization)*. By re-mythologization I mean a radically new perception or total transformation of the image of the black person in terms of the subjective realities of what it means to be black in the world *now*.

A TRANS-RATIONALISTIC VIEW OF REALITY

A second parallel between Humanistic psychology and Black psychology is an awareness of the need to go beyond the more traditional and rationalistic approach to understanding reality. While not denying the value and validity of the rationalistic approach, they insist that a purely rationalistic effort to understand the nature of man denies or ignores significant aspects of human experience. Waldman (1971) comments:

> Man, whose actions transcend the physical laws of nature, cannot be significantly understood if we are to apply to him the very objectifying techniques of the physical sciences that have served well to comprehend and control nature.

Ansbacher (1971) expresses a similar opinion: "Part of the humanistic conception of man is the recognition of man's individual uniqueness which rests on the individual's inner life, his private world, his subjectivity." Ansbacher sees the task of the psychologist as trying to understand the person's uniqueness or subjectivity rather than attempting to reduce it to some hypothetical causes.

Black psychology gives high priority to "soul" and is not apologetic when embracing and confirming the irrational aspects of human existence. The Black psychologist is particularly aware of the contingent character of living in the world. He is aware of the fact of death, of uncertainty and irrationality as a concrete part of human existence. His very life history has often screamed these realities at him. The black child learns daily to cope with frustration, depersonalization and dehumanization. I recall reading Robert Coles' account of such oppression in his book, *Children of Crisis,* in which young blacks relate their experience of entering schools in the South. When I read of this ugliness and inhumanity I was wandering in a beautiful setting in the Colorado Rocky Mountains. I wept as I read. As these children well knew, the black person encounters too much of the irrationality of human existence to deny or evade it.

THE VALUE AND SIGNIFICANCE OF THE PERSON

A third parallel is that of the high priority given to the person and his uniqueness. Humanistic psychology has brought back into clear focus the uniqueness, value and significance of the individual person. Such words as *sensitivity, encounter, self-actualization, personal adequacy* and numerous others keep in focus this emphasis. The emphasis upon the unity or wholeness of the self, upon individual and personal growth, upon subjectivity or the perceptions, attitudes, goals and beliefs of each person, convey this concern for the individual as a unique person. The strong stand against dehumanization, against those beliefs or actions that diminish, limit, distort and stifle human potential attest to the priority of the person in Humanistic psychology.

Black psychology expresses a similar reverence for the worth and value of the person—a concern growing out of the tragic aspects of the black experience, an experience in which the personal identity of the black person has been, more often than not, denied or ignored.

Out of the conflict and struggle experienced by the black person in a society that either represses his search for identity or distorts it, out of such an existence Black psychology has emerged with its concern for the personhood of the suppressed. Fighting hard for his subjective identity in the face of dehumanizing forces often aimed directly and violently at the blacks, the black person needs a positive image of himself that enables him to affirm, discover and embrace not only his own subjectivity and significance but that of all men. Black psychology, as a response to a system which threatens the black person's full emergence as a person, stresses the crucial need for a psychology focusing on the personhood of the black and for those social and political changes which might lead toward the increased dignity and worth of all men.

In conclusion, these parallels between Humanistic psychology and Black psychology suggest that, to some degree, they share a common origin and emphasis. They emerge out of a revolutionary protest against those values and perceptions which diminish rather than enhance human nature. They provide models for a "new psychology" which will confirm the uniqueness of each person as he brings "his thing" to the context of man's striving to give meaning to his existence.

REFERENCES

Ansbacher, Heinz L. "Alfred Adler and Humanistic Psychology." *Journal of Humanistic Psychology.* (Spring, 1971), p. 57.

Coles, Robert. *Children of Crisis.* New York: Dell Publishing Company, 1964.

Ellison, Ralph. *The Invisible Man.* New York: Random House, 1947, p. 7.

Grier, William H. and Cobbs, Price M. *Black Rage.* New York: Basic Books, 1968.

Maslow, Abraham. *Toward a Psychology of Being*. New York: Van Nostrand Reinhold Company, 1968, p. iii.

Poussaint, Alfred. "A Negro Psychiatrist Explains the Negro Psyche." Ned E. Hoopes (Ed.), *Who Am I?* New York: Dell Publishing Company, 1969, p. 85.

Pugh, Roderick W. *Psychology and the Black Experience*. Monterey, California: Brooks/Cole Publishing Company, 1972, p. 3.

Richards, Fred and Richards, Anne Cohen. *Homonovus: The New Man*. Boulder, Colorado: Shields Publishing Company, 1973, p. 11.

Tate, George. "Toward a Black Psychology of the Healthy Personality." Fred Richards and I. David Welch (Eds.), *Humanitas: Educating for the Healthy Personality*. Special Issue, *Colorado Journal of Educational Research*, (Fall, 1972), pp. 21-23.

Waldman, Roy D. *Humanistic Psychology*. New Brunswick, New Jersey: Rutgers University Press, 1971, pp. 90-91.

White, Joseph. "Toward a Black Psychology." *Ebony Magazine*, (September, 1970), pp. 44, 48-50, 52.

HUMANISTIC PSYCHOLOGY AND WHITE RACISM

Elizabeth Rave

Racism exists in America. If you are white and were born in this country the odds are that you are a victim of white racism and perhaps a perpetuator of it. Minorities have been making similar comments for years. Finally in 1968 the National Advisory Commission on Civil Disorders, a high level, federally funded commission, came to the same general conclusion. Since that report, indications are that the split between the races continues to widen *(One Year Later,* 1969). In this paper I explore briefly the notion that humanistic psychology could possibly contribute to rather than resolve the problem of white racism in America.

Is it possible that humanistic psychology can be contributing to the perpetuation of white racism? After all, racism refers to an ingrained belief that the human races have distinctive, innate characteristics that determine their respective cultures. Racism also embraces the idea that one's own race is qualitatively superior and, therefore, has the right to rule or govern others. Certainly there is nothing inherent in the principles of humanistic psychology that implies intentionally the superiority of one race over another. In actuality, humanistic psychology may provide some hope for our increasingly accepting all human beings as equal in worth and value. However, because human beings are first of all human, they perceive such principles in terms of their needs. My concern involves the misinterpretation and misuse of the tenets of humanistic psychology to perpetuate rather than alleviate white racism.

The very nature of humanistic psychology makes it difficult to define the principles with which most exponents of the humanistic orientation would heartily agree. Nevertheless, the application form for the Association for Humanistic Psychology does list four characteristics that appear to be essential areas of agreement for those who identify themselves as humanistic psychologists. Though recognizing there may be some disagreement regarding these four elements, I would like to consider each individually and to illustrate briefly how we might, under the guise of being humanistic, employ each to perpetuate white racism.

SOURCE: Reprinted by permission of the author.

The first characteristic is "a centering of attention on the experiencing *person,* and thus a focus on experience as the primary phenomenon in the study of man. Both theoretical explanations and overt behavior are considered secondary to experience itself and to its meaning to the person." This focus upon experience and the experiencing person has been a vitally needed emphasis in psychological thought. However, it could become a guise for total self-centeredness, a justification for being concerned totally with oneself and only with what I, as the self, am experiencing. "I've got to get myself together first" is the expression that often typifies this posture. To use "getting myself together first" as an excuse for not relating with people of backgrounds other than my own is to allow myself the luxury of looking at and analyzing my own perceptions while avoiding input that might change my way of seeing myself, others, and the world. In addition, while some people are luxuriously "getting themselves together," others are continually struggling to function in environments that are not the most conducive to human growth—and the split between the races widens.

Another misinterpretation of the first characteristic or common element is to equate experiencing with feeling. Humanists do more than sit around and feel. How often have I gone to hear minority group speakers "tell it like it is?" And how often have I felt good about doing that—maybe even a little superior because I was there "taking it" and so many others were not? How often did I leave the talk feeling that because I had "felt" so deeply I was somehow better and had also somehow helped the "problem?" In other words, how often did I do nothing more than hear and feel rather than act on my new awareness? A cathartic release of white guilt followed by no assimilation of new knowledge and, thus, by no change in behavior, does little other than help the white feel better about himself. How tired minorities are of hearing whites say "I understand. I really understand." Understanding is only the first step. If a person really understands the situation of the minority groups in America, he will in some way attempt to effect it by acting on his new understanding. *Feeling concerned* is only validated as authentic where it is embodied in action, when it is extended beyond oneself in terms of active involvement in changing a system that has historically oppressed the blacks and other minority groups.

The second element is "an emphasis on such distinctively human qualities as choice, creativity, valuation, and self-realization, as opposed to thinking about human beings in mechanistic and reductionistic terms." My concern with this characteristic involves the vast majority of humans, in this country and the world, who have limited choices. In fact, the majority of human beings may not even be aware of the concept of choice. In contrast, the majority of humanistic psychologists work in institutions that do not even come in contact with these human beings who are most limited in their choices because of an oppressive socio-economic system that has been imposed upon them. Certainly, it is possible to help create an environment more conducive to expanding choices while identifying with such institutions. I do *not* do that, however, by perpetuating the same conditions. For example, how often have I verbalized a comment such as, "I treat everyone as an individual—that's the way I fight prejudice and racism." Such a statement may be true if a person allows himself to be involved in many different ways and at many different levels with people from different backgrounds. However, how many of us are in situations where we are confronted by numerous individuals of different backgrounds? Unfortunately, too often the persons with whom we work and live are those who represent and confirm our own socio-economic situation—one often oblivious to that experienced by the poverty stricken and suppressed.

When I go to department meetings and university-wide faculty meetings, I meet—for all practical purposes—with people who are cut pretty much from the same mold as I am. When I go into the classroom, I meet with students who are—for all practical purposes—cut pretty much from the same mold as I am. When I walk around my town, however, I see people who are obviously not cut from the same mold as I am. When I visit neighboring cities, I see people who are obviously not cut from the same mold as I am. The point is that it is comparatively easy for me to treat the people I come in contact with as individuals when they are usually pretty similar to me. In reality, however, I cannot really understand the commonalities of humans until I have confronted the differences. If I am doing nothing to help my institution avail itself as a "choice" to people from varied backgrounds, I am perpetuating white racism.

The third element is "an allegiance to meaningfulness in the selection of problems for study and of research procedures, and an opposition to a primary emphasis on objectivity at the expense of significance." We as whites have studied minorities to death—almost literally in too many cases. As Whitney Young used to suggest, the grant money should begin to go to minorities for studying whites. What we don't know and what we don't understand is why we as whites, as psychologists, as human beings, continue to ignore the results of research—in particular that research that demonstrates conditions that are and are not conducive to human growth. Exploring our ability to ignore the results of research would be a tremendous scientific contribution. In addition, why do we continue to believe that we are not part of the problem? Why do we continue to work in institutions without attempting to change the conditions of the institutions? There is need for more studies that give some clues regarding what it takes for a white to incorporate knowledge from research into his behavior!

Even without getting involved in a research project, every individual can and should be studying the institution that he is a part of. How does that institution with which we identify perpetuate white racism? Each institution has favorite concepts that are double binds—concepts that perpetuate the institution and at the same time keep certain people out of the institution. In academic circles and institutions some illustrations of hallowed concepts that are also potentially limiting to groups of people are "quotas on enrollment," "standards," "academic excellence," and "qualified." While such concepts are not innately bad, they can be employed to perpetuate white racism.

The fourth element is "an ultimate concern with and valuing of the dignity and worth of man and an interest in the development of the potential inherent in every person. Central in this view is the person as he discovers his own being and relates to other persons and to social groups." This concept too frequently gets misused and misinterpreted as "I do my thing and you do your thing." Of course, nothing is further from the tenets of humanistic psychology than one doing one's thing when that involves perpetuating white racism. However, if "my thing" means that I should be able to find for me those conditions that are conducive for my development but, at the same time, support conditions which allow "your thing" to worsen, then I am a misguided humanist.

In summary, my main point is that, if I am really concerned with valuing the dignity and worth of humans, I will be actively involved in effecting change any time I become aware of situations that prevent the development of the potential in any person. I will not, in other words, be concerned with my *self* only but rather will be concerned with that *self* in relation to others—and not just others like me.

Humanistic psychology, more than the psychologies which have preceded it, can evolve a theory of social and individual change capable of transforming our society. Hopefully, those who embrace and articulate it will also embody it, also commit themselves to changing a society that presently denies to many their basic dignity and worth as human beings.

REFERENCES

One Year Later. New York: Frederick Praeger, 1969.

Report of the National Advisory Commission on Civil Disorders. New York: Bantam Books, 1968.

THE HEALTHY PERSONALITY AND THE BLACK EXPERIENCE

George A. Tate

The formulation of a viable black psychology of the healthy personality demands a radical rejection or re-mythologization of existing psychological theories that have too often failed to take into consideration, in more than a superficial way, the life-situation experienced by minority groups in America. Despite their contribution to man's understanding of man, such psychological theories too often represent the mainline, white middle-class attitudes and beliefs about what it means to be a healthy or optimally effective person. The specific task of this essay is to suggest guidelines for re-mythologizing—for seeing in a totally new and radical way—the concept of the healthy personality by placing it in the context of the black experience.

Re-mythologization is a term which grows out of the author's contact with Rudolph Bultmann's notion of demythologization. A Christian theologian, Bultmann was one of the chief exponents of Form Criticism, an investigation of the oral tradition about Jesus which had been given literary form in the Gospels. One of the guiding principles set down by the Form Critics was that by removing the editorial embellishments—by stripping away the mythological framework in which the oral tradition had been placed—one could lay bare the essential, actual historical situation out of which the Gospel stories evolved. By de-mythologizing the scriptures, one could understand the mythological content existentially, one could discover the essential life-situation veiled in the Gospel narratives.

Demythologization, then, is the process by which one approaches a body of myths and re-interprets them in light of actual experience (Good, 1966; MacQuarrie, 1960). By reaching inside myth to the core of human realities contained there, the myth is grounded in history and concrete with reality. The myth is an interpretation, a framework of meanings which gives perceived purpose and order to man's experience. The myth-

SOURCE: Reprinted by permission of the author.

ological framework is a map by which man creates a symbolic overview of the territory known as the human situation. However, Bultmann would warn us, along with Wendell Johnson, S.I. Hayakawa and others, that the map is not the territory. Often man, the myth-maker, creates myths which distort or conceal the concrete realities of the human situation which lie unperceived and, perhaps, hidden behind these impressive symbolic structures.

Attempting to move toward a black psychology of the healthy personality, the author sees the process of re-mythologization as going beyond the point to which Bultmann carries us. Re-mythologization calls for *eliminating* the traditional body of myths rather than merely *confronting* them. Bultmann merely confronts the traditional Christian myths and then seeks to re-interpret them in light of the concrete realities or human situations discovered at their core. In like manner, a person working within the framework of traditional, mainline psychological theory may engage in a similar process of demythologization. That is, he may confront traditional psychological theory and seek to re-examine or re-interpret it in light of current human knowledge and experience.

Such a process of re-examination is, however, inadequate and ineffective in seeking to shape or formulate a black psychology of the healthy personality. If the black community is to succeed in shaping an image of the black person as the healthy personality it must view as invalid the traditional psychological theories or myths which are not grounded in the daily realities of the black predicament. What is needed is a new mapping of the territory which the blacks have explored and endured for centuries of struggle and oppression. This means the creation and articulation of a new body of psychological theories, of newly shaped myths which disclose rather than conceal, engage rather than ignore, what it is to be a black person in America. The formulation of such a theory must be the basis for interpreting what it means to be both black and psychologically healthy.

THE FACT OF OPPRESSION

A re-mythologization of psychological theory to ground it in the black experience means confronting the fact of oppression. The new myth disclosing the black person's growth and development toward self-actualization in our society will accept oppression as a given fact. The healthy black person is aware, deeply aware, of the limitations and contingencies placed upon his existence simply because he is black. To be black in America means to wear the scars of oppression. Any psychological theory of the healthy personality which fails to confront and engage this fact is inadequate to address itself to the problem of what it means to be black and in the process of striving to affirm one's full potential to be a human being.

Traditional psychological theory barely alludes to the reality of overt oppression or racial discrimination in America. A concept of self-actualization which naively adheres to the pull-yourself-up-by-your-own-boot-straps myth is blind to the harsh realities of an oppression which, overt or otherwise, minimizes the black person's opportunity to function as a full human being in his own right. In fact, this myth, and others, makes it even more difficult for a black person to be aware of how real and pervasive this oppression is. In addition, he and others may attribute his lack of psychological health and well-being to a "lack of will" or a refusal to "apply himself." Thus, the myth becomes a source of the oppression it refuses to recognize.

Re-mythologization abandons this anemic mapping of oppression and re-sees or re-symbolizes it. It "tells it like it is." It dares to expose the oppression in housing with its symbolization of the "black real estate tax," revealing the limitations placed upon black persons in their search for adequate housing. It exposes oppression in the area of vocational endeavor, an oppression characterized by high black unemployment and a discrepancy between black and white lifetime earnings even though the educational level of both may be the same. Such a situation is conveyed well in the phrase "last hired, first fired." The "separate but equal" slogan articulates the inhumane and horrible inequity regarding the availability of quality education for blacks. "The Twentieth Century black plague" describes the oppression rampant in the area of health and welfare services. The cry for "law and order" too often means the continued oppression of blacks by the American legal system.

THE LEGITIMACY OF BLACK RAGE

The concept of the healthy personality is healthy only if it begins with and is grounded in the facts of the person's existence—the total environment, including himself, in which he has to function. The acceptance of the legitimacy of black rage—of the black man's protest against all those forces that have denied him his identity and a valued place in society—is an absolute element in any black psychology of the healthy personality assuming to address itself to the life-situation of the black community.

Traditional psychology hardly alludes to the reality of this rage. Again, as with the phenomenon of oppression, rage is diffused conceptually by some sort of categorical watering down process. In its most extreme form it sees black rage as some sort of paranoia—a sign of the black man's personal inadequacy rather than an indication that he finds himself displaced, ignored or oppressed in a society inadequately human. This is a clear example of why the author believes that in many, if not most cases, the black psychologist cannot merely demythologize, for this suggests a sort of "retooling" of the traditional theories. How does one retool the labeling of black rage as paranoia? The whole symbolization process of traditional psychology has to be discarded and new symbolizations have to emerge if the black person is to understand fully and deal effectively with his rage and his healthy protest against a dehumanizing environment.

THE NEED FOR SOCIAL ACTION AND CHANGE

The third focus is upon the fact of institutional racism and the need, on the part of the healthy black person, to develop the strategies and methodologies to change society and improve the situation of the black community. These strategies for social change must not be conceived in terms of the value orientation of our present socio-economic system but in terms of values and goals best fulfilling the basic human needs of the black community.

The basic assumption here is that the healthy black person is aware of his need to understand and comprehend the forces opposing and denying his emergence as a whole man and to develop effective behavior patterns to facilitate the changes necessary to maximize his opportunities for increased growth and well-being. This means, of course, increasing and sharpening the skills and capabilities of the black person. The author reminds his fellow blacks that, while it is fine to be militant and confront the system, one needs to extend his awareness and develop the skills to permit him to take maximum advantage of social change. Those who fail to go beyond merely confronting the system may become its victims by having exhausted the energy and resources also needed to secure the black person's autonomy and apply his opportunity to control his own life and destiny toward black goals. Thus, while it is imperative that a black psychology of the healthy personality ground itself in the black experience (his life-situation, history, perceptions, values, goals), it must also articulate a constructive program of social change and action that enables the black person to rise above the syndrome of oppression, frustration, rage and alienation.

To conclude, the black person needs to be aware of the inadequacies of past psychological theories and commit himself to the task of formulating a black psychology of the healthy personality grounded in the realities of the black experience. More specifically, he must be aware of the limitations and contingencies placed upon his existence because of his blackness. Accepting his rage as a legitimate protest against these limitations and understanding the forces which oppose his full emergence as a person in his own right, the healthy black person is one developing and implementing the strategies which will promote the increased adequacy and self-actualization of all blacks. A psychology of the healthy personality which fails to confront the concrete realities of the black experience in America would, if not re-mythologized in terms of black needs, values and goals, confirm the very oppression the healthy black person is called to oppose.

REFERENCES

Good, Edwin M. "The Meaning of Demythologization." Charles W. Kezley (Ed.), *The Theology of Rudolph Bultmann.* New York: Harper and Row, 1966, pp. 21-40.

MacQuarrie, John. *The Scope of Demythologizing.* New York: Harper and Brothers, 1960.

D. HUMANISTIC PSYCHOTHERAPY

THE NEW PSYCHOTHERAPIES

Israel W. Charny

An enormous revolution is going on these days in new psychotherapies and "growth programs," new in content as well as new in delivery systems intended to make psychological help more effective and available to broader groups of our population. There is no question that in most respects the newness is to be valued.

There is much that is wrong with the standard mental-health system. For the relatively few for whom psychoanalytic therapies are well advised, there has been a good deal of genuine help available. However, indications are that only a very small part of the population is likely to benefit from such psychoanalytic therapy. Characteristically, analysis is for people who are able to develop an effective working relationship with a helper, who are bright and turned on by inner experience and symbolisms, and whose wills and strengths of resolution are not greatly damaged by whatever anxiety or other psychological problem they are suffering. As for the finances of psychoanalytic treatment, although any number of practitioners, institutes, and centers made honorable efforts over the years to include a certain number of lower-paying patients (this writer once enjoyed the privilege of fifty-cents-an-hour sessions through a university health service), the overriding facts remain that psychoanalytic therapy is enormously expensive, terribly time-consuming, and restricted to a fairly small number of people who have a great deal of emotional strength to begin with.

There is also much to be criticized about how some of the practitioners of psychoanalytic therapy have gone about rigidifying—and thereby dehumanizing—the beautiful process which they ministered.

The search to discover new helping techniques has been on for many years. Twenty-five years ago Dr. Carl Rogers innovated a basic tool of reflecting feelings back to a person so that he could hear himself. Such reflections were to be packaged in a spirit of "total acceptance." However,

SOURCE: Israel W. Charny, "The New Psychotherapies and Encounters of the Seventies: Progress or Fads?" This article first appeared in *The Humanist*, May/June 1974 and is reprinted by permission of the publisher and the author.

it became clear to many practitioners that the grip of the neurotic, self-hurting unconscious was not so easily released by acceptance of a person as he was, and only a brief range of human experience or behavior could be reopened to new choices through this process of client-centered therapy.

Then came the group therapies with their exciting discovery of the power of group process turned toward supporting emotional growth. However, again it became clear that certain deep—almost "built-in"—personality problems cried for their own private stage on which to be enacted before they could yield to change. So that although the group therapies broadened the base of psychotherapeutic utility considerably, their very effort resulted in underscoring much of the established ethos of psychoanalytic therapy—that it takes a good deal of individual therapy and a good deal of time before much can happen.

There it sat for a good number of years. The mental-health world pretty well solidified around a mix of providing fairly high-quality services to private patients, not bad service to middle-class, clinic, and community-center patients, and a surprisingly varied range of psychological and social services to the lower classes—ranging from terrible and noteworthily punitive to quite good. It was intriguingly common to all of the mental-health professions that they took for themselves a kind of priestly privilege of being dispensers and purveyors of Truth and Knowledge to the less-privileged who had not yet found the real Faith.

Below the surface, however, everything was restless. Inevitably, there were increasing numbers of disquieted and dissatisfied clientele of a therapy that could give significant help to only a small number of people and that was in so many instances a seductive invitation to discover how worthless one was. Even in its better moments, it too often claimed a corner on the market of Truth and Privilege and bred resentment.

In addition, there were too many practitioners who really missed the essence of the quite beautiful process of self-discovery and renewal of experiencing to which they were tending. A certain number of them were the kind of smart and/or conforming students who had done only too well in meeting whatever the paper requirements were of their psychoanalytic courses of training, without ever coming into real inner contact with the mystery and majesty of anxiety as a signal to reach for those parts of oneself that one is most afraid will never be developed. There were others who at one point in their development were fairly growing people, but then, seated on the majestic thrones of their new profession, succumbed to the corruptions of power and the illusion of knowing more than was known. These therapists never connected with the intrinsic challenge and miracle of life, nor with therapy itself as a marvelous miniature of the mysteries of the absurd and the unpredictable that is human life.

In time, the brilliance of the human imagination commanded that new ideas should arise about the freeing of the human spirit. These new ideas have now exploded into a dramatic and far-reaching expansion of modes and models for psychotherapy and growth experience.

Interestingly enough, some of the new variants in psychotherapy involve efforts at a stricter conceptualization of what the truth and correction of emotional distress are about. Such efforts at more objective, scientific thinking arise, in part, in answer to the extreme vagueness and seemingly promiscuous infinity of explanations in the psychoanalytic therapies. Such focusing or narrowing of the frame is intended to focus on key issues of behavioral competence that were obscured in the lush, rich jungle of psychoanalytic thought, where too often no one was entirely clear what disordered behavior was being treated and what was not.

On the other hand, there is also another major revision of therapy that is moving rapidly to the forefront with enormous success, even in creating an entirely new institutional network of growth centers around the world, and it has as its calling card not greater certainty but greater sensitivity, empathy, contact, and closeness.

RATIONAL-EMOTIVE THERAPY

Prominent among the "corrective methodologies of certainty" is the rational-emotive school of psychotherapy pioneered by the indomitable Dr. Albert Ellis. In his characteristically clear-thinking style, Ellis hammers away at the fundamental proposition that all emotion represents inner thought and that the many forms of distressing inner experience to which people are subject in fact derive from statements that they are making to themselves in unrecognized thought processes. For many philosophical thinkers, Ellis is trapping one side of the truth that emotion and thought are correlatives or opposite sides of the same coin. Both indeed are always present, and therefore Ellis' argument that thought is always operative in connection with distressing emotion is valid, but the deeper truth is that thought and emotion each add a side of experience the other cannot encompass.

Be that as it may, with this one tour de force, Ellis has reopened for every human being the possibility of being the author or master of his own destiny, one of the fundamental objectives of all psychotherapy, of course. With his one tour de force, Ellis also hooks into that most powerful discovery of psychoanalysis—that all of us carry within our own selves inner styles of self-hurting and ways of pushing ourselves around that derive from a complicated system of our past reactions to how our parents were relating to us in our formative years. Bypassing rich but oh-so-complex processes as introjection and incorporation, and the whole psychoanalytic machinery of transference where the patient re-creates much of his basic relationship-style with his troublesome parents via his relationship with the therapist, Ellis hammers away at the messages a person gives to himself. Very prominent among these false messages, he claims, and again with singular accuracy, is the notion that one must feel badly if one does not compare well to others, as if the golden calf of one's public image is virtually more precious than all of one's being. He teaches that the pursuit of this elusive golden calf is fated to yield disappointment and dissatisfaction. All who would dance around the calf are setting themselves up for any number of inner messages to the effect that they are failures, incompetents, and worthless people.

This writer has seen that the shorthand, directness, yet truthfulness of the Ellis notions can provide handles for people who have been floundering endlessly in an uncovering psychoanalytic therapy and that they offer a real promise of ownership of oneself and mastery of one's own psychological future to people who would otherwise forever be awaiting release from their dibbuks or transferences or hangups by powers greater than they—outside of their own selves.

Yet, jumping on the bandwagon of these fine notions came a whole variety of Certainty Peddlers, all too ready to announce the new Torah and the new Science. At the psychoanalytic therapists, they scoff relentlessly: "Woe unto the dream-tellers, interpreters, and feeling-tracers." Instead, they propose glibly that all will now be well for those who, all too simply, identify their inner thoughts and how these set them up for their own undue hurts.

In addition, we find that the machinery of rational-emotive therapy has little in it of warmth or tenderness—or a mood of nonverbal contact with inner experience. The terrible nonverbal pains that abound in so many human problems, such as various psychosomatic conditions, do not touch these new rationalists. The kind of courage and depth of person that may grow out of contending honorably with one's anxiety over a period of time is not important to them. Anxiety is to be banished. Pain is to be a thing of the past for all those who decode their inner messages to themselves in Rational Utopia.

BEHAVIOR MODIFIERS

Another major entry into the sweepstakes of the new psychotherapeutic certainty are the behavior modifiers. They arrive out of the honorable tradition of the experimental laboratories that spawned them. Theirs is the whole revolutionary notion of modern science that man can ask objective questions, to which he then offers hypothetical answers, which he then proceeds to test through rigorous and objective experimentation. Thus, for a person afraid, behavior modification analyzes the com-

ponents of a person's fears and slowly but surely offers a sequence of vac-
cinations or desensitizations to the sufferer, much as an allergist will do.

Say you are having trouble in your sexual functioning. The problem
is how to improve your functioning. It is not important what causes your
hangup. It is important to talk of your scare and anger toward your
spouse. It is not important to analyze the self-protective mechanism by
which you quit on yourself before being fired. What will work best is to
practice improving your reaction time, as in the experimental psychology
laboratory of old. So you simulate through fantasy a ladder of sexual experiences, and you stretch yourself ever so gently from one stage to the
next. Accompany your imagery with pleasant thoughts. Watch for negative reactions that are a sign you are not ready for this stage. Slowly,
slowly, until your weak behavior has been modified and you are now a scientifically certified Kosher Lover.

Scared of riding on an airplane? Okay. We'll start by thinking of
going to the airport. No, no airline trip today. Not even buying a ticket.
Several sessions later: All right, shall we go for a ticket today? This is a
therapy of rehearsal with a friend and guide and tutor in the person of the
therapist. It is the kind of rehearsal that is characteristic of all learning
sequences, much as we once all learned to walk. So many of the challenges of our adult lives seem to jump out at us when we're not ready, yet
they demand our total presence. At long last, here is a way of rehearsing
for life.

A contrast to this careful gradation of building to experience-read-
iness starts from the entirely opposite side to explode one's worst fears
with a flourish! What is the worst you can imagine? Being consumed in
the act of intercourse? How? Your lover's body swallowing you up whole
to the point where you don't exist anymore? Okay. Imagine just that.
Yes. Let yourself go entirely. Okay. Here we go. You're getting anxious.
It really frightens you. Fine. Good. That's a good sign. Here the notion is
that exploding one's deepest fear, taken to its very absurdity, will free
people from the paralysis that they normally suffer from fear of their
worst fantasies, which they never really test out and therefore can never
correct. This kind of behavior modification gets the worst over with right
in therapy, as it were.

The behavior-modification people have, however, demonstrated gi-
gantic prowess in offering new concepts for the management of controlled environments, such as institutions. Utilizing principles of reinforcement through reward and selective punishment or deprivation (if
you are ten minutes late to the dining room you lose two tokens in the
canteen economy, for example, but if you are on time you gain a token),
they have provided new hope for any number of sterile, self-hating, bankrupt, and authority-ridden institutional environments.

Yet, the devotees of behavior modification, too, very often spring to the platform of Finality and announce with decisive assurance that Freud's way is no way, that inner feelings are no more than cues to a repertoire of behavior responses that are to be sequentially analyzed and then reorganized or modified.

Two-year-long psychotherapies for the spirit? Nonsense! Send me your ailing for as little as weeks and months. Relationship problems? Ridiculous! Let's take a look at the behavior and what kind of expectations you communicate to one another and reinforce for one another. It makes no difference that you are afraid of yielding to love for fear that you will later be hurt. What does matter is that, when your spouse yells back at your provocativeness, you are reinforced by the attention and gratification of your power needs; so we want to teach your spouse not to rise to the bait. An underlying depression (over feelings of being unloved) in a child with a behavior disorder? Forget that! The important thing is to see that the child is quietly and firmly limited in his rammy behavior. Use a time-out room. Turn off the bad behavior, quickly and rapidly. Reward good behavior. We'll forget about the quiet caring that you haven't known how to offer.

So, again, we have, on one hand, an exciting broadening of the horizons of knowledge and the technology of helping. The behavior modifiers remind and teach us to ask more-specific questions and to conceive of the specific learning experiences that so many of us human beings need when we want to attempt new behaviors and want to reduce our fears of the unknown. On the other hand, again the door has been opened to all those True Believers who would reduce all experience to the particular dimension of learning to which they are privileged to tune in.

Worst of all is the haunting feeling that all manner of basic human issues have been brushed aside. Caring. Wanting. The morality of taking a stand on real issues in one's life. Hostility. Jealousy. Perhaps the behavior modifiers are bringing us to the ultimate triumph of science, freeing us from the nonsense of a non-existent Soul; but now that such scientific Heaven on Earth is here at last, to many of us so much of it seems heartless.

THE ENCOUNTER MOVEMENT

No less sure of themselves, yet far more blossomy and red-cheeked with warmth and enthusiasm, are another group of innovators of new techniques for facilitating growth, not so much by objective answers but through human contact, sensitivity, and caring.

There is no question that from a business standpoint the growth-center movement and its parent intellectual progenitor, humanistic psychology, are off to a resounding start. It only takes a regular reading of the mailings of a sampling of some of the well-established growth centers all around this country, and the world, to see that they now provide for a steady, loyal, and growing clientele.

For a whole variety of reasons, more and more centers in the last few years have been emphasizing in their promotion that their groups are not intended to serve as psychological or psychiatric treatment for people suffering from known neurotic or mental disorders. Not a few centers request that enrollees who are presently in psychotherapy secure a note of approval from their psychotherapist. Still, the feeling persists that many of these disclaimers grow out of a kind of business and social sense of self-protection, particularly for those centers whose staffs include many leaders who are not mental-health professionals—that is, they are not psychotherapists in practice who are accustomed to accept responsibility for the management of their cases. (This is not to imply that a therapist is responsible for the outcome of a case, but the therapist is indeed responsible for the quality of his work and what he purports to offer his patient.) The problem for the growth centers has been that they may appear to be offering treatment for weary and upset neurotics, and what if such people then enroll in courses and (a) don't get better, (b) get worse, (c) get horribly worse, precisely as a result of being offered opportunities of emotional intimacy, (d) flip out dramatically in a psychotic break or suicide.

The latter dire outcomes have been reported with significant frequency following experiences in growth-center groups, though it should be cautioned that some of these reports have been the result of rumor, exaggeration, and hysteria, as well as the professional envy of colleagues. Still, there has been at least one careful study of the outcome of growth-group experiences (Encounter Groups, by Lieberman, Yalom and Miles, Basic Books, New York, 1973), that did report a number of psychiatric casualties; and most responsible observers acknowledge that the sudden and large number of contact opportunities that growth groups pride themselves in offering may be very heavy fare for certain people suffering long-term emotional starvation. There also is no question that there are instances of very poor management of contact opportunities by leaders of certain groups.

When all is said and done, the feeling nonetheless persists that what growth people really feel they are offering is very much a treatment experience and a more profound growing experience than they believe takes place in many of the psychotherapies. However, they cannot allow themselves to use the language of therapy because of the sociologic or institutional no-no's that demand that therapy be done in the offices and institutions of duly certified therapists in the traditional mental-health professions.

What the growth movement is saying is that psychotherapeutic crying over either ancient hurts or one's current emotional isolation does little more than reinforce them. What human beings need is a full-bodied measure of touch and encounter of one another. Experiencing the beauty of one's humanity in the here and now and in concert with the beauty of others' humanity does more to reenergize people and revitalize their present lives. So men and women gather together to focus on this quality of experience and that zone of sensation. They gaze soulfully into each other's eyes, tap one another's backs, buttocks, and heads. They dramatize and act out scenes of yesteryear and, by the reenactment in the here and now in the company of significant others, seek to transform the past into an immediate experience that will wash away the hurts, frustrations, and blockages of yesteryear.

On balance, there is a great deal to be said for the encountering experience. There is much to be said for any setting that offers a forum to those of us who are hurt and lonely and want to reach out to others, to any setting that makes room for the courageous and the brave to explore and risk new relationship experiences, and certainly to any group that offers practice and supervision to those of us who are unknowing, untrained, and untutored in social relationships.

In my own psychotherapeutic practice, I consider the availability of encounter groups in the community a very important resource for any number of people for whom the psychotherapeutic experience in itself, however meaningful, cannot provide real-life opportunities to experience with peers the simple rudiments of helloing, good-byeing, embracing, wanting, accepting, and being accepted.

However, there are also other sides to the coin of the encounter process. In any number of ways, it is a phony coin. It is a coin that invites the worst of the money changers into the act. And it is often a short-changing coin.

One problem with encounters is the very glow of contact and warmth they turn on in lonely people who are otherwise caught up in complex defenses against contact. People may admit long-forbidden senses of sensuality, warmth, and excitement in the encounter experience, but what then may follow the high of being touched by love and life—lasting forbidden fruits, as it were—is a tremendous demoralization and panic.

There is also a clear-enough faddism in the growth movement that spawns encounter addicts and hucksters who claim that it is the royal road to lifelong human warmth, devotion, and togetherness. In the afterglows of what were perhaps very lovely experiences at the time, it often becomes clear that encounter power is not sufficient to remove many blocks, lack of confidence, and especially lack of know-how for handling *conflicts* in intimate relationships. Take a person who is saddled with an inner feeling of being fundamentally undeserving, or "bad," if you will. What often happens in encounters is a pseudo-intimacy in which there is a "high" from some measure of contact with others, but without really exposing and experiencing the objectionable and the fearsome in oneself; after the ball is over, there may well follow a serious depression.

Now we need to speak of the leadership of encounter groups. The movement has attracted many fine, creative, and truly searching minds from the mental-health professions and various behavioral sciences. In some growth cafeterias, the menu is well planned, expertly cooked, and tastefully served by otherwise experienced psychotherapists, who know not only of joy but of psychological defenses, that is, how pain follows on our getting closer to the very experiences we most fearfully desire and how too rich a diet can induce nausea. These leaders know that conversion experiences to a new ideology of growth are not the same as earning and owning inner changes in oneself.

However, in a great many instances, the leaders of encounters are *not* trained psychotherapists. On one hand, this democratization of encounter offers a living representation of the truth that becoming more human, intimate, and free is possible for all of us. Humanistic development need not be purchased at expensive salons, nor need it be gained via secret rites to be dispensed by a handful of high priests. The potential for humanness lies latent in all of us. Those who would teach and lead others to their inner resources may otherwise be teachers, ministers, actors, or shoemakers, secretaries, laborers, plumbing-supply salesmen, or square-dance callers on nights when they are not leading encounters. This is a heady heresy for a culture that otherwise panders to the impressiveness of its doctors and authorities ("I'm going to see a big specialist . . .") and that has not known how to cope with the power corruptions of its specialists. The encounter or human-growth movement represents a humanization and democratization of mental-health experiences that contrasts with the too common mystique of expertise and priestly claims to private ownership of difficult-to-understand personality processes by elitist professional groups.

Unhappily, the price of such welcome democratization is a good deal of nasty and dangerous bastardization. Not infrequently the leaders of encounter processes are or become undisciplined, narcissistically hungry, power-desirous shamans, charlatans, con men, and medicine men. Ironically, the excesses, carelessness, or exploitation with which these leaders are charged are matched by a surprisingly tawdry record of the same behaviors by entirely well-established, diplomaed mental-health practitioners. For example, it is no longer a closed secret that there are frequent instances of patients in psychotherapy being engaged in sexual intercourse by their therapists. Granted, some serious thinkers in the field have spelled out the considered possibility that some such encounters were or could have been planned to offer the patient a constructive enough learning experience, but the fact remains that the larger number of instances read simply and blatantly as sexual seductions no different from any other sexual seductions, except as they trade on and then forever compromise the very special set of meanings attached to the contract between patient and psychotherapist. Still, there is some comfort in knowing that when an accredited professional mental-health therapist sleeps with a patient, he is at least risking his career to censure by his colleagues and professional society, perhaps also risking his very license to practice. However, when the seductions issue from operations outside the pale of professional and legal controls, there is an alarming feeling of paganism and demagoguery running wild.

One instance of a growth-group leader using his position as a launching point for raunchiness concerns a very upset woman in my own practice. She is a courageous person, who at the time was waging a battle virtually to stay alive, and there was also a complicating factor that her funds for therapy were very limited—so much so that we abbreviated the traditional forty-five-minute session to a single half-hour session each week. I proposed to her that she join an encounter. Her individual therapy was being devoted to a rock-bottom focus on how she could break a vicious pattern of feeling trapped, betrayed, and worthless. I recommended to this good lady that she join a group with whom she might enjoy experiences of tenderness and closeness and support that could never be matched in any number of hours of individual therapy.

As luck would have it, the good lady returned from her very first session to report that following the end of the session the group leader asked her to stay on and forthwith proceeded to recommend sexual intercourse to her.

My already overstimulated patient was then quite shocked when my response to her information was, in effect, "Great, you have a marvelous opportunity. It's come to you on a silver platter. We couldn't have created something like this on our own for love or money."

"What do you mean?" she asked with shocked incredulity. "You don't expect me to go back there again, do you!"

"If you mean do I want you to go back and sleep with him, the answer is, 'No.' " I said. "If you mean do I think you ought to go back and just plain participate in the group and ignore what happened, the answer is again, 'No.' What I do mean is that here you have a fantastic opportunity to go back and give this man hell—and to do it as part and process of your experience in the group. You and I both know that you went through your entire childhood hardly saying boo to all the unfairness and uncaring that came your way. You just took it all and absorbed the punishment to a point where you yourself ended up believing that you were undeserving of respect for your person. This s.o.b. has given you a rare opportunity to go back and give him everything that he deserves for trying to use and for violating your dignity." P.S. She went. Not too long afterward the leader was dropped by the center.

It is not only instances of manifest excess that are in question, however. There are fundamental scientific questions yet to be worked through about just what are appropriate kinds of growth-group experiences for people at different stages in their lives. The fact that there are some psychiatric casualties following encounter groups in itself is no condemnation of growth groups. All of life leaves casualties. Virtually all therapies leave casualties. Still, there is a sense in which the risking that takes place within the context of a disciplined search for new knowledge is different from casualties in a faith-healer's tent; and while the entire growth-center movement is not an irresponsible medicine show, it has not yet really emerged as a self-researching, self-disciplining group.

As for the quality of encounter-group leadership, it isn't only instances of brazen exploitation of people's hopes and fears, such as sexual seduction, but the whole question of the stage that the growth group offers to the charismatic leaders who are really more concerned with leaving the imprint of their narcissism on their clientele than with knowing how to evoke the growth of the other person. Certainly this is the impressive conclusion of the studies of Lieberman and his colleagues, who found that real personal change was more likely in groups that were led by quieter, process-centered leaders than in groups that were conducted by flamboyant and colorful leaders, however brilliant and knowledgeable, whose unconscious motivation was to project their own presence on their groups.

FAMILY PSYCHOTHERAPY

Another major innovation of these years was family psychotherapy. This approach of treating family groups, rather than focusing on the individual patient in the tradition of medical problems, sprang into life in the late fifties. It is generally acknowledged that family therapy was spearheaded by psychiatrist Don Jackson and his colleagues in California who were working on innovative family treatment of schizophrenics. In the process, they contributed brilliantly to our understanding of the psychological genesis of schizophrenia as a disordered system of family communication characterized especially by the "double binds" of the patient—who is simultaneously told yes and no about how he is to feel and act.

As is typically the case in man's inventions, at the same time other pioneering explorations of family therapy were taking place. One story of the early era is that psychologist John Bell, then of the National Institute of Mental Health, was visiting the famous English psychiatrist John Bowlby and, as luck would have it, was at Bowlby's clinic at a time when an entire family group was being seen together. Dr. Bell believed that this was a treatment style that was regularly used. He was so intrigued that he thought about it all the way back to America, where he then embarked on his own explorations of family therapy with problematic adolescents. Only later did he discover that the family interview he had seen at Dr. Bowlby's office was an isolated instance in a situation where, because the traditional parallel treatment of child and parents was bogging down, the family was brought together in an effort to see where the resistance to treatment lay (which was also innovative, but not unique and not as far-reaching as Bell had imagined).

Another story of the early days of family therapy came out of a traditional mental hospital where schizophrenic patients were being seen in group therapy, and their relatives were being seen in a parallel group along the traditional lines of helping the relatives to understand the patient in their midst, how to approach their patient-relative, and so forth. It is not quite clear how and why the suggestion was made, but somebody proposed that the patients and relatives be seen in a group session together. Several observers who had not been working with either group reported that they were unable to tell the patients from the relatives! This was quite an astounding observation in those heydays of belief in an objective psychiatry, when it was assumed that people who were remanded to psychiatric hospitals were quite obviously "crazy" and different from people outside, or else they would not be hospitalized by fair, modern-day psychiatrists.

It was this dramatic phenomenon of what happened when "crazy" patients and their ostensibly "non-crazy" relatives were brought together that propelled family therapy forward to win staunch adherents around the country. From one setting and then another, there began to issue reports that, when a longtime psychotic patient—withdrawn, bizarre, hallucinating, or what have you—was brought into the setting of his family and treated as a member of a group of people who were full of feeling for one another, in a brief time the psychotic patient would shift over to an almost-forgotten semblance of rational, nonpsychotic talk and behavior. Furthermore, paralleling this amazing shift, there often issued an upsurge of upset and even strangeness in apparently healthy relatives.

The "trick" quite simply was that the family therapist chairing the family meeting would relate to the various behaviors of the patient as symbolic messages of feelings he experienced toward his family. Similarly, the therapist would pick up the tonal, gestural, and other emotional qualities of the seemingly innocuous remarks addressed to the patient by his family. The therapist would then reflect or mirror back what the patient and relatives were "saying" to one another. As we now know even more clearly, the therapist was attacking the covert scapegoating of the patient and the patient's acceptance of a scapegoat role that underlies much psychosis. Here was not a sickness selected at random to visit upon the patient, but an assignment of roles agreed to in an unwritten but powerful contract between family members.

The therapist's offer of equality was sufficiently inspiring to some patients that they were able to give up their sick roles, at least temporarily. Even if the patient subsequently did not stay sane (freedom from being a victim is not won by just one trip to a therapy shrine), seeing this kind of a once-in-a-lifetime movement of a "crazy" person, who previously had given up on life so totally, was a never-to-be-forgotten experience that compelled the therapists who were privileged to be present, and then the many who heard about these minor miracles, to go on researching the new procedure of family therapy.

Among the major cornerstones of family therapy are these beliefs:

It is the family system that brings psychological illness to one or more of its members.

It is the family that the symptomatic "ill" person is addressing by way of his symptoms in a veiled protest of the injustices and unresolved problems in the family.

Often, emotional and moral integrity in the ostensibly healthier members of a family is more seriously lacking than in the presenting patient; and, paradoxically, these people may be free of clinical symptoms precisely because they are managing to exert an oppressive power over the patient in their family through which they prop up their own emotional functioning.

Much of an emotional problem is caused by a failure to work through hostility toward relatives, oftentimes this hostility is repressed but plays a vicious subterranean (unconscious) role, and other times the hostility is so excessive that tenderness and caring are blocked out.

Family therapy provides an actual living forum for the airing of hostilities and also for renewing affectional connections with one's intimates, who in the final analysis most of us want to love.

A fascinating thing happens to the therapist in family therapy. Don Jackson wrote in one of his early papers that it was too early to evaluate the significance of the impact of family treatment on patients, but all of the therapists who participated in the new family therapy were feeling much better!

What happens for the therapist in the family therapy is a greater experiencing of oneself as a person—as husband, wife, former child, present parent. In the therapy room is a family just like the therapist's. Here and there may be an identifiable presenting patient but, as we have seen, what soon happens—not only in terms of presenting symptom pictures but on a more intrinsic level—is that the essential human dilemmas and absurdities come forcefully stage front, and therapist and patients together are left gaping in fascination at the mosaics of loving and hating, approaching and avoiding, tenderness and harshness and fairness and unfairness, and so on, of our human lives.

It is one thing for the therapist to continue, as he should, to play his professional roles—as a resource person to facilitate communication in the family group, as a mental-health clinician knowledgeable in the dynamics of how one person comes to be unable to function for himself, as an experienced therapist who knows that patients and family groups can change in a direction for the greater welfare of them all. Insofar as the therapist continues to serve these other functions, he occupies a role that is very different from that of the participating family members. Yet the essentially humanizing and democratizing quality of sharing with fellow human beings the everyday concerns of family living, which are inevitably so like the problems in the therapist's family, creates an atmosphere and tone for the therapy in which the therapist is likely to see himself as a peer of his patients.

From the very beginning, family therapy differed from the traditional, if only in response to the seating arrangement. When a therapist and family sit together, the scene is quite different than when a senior therapist sits qua doctor with an individual patient. It is also less likely in family therapy to find therapists sitting behind traditional desks.

Not that a therapist cannot pompously preside at a family-therapy session if he is dead set on it. Nor is it against the rules for a therapist to come across as a human being in a one-to-one therapy, and many do—including even a good number of psychoanalysts, despite the fact that the analysand is in an especially dependent posture on the couch. It is quite possible even for a traditional therapist to convey, however soundlessly, his human connection and ultimate peer relationship with his patient. However, there is a more essential everydayness to family therapy in its convening and seating of a group in which apparent nonpatients far outnumber the one or so symptom-bearing patients, where a variety of ages and sexes are meeting together in a kind of town-meeting relationship about processes that are ultimately universal to all groups of people in their interrelationships with one another.

More and more family therapists see as almost inherent in the process of their work with the family group the therapist's much more flexible and open use of himself as a person: alternately caring, sad, happy, angry, even seductive and challenging. In some cases, as in the brilliant and lovable work of Carl Whitaker, the University of Wisconsin professor of psychiatry, who is in great demand as a lecturer and workshop leader all around the country, there is even the use of the paradoxical and the absurd, which he compares to the process of *koans* in Zen. Whitaker heightens the absurdity that is inherent in human life to such a point that family members are paradoxically freed to look for new solutions outside of the ruts into which they have fallen and from which they feel there can be no escape.

So many of us get ourselves into angry, negative, or controversial relationship situations we never really wanted, but we feel doomed, and then we do not know what to do to get out of them. By taking the absurd to the extreme—"Why don't you move out of the house and let the children fight it out themselves?" the therapist may ask; "You should give her all your money, checkbooks, and securities," he may propose—rigidities and locksteps may be broken.

Such heightening of paradox and absurdity on the part of a therapist has in it many qualities of control and use of power that at face value are quite undemocratic. The use of such a technique certainly challenges a therapist to be deeply sure about his conscious and unconscious purposes in confronting people with the really painful extremes of their life choices. However, insofar as the therapist is putting the issues right out in front, in a certain way he is much more out in the open even in his presentation of the absurd than he is in traditional psychoanalytic treatment where, for great stretches of time, he remains reserved, distant, and calculatedly unreal.

In any case, this whole style of treatment is a very radical one, at the moment safe only in the hands of a master. For the most part, the process of family therapy concentrates on the therapist being leader, facilitator, encourager, guide, and model for genuine communication of positive and negative feelings in a family group.

From the point of view of sheer economy of time and money, the delivery system of family therapy is impressive. In traditional individual psychoanalytic therapy, all too often it has emerged that treating one person is at best a prologue to subsequent treatment of other members of the family. Treat a husband, and before long there is the wife requiring help. Treat one child in the family, and it is the frequent experience of therapists that, when that child gets better, another child takes on symptoms and requires help. Besides, if one views psychological symptoms at best as outer shows (reminiscent of Plato's cave, for those who enjoy the parable) of inner issues of relationships between members of the family group, it follows that sooner or later it behooves the entire family—if not all families—to take a good look at the ways in which they are doing their loving and feuding. Family therapy says: Let us stop the absurd one-by-one therapies over interminable years and get down to meaningful experiences with the entire family group at once.

Most family therapists now work fairly comfortably with flexible combinations of individual and family treatment, so that family therapy does not preclude utilizing time-honored techniques of psychoanalytic therapy in conjunction with the family process. Earlier in the emergence of the new family therapies, there was a danger of a new kind of ortho- doxy arising that would insist on all people being treated only in total family groups. Unhappily, rigidifiers and seekers of Absolute Truth abound in all camps. Fortunately, the danger of such orthodoxy has for the most part been averted, and there is now a healthy and even de- lightful flexibility about much of family therapies.

Very much related to the unfolding of the family therapies are new trends in marrage psychotherapy through flexible integrations of sessions for the couple together and each spouse separately, also through what many therapists consider an enormously powerful medium—mar- ried-couples group therapy. Although so-called marriage counseling has been around for a fair number of years, for a long time this field was char- acterized largely by a search for compromise, appeasement, and a fairly simplistic notion of communication between husband and wife. With the advent of the family therapies, and the entry of a good many psycho- analytically trained therapists into family treatment, a new vital thrust in marriage counseling has emerged. This is an effort, which many call "marriage therapy," to unravel the interlocking or complementary need- systems of the two partners: the spouses fit together originally in an effort to compensate for each one's weakness through the strength of one another, and then, increasingly, dissatisfaction and conflict erupt as the contract is no longer satisfactory to the growing needs of each partner.

There also is a broadening interest and enthusiasm in recent years for so-called family-life education programs, namely, where treatment agencies and any number of societal institutions, such as the church, even the school, reach out to a broad spectrum of people in the commu- nity, who do not have to define themselves as "patients" or as otherwise troubled in order to qualify for the program of learning ways of interact- ing in marriage and family life.

What of limitations of family therapy? As always in the affairs of man, there are some devotees of family therapy who jump on this new mode of therapy as on any other bandwagon and make fetishistic medi- cine-man pitches for a guaranteed efficacy of family therapy for just about all boils, warts, or dandruffs.

Further, although one can get to a fair amount of the angers and turn-offs in the family through family treatment, there is the likely short- coming of missing those end-of-the-road personality issues (whether of the "patient" or "nonpatient" in the family group) that really demand the surgical, probing depth that is the milestone of accomplishment of good psychoanalytic therapy. Thus, it is one thing to identify how fearful some family members may be of being turned down in matters of the heart and how to protect themselves—they may avoid trying for love, or they may seduce anger, which will guarantee that they will never be loved and then rejected. Identifying such patterns in family therapy may bring a certain measure of relief and change; but if the pattern of defense is deeply rooted and the deep need for playing it safe and avoiding hurt grows out of unresolved hurts in childhood, what is needed is the kind of change process that psychoanalytic therapy prides itself on. The question then becomes how wisely and how effectively family therapy practitioners know how and when to combine individual- and family-treatment techniques.

Another problem with family-treatment techniques concerns those situations where separateness for an individual is preferred. For example, in the instances where teenagers or young adults are so busy at the emotional job of separating from their past, putting them together in family therapy with their pasts may do them a disservice. There are profound differences in the family-therapy camp on this issue. Some claim that the best thing to do is to help the young person do his separating from the family right there with the family. Others claim that the contradiction of putting people together who really should be apart cannot be resolved in family sessions, and that such people need to be able to have most if not all of their therapy on their own. There are also many different situations in which an individual spouse very much needs to differentiate from the other; and while some of this work can be done in family sessions by focusing on the unseparateness and helping the couple to experiment with newly separating ways, some of the counseling work should be done separately. Thus, frequently, an exploratory affair in marital life may in a larger perspective be a fairly healthy milestone of experiencing oneself, which then offers people a basis for an even deeper recommitment to the marriage. Many such affairs should *not* be talked about with one's spouse. Of course, there are also any number of instances where the process of treatment is part and parcel of a process that unfortunately must lead people to separate and divorce, and these to a large extent properly call for individual sessions.

Knowing how and when to utilize the new methods of family treatment is important but does not involve the dangers of a potentially damaging therapy. Nor are family therapies likely to miss major issues in a person's psychology, such as is the case with some of the other new growth modalities that pick restricted ranges of human experience (such as the focus on loving, without dealing with anger, in sensitivity or encounter groups, or the approach to symptom correction in behavior modification, which does not deal very much with the inner spirit or character of a person).

On the whole, family therapy appears to be a sound and exciting addition to our therapeutic tools, but there is much to learn of how and when to utilize family therapies.

GESTALT THERAPY, TRANSACTIONAL ANALYSIS, AND PARENT EFFECTIVENESS TRAINING

We will treat somewhat more briefly, though respectfully, three other new therapies on the scene that certainly deserve understanding: Gestalt Therapy, Transactional Analysis, and Parent Effectiveness Training.

Gestalt Therapy techniques are finding very wide acceptance among therapists and growth leaders and are rapidly being incorporated into many other frameworks. In terms of maintaining its own separate identity the Gestalt school will probably fade out, and perhaps this is a tribute to its greater authenticity. The Gestalt focus, as pioneered for many years by the late Fritz Perls, addresses itself to a total dimension of experiencing as more important than intellectualizing, thinking about, or remembering experiences—all such secondary functions introduce barriers between the person and his actual experiences of being what he is and was, and what he will now wish to become. Thus, a favorite Gestalt technique is, instead of talking about one's feelings toward one's mother or father in the past, to act as if one is addressing the mother or father in the same room, sitting in yon (empty) chair. Anyone who has tried this experiential maneuver soon discovers what an enormous difference there is between *talking about* and *living out* even simulated reconstructions of an experience.

The Transactional Analysis people, generally referred to as TA, emphasize our learning to differentiate between Child and Parent and Adult modes of functioning. The Parent talks down to the Child. The Child is the recipient of Parental talking down. The Adult is the independent agent who operates for and out of his own dignity. By reducing many, many complicated behaviors to such interacting roles, which they diagram much like football plays, the TA people do an enormous service. Too much of psychotherapy is bewildering, confusing, and elitist. The TA people focus on a very powerful and central process, namely, the definition or assignment of dignity values in an interpersonal interaction, and thus bring rapidly within the reach of millions of people enormously valuable tools for changing many maladaptive behaviors. At the same time, the TA people have suffered from the same kinds of excesses of cultism and oversell that characterize so many new movements.

TA is a very effective way of organizing our understanding of some important human experiences, but not all of human experience. It is a way of addressing certain major issues of the equality of people, but it does not address the full range of issues, of fright, unsureness, loving, and so forth. A particularly glaring void in TA theory concerns not the Child that was in all of us, and he still may be hanging on in our grey-haired years, but *real* children. TA seems to begin at age eleven or twelve, and does not have a language to deal with the necessity of real children's dignity equalities.

This void may have been filled by another entirely unrelated but extremely useful new system that very much concerns itself with the realness of children as people who need to be heard and respected. This is Thomas Gordon's Parent Effectiveness Training (PET). Focusing on some fairly simple techniques of "active listening"—which means hearing what the child is feeling and then reflecting back to him his message and a "no-lose" approach to working out problems and conflicts with children. PET courses are offered all around the country to help parents develop nonpunitive, encouraging ways with their children. Again, in contrast with the chaotically bewildering mystique of traditional psychotherapy as to what constitutes parental effectiveness, here is a commonsense, teachable, practicable system for being fairer, more decent, and more helpful to kids. There is no doubt that PET works. What is also relevant, however, is that it opens the door to experiencing even more deeply the real unresolved issues of personal development in both the parents and the children. More sophisticated teachers and practitioners of PET find that it is a marvelous introduction and stimulus to subsequent psychotherapy of child and/or family. It is especially to the credit of Dr Gordon's PET that it works for many people who never would have made it either *to* or *through* traditional therapy with its unwitting bewilderment, confusion, and indirect put-downs of people.

CONCLUSION

Are we now entering an era of healthy democratization in both philosophy and delivery system of treatment and growth? Or are we coming into another era of faddism, of which there are so many in the history of human events? Or are the new therapies of these mad seventies a combination of both a welcome democratization and a pleasure-seeking faddism?

How deeply do these new helping techniques go? Are they essentially *feel-better* techniques that relieve people of pain—these too have meaning in human events, but they are different from therapies that generate a deep learning, which people then hold on to for many years. Do any of the new helping techniques have the potential of a depth similar to the best psychoanalytic therapy?

Do the new helping techniques free the new creative talents in the helping fields? Or do the new therapies and growth centers open the door to untrained, unaccredited leaders who are not checked by standards of professional responsibility and who do not have a commitment to long-term research and evaluation of their new helping techniques?

Clearly these questions admit no simple answer for *any* of the new helping processes—or the old! We have been touching on the strengths and weaknesses in each treatment or growth process; and it seems clear that we are having a marvelous but terribly gawky explosion of new ideas, delivery methods, and leadership resources, all of which point toward an enormous new flexibility and rich potential for helping, and all of which also have an enormous potential for faddism, cultism, idolatry, lowered standards of professionalism, and dilettantism.

The explosion of new therapies of the seventies represents and brings to the old existing psychotherapy establishment a new insistence on people caring, also a new involvement of the therapist or leader and a new concern with what really goes on in human interactions. In addition, what has been true of virtually every new therapy over the years is that the new explorers, practitioners, and adherents bring to the ministering of their new therapy a quality of caring, if not for their patients then for their patients as recipients of the new therapy they wish to advance (although this distinction often is blurred and lost to the minds of the therapists). Characteristically, all new therapies on the mental health scene report excellent results during their first few years, including electric shock, insulin shock, and other such therapies that leave most growth-oriented, psychotherapy-caring people aghast. The big question is what happens after a few years when the newness of the "honeymoon" is over and the treatment procedures in a sense are stripped to the bare essence of what they have to offer their client population. No longer is there the same enthusiasm or striving on the part of the therapist. Also, by this time, there will have arrived on the scene any number of "camp follower" therapists and leaders, who do what they have learned from others one is supposed to do, without that much excitement, involvement, or sense of exploration; so that the best in the once-new therapy now has to emerge notwithstanding the banality of such pedestrian, unimaginative therapists.

The new therapies of the seventies demonstrate excitingly that it is possible to translate complex, previously all-too-mysterious processes into concretely meaningful steps and tools for everyday human beings in their everyday lives.

This is an enormous breakthrough, and in its own way it is a challenge to the more traditional depth-seeking therapies to evolve new ways for the consumer-patient to go about helping himself in his everyday life. Too much of psychoanalytic therapy has pretended to priestly rites of knowledge that will always remain better understood by the therapist even long after the analysis is over.

The new therapies add considerably to our understanding of several fundamental behavior processes. Thus, the rational-emotive therapist has much to say about the utter nonsense of how much we conduct our lives with an eye to what others will think of us, and about how we should understand the many ways in which we get trapped when we fear fear and then complicate what might be a briefer process of anxiety by tensing up so much against our anxiety that we end up less able to rid ourselves of it. The TA people teach us wisely of our being driven by Parent-like preachings and finger-wagging here, there, and everywhere and of our alternately running, surrendering, suiciding, and adopting all manner of slave styles other than being ourselves—adults, living for ourselves, with our own real talents and interests. Family therapists teach us not to get lost in a world of inner psychological dynamics without moving resolutely to explore and experience with our family our hurts, angers, longings, and frustrated wishes to love. The behavior-modification people say that we should not get lost in mumbo jumbos of internal psychological phenomena without looking at just what behavior it is that we want to change and then objectively examining the conditions under which such behavior arises, so that we may then utilize established scientific procedures for breaking up the sequence of behavior we want to modify.

On the other hand, like in much of psychoanalysis, there is also in all these new therapies an assumption that man's behavior is reducible to "straight-line understanding," that is, patterns of cause and effect or sequences where one step inevitably leads to another. Whereas the truth may well be that, although *some* human behavior is straight-line, a good deal of human behavior, especially perhaps the spirit-essence of human experience, may be laid out in Nature's Grand Plan quite differently. Perhaps we are "wired" in part for contradictions or paradoxes, or perhaps we are designed in Hegelian dialectics. Perhaps we are in part an absurdity. Perhaps we are all of these together: a brilliant master-system built of subsystems of logic, contradiction, paradox, dialectics, and absurdities. Thus, a peaking of marital love, say, is necessarily followed by negativity and hate, which then build to a new tension of love and hate, and finally to a new synthesis in a peaking of closeness and release. Certainly there are all too numerous graduates of essentially very successful psychoanalyses who for themselves have come to the conclusion that it is not simply the unraveling of their hang-ups that makes the difference, but a kind of constant focus on the joy and dignity of being oneself, even as one continues to suffer any number of upsets in discovering the utter insanity and absurdity of one's spouse, children, the entire world (as well as one's own dear self). However, the trick is to see these as the other sides of the beauty and grandeur of all human beings and not be flipped out by the unfairness of life.

It may therefore be built into *all* treatment models that there must be at least some inadvertent medicine-man ballyhoo. It would therefore behoove all prudent seekers of truth to respect and enjoy all new understanding, but remain open to the never-ending discovery that there is so much that we cannot understand; and no steps should be taken to spare us the pain and joy of discovering further.

The new therapies develop marvelous new technologies for freeing so many more people, more rapidly and more optimistically, from various blocks to free utilization of their energies and talents. Where previously a person afraid of flying in an airplane might, in theory, spend several years in a wide-ranging psychoanalytic therapy, now there are behavior-modifying helpers who focus systematically on reducing the fear in a brief period of time. Where previously we offered only long, lonely routes of therapy to lonely, frightened, unconnected people who did not know how to try for social contact without the strain of their effort reinforcing their sense of not being able to cope with social contacts, there are now encounter groups, in which the warmth and individual attention and the sense of communality that grows out of sharing simple experiences of touch, offer quite rapid, new contact experiences. Where previously endless additional hours of analysis were prescribed for surges of frightening anxiety, rational-emotive therapists now cut through to teach us directly, first how not to be afraid of anxiety and then how to trace the inner message of anxiety to the statements we actually are making to ourselves—often that we are fearful of how we are appearing to others. In effect, insofar as each of the new therapies clearly taps a truth that can free blocked human development and unleash mysteriously beautiful human energies that were being checked, each of the new therapies vividly represents an important new way of freeing human potential.

Yet, the questions remain: Just how effectively does any given therapy or growth process free inner energies? For how long? What kinds of blocks does a given treatment reach best? Which therapies open the door to a momentum of further freeing experiences—not only in therapy, but in embrace and struggle with one's family and peers. In tougher pragmatic terms: Which therapy toughens us up best for lives that will always be beset with problems, inequities, and a never-ending series of absurdities that many of us see as intrinsic to the human condition? No matter how hard we try, we ourselves shift from one side of our humanness to another, and those we live with are busily engaging their own many sides of humanness. At this point, the "psychophysics" of such movement from one side of our humanness to another are only vaguely recognizable. No matter which psychological therapies we undergo, and no matter what books we read, conflict, dissatisfaction, injustice, betrayal, failure, and challenge abound at every point in life.

From this point of view, perhaps the best question is: Which of the psychological therapies prepares man the fullest for the absurdities of his life?

Insofar as faith, optimism, and courage are the necessary qualities for facing crisis, all therapies that help us feel better about ourselves are good for us.

Insofar as success in breaking an inhibition or block gives us reason to trust ourselves to work our way through still the next block or problem, all therapies that help are useful.

Insofar as therapy invites the illusion that those who would live according to the truths of this or that psychological faith or guide to living doubtless will be freed from further hurts, disillusionment, and unfairness, that therapy—new or old—is dangerous. At best, people do gain a sense of safety and security in conforming and identifying with their doctrine and its adherents, but they pay a price of blindness to many processes of reality. At worst, people beguiled by orthodoxy are set up for a cruel crisis of faith when their mythology is finally shattered by life's relentless truths.

As we see it, some of the new therapies and some of the best aspects of traditional psychoanalytic therapy address themselves to just this critical issue of preparing people to tolerate pain, to search ingeniously for alternatives, to draw on deep wellsprings of courage when the never-ending crises of life strike.

Interestingly enough, the very helping process of psychoanalytic therapy is cast in a mold that seeks to create new crisis and then to teach the patient how to manage crisis with a deep inner resourcefulness. It is only a temporary ploy that the distressed or uncomfortable patient is initially offered support and relief. The essential structure of real psychoanalytic therapy is that the therapist—very much like a Zen master!—then leads the patient to the discovery that there really is nothing available to him from the therapist. The therapist puts out a huge dose of silence, a huge dose of frustration of every dependent wish. He turns away from cries for sympathy. The paradox is that the frustrations and turnaways are rendered not in overt cruelty, but against a background of silent, wordless compassion and interest that somehow reaches the beleaguered patient as he finds that no matter how clever he is, no matter how appealing, no matter how madly symptomatic, the disciplined therapist will not act to take away the pain of his fellow human being. Finally, out of the unfathomable pain of aloneness, hurt, rage, and fear that the end has come, grows a deep wellspring of courage and discovery of one's dignity and strength, a profoundly humbling but enlivening realization that all of life is marked by being alone, till the day we die alone. Along the way, we may properly seek the presence of people who, through their own humanity, do care to some extent, but neither they nor we can transcend our humanity to live or die for one another.

From this point of view, in evaluating new therapies and encounters—the quick and easy, the rigorously rational, the enticingly warm reconnecting to family members, learning to be more of an adult, finding no-lose solutions with our intimates, and so on—*all* fall short of making us realize that we will never be complete, never safe from pain, and that paradoxically this is the jumping-off point for the discovery of the greatest strengths in us.

From this point of view, virtually all of the new therapies are dangerously seductive, and from this point of view, the well-aged wisdom of psychoanalytic therapy looks better than ever. However, one would hope that the new therapies will in turn contribute to a new psychoanalytic therapy: in which the soundless, depriving, Zen-maddening qualities of therapist reserve are enriched with still deeper qualities of feeling for and with the other human being; where the therapist will leave his silences more often, where long stretches of soundlessness will be sprinkled with good counsel and fellowship; where transference work will be periodically put aside for specific habit-retraining exercises, especially for particularly disabling symptoms that might be substantially relieved; where learning experiences in settings other than the analytic therapy will be encouraged, such as attending encounter groups and PET courses; and where genuine direct communication experiences with one's contemporary family and family of origin will be encouraged and sequences of family therapy sessions integrated with the individual therapy. In this sense, even if many of us still return to the ancient therapy for training in depth of our potential human courage, it should be a psychoanalytic therapy that has been advanced by all of its offspring and all of its rebels to be more humanizing, more democratic, more on guard against its own fetishes and idolators.

We conclude that everyone, but *everyone*, is clearly the richer for the burgeoning of all the new therapies of the seventies. It is for the consumer-patient and seeker of growth to know that, as in buying automobiles, no manufacturer does everything right. Each type of car has its advantages and disadvantages. Each innovation brings its new freedom and its unpredicted difficulties. There are also any number of otherwise successful cars that a responsible manufacturer needs to recall. There also is always the unknown of the frequency-of-repair record as cars get older. In short, select therapy and growth experiences wisely.

THE COUNSELOR: EDUCATING FOR THE BEAUTIFUL AND NOBLE PERSON

Fred Richards

During the past three decades psychologists have focused increasingly upon the healthy personality to clarify, define, and objectify the optimal end of the growth process in human nature. A vital part of this revolutionary reconstruction of the image of man has been a re-evaluation of the counseling relationship and a new model of the counselor or helper as one becoming fully human, fully growing and fully functioning in every aspect of his life. Systematic exploration into the interpersonal dynamics of the therapeutic process and the facilitative dimensions of counselor functioning suggests that the more effective counselors are also the more fully human, the most actualizing. Such research findings challenge us to devise counselor training programs which have as their main thrust the facilitation of the maximum growth of the trainee. They urge us to employ training programs educating for what Landsman (1968) calls the "beautiful and noble person."

Thirty years ago, Carl Rogers presented a paper entitled, "New Concepts in Psychotherapy," which attempted to formulate a newer approach to counseling and therapy. Rogers' approach emphasized, as we know, the profound significance of the counselor/counselee relationship and the human qualities of the counselor. Years later, Rogers (1967, p. 181) wrote:

> Some years ago I formulated the view that it was not the special professional knowledge of the therapist, nor his intellectual conception of therapy . . . nor his techniques, which determined his effectiveness. I hypothesized that what was most important was the extent to which he possesses certain personal attitudes in the relationship. I endeavored to define three of these which I regarded as

SOURCE: Fred Richards, "The Counselor: Educating for the Beautiful and Noble Person," *Colorado Journal of Educational Research*, Fall 1972. Reprinted by permission.

basic—the realness, genuineness or congruence of the therapist; the degree of emphatic understanding of his client which he experienced and communicated; and the degree of unconditional positive regard or non-possessive liking which he felt toward his client.

Rogers' theoretical formulations focused on those personal qualities characteristic of that person other humanistic psychologists were beginning to define as the "ultimate" in human growth and development. These psychologists were seeking to postulate an ideal image of the most human realization of man's potential. During thirty years of exploration and research into what man may become or could be, Rogers and others have variously described this human potential as: self-actualization, integration or individuation, adequacy, authenticity, fully-functioning, the transparent self, the beautiful and noble person. While their descriptions have varying emphasis, the authors agree that the human being they describe is one "realizing the potentialities of the person . . . becoming fully human, everything that the person can become" (Maslow, 1968, p. 153). These various descriptions of full humanness appear to converge at one point: the truly healthy personality, in part, can be operationally defined as a person functioning on high levels of empathy, genuineness and positive regard. As Maslow (1970) points out, it has become "clearer and clearer that the best 'helpers' are the most fully human persons . . . the best way to become a better 'helper' is to become a better person."

Descriptions of the healthy personality by humanistic psychologists emphasize the convergence of these personal qualities in the superior person.* Describing the qualities the effective counselor communicates in therapeutic relationship, Rogers (1967) writes that the counselor can sense and identify with the client's private world of inner meanings and feelings and communicate his understanding at levels where the client is vaguely aware. The effective counselor is openly, freely, spontaneously himself; he is genuinely there, authentic, *sans* a front or facade. He also accepts, respects and cares about his client in a nonpossessive way. He is warm and caring. He does not judge or evaluate the client, but lets the client *be*.

Landsman (1961, 1967, 1968) describes the beautiful and noble person or the best self "as an individual's functioning on the highest levels of his uniquely human characteristics" (1967, p. 32). Intelligent, productive, self-actualizing, he is the "helper" possessing the qualities of warmth, kindness, gentleness, courage, and compassion. He has sharp, accurate perceptions of reality. He accepts, likes, enjoys, expresses and

---

*See Welch and Rodwick, *"Communicating the Sciences: The Scientist as a Healthy Personality."*

understands himself. Joyfully, passionately, fully, he goes out to meet, experience and respond to his world. Deeply caring and committed to the growth and well-being of others, he is the compassionate, facilitative helper (Landsman, 1968).

In short, the effective counselor is the compassionate person at the positive end of the passionate-productive-compassionate continuum describing the growth process of Landsman's beautiful and noble person, (Landsman, 1968). It appears that counselor training programs committed to producing effective counselors should have as their goal the maximum growth and full humanness of the trainees.

Research on the facilitative dimensions of empathy, genuineness and positive regard have produced results with important implications for the structuring of counselor training programs. Research by Carkhuff (1967), Carkhuff and Berenson (1967), Carkhuff and Truax (1966), Pierce, Carkhuff and Berenson (1967), and Truax and Carkhuff (1964) found that low levels of counselor functioning have deteriorative influences on client personality change and that high levels of therapist offered conditions evoke the greatest constructive change in the client. That is, counselors both promote and inhibit or retard the growth of their clients! Alexik and Carkhuff (1967) found that low level functioning counselors are manipulated by the client's depth of self-exploration. In one study, Kratochvil, Aspy and Carkhuff (1967) concluded that the counselor's direction of growth or change in levels of functioning had a profound effect upon constructive changes in the client. Foulds (1969) found that counselors communicating high levels of facilitative conditions are more self-actualizing than low functioning counselors.

Carkhuff and Berenson (1967), Carkhuff, Kratochvil, and Friel (1968) and Pierce, Carkhuff and Berenson (1967) found that training programs function at the level of the trainers who conduct them; the levels of trainer or supervisor functioning may facilitate or retard the trainee's level of functioning and constructive personality change. Bergin and Solomon (1963) concluded that graduates of training programs functioned at unusually low levels. Carkhuff, Kratochvil and Friel (1968) also found that graduates of training programs function at lower levels than they did when first entering the program, and that the more and less adequate trainees left the program while the middle or average range of trainees remained.

The above mentioned research findings must be viewed with some caution, however. Combs (1970, p. 7) correctly warns that counselor "training programs must concern themselves with perception and less with acts and methods." Researchers emphasizing the latter too often attempt to measure the interpersonal functioning of the counselor/subjects while employing an approach greatly lacking in the dimensions of inter-

personal functioning they seek to measure. Often little or no consideration is given to the perceptual organization or personal meanings of the
behavior who is the subject of the research. The counselor/subject's level
of functioning is evaluated in terms of whether or not his verbal behavior
conforms to the expectations of the rating scales designed by researchers
who consider themselves "the experts." On the other hand, it is incorrect
to assume "that the way to become expert is to do what the expert does."
(Combs, 1964, p. 371). It is also true an effective counselor is not necessarily a person who employs any particular method. An effective counselor is one whose methods fit him (Combs, 1970, p. 6). Often the basic response repertoire of the counselor/subject—his particular "method"—is
considered ineffective or low functioning because the researcher fails to
consider important what causes the subject's behavior, i.e., his perception and not the researcher's perception of the client and the situation.

Even though the above research into the interpersonal dynamics of
the counseling relationship has its evident shortcomings, it alarmingly
and convincingly suggests that present training programs may be educating for mediocrity rather than human magnificence, may be producing
"nonhelpers" rather than helpers. Mediocrity, even though it has a professional polish, is not enough. Training programs not honestly committed to educating for the best, the ultimate realizations of human
growth and development, become part of the very interpersonal environment that drives a client to the counselor in the first place.

Having commented on the chronic lack of healthy, human nourish-
ment available in our society, Carkhuff and Berenson write, (1967, p. 1):

> The hope, it would appear, lies in the development through both
> training and constructive personal change, of the whole per-
> son/counselor, the person who does not view counseling and thera-
> py as distinct from life, but rather, counseling as a way of life. The
> only reasonable starting point from which to increase the quality
> and quantity of nourishment in all human relationships is the whole
> counselor, a person acutely aware of his own experience.

The whole person/counselor is both competent and compassionate. He is
a grower, one committed to his own personal constructive change and the
growth of others. He has vast resources, is fully alive, full of energy and
zest for life. He employs a thorough knowledge of research and research
tools to discriminate and communicate high levels of facilitative conditions (Carkhuff and Berenson, 1967). Briefly, he is self-actualizing; he is
passionately, productively, and compassionately alive.

What kind of training program would best educate for such a man?
Carkhuff and Berenson and others suggest an integrated didactic and experiential approach to counselor training with a focus upon the trainee's

personal growth and self-actualization, (Carkhuff and Berenson, 1967; Carkhuff, Kratochvil and Friel, 1968; Carkhuff and Truax, 1965a, 1965b). The training program would provide a "living, flourishing, productive pocket of health" where trainees would interrelate with trainers who would be models of the effective whole person/counselor, models of the person who "is involved in a life long search for actualization for others as well as for himself, and is readily amenable to the sharing of his search with others" (Carkhuff and Berenson, 1967, pp. 205 and 46).

A program characterized by the above and providing vast opportunities for evoking behaviors ascribed to Landsman's beautiful and noble person has exciting possibilities. Landsman's systematic exploration of positive experiences suggested to him the fascinating possibility "that the maximization of positive human experience is perhaps the key to the maximization of self-actualization," (Landsman, 1961, p. 51). He postulates an experiential continuum which describes the growth process of the self-actualizer moving beyond normality toward superior functioning as the beautiful and noble person, (Landsman, 1968). Landsman clearly insists that the first phase, the passionate-self-positive context, is absolute; a positive attitude toward self is a necessary basis for movement toward higher levels of functioning on the continuum. The second or productive phase is characterized by increased productivity, efficiency, single-minded commitment of one's resources, talents and energies to personally meaningful tasks or goals. Here the mode of productivity is that most expressive of one's essential personality. The third phase, the compassionate person, is the highest level. Here one is the socially effective person, the exciter, the growth facilitator, the loving-caring person. Here one is, if you will, the whole person/counselor.

The following only suggests possible directions for a training program which would operationalize or confirm Landsman's continuum. No effort to outline a complete program is intended. What the authors attempt to do here is to give a brief overview of what might well be the emphasis in each phase of a program. The selection of staff members and students is considered only briefly, although some research has attempted to deal with this problem, (Whiteley, Sprinthall, Mosher, Donaghy, 1967).

It is assumed that the counselor trainers or supervising personnel would be some of the best persons available, those functioning on higher levels and actively and continually committed to their own growth. Selection of counselor-trainees should include a candid discussion of the risk factor implicit in the growth-process emphasis of the program. Important is that prospective counselor-trainees choose to participate in such a process only after exploring and sharing with one or more members of the staff their own perceptions of what such a program means to them. Counselor-trainees accepted into the program would become involved in an intense mini-program, a one to three week session reflecting both the climate and challenge of the full program. The mini-program would function as an experiential selection phase, a selection process grounded in the very qualities of interpersonal functioning the program hopes to facilitate and one that provides an opportunity for students to leave the program, if they choose to do so, after an intense and personal interaction with other students and the staff.

THE PASSIONATE SELF PHASE

A conscious committed effort to create a climate of non-evaluation, non-threat and unconditional positive regard. A real attempt on the part of all personnel to communicate high levels of the facilitative conditions to the trainees. A commitment to the creation of community celebrating the separateness and uniqueness of each individual. A commitment to being, working, playing and sharing together to facilitate the maximum well-being of all concerned.

The emphasis should be upon dialogue in community with others, the discovery of significant others among the staff and students, sensitivity training, encountering, confronting, being with oneself and others, joy, closeness, sharing, mutual acceptance and respect, spontaneity. Students would help others to discover their potential creativity by sharing unique talents and skills, would design their own "program" of ongoing growth as the whole person/counselor, would strive to increase their openness to others, themselves and the world. They would meet with other students and staff members to discuss ideas, share insights, or self-disclose and listen to the self-disclosures of others. Students would be encouraged to set aside time each week to meditate alone, sit quietly, walk, hike and simply enjoy learning the art of responding more fully to their inner selves and their environment.

Students would keep detailed cumulative records or journals of their experiences with self, others and the world, would share these records or journals with significant others, and would use them to better perceive and understand more deeply their own growth process. They would participate in preparatory seminars to explore the personal meanings and implications of the passionate-productive-compassionate continuum and related areas in psychology, literature and other fields. Important here is that each trainee's experience frees him increasingly to explore and share his changing perceptions of himself and others. Such a climate would be an invitation to explore his feelings of personal adequacy and more toward accepting any and all aspects of his perceptual world. A goal of such seminars would be to give the students a personally meaningful overview of the process in which they were personally involved, enable them to perceive their unique and separate, though perhaps shared, experience of the process, and give them a sense of being an accepted member of a community committed to the growth and well-being of *all* its members.

THE PRODUCTIVE SELF PHASE

This phase would build upon, grow or emerge out of the former phase. In the first phase trainees would be helped, through extensive interaction with staff members and other students, to realize that their process of self-exploration and self-discovery may move forward on their terms and that it is at times a very slow and laborious one. Consequently the decision to move forward would be a shared one. The trainees would only move into the second phase when adequate enough to do so and when such movement was personally meaningful. Thus the length of each phase would vary according to how the trainee perceived his own growth experience after sharing his perceptions of the experience with significant others.

In the productive-self phase the emphasis would be respectable but creative research in areas dealing, directly or indirectly, with personal blocks to further growth, personal problems, conflicts, meanings, urges toward growth experienced by the student in the initial phase of the program. Productivity with significant others would be emphasized, also the increased realization of goals or the satisfaction of needs newly perceived in the first phase and now a personally meaningful basis for research, new projects and new directions in one's program.

Students might work extensively with research scales to increase their ability both to discriminate and communicate a core of facilitative conditions to others. Rather than a mechanistic use of the scales in which the trainee attempts to become a carbon copy of "the effective counselor" by "learning" or mimicking taped responses rated high on the scales, the trainee would function in terms of *his* initial and changing perception of how *he* sees the various levels of functioning as defined by the observational instruments. Most important is that the trainee become his instrument, that he increasingly becomes "a person who has learned to use himself as an effective instrument" (Combs, 1964, p. 373). Working extensively with the scales the trainee would seek to acquire a deep awareness of how *he* functions most authentically as a helper.

Trainees would also work with video and/or audio tape-recorded examples of therapists functioning at different levels of facilitation. They would also participate in sessions in which each student would respond to the taped sessions of supervising staff members and students who, at the compassionate-self phase, would be actively involved in the counseling experience. Again, it is important that such "evaluation" take place in an atmosphere of trust, acceptance and respect, that the facilitative qualities considered characteristic of the whole/person counselor be equally that of the program in general.

The second phase student-trainees would role play as both "counselor" and "counselee." Immediate feedback from video and/or audio tapings of these sessions would be evaluated by those who volunteer to be taped and by fellow students. Students perceiving themselves as functioning at low levels on the core of facilitative dimensions would role play as "counselees" with those students functioning at higher facilitative levels serving as "counselors." As student "counselees" increase their sense of adequacy they would move into the role of "counselor." Both "counselors" and "counselees" would record, by using journals, cassettes, charts, etc., their change in levels of interpersonal functioning. They would continue to keep journals—an extension of the first-phase journals—which would relate their levels of functioning to their understanding and perception of their personal growth.

In this phase, as in all phases of the program, the educative process would be always an active participation in one's own growth and the growth of others. As aspiring helpers in a counselor training program they would be helpers in their relationships with one another. In the context of the experience of community nurtured in the first phase, evaluation of trainee functioning in the second-phase taped sessions is intended to be facilitative rather than threatening. Mistakes would not be failures but the cutting edge dimensions of one's personal growth process to be accepted, disclosed and assimilated into one's perception of himself and his role as a helper. To view the instruments as a means of "degrading" rather than facilitating the trainee to grow and learn in a climate of non-threat would be inimical to the training program suggested here. In fact, if the selection of students for the counseling program, viewed here as a vital and significant phase of the program, could distinguish between "growers" and "non-growers," "failure" in the context of such a climate might be a near impossibility. Perhaps no significant data is available on this matter because an educative process pregnant with vast opportunities for positive facilitative experiences toward the increased actualization of the student has never been tried!

THE COMPASSIONATE SELF PHASE

This phase would again be an extension and continuation of the first two phases. But the emphasis here would be the active involvement of the trainee in the counseling relationship. He would function as the compassionate helper. Phase-two students' evaluation of the trainee's video and/or audio taped sessions, done in a climate of community and mutual helping, would give the trainee immediate feedback. The trainee would focus his passion and productivity on the increase of his capacity to function as an effective helper in every facet of the program. He could assist in research and carry out his own; he might extend his role as helper by co-leading seminars with staff members and by advising or assisting students participating in earlier phases of the program.

Using his own cumulative records or journals, tape-recorded sessions of his second-phase "counseling" and third-phase counseling experience, the student would do an extensive self-evaluation of his own growth process and his perceptions of his increased professional competence as a helper—an evaluation of himself as a whole person/counselor. This analysis or self-evaluation would be extended and supported by personally meaningful research in counseling psychology and related areas and/or a project of excellence whose focus and form would be determined by the needs of the student. The project of excellence would be an extension or expression of the unique concerns and directions of each of the counselor-trainees and a contribution to the counseling field. It would be an integration of the various aspects of the total impact of the trainee's experience and involvement in the program. Important here is that the student obtains a deep cognitive/affective or personally meaningful understanding of *his mode of counseling,* that his own unique mode is related, by him, to the total counseling field, that he become increasingly aware of himself as the whole person/counselor, that he gain insight into the unique direction of his own development and growth, that he knows what he's about, where he's been, where he is, and where he can and may be going.

Participation in a training program that strives to achieve and practice the same high levels of interpersonal functioning it desires of its trainees would, it is hypothesized, free the trainees to discover and begin to develop their own maximum potential for becoming effective facilitators of growth. Hopefully, the trainee's experience in the counselor training program will prepare him to function not only as an increasingly effective counselor, but as an increasingly effective human being as well, as the beautiful and noble person.

REFERENCES

Alexik, Mae and Carkhuff, Robert R. "The Effects of the Manipulation of Client Depth of Self-Exploration Upon High and Low Functioning Counselors." *Journal of Clinical Psychology* (1967), No. 23, pp. 210-212.

Bergin, A. E. and Solomon, S. "Personality and Performance Correlates of Graduate Training." *American Psychologist* (1963), Vol. 18, p. 393.

Carkhuff, Robert R. "Toward a Comprehensive Model of Facilitative Interpersonal Processes." *Journal of Counseling Psychology* (1967), Vol. 14, No. 1, pp. 67-72.

Carkhuff, Robert R. and Truax, Charles B. "Training in Counseling and Psychotherapy: An Evaluation of an Integrated Didactic and Experiential Approach." *Journal of Consulting Psychology* (1965), Vol. 29, pp. 333-336. (a)

Carkhuff, Robert R. and Truax, Charles B. "Lay Mental Health Counseling: The Effects of Lay Group Counseling." *Journal of Consulting Psychology* (1965), Vol. 29, No. 5, pp. 426-431. (b)

Carkhuff, Robert R. and Truax, Charles B. "Toward Explaining Success and Failure in Interpersonal Learning Experiences." *Personnel and Guidance Journal.* (1966), Vol. 44, No. 7, pp. 723-728.

Carkhuff, Robert R. and Berenson, G. *Beyond Counseling and Therapy.* New York: Holt, Rinehart and Winston, Inc., 1967.

Carkhuff, Robert R., Kratochvil, Daniel, and Friel, Theodore. "Effects of Professional Training: Communication and Discrimination of Facilitative Conditions." *Journal of Counseling Psychology* (1968), Vol. 15, No. 1, pp. 68-74.

Combs, Arthur W. "The Perceptual Approach to the Helping Professions." *Journal of the Association for the Study of Perception.* Vol. V., No. 11, Fall, 1970. pp. 1-7.

Combs, Arthur W. "The Personal Approach to Good Teaching." *Educational Leadership* March, 1964, pp. 369-377, 399.

Foulds, Melvin L. "Self-Actualization and the Communication of Facilitative Conditions During Counseling." *Journal of Counseling Psychology* (1969), Vol. 16, No. 2, pp. 132-136.

Kratochvil, Daniel, Aspy, David, and Carkhuff, Robert R. "The Differential Effects of Absolute Level and Direction of Growth in Counselor Functioning Upon Client Level of Functioning." *Journal of Clinical Psychology* (1967), Vol. 23, pp. 216-217.

Landsman, Ted. "Human Experience and Human Relationship." In *Personality Theory and Counseling Practices.* First Annual Personality Conference, University of Florida, Gainesville, Florida, January 5, 6, and 7, 1961, pp. 42-52.

Landsman, Ted. "To Be or Not To Be . . . One's Best Self." In *To Be or Not to Be . . . Existential-Psychological Perspectives on the Self.* Sidney M. Jourard ed. University of Florida Social Sciences Monograph No. 34. Gainesville, Florida: University of Florida, 1967, pp. 37-49.

Landsman, Ted. "Positive Experience and the Beautiful Person." Presidential Address, the Southeastern Psychological Association, April 5, 1968.

Maslow, Abraham H. *Toward A Psychology of Being*. Second Edition. Princeton, N.J.: D. Van Nostrand Co., Inc., 1968.

Maslow, Abraham H. "Introduction" to new edition of *Religion, Values, and Peak Experiences*. New York: Viking Press, Fall, 1970. (mimeographed copy from author)

Pierce, R., Carkhuff, R. R., and Berenson, B. G. "The Differential Effects of High and Low Functioning Counselors Upon Counselors in Training." *Journal of Clinical Psychology* (1967), Vol. 23, pp. 212-215.

Rogers, Carl and Stevens, Barry. *Person to Person: The Problem of Being Human*. Walnut Creek, California: Real People Press, 1967.

Truax, Charles B. and Carkhuff, Robert R. "The Old and the New Theory and Research in Counseling and Psychotherapy." *Personnel and Guidance Journal* (1964), Vol. 42, No. 9, pp. 860-866.

Whiteley, John M., Sprinthall, Norman A., Mosher, Ralph L., and Donaghy, Rolla T. "Selection and Evaluation of Counselor Effectiveness." *Journal of Counseling Psychology* (1967), Vol. 14, No. 3, pp. 226-234.

CHANGING PERSONAL WORLDS: A HUMANISTIC APPROACH TO PSYCHOTHERAPY

Sidney M. Jourard

Everything depends on what you believe man is like.[1] If you assume that man is something like a machine, that assumption is, in a way, not an assumption alone. It is sort of an invitation and a prescription to man to be in the world in ways that mimic a machine. Man seems to me to be a very peculiar creature: he can conform himself to all kinds of images, because he doesn't have any rigidly fixed nature or design to determine how he will be in the world, how he will act, and how the world will be for him. Now, if you assume that man is a being like a monkey or a pigeon, then that too is a kind of invitation that a person may accept.

I have been exploring with as much vigor and ingenuity as I know how the implications for living, for doing psychological research and for applied psychology when I assume that man is *human,* and hence more like me than a machine, monkey, or pigeon.[2] One implication of this assumption is that, as I learn something about myself, I will have learned a certain amount about you. When I assume that you are a being something like me, this will influence the way I interact with you when you are my friend, a member of my family, my student, my research subject, or when you're my patient. I'll probably address you truly in the second person, as "you," rather than speak to you in the pretense that you are indeed a "you," a being something like me, while in my imagination I'm really talking to my colleague who truly is "you" to me. He and I are talking about the "him" which is "you": you exist for us in the third person from this perspective.

SOURCE: Reprinted by permission of Antoinette Jourard. A version of this paper was presented at a Cornell University symposium on "Humanistic and Behavioristic Approaches to Personality Change," May, 1972.

Now I will explore the theme of changing personality, which might also be called changing behavior, or changing experience. Actually, I prefer the title "Changing Personal Worlds: A Humanistic Perspective."

First, we'll concern ourselves with the theme of personality. From my point of view, the term "personality" simply means *one's ways of being a person.* To be a person refers to a way of experiencing the world and a way of acting upon the world.[3] You can turn that around, and say that to be a person is a way for the world to be experienced and acted upon. If you have two persons present, you have two ways for the world to be experienced, and two ways for it to be acted upon. When I say "experienced," I'm using the term experiencing in the phenomenological sense: that is, I am referring to the different modes of experiencing, which include perception, remembering, thinking, imagining, fantasy and dreaming. These are all ways for the world to be experienced by persons. Each one of us embodies a way for the world to be perceived, thought about, remembered, imagined, and so on.[4] But your experience is a determiner of your action. As you change your ways of experiencing the world you'll also be changing, to some extent, your ways of acting in the world.

The theme that I am addressing, then, is how does personality change occur? How might somebody foster it, or facilitate it, or make it happen, or help it happen, when we talk about man, not as a "him" or an "it" in the third person, but as a "you," as someone who exists for me in the second person, and for himself in the first person. Personality change, when viewed from the perspective of a humanistic perspective on man, entails some disengagement of a person from his present ways of experiencing and acting in the world, followed by an opening of his field of experience to new dimensions of experience that were always possible but were not yet realized, followed then by a reentry into one's situation in order to make it more livable. This is a view of personal change that has gradually been emerging from my own thinking and my own research.[5]

Let me address the theme of *trying* to facilitate or invite change in another person. This is what a professional counselor and psychotherapist does.[6]

A psychotherapist can be seen as a repairman, as a trainer, as a doctor, as a guru, as a zaddik—each model or metaphor calls for him to do or be in some ways and proscribes some other ways. I refer you in this connection to Kopp's recent book.[7] Here I want to explore the image of a psychotherapist as a specialist at transcending, one who has displayed expertise at transcending some aspect of facticity to which men have hitherto adjusted. The master learns to liberate himself from dehumanizing forces, freeing himself thus to lead a life that he has chosen. He is then in a position to show others how he did it so that they might do it too. His technique, if he has any, is to serve as a model, to show off, to make himself transparent. This view of the therapist is not meant to replace other models, simply because it cannot. But I intend it, rather, to supplement prevailing images of therapy and to invite more psychotherapists to explore the therapeutic possibilities of modeling, of being a model.

Let me just make a digression at this point. We're talking about trying to foster or invite personal change, change in a person's way of being in the world. This presumably is what psychotherapists are supposed to be skilled at doing. There are two ways to approach this. If one experiences the other individual as "him," in the third person, then one's approach to personal change almost necessarily calls for techniques of manipulation, influence, hypnosis, shaping, doing something. From a broader perspective you can say that this is the exercise of power *over* another, when one experiences the other in the third person. When one is inviting change by example, then the other individual exists in the second person, as "you." Other metaphors make sense; one is seducing, one is showing off, one is inviting, one is challenging.

Let's just pursue this. Modeling, (showing off) can be seen as a case of *the attribution of power and strength* to somebody. To attribute one's own capacity to cope to another person is what is implicit in the act of modeling, in letting another person see how you've done it. I'll develop this question in several ways here. We can just ask this question, "To whom do you attribute the power to change your situation: to another person? to yourself? to God?" This question is decisive. If we think of modeling as a special case of attributing power to others: power to cope, power to transcend, it brings therapy into the possibilities of research by techniques that already have been developed in social psychology by people like Fritz Heider[8] and Ronald Laing.[9] One has to become interested in the whole logic and theory of attribution. How do I experience you? What power or capacity to cope or to grow do I attribute to you? Do I see you as a creature inhabited by forces over which you have no control, so that you need my power to help you control it? Or do I experience you as someone with the capacity to cope with damn near anything? If a person becomes a patient, it's because he has clung to a way of experiencing himself, others and the world, and he has clung to ways of acting in the world *which no longer are life-giving*.

When a person is suffering, it is almost *prima facie* evidence that his ways of being are no longer viable. They are no longer effective in sustaining well-being and growth, and it is time for him to change some aspect of his world.

Let us explore just what it is that we think needs to be changed. If one addresses a person with the resolve to alter his behavior, to extinguish or shape it (this terminology comes from a behavioristic approach to the study of man), this can alter that person's experience of power. But the question is, *whose* power is a person experiencing when he has altered his behavior at the instigation of some expert at behavior change? He may have his view confirmed, that *the other person's* theories and powers are very powerful indeed, but it may not enhance his own sense of his own powers, or his felt capacity to change his world and his situation at his own initiative. As for myself, I resolutely refuse to see another person as one who is condemned to weakness or as one whose existence and growth is dependent on drugs, doctors, or on charting his responses. I insist on seeing the other person *as a person* who has the capacity, when his life has reached a stalemate, and he is no longer living in viable ways—*I see him as one with the capacity to transcend that,* to cope with that, to withdraw, get a better picture of what is going on and charge right back into the situation and change it in some non-destructive way so that life is more possible. And I see the great psychotherapists (or psychotherapists whom I see great) as specialists in coping with some dimension of facticity that most people yield to or accommodate themselves to. The great therapists stand as living proof that that which has subjected most other men is to them a challenge that they have tamed or transcended. By so doing, they are living exemplars of the possibility that you and I and anybody else can do it.

Everything can be a metaphor for anything else. For instance, you can see me as a tiger or a monkey. Or a woman can be seen as an iceberg or an inferno. Metaphor and simile and analogy are all tokens of a vital imagination and these release man from the hypnotic spells of perception and memory. Every metaphor is an invitation or a challenge to transmute what is perceived or remembered into the metaphor. As soon as one envisions a different self and a different world and begins to make them actual, then the present self and world become a kind of metaphor, a pale simile for the world to come.

A therapist can be seen as a metaphor for the patient. His way is a possibility for the patient if he shows how he did it, how he tamed some facticity, how he emancipated himself, healed himself, perfected himself. From this perspective, the patient is his therapist *manqué*.

The most obvious implication of this view is that it really doesn't matter in what theoretical school a therapist has been trained, nor do his techniques matter. What seems crucial to me is that he be a continually growing person, that he be continuously engaged in the struggle between his freedom and the facticity amidst which all of us live. The effective therapist is, perhaps, adequate at taming most of the facticity he encounters but he is magnificent at coping with some one dimension of it so that he is heroic and graceful in his victory. Such a person is proof that a mere human can do it, almost as if to say, "If I can do it, so can you" or "If he can do it, so can I and you."

My flying instructor—I take flying lessons—is a boring man outside of the airplane. He speaks in a monotone, his personal life and his political philosophy, as I know them, are unimaginative and stereotyped. To me, however, he is a hero, the master of flight, a tamer of gravity, a birdman. He holds a certain charisma for me. He's willing to show me how he does it and I'm learning and oddly enough he shows me how it's done by imitating a teaching machine. As we sit in the airplane, he gives me "frames." He offers frames from a program instruction booklet that change you from a groundling to a pilot. I don't, however, consult with my flight instructor for help in how to live my marriage, my professional life, or my life in the community in ways that would preserve my eccentricity and magnificence.

I invite you, now, to look with me at some psychotherapists whose careers seem to me to be evidence to support the hypothesis that I've been presenting, that the great psychotherapists are exemplars at taming and transcending some aspects of the factical world that subjugate most of us.

The hypothesis seems obvious to me. To assert that some other factor such as training, tricks or techniques are the only effective agents in psychotherapy, teaching or influence seems to me to be stupidity, bad faith, or a futile quest for the means by which little men can pretend to be larger men in order to influence others out of proportion to their merit. I might add, be careful whose techniques you use, because you may not be person enough to use them properly. A corollary to this hypothesis is that a psychotherapist cannot himself lead a person to a freer and more enlightened existence than he himself has attained or can imagine for himself and is presently seeking. According to this view, he leads and influences his patients like the Israeli officers who do not say, "charge," they say "follow me."

Now let me turn to what I call the "exemplary magnificence of some psychotherapists." We'll start with Freud. We could actually start with Moses but Freud is a good place to begin.

Freud mastered some forces which could have prevented him from becoming the man who invented psychoanalysis. He suffered "Portnoy's Complaint," as millions of people in the West have—a seductive, doting mother and a father who was both strong and weak, loved and feared. The result of struggling with such conflicting parental demands has been neurosis and diminished growth for many. Freud's courage lay in facing his recollections and fantasies, his sexuality, his anger and discovering that one's past need not preclude fuller functioning, whether it was genital, intellectual or physical functioning, in adult years. I believe he was most effective as a therapist with persons whose suffering grew out of anti-growth forces comparable to those which he himself had tamed. The therapeutic technique he taught others has not been notorious for its effectiveness. Freud showed in his very person that it's possible to marry, make love, raise children and defy all kinds of social pressures in one's time and place in spite of having been raised as a middle class, minority group member with parents whose demands and expectations were not always compatible with the free flowering of individuality. I suspect he might have helped his patients more swiftly—he sometimes kept patients seven years or more—if he were not so shy and so reluctant to share his experience with his patients.[10] It's interesting that Freud apparently was never so effective with older people as Jung was, people who had already struggled through their childhood hangups but were finding life meaningless in their forties and fifties, not because of unresolved Oedipal problems but because life, as an adult, had reached the end of its tether. It was time to let go of those forms in order to go forward.

Now I'll discuss the magnificence of Hobart Mowrer. Mowrer was not helped with his incapacitating depressions by more than seven years of orthodox Freudian therapy. He lived into adult life plagued with guilt over some childhood peccadillos and adult transgressions against his own ethical and moral standards. Hobart Mowrer doesn't mind my presenting this information because he has already put it in the public domain. There are millions of people who have to try to live a meaningful and rewarding life though they are possessed, notice what I say, they are possessed, they don't possess, they are possessed by a powerful, puritanical conscience. What Mowrer found to be ultimately and recurrently therapeutic was absolute openness and transparency before all those with whom he dealt. For him to lie, even a little, was analogous to a heroin addict who in the process of trying to get rid of the habit decided to take just one little wee shot. And so Mowrer developed his integrity group psychotherapy. He participates continuously in an ongoing small group to help him stay on terms of authenticity with himself and others. Mowrer showed that the temptation to lie and to cheat, to misrepresent one's self can be tamed, thereby averting profound guilt and depression for those who are afflicted with a similarly puritanical conscience.

Now let me mention Carl Whittaker and R. D. Laing. I suspect that Ronald Laing and Carl Whittaker enjoy the kind of experience that many of their colleagues call schizophrenic. They can maneuver effectively in the conventional world despite or because of the fact that they are capable of such transcendental experience. If the average person is terrified by the experience of the dissolution of his world and his identity, then he must repress his capacity for enlarged experiencing, thereby limiting his capacities for growth and for functioning. (Whittaker is Professor of Psychiatry at Wisconsin, Ronald Laing is probably one of the best known writers on themes relating to living life and a very competent, practicing psychotherapist.) Both these men show that it's possible to be effective in personal and professional life and to live with one's possibilities for madness, which they see as an opportunity for either the destruction of one's world and letting it stay there or the beginnings of an enlarged world in which one can live more fully.

Let me mention Alfred Adler and Eric Berne. I believe that we can look at Adler as a person who in his lifetime suffered from other people's efforts to make him feel inferior, to put him down. Many people yield to others' suggestions that they are worthless and they live only half-lives because of such yielding; and everybody has been victimized to one extent or another by someone who can say, "Oh, you're looking very well *today.*" Adler recognized the games that were being played with him, and the self-defeating counter-games he was playing, and so he became a *Magister Ludi,* a master of the game. He was able then to help others who grappled with the same dilemmas. He strongly influenced Eric Berne in the process. Now, because of the writings of Adler and Eric Berne, millions are shown how people try subtly to gain control over one another's existence and how one can gracefully get on with life in spite of such games or, better, without them.

Now let me mention the founders of various self-help, non-professional groups. The alcoholics and drug addicts and obese people who "kick" their self-destructive addictions in order to live more effective and meaningful lives are living testimony that addictions can be tamed. The way of life which the founders of Synanon, Alcoholics Anonymous and Weight Watchers developed is teachable or demonstrable. The way of life that they embody does tame the urge to engage in self-destructive behavior. I see a similar dynamic at work in Women's Liberation and in the various Black movements. Some one person understood and mastered the forces which were controlling people as a master controls his victim. The liberated woman and the self-respecting Black both attest that the forces which were diminishing the victims could be transcended.

Fritz Perls, the founder of gestalt therapy, discovered that there were many factors operative that could prevent a person from living fully in the immediate present with all senses and moods of experiencing fully active and with the freedom to act spontaneously. He identified these factors and spent his personal life taming them. He was himself, in person and beyond any of his writings, living testimony to man's determination, as well as his power, to struggle to transcend and prevail over forces that would diminish his sense of vitality. And he was able to show many people how it's done.

Victor Frankl impresses me, not so much by his therapeutic theories, but by the very fact of his survival as a magnificent human being, in spite of the Nazi effort to incinerate him. Frankl was able, daily, to find *raisons d'être* reasons for living, when all about him in the death camp others were giving up, or permitting themselves to be killed by Nazis or by weakness.

Now I would like to look at some behavioristic psychologists—Skinner, Ogden Lindsley, Professor Wolpe, Eysenck and my colleague Pennypacker. They too are all exemplars of a certain kind of magnificence which I take to be the discovery of techniques for teaching others how to analyze large behavioral units into manageable bits, the better to control it. It's unclear to me yet how effective these men are at attributing power to patients. I think they believe power resides in the idea of behavior modification, or the various conditioning theories and techniques. What I found most fascinating about the whole field of behaviorism or behavior science is that its appeal is to those who are most fascinated with the problem of management and control of somebody's behavior.

Now I'm most familiar with the efforts of my colleagues at Florida where we have a very flourishing division of behavior management within our department. My colleague, Pennypacker, has hundreds of people "managing" reading-behavior. He trains one group of students as "managers" and they have questions on three-by-five cards; students read chunks of a book, and then chart the number of correct answers they get in five minute episodes. They all get straight A's because they can answer questions efficiently. It's still not clear yet what this kind of monitored studying does to the capacity of the student to tackle large challenges.

I have to share with you an amusing anecdote. Pennypacker and I are very good friends and colleagues and have been for the past ten years; we each were compulsive smokers. He and I both were smoking two ounces or more of pipe tobacco a day every day, inhaling every puff. We were totally addicted. About two years ago I decided to quit. But as an addict, I had withdrawal symptoms. I became terrified. I asked myself, "How can I quit? I know what, I'll do what Hank Pennypacker does, I'll count something. I'll count puffs, chart it, and establish a base rate."

I then said, "The hell with it, that's for children and animals, and I'm neither. I will trust in my own theories." I was interested in yoga, and I developed this technique for stopping my smoking out of a Hatha Yoga exercise. I kept my pipe in my hand at all times; every time I got an urge to smoke, I would take a slow yoga breath.[11] If the urge persisted, I would do another one. That first day I had to do about fifty cycles of that but then the second day it was cut to twenty-five, and the third day about a dozen, the fourth day about half-a-dozen and the fifth day two or three. That was it, there was no more. I have not smoked for two years now, and I have had no urge to resume.

Pennypacker believes in his own techniques and he keeps careful count. He has a wrist counter, and he's on to cigars now and he's trying to bring his urges and the cigar under stimulus control. It's hilarious. He has one of those little buzzers, a one hour buzzer. You can set it for an hour or half-an-hour. At executive committee meetings we'll be talking away about the policy of the department and all of a sudden buz-z-z-z. Pennypacker will whip out a cigar, but my colleagues all start drooling like Pavlov's dogs because you never know what's being conditioned with what.

I want to explore, briefly, some of the implications of this hypothesis for psychotherapeutic practice. What I'm saying, incidentally, extends to some of the so-called humanistic growth promoting techniques that you read about or involve yourself in—encounter groups, yoga, the various sensitivity training techniques—they all share something in common with the thesis that I'm presenting here: a refusal to yield to the path of least resistance which is one way of saying "being determined." They share a struggle, in other words, to disengage from that which was controlling you in order to discover new possibilities of one's self and of the world in order then to dive back in, as Odysseus returned to Ithaca, to make it fit for a grown man to live in.

I think its high time we stopped regarding people who aren't able to get on with life as sick because we may then feel it's essential to cure them. Better to regard them as sickened or, better, as unenlightened and subdued or misguided. In such cases, one can enlighten, encourage and guide more appropriately. Clearly the sickened ones have not known how to transcend the forces which sicken people.

How elegant if those committed to healing and helping would themselves be exemplars of the ways to live that maintain vitality and foster growth. Now to whom do professional psychotherapists turn for help when they find themselves in some sickening or dispiriting impasse in their lives? Do they seek yet more analysis or client-centered therapy or behavior modification or Gestalt psychotherapy? I don't. Instead, I pull back, I withdraw from the ways in which I'd been living up to that point and through meditation or conversation with an honest friend or travels to get away from the scene, try to get a perspective on my situation. I try to reinvent my situation and my ways of being in it in some enlightening ways. This takes time, so I need to be able to put up with depression and boredom and some anxieties. I'm glad to get all the forebearance from friends and family that I can get during this time of withdrawal in order to reinvent myself. I don't want to be healed. I just want to be left alone or talked to as a human being. If I turn to psychotherapists it's not because of their technical orientation but because I know them as persons, and I respect their prowess at coping graciously with dilemmas which presently overpower me.

I struggled with the realization that others see me as middle-aged. I've got bifocal lenses, I have gray hair, I'm in my forties, and my children are nearly grown. I arrived at a kind of impasse that Jung has described with considerable vividness. I and a lot of my colleagues and friends find ourselves in this particular bind, and as America becomes increasingly affluent, people will arrive at this bind at younger and younger ages—in fact, they already are. Then the question is, how then do you cope in life-giving ways with an impasse of this sort? I turned not to psychotherapists but to one of my colleagues who happens to be a sleep researcher. He has handled this possibly devitalizing time of life very graciously and even with elegance. It was in conversation with him that I coined the statement of an immortal truth which might catch on: "Middle age is definitely not for children." But just as one does not send a student who wishes to learn dancing to a voice teacher, I think it's ridiculous to send someone who can't control his urge to drink to someone who's expert at overcoming his dead parents' influence on the way he lives his adult life.

If I were suffering because I had to spend my time struggling against an impulse to dissociate and hallucinate, I wouldn't seek the help of someone skilled in controlling anger: I would want to consult with an acknowledged madman who has proven his ability to pass in the straight world. I want him to show me how he did it and to supervise and challenge me as I try to find my way.

Here then is an argument for psychotherapists, and for that matter, counselors and encounter group leaders and teachers to examine themselves and answer the question, "In what ways am I magnificent, what aspects of facticity do I transcend with the greatest elegance?" If we can answer these questions then we might be able to help others in a more direct way once they came to trust us; and they would if we were trustworthy. This is an invitation to psychotherapists to share with their patients not just technical expertise—which is what one applies in the third person as one talks about it in the second person to one's true peers—but also their ways of staying alive and vital and growing when all about them others are devitalized. Sharing this when it becomes relevant is the dialogue that I call psychotherapy.

Perhaps a new system of classifying specialists is implicit here. Imagine a brochure which listed the names of all the therapists, not by their theoretical orientation but by the kinds of dilemmas, backgrounds and crises that they had faced and transcended. This actually does have some far-reaching implications. You know how they have computerized dating and mating. You fill out a card; you like chess, you like horseback riding and this music and that literature and you shuffle the cards together and the computer drops out the names of five or ten possible people. Well, I don't see why it wouldn't be possible in a neighborhood or a community to identify the people who are just superb at transcending some dimension of facticity so that when someone is overwhelmed or near suicidal from it, you call Aunt Molly, or the bartender or Uncle Willy who is good at it, and he comes over, just as in Alcoholics Anonymous when someone is ready to take a drink he calls a buddy and they sweat it out together. One could identify those people who had tamed the facticity that is subjugating somebody else and they might then avert the necessity of a great deal of professional care.

Let me conclude by saying that there is a sense in which I regard efforts to foster change in another by environmental control or by shaping techniques or by any means that are not part of an authentic dialogue as in some ways pernicious and mystifying, probably not good for the well-being and growth of the persons to whom these efforts are addressed; and probably not very ennobling for the people who practice them.

NOTES

1. It seems to be the case that we seek to understand the unknown by comparing it with aspects of the known world which it resembles. Psychologists since Wundt have compared aspects of man with chemical compounds, animals, machines, hydraulic systems, etc. I am proposing that we explore the resemblance between a person's experience of himself, which he knows directly, and other aspects of the world. In short, I am exploring a new kind of anthropomorphism.

2. Several months after this talk was given, I obtained a copy of a recent book in which "an anthropomorphic model" of man is explored as a basis for explaining man's social behavior. See Harré, R. and Secord, P. F., *The Explanation of Social Behavior*, Oxford, Basil Blackwell, 1972. This sophisticated essay in the philosophy of science made me see more clearly that the use of myself as a conceptual model guided my conception of psychology as I wrote it, especially in my book *Disclosing Man to Himself* (Van Nostrand Reinhold, 1968).

3. This definition is adapted from that provided in Laing, R. D., *The Politics of Experience*, New York, Ballantine Books, 1967.

4. Cf. Jourard, S. M., *Disclosing Man to Himself*, especially pp. 174-177.

5. Jourard, S. M., *Ibid.*, pp. 111-120; 152-172.

6. Parts of the following remarks are from a forthcoming paper of mine; see Jourard, S. M., The transcending psychotherapist. *Voices: The Art and Science of Psychotherapy*, 1972.

7. Kopp, S., *Guru: Metaphors From a Psychotherapist*. Palo Alto: Science and Behavior Books, 1971.

8. Heider, F., *The Psychology of Interpersonal Relations*, New York: Wiley, 1958.

9. Laing, R. D., *op. cit.*

10. There is something pernicious, to me, about viewing people with difficulties in living as sick and weak. This seems to be a case of the attribution of weakness to a person, who then experiences himself as weak and helpless.

11. I would inhale slowly, to the count of 8, hold the breath for 8 counts, release it to the count of 8, and await the next inhalation for the count of 8. This constituted one breathing cycle.

REFERENCES

Harré, R. and Secord, P. F. *The Explanation of Social Behavior*. Oxford: Basil Blackwell, 1972.

Heider, F. *The Psychology of Interpersonal Relations*. New York: Wiley, 1958.

Jourard, S. M. *Disclosing Man to Himself.* Van Nostrand Reinhold, 1968.

Jourard, S. M. The transcending psychotherapist. *Voices: The Art and Science of Psychotherapy.* 1972.

Kopp, S. *Guru: Metaphors From a Psychotherapist.* Palo Alto: Science and Behavior Books, 1971.

Laing, R. D. *The Politics of Experience.* New York: Ballantine Books, 1967.

SECTION III
COMMUNITY

Community. America seems to be a culture everlastingly on-the-road. Our mobility is astounding. Some say that our lives have become a process of trading in our jobs, homes, cars, and even our marital partners every three or four years. Our ties, our roots seems to be slipping away as we become increasingly mobile and families separate, leave the cities and towns of their birth and find their lives elsewhere. This breakdown is not only one of physical community but of psychological connectedness as well. How will we confront this issue of the breakdown of the past as we move into a future that remains largely unknown and unpredictable?

Some of these issues are discussed in the section on Socio-Cultural concerns. Many of the great issues of the day—population, cities, racism and the family—may defy solutions. Sometimes the very solutions themselves create greater problems. Yet this section tries to come to grips with such problems, and the problems of America's future.

What is the good society and how can we move toward it? So much of our life is manipulated by the assumptions we make and the assumptions of others that it is sometimes necessary to think back to where we started and what goals we truly wish for ourselves as a people. How can we create a society in which our social and individual growth are fostered?

Some of us have tried to create intentional communities which preserve and promote human dignity and worth. Others have tried to salvage marriage and family life as traditionally experienced. Still others are encouraging us to explore new ways of understanding marriage as we move into the future.

The family was once concerned primarily with the rearing of children. This aspect of life has also come under scrutiny as population has risen steadily throughout the world. Many couples now choose not to have children. Those that do choose to have children are challenging physician-dominated practices and have increasingly moved toward "natural" childbirth. Once those children are among us, the issues of childrearing continue to confound us. We are called the best read and most confused generation of parents in history. The confusing practices in the home and in the religious and educational institutions that profoundly affect our lives have created, some say, a vast spiritual chasm in our lives.

The religious questions remain among the most important in our lives. The answers we have sometimes settled on have often been too pat, too easy and in the long run too damaging to remain unchallenged. Religion can be a crucial part of the human question and it continues to be a vital part of our concern for community.

Our schools have become battlegrounds for competing political and philosophical positions. The wars take their toll and too often the casualties are the dedicated teachers and administrators who genuinely care for the lives of children. Certainly, the question of the psychological health of children in schools is a real one, and one with which humanistic educators continually grapple.

This section is primarily concerned with our socio-cultural future and the issues of the future that might concern the community of human beings in our great institutions, such as marriage, the family, the churches and the schools. It gives a feeling for how humanistic thinkers view the vital social problems of the present and their concerns for the future.

SOCIO-CULTURAL
CONCERNS

SOME SOCIAL ISSUES
WHICH CONCERN ME

Carl R. Rogers

I have never been a joiner, or a supporter of CAUSES. I know some people who sign every petition, who sponsor every worthy cause. I respect them, but it is not my style. All my professional life I have preferred to work in the areas in which I have competence, endeavoring to bring about constructive change in those areas. I have been a revolutionary with a narrow focus. Thus I flatter myself that I have helped to cause healthy change in the field of counseling and psychotherapy, in the conduct of encounter groups, and perhaps most broadly, in our educational institutions. But I have never before spoken out on the broad spectrum of social issues which face our society.

Now, however, I believe our culture is facing a life and death crisis on many fronts, and that I have an obligation as a citizen to speak out. I am frightened about our destiny as a people, as a nation. So I want to take as clear a stand as I can on a variety of issues, including our insane wars, which I shall leave to the last. I recognize very well that I am no expert in most of the fields I shall mention, but I shall simply voice the attitudes and views of one deeply concerned person.

There is one other preliminary comment I wish to make. I have never been fond of those who do no more than "point with alarm." It is easy enough, for example, to stir up emotions by picturing the many millions on this planet who do not have enough to eat. But I do not have a high regard for those who point this out, unless their "pointing with alarm" is accompanied by some statement of the means which would move us toward ending the tragedy. Consequently, I will discuss only those issues for which we have much of the know-how, or technology, or funds to solve. What seems to be lacking in each case is the choice, the intent, the purpose, the determination to work toward resolving it. These are issues which, in every case, we could move toward solving if we had the in-

SOURCE: Carl R. Rogers, "Some Social Issues Which Concern Me," *Journal of Humanistic Psychology*, Fall 1972. Reprinted by permission. Reprint requests: Carl R. Rogers, PhD, Center for Studies of the Person, 1125 Torrey Pines Road, La Jolla, California 92037.

dividual and collective *will*. To mention one example, I am not going to discuss pollution because it appears that we have, as a nation, already *made* the decision to tackle that problem. I don't deceive myself that it will be easy, or quick, or that we may not lose. But at least we seem to have made the all important *choice*, and this decision is fully as significant as any of the technological steps which will follow.

Enough of these provisos and qualifications. I want to move on to some of the problems which give me great concern. I regard it as desperately necessary that we rethink our priorities and our allocation of funds.

INUNDATED WITH PEOPLE

One of the most astonishing sights I know is to see the graph of world population since the beginning of recorded history. For centuries and millennia it remained almost flat, creeping upward very, very slowly. Then, with the advent of scientific medicine and the reduction of the death rate, the curve begins to sweep upward and off the chart with currently an almost straight upward climb. It is not just this astonishing curve that I would like to comment on, but what it means for us.

Let me try to make it a bit more personal. When I was 13, the population of our country was 100 million. It had taken 125 years to grow from the 4 million of 1790 to that first 100 million. When I was 65, 52 years later, the population was 200 million. If I should live to be 87—and I don't think I want to—the population will, according to prediction, have increased to 300 million. The last 100 million increase will have taken only 22 years, instead of 125 (unless the present sharp drop in birth rate continues).

Why have we not felt this as an urgent problem? Because in this country our incredible technological advances (leading also to unbelievable pollution) have more than kept up with the population growth, and each individual of the more than 200 million is probably, on the average, more affluent than when we numbered 100 million.

But take an example from an underdeveloped country which is typical of many—India. That country has made astonishing strides. In agriculture improved high-yield rice and grain have been developed; in industry the rapid expansion of all kinds of manufacturing plants have enormously increased production. And what is the result? On the average, each person in India is closer to starvation, less well supplied with the necessities of life than he was before these programs started. In spite of significant government encouragement of birth control, the population increase has been so great that it more than eats up every gain that has been made. Running with tremendous energy, India cannot even stay where it is, but is tragically slipping backward.

The noted demographer, Philip Hauser, writing in 1968, gives figures which predict that, by a conservative estimate, the population of the more developed countries will increase by 90% in the next 50 years, but that the underdeveloped world—Asia, Africa, Latin America—will increase by 240%. Thus the heaviest burden will fall on those least able to bear it. All the projections indicate that in the coming decades, the developed countries will become richer and richer because they will be able to handle their population problem, while the underdeveloped countries will have less and less food and material goods for each citizen. It will be a world of affluent "haves" and increasingly needy, frustrated, bitter "have-nots." For more than half the world to be populated with largely unwanted, often unloved, certainly ill-fed and poorly cared for persons, looking enviously over the fence at our affluence, or surviving on our charity, is not a pretty picture.

One reason we often fail to see the urgency of the situation is that we fail to visualize the consequences. We speak of population doubling in 20, 30, 40 years, depending on the country. But we often fail to realize what that means. Even to hold on to their meager standards, there must be twice as much food, twice as many homes, twice as many schools, twice as many highways, twice as many buses or trains or planes, twice as many doctors and hospitals—and on and on and on. And how can an underdeveloped country meet this tremendous demand? It cannot!

I haven't given so many statistics in years! I'll stop. But I do want to bring home the point that this is a desperate social problem though by and large in this country we do not yet recognize it. In less developed countries it defeats every effort at reform or improvement of the quality of life. Since writing the foregoing, I have received a letter from a friend who has been in India. Two sentences will suffice. ". . . They have doubled food production in the last 5 years, but population is still outpacing growth of resources. Life is still cheap."

In spite of all this, population increase is a problem which we have the technology to solve, and that technology is improving all the time. The pill and the intrauterine device will soon be superseded by better methods. Psychologically it is no longer a taboo subject. One would expect to find psychologists and educators actively at work, studying the attitudes which promote large families, the religious and other reasons which still stand as barriers to population control. We would expect to find educators, beginning at least with high school, providing materials which point up the urgency of the problem and making certain that every young person not only knows all the latest birth control devices, but has easy access to them. But no, neither the professionals nor the laymen have yet made the choice to move in such directions. We do not give it nearly the priority given to the ABM system, as indicated by the funds allocated. Yet the problem is definitely more pressing than our so-called defense by the ABM.

OUR CITIES

Our great cities concern me deeply, but the facts are well known and I will not bore you with them. Our large urban centers are seemingly un-governable, choking on their own traffic, becoming insufferable garbage-littered ghettos, and are rapidly becoming financially as well as psy-chologically bankrupt. All that is known. Yet, according to Barbara Ward (1967), British economist, by the year 2000, 80% of us will be living in such cities. Chances are that over 200 million people will be living in—a new term—a megalopolis. One will be the eastern seaboard, Boston to Washington, D.C. One will be the western coast, from San Diego to San Francisco; and one will be in the middle west, stretching from Chicago to Pittsburgh.

In this incredible influx into the cities, it might be well to consider some lessons learned from a study of rats. (Imagine me invoking a rat study!) A number of years ago, John Calhoun (1962) carried on a cleverly designed experiment with a rather large number of rats. I won't go into details. Some portions of the experimental area had narrow entrances, and one dominant male rat could keep any others from entering. (Sorry about that, Women's Lib!) But the central area was available to all and could not be dominated. All the rats in every area had sufficient food and water (privileges not extended to our city dwellers) and were free to breed as they wished. A few findings give me pause.

The rats multiplied, of course, but in the areas controlled by a dominant male, overcrowding was not excessive and life was reasonably normal. In the central, uncontrolled area, there was serious overcrowding and this was accompanied by poor mothering, poor nest building, high infant mortality, bizarre sexual behavior, cannibalism, and often com-plete alienation, some rats behaving like zombies, paying no attention to others and coming out of their solitary burrows only for food.

More ominous still, the central area, with all its bad conditions, had a certain magnetic pull. Calhoun called it a behavioral sink. The rats crowded together in it. A feeder would be ignored unless there were other rats eating at it. The more rats at a feeder, the more others would crowd in. Females in heat would leave the protected areas and head for the central area, sometimes not returning at all.

The resemblance to human behavior is frightening. In humans we see poor family relationships, the lack of caring, the complete alienation, the magnetic attraction of overcrowding, the lack of involvement which is so great that it permits people to watch a long drawn out murder without so much as calling the police—perhaps all city dwellers are inhabitants of a behavioral sink, cannibalism and all.

We have not availed ourselves of the alternatives, which are known and feasible. Corporations are, in considerable numbers, moving their offices out of spots like Manhattan, but that could simply mean making big-city slums out of places like Greenwich, Connecticut. What we need is to turn loose some of our city planners, or better yet, unleash creative innovators like Buckminster Fuller, scrap our obsolete building codes, and instruct these gentlemen to build small urban centers, designing them for human beings and human life, not simply for profit. We could build smaller cities with great park and garden areas, with neighborhoods of all races, all economic levels, which would promote humanization, not dehumanization. It would have to be such an attractive place for human beings that it would overcome the magnetism of the behavioral sink. The schools, for example, could be built along totally new lines, not only informal seating and pleasant surroundings, but planned from the first on the basis that most learning will go on either in the community, or as a result of self-directed and self-initiated learning on the part of the student.

To be sure, there would be frictions between races, ethnic groups, between persons with very different value systems, in these human cities. But the behavioral scientist could help to meet that challenge with communication workshops, with encouragement of learnings from the distinctive contributions of each group to the others. We could help people to listen—and to understand. The human planning—both before and during the building of such a community—would be fully as important and as well financed as the architectural planning. It would involve the families, the schools, the recreational facilities, and would be a crucial and continuing aspect.

We know how to carry out every aspect of what I have proposed in regard to our cities. The only element lacking is the passionate determination which says, "Our cities are inhuman. They are ruining lives and mental and physical health at a devastating rate. We are going to change this, even if it costs us money!"

WHAT OF MARRIAGE?

To me it seems clear that conventional long-term marriage, as we have known it in this country, is either on its way out or will be greatly modified. In California, which often points the way for other parts of the country, there were, during 1970, 66 couples dissolving their marriage for every 100 couples marrying. And in Los Angeles County, essentially in the city of Los Angeles, in 1971, 4 couples were applying for a dissolution of their marriage, while 5 couples were obtaining licenses to wed! A failure rate of almost 79%!

Curiously enough, I am not very concerned about this because I believe that the partners often find that the dissolution of the marriage constitutes a step toward their own growth. Then too we are actively exploring alternatives—often in groping, uncertain fashion—but nonetheless searching for new ways. Couples are living together without marriage or children. Communes are trying to establish extended families. Some are trying multiple marriage, with each married to every other, and discovering how difficult it is. In a few instances there are households of three adults. There is more open extramarital sex. There is talk of marriage as a renewable three-year contract. The path is open for a wide variety of experimentation. The one thing that is clear is that we are seeking man-woman relationships which will have permanence only to the degree to which they satisfy the emotional, psychological, intellectual, and physical needs of the partners. They must be mutually enhancing and growth-promoting if they are to last. I believe we are making some progress in that direction (with very little help from behavioral scientists).

There are two issues which do concern me about marriage. The first is the incredible lack of any attempt at education in the field of interpersonal relationships, which would help young people to face realistically the problems they will meet. I was interviewing a young couple recently, both of whom had attended college. They had lived together for three years and then married. I was curious as to the elements in this decision. I learned that this was the story. They quarrelled all of one evening—a rather common occurrence—and finally the man told her to pack up her things and leave. She said, "I will not! I belong here as much as you do." He paused a moment and then said challengingly, "Well, then do you want to get married?" to which she replied, "O.K." It developed that there was a rationale of sorts behind this bizarre decision. He believed that if they married, marriage would be the miracle which would resolve all their difficulties. He was surprised that it had not, and only during the interview did it seem to dawn on him that perhaps achieving a satisfactory marriage might take time and effort! It angers me that neither of these young people had received the slightest education in man-woman relationships, though naturally they had learned the *valuable* things like mathematics and foreign language. Here again we have all the necessary know-how, but we define education so narrowly that it excludes everything about living.

Education is the one field in which feedback from "the consumer" is utterly disregarded. Our educational institutions were born at a time when intellectual stimulation was terribly important, since ordinary life supplied all the other ingredients of learning. But school has increasingly *become* life, and education which operates only "from the neck up" is becoming irrelevant to real learning, as our young people are shouting so loudly. But psychologists are the last to listen, in their headlong (and futile) race to become a "hard science." Hence the thought of education oriented toward human relationships, toward marriage partnerships, is anathema to most psychologists, although this would seem to be the very field in which they might and should contribute.

The other issue regarding marriage which troubles me is that we have been both unimaginative and irresponsible regarding children, particularly children of divorced parents. First the child is torn by the stresses between his mother and father, and has no extended family to which to turn. Then he finds that we usually label one parent guilty. Next we shuttle the child back and forth between the two warring adults. Small wonder that psychological problems develop. Yet we know, quite accurately, what children need—continuing love and caring, a sense of stability, several sources of support and care, and a feeling of being trusted. We have experiments like the kibbutzim to observe and from which to learn. We *know* enough. We have just never made the decision that we wish to *act* on behalf of the welfare of our children. We prefer, as a nation, to spend our money on war and preparation for war.

RACISM AND MINORITIES

Running like a fever through all our culture are the attitudes we hold, mostly at the unconscious level, toward blacks, chicanos, Indians, and other minorities, including women, who while not a statistical minority, are treated as one. We know something of how to attack the roots of this problem. I have learned enormously from the few black-white encounter groups I have facilitated, and have learned that the bitterness and rage which exists can be expressed and prove constructive. I have learned even more from the much more extensive experience of two of our staff members, Dr. Norman Chambers, a black, and Dr. Lawrence Carlin, a blond Nordic if I ever saw one. They have worked with many black-white groups and with some chicano-anglo groups. They have found most helpful a simulation game they invented called "Pleasantville." Pleasantville is the home of a new industry which is employing many black workers new to the town. Everyone is given roles, the whites usually being assigned more conservative roles than they would normally play—the head of the real estate board, the local union leader, the school superintendent, the president of the women's club. It's just a game—everyone knows that. But the whites are astonished at the ease with which they can express the most bitter anger toward the invading blacks. They have gotten in touch with unknown aspects of themselves. "I never knew I had such feelings," is a very common reaction. Meanwhile, the game gives the blacks permission to voice their rage, and the polarization is out in the open for all to see.

The outcomes are an experiential, gut-level learning of racist attitudes on the part of the whites, and a rare opportunity for honest confrontation on the part of the blacks. The surprising finale is that they tend to become persons to each other, and can talk openly and freely of things they dislike and like about each other without reference to stereotypes or skin color. It becomes a much more direct, honest dealing with one another as individuals. They tend to leave the game experience feeling deeply educated.

I describe this because I happen to know of it directly. It is not the only approach which could be made, but it is a start. Carried out with black and white community leaders it would lead first to direct dealing, and then to mutually agreed decisions, which, because they were personal and real, would be carried out. Isn't this worth the price of the scores of helicopters shot down over southeast Asia? I believe that programs of this sort should be expanded a thousand-fold.

THE GREENING OF EDUCATION

I have talked and written so much in recent years about our dying educational institutions that I hesitate to repeat any of what I have said. There is just a slim chance that our schools and colleges may change rapidly enough to escape total irrelevance, and total death. I would like to focus on some of the signs which show that we know perfectly well how to resolve the educational problem if our medieval faculty members had the will to do so.

When I wrote *Freedom to Learn* in 1969, I hoped that it might make some small dent in the education system. In it I tried to show, by examples, how educators could be personal, innovative, and facilitative of learning, even within the antiquated system. I certainly did not foresee that by 1971 it would be selling by the thousands, nor that one public school system alone would purchase 500 copies for its teachers. All this shows is that many in the system have eagerly been looking for new ways. The archaic educational giant is at least stirring in his sleep. He might even move.

The most dramatic proof that we have full knowledge of how to bring education not only into the twentieth century but even into the twenty-first, is contained in the rapid change taking place in the public schools of Louisville, Kentucky (Project School, 1971). This is an inner-city school system in which the situation two years ago could only be described as horrible. A few facts: Eighty-three per cent of the pupils were below the national norm in achievement; this figure was increasing each year, which means that learning was decreasing each year; they were among the highest in the nation in school dropouts, delinquency, teacher turnover; the area was 60% white, 40% black, 34% with incomes of $2,000 or less! You get the picture. A five-man Board of Education (3 white, 2 black) hired an innovative superintendent, Newman Walker, who brought in a central office staff determined to improve the conditions for learning. Fourteen of 55 schools were set apart as a special pilot project, but all schools were encouraged to develop plans for change. In the pilot schools, principals and teachers were accepted only if they whole-heartedly wanted to be a part of an experiment. Among other things, they agreed to full and free communication regardless of rank, to a reliance on consensus rather than coercion, to decisions made on the basis of competence rather than personal power, to a classroom atmosphere created in which feelings had as much of a place as task-oriented behavior.

Then, during a six-month period, 1600 administrators and teachers were enrolled in workshops and encounter groups concerned with communications, human relations, and organizational development. The Board of Education, the superintendent, and his central office staff were among the first to take part. One of the aims was to put into the classrooms teachers who were real to their students, who felt a warm liking for these largely underprivileged youth, and who had a clearly empathic understanding of the feelings and problems of these individuals.

It is too early to know the final outcomes, but the ferment is tremendous. The schools are no longer jails, but exciting places to be, as I know from my visits. They are facing many problems, but the problems are how to bring about change, how to live as a process, not how to prevent change. Preliminary findings already show that in the experimental schools the steady decline in reading, for example, has been halted, and that there have been sharp decreases in vandalism and school dropouts. I believe that this is the most promising, broad-scale venture in public education in the United States today. We know at least one way to resolve even the disasters of an inner-city school system, once we have determined we will do so.

A POLICE STATE?

I am very frightened by what seems to me a steady drift toward an authoritarian state. It was only a few years ago that I heard a foreign-born faculty member express the idea that the United States was so much like pre-Hitler Germany that it frightened her. At that time I thought her fear exaggerated. Now the signs of a growing trend toward a police state are there for all to see.

I would like you to engage with me in a fantasy. Put yourself back in 1962, trying to remember what you were doing, and if possible, what your attitudes were. Suppose that this was 1962. Imagine that in 1962 I was telling you about a country in which these events were taking place:

> Students, both rebellious and completely innocent, have been tear-gassed, beaten, and killed by police and militia;
>
> Members of a militant dissident party have been shot in their beds by police;
>
> Major trials are not for acts committed, but for conspiracy to commit such acts—in other words, one can be found guilty of an intention;
>
> The military, as well as the legal espionage agency, is spying on thousands of citizens, who are breaking no law, committing no illegal act, but simply show a *possibility* of being critical of the government;
>
> Young men by the thousands are deliberately refusing to serve in the armed forces and are risking the consequences;
>
> Every major city and state is training police and soldiers to suppress citizen riots, revolts, and uprisings; armored cars and tanks are sometimes brought into cities for the same purpose;
>
> Brilliant and dedicated student and religious leaders, and leading members of minority groups are serving prison terms for defying the government;
>
> And to end on an ironic note, persons are harassed and arrested by the police for no other reason than wearing unusual clothing or having let their hair grow.

If I had told you about such a nation in 1962 you would be casting about in your mind asking what nation could be so ugly and so awful; so utterly dedicated to the use of coercion and the power of the police and the military; so oblivious to individual rights; so unresponsive to demands for change; so completely totalitarian in its spying, its oppression, its use of force alone as the instrument of government. It is humiliating beyond words to realize that we are that nation in 1972.

What do we do? What can we do? A small number of young people are turning to violence—mostly violence intended against property. So bomb threats, and explosions, and window-smashing, and even sniper fire have become a part of present-day America. I can understand how an individual would become so bitter, so desperate to bring change, that violence would seem like a possible channel of action. But I deplore his strategy. In the present situation violence is almost certain to have just one major outcome—repression. Its most obvious result would be to bring in a totalitarian regime, which could take generations to undermine.

WHAT NEXT?

What can we do about all this? My answer is my version of Reich's (1970) thesis in *The Greening of America*. Like every original idea, his has been strongly criticized, but I believe its central thrust is sound. When enough of the people think through and believe, and most importantly *live* a set of convictions based on a new value system, present institutions must change or fall.

Let me spell that out a bit more precisely, not in Reich's terms but in my own. In 1969 I gave a talk on "The Person of Tomorrow" spelling out some of the characteristics of the new, powerful person emerging in our culture, and the vital, different set of values he both maintains and lives. I stressed his hatred of phoniness; his opposition to all rigidly structured institutions; his desire for intimacy, closeness, and community; his willingness to live by new and relative moral and ethical standards; his searching quality, his openness to his own and others' feelings, his spontaneity; his activism; and his determination to translate his ideals into reality. I have had no reason since to materially change that picture, except that for a time I feared that he was turning toward violence, which I see as the road to the annihilation of all hope for change, or toward drugs, which would essentially be escape. But those fears have recently diminished.

I have been strongly criticized for the views contained in that talk. I feel some of the criticisms are from people who simply hate to face what is occurring in the lives of our young people. They prefer to get angry and "point with alarm." But some of the criticism is based on the fact that my description of the person of tomorrow applied to only a very small minority of the young, and to only a minute proportion of their elders. I have thought seriously about that criticism, and I believe it is correct. I am talking about what is, numerically, a relatively small number of people. But I believe, intuitively if you wish, that these people constitute the change agents of the future.

What research evidence can I bring to bear to justify this view? Frankly none. But historically it has been shown again and again that a small group of individuals, believing deeply in a new set of values, or a new picture of what the culture might be, has an impact far beyond its numbers. One could name the 12 disciples, the small dedicated group of early communists in China or Russia, the early organizers of the labor union movement in this country, or Martin Luther King and the black woman who sat in the front seat of the bus in Montgomery. When some part of a culture is decayed at the core, a small group with new views, new convictions, and a willingness to live in new ways, is a ferment which cannot be stopped.

I have even felt this in my own professional career. The time was evidently ripe for the idea that the resources for health lay in the client, not in the therapist, and only needed the proper psychological climate to be released and utilized for growth. No man or small group could have possibly wrought the changes which have since occurred. The view of the therapist as the expert was already beginning to decay, and the new view—like a surfer catching a wave at the right time and right angle—swept along into other areas far removed from therapy, and having an impact such as I could not possibly have dreamed.

I have exactly the same feeling about the person of tomorrow that I have had about the civil rights leaders, or about my own central thesis of 30 years ago. I feel very sure that his values will prevail. The person of tomorrow is the wave of the future. Take such a small example as the astonishing changes in the armed forces personnel regulations. Did the military brass undergo a liberal conversion? Of course not. But they are realists. They recognize that no one can govern for any length of time, not even a military commander with theoretically unlimited power, without the *consent* of the governed. And so long hair, informality, and discussion are being permitted, simply because those on the lowest rungs of the military ladder believe such things should be permitted. It is as Reich would say, Consciousness III at work. (Even I was surprised when I saw a Navy seaman wearing a full beard and sideburns!)

I read such writers as Reich, Philip Slater (1970), whose subtitle is, I think, more to the point than his title, "The Pursuit of Loneliness: American Culture at the Breaking Point," and though I do not entirely agree with either of them I believe these are the prophets of the future, along with others such as Theodore Roszak (1969) in his "The Making of a Counter Culture." I believe these writers are essentially correct in predicting that our American way of life will be radically altered by the growth of a new value system, a new culture in which feelings and subjectivity and openness (rather than hypocrisy) have a prominent place, alongside intelligence.

We are going to have a new America, in my judgment, an America of change and flow, of people rather than objects. We have the know-how, the skills, to bring about this new America. And now, in an increasing number of significant persons, mostly young but also older, we have the determination and the will to bring it into being. I think it is not unrealistic to believe that there will come into being a portion of the global community, residing on this North American continent, of which we will no longer be ashamed, but in which we will feel a quiet, peaceful pride.

REFERENCES

Population Explosion

Hauser, P. Population. In Foreign Policy Association (Ed.), *Toward the year 2018.* New York: Cowles Education Corp., 1968.
The next ninety years. Proceedings of a conference sponsored by California Institute of Technology, Pasadena, Calif., 1967.

Urbanization

Calhoun, J. Population density and social pathology. *Scientific American,* 1962, *206* (2), 139-150.
Ward, B. Speech to members of "California Tomorrow," San Francisco, Calif., 1967.

Marriage

Rogers, C. *Becoming partners: Marriage and its alternatives.* New York: Delacorte, 1972, in press.
Rogers, C. R. Interpersonal relations in the year 2000. *Journal of Applied Behavioral Science,* 1968, *4* (3), 265-280.

Racism and Minorities

Personal reports from Dr. Norman Chambers and Dr. Lawrence Carlin, both of the Center for Studies of the Person, La Jolla, Calif.

Education

Dickenson, W., et al. A humanistic program for change in a large city school system. *Journal of Humanistic Psychology,* 1970, *10* (2), 111-120.
Project school first year report, *Tall Oaks,* 1971, 2. (1), Louisville Public Schools, Louisville, Ky.
Rogers, C. *Freedom to learn.* Columbus, Ohio: Charles E. Merrill, 1969 (Chapter 15 and Epilogue).
Rogers, C. *Carl Rogers on encounter groups.* New York: Harper & Row, 1970.

The War and the Police State

Galbraith, K. A decade of disaster in foreign policy. *The Progressive,* 1971, *35* (2).
Knoll, E. Melvin Laird: Salesman for the pentagon. *The Progressive,* 1971, *35* (4).

Schell, O. Silent Vietnam. *LOOK,* April 6, 1971, p. 55.
Symington, S., et al. *Report of subcommittee on security arrangements and commitments abroad.* Washington, D.C.: U. S. Government Printing Office, 1970.

Concluding Portion

Reich, C. *The greening of America.* New York: Random House, 1970.
Roszak, T. *The making of a counter culture.* New York: Doubleday, 1969.
Slater, P. *The pursuit of loneliness: American culture at the breaking point.* Boston: Beacon Press, 1970.

EUPSYCHIA—THE GOOD SOCIETY

Abraham H. Maslow

Mr. Thomas: "Dr. Maslow, during the next few minutes we are going to be talking about good societies and about your ideas on the psychological foundations of good societies. I remarked as we were coming into the studio that these were rather peculiar times to be discussing Utopias. Utopian societies have traditionally been descriptions of economic achievement—a place where the material needs of food, clothing, shelter, were completely filled. Why, then, in America where we have apparently solved these material problems, do we still feel compelled to reach out, to define better societies? Why are we dissatisfied? Why do we go on imagining Utopias?"

Dr. Maslow: "I think we're simply witnessing a human phenomenon that has appeared down through the ages. What man does not have, he struggles for. When the need is fulfilled, he moves to a different and higher need. The picture of the ideal society reflects the level of poverty or wealth of the current culture and, incidentally, of the individual's own concept of how rich *he* is, and how rich he wants to become. The fact that America is very rich—that all the things for which most cultures have struggled throughout history have been achieved here—is tending to push our thoughts to higher needs and therefore to higher levels of frustration."

Mr. Thomas: "Would you say something about the difference between 'higher' and 'lower' needs?"

Dr. Maslow: "Well, I think most psychologists now agree that our needs are arranged in a kind of hierarchy, with food and shelter the lowest on the scale. When our bellies are full and we are sheltered, we turn towards the problems of safety and security in the world. We want a good police force and good doctors. Then, we think of education, and we want good schools. This reminds me of that old cartoon where the wife says to

---

SOURCE: A. H. Maslow, "Eupsychia—The Good Society," *Journal of Humanistic Psychology,* Fall 1961. Reprinted by permission.

the husband 'You are always wanting what you haven't got,' and he answers, 'Well, what else can you want?' "

"Now, I think of love as a higher need, and beyond love there are the still higher needs for respect from others, for self respect, and so on. You can see that the higher the need, the less it is directly related to the basic material and physical needs. For these reasons I think it is entirely valid to be imagining better societies in America at this point in our history; but, I think we are now ready to conceive of a 'Eupsychia'—a psychologically healthy culture—rather than just another materially-based Utopia."

Mr. Thomas: "It seems to me that many people stay at the material level, building up stronger and stronger motives to gain more and more material possessions, even though they are aware, at least vaguely, of these higher needs. How does one become so aware of these higher needs that there are motives to act on them?"

Dr. Maslow: "This is a problem of ignorance or of pathology. We psychologists must conclude—on the basis of extensive clinical studies—that the person who continues to build up wealth after his needs are satisfied is actually looking for something else. The possessions perhaps symbolize the power or the respect he is seeking; or he may feel unconsciously that wealth will make him a more lovable or attractive person. We would simply call this neurotic, or, possibly ignorant.

"A good example of this is the history of what trade unions have struggled for over the years. In the old days, perhaps sixty years ago, a union struck for food. Now that union laborers have more money, more food, and many other benefits, what are they striking for? If you dig below the surface, as some labor union economists are doing, it appears that unions are following the hierarchy of needs that I have been talking about. First they struck for food, then for security; now I think we could say that unions are striking for self respect—for a feeling of being masters over their own fate, for power rather than powerlessness."

Mr. Thomas: "What about these two words, 'power' and 'powerlessness'? Certain social critics—Erich Fromm comes to mind—have been very much concerned about the isolation of the individual and his feeling of powerlessness. What do you mean when you talk about the need to feel power?"

Dr. Maslow: "Again, I would define power as the feeling of self-respect, especially in males. Or, you could say the feeling of having some control over fate, of not being a helpless tool, a passive object, a cork on the wave which is tossed here and there by forces out of control. This characterizes power as a very healthy, straightforward trait, a very desirable thing for any human being.

"Then of course psychologists can talk of power in a pathological sense as something for which people *think* they are looking, but which is actually a symbol for something else."

Mr. Thomas: "You've made a distinction between 'good love' and 'good power,' and between 'pathological love' and 'pathological power.' This leads me to ask what you as a psychologist know about the 'good side' of people. I've heard and read a good deal about the 'evil side,' what do we know about the 'good side'?"

Dr. Maslow: "From a strict scientific point of view, using classical traditions of scientific exploration, we "know" very, very little. However, there are pilot studies of one sort or another in this area and I feel we are gaining a level of knowledge that will allow some generalizations. Actually , we have a huge mass of clinical knowledge—we shouldn't overlook the fact that most psychotherapeutic cases go from 'bad'-to 'better'—from 'less healthy' to 'more healthy.'

"My own research was simply to pick out the healthiest people I could find, and then to study them directly. It was a small sampling, for there certainly aren't very many truly healthy individuals in this society. I just tried to find out what they were like. How did they feel? What kind of humor, interpersonal relations, families, demeanors did they have? What were their relationships to society? These were the kind of questions I asked, and I found to my satisfaction that it was possible to make some important preliminary generalizations from their answers—generalizations which on the whole have stood up remarkably well in the light of my own additional findings since then, and of those of many other psychologists which have accumulated during the fifteen years since this survey was first carried out."

Mr. Thomas: "And what were some of these generalizations?"

Dr. Maslow: "Well, for instance, just to pick out the most important ones, it was very clear in my pilot study that either the most important or one of the most important characteristics of psychological health was simply the ability to perceive clearly—that is, to see the truth, to penetrate falsehood, phoniness, hypocrisy, and so on. This was very clear and has been supported a dozen times over by other people, by the results of psychotherapy, which is after all, an effort to make a good man, too. This is pretty clear now; I think it is safe to say that psychologically healthy people are just more perceptive, they can see the truth more clearly, they are less fooled by masks, conventions, and expectations. They can penetrate through to the truth more easily, more clearly."

Mr. Thomas: "I guess this leads to the next obvious question, then: What is the factor in psychologically healthy people that permits them to be more capable of this perception?"

Dr. Maslow: "We don't have the time to talk about it at length, but for our purposes here we can call it a unique lack of fear. It is *fear* that puts blinders on our eyes and that puts shackles on us. You could also call it anxiety, inhibition, or lack of confidence. Whatever the term, it is the main psychological block to a Eupsychia—a society of psychologically healthy people.

"I might then go on and describe the second most important characteristic of healthy people—and the second basic foundation of Eupsychia—as spontaneity, or the capacity to function fully, to live with a certain naturalness, simplicity, lack of artificiality or guile."

Mr. Thomas: "Dr. Maslow, this word "spontaneity' is quite common in much current popular literature. I would see the word as being tied in with the concept of creativity. Would you see it this way?"

Dr. Maslow: "Very definitely."

Mr. Thomas: "Would you sort of nip the two concepts together for us?"

Dr. Maslow: "Being creative is being spontaneous—and it takes courage. Certainly one aspect of the creative person is that he must be strong, or let us say, unafraid. The creative person sticks his neck out when he has an idea. He may be defying the whole culture, even the whole of history. He is saying that what everyone accepts as the whole truth just isn't good enough. He is evidencing a certain defiance and perhaps a certain loneliness. To maintain this spontaneity—and thus, creativeness —he must overcome the fear of being in this very vulnerable position. Since we are all creative to some extent, perhaps those of our culture who evidence creativeness are simply those people with the ability to overcome a fear of spontaneity."

Mr. Thomas: "The fear is always present then, but the successful person is able to overcome it and 'be spontaneous' and thus 'creative'?"

Dr. Maslow: "Yes. When he overcomes his fear he can then permit what is inside of him to emerge—even if other people laugh at him, even if he looks ridiculous, even if his emerging idea is a mistake, as so many creations are, and he has to throw it away and be laughed at even more for this. He must be strong to withstand this.

"Now in our Eupsychia, where everyone by definition would be psychologically healthy, everyone would be able to handle spontaneous ideas, and because there would be fewer personal hostilities there would be very little fear—and thus great spontaneity and creativity. People would trust themselves; they would look forward to new ideas, to novelty, to change. There would be no need to hang on to the past—people would happily adapt to changing conditions.

Mr. Thomas: "This certainly runs counter to the 'utility' or 'usefulness' concept commonly held in our culture—the idea that the end product is the important thing, not the means or the 'doing.' We tend to regard education as a tool. We are always concerned about the use to which it will be put, about how much added income will result from it. I gather, from what you are saying that the end product of the creative process may *not* be the most important part of it. Aren't you somewhat in conflict with these traditionally held values?"

Dr. Maslow: "Well, I think the old notions of 'usefulness' are breaking up a little, not only because academic people and intellectuals object to it, but because the government and many industries are finding out the hard way that there is no system, no easy way, no method for generating really new, creative ideas. Industry is embarked on a five billion dollar annual quest for research *results.* They are finding that emphasis on use literally kills off creativity. They are learning to relax a little and wait for the really new, useful product. It is kind of a package deal—the great creative break-throughs come when the people who play with ideas are perfectly willing to make lots of ludicrous mistakes. It is from the people who can toss these mistakes aside and go on, who dare to think in a crazy, unusual way—it is from these people that really new, useful ideas and things come, and often as a by-product. Incidentally, it is the same way with happiness; it usually comes as a by-product—you don't 'get happy' by looking for it directly."

Mr. Thomas: "It seems to me that this 'non-utility' concept might also run counter to an image many of us carry about psychologists who do 'adjustment' work in industry, in schools, and as family advisors. What is your reaction to the adjustment concept of psychology?"

Dr. Maslow: "I would say that in the last ten years, most if not all, leading theorists in psychology have become anti-adjustment."

Mr. Thomas: "There are, of course, many 'adjustment' practitioners, are there not?"

Dr. Maslow: "Well, this is another story. The theorist can live in his own ideal world. He conceives the ideal, and to him adjusting means adjusting to an ideal culture. But we know the culture is not perfect. We have learned to ask whether we are going to advocate adjusting to the dope addicts down the block, the Nazis around the corner, or the Negro haters in the next city. To be adjusted to stinkers is to be a stinker yourself. A requisite of Eupsychia is that adjustment is a neutral concept. To adjust to good would be good; to adjust to bad would be bad. Theoretically, the problem wouldn't come up in Eupsychia.

"Instead of cultural relativity, I am implying that there are basic, underlying, human standards that are cross-cultural—which transcend cultures and which are broadly human. Without these standards we simply would have no criterion for criticizing, let us say, the well-adjusted Nazi in Nazi Germany."

Mr. Thomas: "You would say that without certain standards, you couldn't criticize the Nazi because his adjustment would be simply a reflection of the culture in which he finds himself?"

Dr. Maslow: "Yes, we need principles which stand above cultures and which can help us evaluate any culture, any human behavior. Then we can criticize the Nazi for just being adjusted—for not fighting a bad culture. As I mentioned a few minutes ago, we're looking for these principles in the healthiest people we could find."

Mr. Thomas: "Aren't these principles the same basic values that every religion and philosophy has attempted to find—a quest as old as cultures themselves? How does your approach as a psychologist differ from the philosopher or theologian?"

Dr. Maslow: "I think my approach differs tremendously and the difference can be stated very, very simply. It is certainly true that mankind, throughout history, has looked for guiding values, for principles of right and wrong. But he has tended to look outside of himself, outside of mankind, to a God, to some sort of sacred book perhaps, or to a ruling class. What I am doing is to explore the theory that you can find the values by which mankind must live, and for which man has always sought, by digging into the best people in depth. I believe, in other words, that I can find ultimate values which are right for mankind by observing the best of mankind. If under the best conditions and in the best specimens I simply stand aside and describe in a scientific way what these human values are, I find values that are the old values of truth, goodness, and beauty and some additional ones as well, for instance, gaiety, justice and joy. I do not say we should look for goodness because we *ought* to, or because there is some principle outside of ourselves that tells us to. I am saying that if you examine human beings fairly, you will find that they themselves have innate knowledge of and yearning for, goodness and beauty. Now there is an important reason why we don't see more of these good instincts; we are afraid of them, we tend to block their expression—the fear that I was mentioning earlier—even though we have a deep yearning for their expression. Our task is to create an environment where more and more of these innate instincts can find expression. This is what would characterize Eupsychia."

Mr. Thomas: "You would say then that this theory refutes the concept of the completely malleable personality—the so-called blank slate?"

Dr. Maslow: "Oh yes. Most psychological theorists have given that up. Some version of biological theory, or instinct theory, or basic need theory, or whatever you want to call it, is absolutely necessary for such a conception as I've outlined. Furthermore, I am saying that these basic needs are good, and that careful study of them will provide the values we need by which better societies can evolve."

Mr. Thomas: "Even such broad complex concepts as justice? Is this a constituent of all people and all cultures, in the same way that your concept of goodness is a cultural universal?"

Dr. Maslow: "Yes, I would say that every known culture has some kind of concept of justice."

Mr. Thomas: "What are some other universal constants of cultures?"

Dr. Maslow: "Another example is responsibility to certain other human beings. Every culture limits whom you can kill, to whom you can be hostile or kind, the persons to whom you have duties and obligations. Of course this is a cross-cultural generalization, but I would say that every culture has some kind of cosmology—call it religion if you prefer—some picture of the world and man's proper relationship to it; in other words, a philosophy, good or bad, true or false."

Mr. Thomas: "You mean that despite "good" cosmologies, philosophies, religions, value systems, a culture can still be 'bad'?"

Dr. Maslow: "Yes, we certainly know that throughout history cultures have attempted to exterminate one another, to maintain and advance their particular brand of cosmology. The good impulses within people are easily warped by cultures—you never find them in their pure state. The people within a culture may, deep within themselves, hold the universal constant of justice. Within the framework of a bad culture it can be twisted into an instrument of evil."

Mr. Thomas: "It would follow, then, that your Eupsychia—the ideal community of healthy people—would have an emphasis opposite from most Utopian ideals. A Utopia has usually been a good community, a good system, which produced the good life. You are saying that in Eupsychia, good lives will produce the good culture."

Dr. Maslow: "Well, let me say that creating an imaginary culture, a Eupsychia, is a game that I enjoy playing. At the same time it is a game from which very serious consequences can flow; all the more if I can remain spontaneous about the concept and let the fantasies roam free. On the other hand, I certainly must remain realistic and ask myself why so few people press for truth, beauty, and goodness, when these impulses are in all of us. Though we have a tendency, a yearning for these basic values, what keeps them from us? Are they strong enough to produce Eupsychia?

"I just said above that these impulses—these innate values—can be easily warped by a culture. But there is also another reason that they seem to appear infrequently; we tend to fear them. This fear—and rejection—of values is now occupying me theoretically; it has already occupied many psychologists for a long time under the general heading of psychopathology. For myself, I call this 'countermorality.' We know a great deal about why man, when given a choice, chooses evil over good—why he fears ultimate values—from the studies of psychopathology."

Mr. Thomas: "Would you expand on that—on 'fear of ultimate values'?"

Dr. Maslow: "Well, one example I can speak of is that we are really *afraid* to be nice, to be decent and tender. One psychologist wrote a chapter on this entitled 'The Taboo On Tenderness.' We are afraid to be boy scouts, to be soft—especially the men in our culture. One reason for this—one which impresses me very much and has changed my thinking and seems to be a very valuable tool—is that these ultimate values, or instinct-like needs (or call them biologically-based left-overs from our animal heritage); these are *not* strong, *not* overpowering as everybody has always thought but rather they are very weak, subtle, delicate. They can be easily overcome by a culture gone bad; for example, a culture that has built up an over-tough conception of masculinity which suppresses impulses such as love, kindness, and tenderness. These instincts are easily overcome by learning, habit, tradition. Part of the job of Eupsychia would be, *not* to protect itself from instincts, as Freud would have it; but rather to make society into an environment which would encourage instinct strengthening and would call out and use these valuable elements which are so feared, so delicate, so easily overcome and so mistrusted."

Mr. Thomas: "Now you're talking about the instincts for good, not the evil instincts?"

Dr. Maslow: "As far as I know we just don't have any intrinsic instincts for evil. If you think in terms of the basic needs; instincts, at least at the outset, are all 'good'—or perhaps we should be technical about it and call them 'pre-moral,' neither good nor evil. We do know, however, that out of the search for fulfillment of a basic need—take love in the child for example—can come evil. The child, wanting his mother's exclusive love, may bash his little brother over the head in hopes of getting more of it. What we call evil or pathological may certainly arise from, or replace, something good. Another example is the little squabbles among children; all the fighting they do about who should do what, about dividing up the chores, ultimately can be seen as a distorted expression of a very powerful need for fairness and justice."

Mr. Thomas: "It seems to me that Eupsychia would be a good place for the nurture of these good instincts. But the question I have is, that if these instincts are so weak and easily damaged, how can we bring them out before we have Eupsychia? How, in our present cultures, can we work toward the healthy society?"

Dr. Maslow: "The primary technical tool we now have for doing this, and I suppose the best way for doing it, is by psychoanalysis or by some other form of depth analysis with the help of a skilled person. However, since this is not a very practical suggestion for most of us, certainly not for most of mankind, we must turn our attention more and more to mass techniques of helping the person to discover this precious human nature deep within himself—this nature that he is afraid of expressing. Education, for example, certainly should help the person discover his own human nature, as should self-therapy. Self-therapy is applicable to all of us, although it is an extremely difficult job; we have only a few guide lines, a few models. One good guide, one which I frequently recommend to my students, is a paperback by Joanna Field called *A Life of One's Own*. It is a model for self-search and a description of a technique for doing it. Another good help is a book by the same author but under her own name, Marion Milner, *On Not Being Able to Paint*.

"In general, the consequences of psychotherapy are moves toward better values. The person in successful therapy generally comes out a better citizen, a better husband, a better wife—certainly a better person. He is more perceptive and more spontaneous—this practically always happens. These results are achieved through self-knowledge—the main path to discovering within ourselves the best values for all mankind. The more clearly we know these values, the more easily, spontaneously, effortlessly we can grope toward them.

"Let me put it in an old-fashioned way. One of the results of good psychotherapy is to be better able to decide between bad and good, and between the beautiful and the ugly. It's like learning to have better taste; and this, again, is via self-knowledge. You can also put it the other way around; if you think of all these therapies as simply uncovering something which is there beforehand—and that is what good therapy is supposed to do—what is uncovered is what we in our culture today call good values."

Mr. Thomas: "Doesn't it follow from this, Dr. Maslow, that the person undergoing therapy in his search for a good life must somehow reconcile all the external pressures with this image of the good as it develops? And isn't this becoming more and more difficult in our culture?"

Dr. Maslow: "While it is certainly true that cultures can block innate impulses which are good, I hope I won't sound Pollyanna if I say that the cultural pressures are really not as pressing as people sometimes make them out to be, at least in America. It is very frequently possible, especially for the young person who doesn't yet have many commitments, to simply get off the merry-go-round—to say 'nuts' to cultural pressures. In our open society this is possible; you can just about pick your way of life, you can choose something which won't trap you. It is, of course, a different story for the middle-aged man or woman. They are already committed to so many things that about the only thing that therapy can do for them is to give them strength to bear with fortitude what they have to bear.

"I would say that most psychologists regard this talk about cultural pressures as a kind of alibi. It's like saying 'poor me, I'm so helpless, I must do what I'm told.' But this is phony, especially when you're young; you don't really have to do what you're told. Does this sound too extreme to you?"

Mr. Thomas: "No, it doesn't, but I'm curious about how many of the young people you know through your work at Brandeis University would be willing to kick that part of the culture which was blocking them—let's say, preventing healthy growth. How many would say 'nuts' to the culture?"

Dr. Maslow: "Well, it is true that young people are more afraid than healthy older people these days. They have to be helped by having alternatives set before them. They then become involved in debates over the classical thinkers; they compare this bill of goods, this way of life with that way of life, and then they have to choose. Sometimes the culture is not the unanimous choice.

"I would guess, to answer your question, that about one-third or one-fourth of our students are what you'd call struggling, groping, earnest, self-making, self-creating individuals. These are the students that will retain all the possibilities of growth and development throughout the rest of their adult lives."

Mr. Thomas: "I would say that this is an impressive number."

Dr. Maslow: "Yes, it is a large proportion from one point of view. And of course Brandeis students are very bright, very carefully selected. From another point of view, however, you can certainly feel sad about the majority, the students who will walk through their studies. They may do well—get good grades, do what they are supposed to do. They learn, but in a passive way, without really deciding on a life path. They just play along with what is laid out for them. You might say they accept the dominating elements of the culture—*both* the good and the bad—without choosing, without questioning too much. Of course, in that sense they become educated, but not all educated people are wise—not all educated people keep on growing. As someone said, 'Any dope can have a high I.Q.'"

Mr. Thomas: "What would be the major function of education in Eupsychia? Or better yet, why not just tell us more about Eupsychia?"

Dr. Maslow: "The way you ask the question, it sounds as if it exists! It occurs to me now that perhaps it really does in one sense. I'll mention this in a moment. As I said earlier, the way I started playing the game was after studying self-actualizing people and learning how they behaved with each other, interpersonally, and with their families, their children. I observed that their relationships with other people showed certain differences from the average. I groped toward these differences, tried to formulate them, tried to get them clearer in my own mind. It was from this search that I began to wonder what the world would be like if all people had developed to the level of maturity and wisdom of these healthy people. Or, what kind of a culture would be generated by a thousand of these mature individuals if they were placed on a desert island and not confronted with outside cultural forces. What kind of values would they have?

"My answers—tentative of course, but nevertheless very provoca-
tive—grew from my studies of psychologically healthy people. It appears
that there would be a very great respect for individual differences—more
permissiveness for other people to grow in their own style. In this sense it
would certainly be a democratic culture. The trend might even be toward
what the philosophical anarchists used to talk about. Certainly there
would be less crime, less impulse toward it, less need for it. There would
perhaps be no laws or constitutions, except those written to protect the
society against the insanities, the feeble-mindedness, the illnesses which
can produce evil; brain fever, for example, which produces uncontrollable
hostility, and so on. But these laws would be in the background. We certainly wouldn't need armies. Our isolated group of healthy individuals
would certainly transcend nationalism, our great curse at present—the
local patriotism which may kill us all yet. I know from studying these
healthy individuals that they have less of the so-called 'national character'—that is, in a certain meaningful sense, they are international
people."

Mr. Thomas: "Because they find less *need* to be 'national'?"

Dr. Maslow: "Yes, they feel brotherly towards all mankind—and especially toward their own kind of healthy person, whether he happens to
be Japanese, German, American, or Russian. The truly healthy people all
seem to be members of the same culture. It is in this sense that Eupsychia exists already. In the middle of the messy cultures that we have
today there may be a thousand of these healthy individuals; the new
Eupsychia. I'm sure they could get along with each other very, very
nicely. I've seen it happen on a small scale."

Mr. Thomas: "Our time is about up, Dr. Maslow, and before we
close this very interesting discussion, let me ask you if you know of
people in other disciplines—economists, political scientists, anthropologists—who share this idea. Is there a journal of communication?"

Dr. Maslow: "Yes, there is a good deal of correspondence between
people in many different fields. One periodical published on the West
Coast called *Manas* carries articles from many disciplines—psychological, sociological, philosophical, religious—all pressing toward an understanding of better men and better cultures. Then there is the new
Association for Humanistic Psychology which will soon be publishing a
journal."*

Editor's note: The first issue of the *Journal of Humanistic Psychology* appeared in April,
1961.

The *Association for Humanistic Psychology* is now organized—see Editor's Preface
in *Journal of Humanistic Psychology*, Volume 1, Number 2.

MARRIAGE, FAMILY
AND CHILDREN

MARRIAGE IS FOR LIFE

Sidney M. Jourard

The title of my article has nothing to do with chronological time. When I chose a title "Marriage is for Life" I meant that marriage is to enhance life, and it is not so much an answer as it is a search. I want to direct my remarks to that search, the search for life itself.

IDEAL (AND FALSE) IMAGES OF MARRIAGE

The image of the good marriage is perhaps one of its most destructive features. The ideal marriage is a snare, a trap, an image the worship of which destroys life. The ideal marriage is like the ideal body or any other ideal, useful only if it engenders the divine discontent which leads to questing and authenticity. Whose image of a way to live together will guide a relationship? This is a question relevant for a president and his electorate, a doctor and his patient, a parent and child, a researcher and his subject, or a husband and wife. Shall it be an exercise in the concealment and display of power or a commitment to dialogue? Failure of dialogue is the crisis of our time, whether it be between nation and nation, us and them, or you and I.

I had thought of putting together a book of my several writings on marriage, education, psychology, politics, and business and entitle it "Disaster Areas," for that indeed is what they are. The state of marriage and family life in this country can easily be called a disaster. I think it stems in part from unrealistic expectations and in larger part because of a culturally induced arrest of growth in adults. Perfectly good marriages are ended because something has gone wrong. Actually, I would say they are ended right at the point where they could begin.

There are two fallacies perpetuated which keep the disasters happening. One is the myth of the right partner. The other is the myth of the

SOURCE: Sidney M. Jourard, "Marriage Is for Life," *Journal of Marriage and Family Counseling*, July, 1975. Reprinted by permission. Taken from tape recording of plenary address at the annual meeting of the American Association of Marriage and Family Counselors and the National Council on Family Relations, October 26, 1974, St. Louis, Missouri. Sidney M. Jourard, PhD, Professor of Psychology, University of Florida, Gainesville, FL, was accidentally killed December 2, 1974.

right way to act so as to ensure peace, joy, and happiness. People believe, or are led to believe, that if they just find the right partner, the right answer to the riddle of their existence will be found. Once having found the right person and the way of relating that is satisfying at this time, the partners try to do everything to prevent change. That's tantamount to trying to stop the tide. Change, indeed, happens, but it happens underground, is concealed, and then it's introduced and experienced as a catastrophe. Instead of welcoming it, the partners find it devastating. Each may then seek to find someone who will not change, so that they never need face the need to change themselves.

MARRIAGE AS DIALOGUE

Marriage at its best, according to the image that is making more sense to me, is a relationship within which change is generated by the very way of relating—dialogue, so that growth as well as identity and a sense of rootedness are engendered. Change is not so much a threat as it is the fruit of a good marriage, according to this image. Marriage is for growth, for life. It's a place to call home, but like all homes one must leave it in its present form and then return, and then leave it, and then return, like Odysseus, leaving Ithaca and returning.

Kierkegaard refused to marry and thereby defied the nineteenth century. I have refused to divorce, and I defy the twentieth. When one marriage in three is dissolved, or maybe it's 2.6, to remain wedded to the same spouse is virtually to live an alternate life style. If so few marriages endure, then something is non-viable about that way of being married. I have tried in the 26 years of my marriage to be married in the ways designated by tradition, by the mass media, by my friends, by textbooks on marriage, by my wife's image of a good marriage, and none of these ways were for life. None were life-giving, but were rather images, or better, idols. To worship idols is idolatry, a sin. To worship means to live for, to sacrifice what is of ultimate value. To worship an image of marriage is like any other idolatry, the expenditure of one's own life, time, and vitality to enhance the image. That such marriage is disastrous is self-evident. When it endures it becomes a major cause of psychological distress and physical illness in our land.

Conventional medicine, psychiatry, and psychotherapy, and for that matter, marriage counseling and family counseling, frequently function very much like combat surgery. The illness and suffering which reach the healers stem from the stress and "dispiritation" engendered from inauthentic family relationships. Laing and Esterson documented the way a family image can be preserved at the cost of one member being scapegoated as a schizophrenic (Laing and Esterson, 1965). The wards for cancer, heart disease, gunshot and knife injuries, suicide attempts, and

other stress ailments provide evidence that non-dialogic family life engenders unrelenting and destructive stress. To be married is not an un-
mixed blessing. If marriage is hell, and family life is a major cause of
disease, which indeed it is, why stay in it, or get in it?

Is the family dead, as David Cooper observed (Cooper, 1971)? If it's
dying, should we then kill it, put it out of its misery?

What do people do who have tried marriage and then gotten out of
it? The overwhelming majority remarry, and try to live the second, third,
or seventh marriage in a way that is more life-giving for the self and
others than the first. Frequently, these marriages "fail," as did the first,
and I put "fail" in quotes, because I don't think marriages fail; I think
people fail marriages.

Wherever I go in this country I get uncomfortable. I think it's more
so in California than elsewhere, and it's not with smog or even the inhabitants of Orange County, but with the people one encounters everywhere.
I am a trained and rather experienced psychotherapist, tuned in to the
non-verbal expressions of despair, loneliness, anguish, and need. So
many of the adults I encounter casually or in depth are suffering a
rupture of their last lawful or common-law marriage, and are desperately
looking for a new one or despairingly avoiding all but superficial relationships in order to avoid risk. The silent shrieks of pain deafen me. To be
married is for many boredom or hell. To be unmarried, legally or un-
legally, as many experience it is hell and despair. Is there an alternative?

Everything depends on the model or metaphor which defines the
marriage one will live, seek, grow in, or die from. There are lethal images
of marriage and family life, and there are life-giving models. I take it that
enduring, growing relationships are essential for truly human life and for
personal fulfillment and growth. I take it that happiness, pleasure, or
growth if sought as ends in and of themselves will not happen. They are
by-products of a fully-lived life. A life lived in continuing dialogue with
some few others will encourage, even force growth.

I take it as true that there is no way to go through life without some
pain, suffering, loneliness, and fear. We can help one another minimize
the shadow side of life; none can avoid it completely. To seek to avoid
pain at all costs is to make an idol out of pleasure or painlessness. To
avoid solitude at all costs is to make an idol out of chronic companionship. To avoid anxiety and depression at all costs is to make an idol out of
safety and elation. To have to achieve orgasm with somebody in particular is to make an idol of that person or of the genital experience. To
sacrifice everything for the breathless experience of being in love is to
make an idol of breathlessness.

Many people live in such idolatrous fashion. They marry for those
ends and divorce when the other side of reality creeps or bursts into the
magic circle, only to seek another playmate or protector in relation to

whom the idol may once again be worshipped and the sacrifice of life continue afresh.

Marriage as dialogue through life is for me a viable image, one that engenders life and growth as the conversation unfolds. Dialogue for me, as for Martin Buber (Buber, 1937), is the appropriate way for human beings to be or to strive to be with each other, not imposition, power plays, and manipulation. Family life is an appropriate place for dialogue to be learned and practiced. And through dialogue it's a place to grow in competence, self-sufficiency, and self-esteem.

To me the great failure in marriage as in American education is that neither institution as lived and practiced fosters enlargement of self-respect, respect for others, or growing competence in the skills that make life livable. Deception, manipulation, bribery, and threats are as American as apple pie and mother. These skills are learned in relation with Mum, Dad, the teacher, or the teaching machine.

There is, as near as I now know, no assured way to practice marriage as dialogue except by living it. As soon as a relationship becomes habitual, dialogue has ended. Predictable, habitual ways for people to act with one another are simply non-verbal ways to say the same things to one another day after day, year after year. Habit is the great anesthetic, the annihilator of consciousness.

Non-dialogic ways of being married are either exercised in a chronic struggle for power and control or they are harbors to escape those aspects of life that would engender growth. Some people stay married so they will have someone to control. Some people stay married so they will have an ear to talk into. Some people stay married so they can suffer or make their partner suffer. Most curiously, some get divorced when their partner will no longer be controlled, will no longer listen, or will no longer consent to suffer. The other's changes may be, indeed, a sign of the other person's personal growth. The one who gets a divorce may find yet another partner with whom control can be practiced or who will listen to undisciplined chatter with apparent interest or who will accept pain.

All this is by way of saying that I think in America and in the countries that follow the example set by the American way of life, we expect more out of marriage than it could ever deliver and we expect the wrong things. God, in Her infinite wisdom, so designed us that we are of two kinds and we find one another irresistible at various stages in our lives, so much so that we decide to live together. So far, so good. It's joyous to find another person attractive who finds you attractive, then to make love, even to have children.

Then the honeymoon ends and the marriage begins. It is at this point that I think most divorce happens. We are hung up on honeymoons. My honeymoon was a disaster. I knew next to nothing about tenderness and solicitude, sex, women's sexuality, my bride's sexuality. I was incapable of dialogue. I wanted to be seen in a certain way. I needed my wife to be a certain way, and obliging girl that she was, she obliged. She seemed to be the kind of person she thought I thought she was, the kind of person she felt I would like. We carried out this double masquerade for about three years. It took me that long to cheat. By seven years I was an accomplished dissembler in the realm of my sex life, not my love life, where I was a truthteller in all realms except that.

With our first separation I had a modest collection of female scalps, so to speak, to my credit and my wife, to her credit, after the shock of disclosure wore off discovered the dubious joys of semi-guilty infidelity. Through some fluke, though, within a month of a decree of divorce, we decided to resume our by now somewhat scarred relationship, rather wiser and more honest with one another about who we were. This openness for those not practiced in it was pure hell. It was painful, I assure you. It was painful for me to learn that my wife had a mind, a perspective, and feelings of her own different from mine. She was not the girl I married; in fact, she never was. I married my fantasy, and so did she. She had some coping to do, discovering that I was not the saint I had once seemed. She learned I was, and still am to some extent, a scarcely bridled privateer, a pirate, and adventurer, barely domesticated to her or American conceptions of married males.

How do two or more eccentric and energetic people live together? With humor or not at all. I did not become selectively gelded upon marriage. The more I reflect upon it, the more I like myself, having had the courage to pursue those ways of keeping vital and alive as non-destructively as I did. I could have done worse. I could have sought a divorce or have been divorced by my wife. If the first three years were the honeymoon—actually only about one year was honeymoon—boredom and pretense at joy in our sameness is a better description of our next two years. My cheating was the beginning of a marriage with some authentic companionship, some lying and getting on with the career, and the experience of living with several very young children. This marriage or this way of being married lasted until seven years when I experienced the death of my father, the completion of my first book, and the dreaded disclosure of my rather complicated affairs with several other women. Here was a real opportunity to be taught a lesson or to learn a lesson. I didn't divorce, however, nor did my wife divorce me, because we retained some recollection of affection between us, we had some children to care for, and a vast amount of anger and mutual reacquaintance to go through. It is, I assure you again, a painful experience extended through time to make yourself known to the person with whom you live and to learn aspects of her experience, attitudes, hopes, fears, and so on which shatter your image of her.

But my marriage and family life were not all my life. I had friends, other interests, and I pursued these, as did she. My life did not begin when I met her nor end when we were out of contact with one another.

My third marriage to her began with hope and resolve, as we struggled to find some enjoyment in living and to care for our children. I suspect we were growing in experience, self-sufficiency, and self-esteem. I hesitate to use certain words, but I'll say them. The point I was going to make is that marriage and family life is a wonderful place to learn shit, fecal detritus, because if you don't know shit, you have not lived. But if that's all you know, you have not lived.

I don't know how many marriages I have had by now, but I am married at the present time to a different woman of the same name in ways that are suited to our present stage of growth as human beings. I am not breathlessly in love with my wife, nor is she with me. Now, she read this and there are some asterisks in her handwriting. It says, "Maybe not breathlessly, but I do love you now with more intensity and depth and true caring than I ever have in my life."

When we spend a great deal of time in one another's proximity, we can both know irritations, even rages of astonishing intensity. It is difficult for two strong and passionate and willful people to share space and time without humor and respect for the other, even though she is wrong, as from my point of view she is. It would be so much easier for me to divorce her and to live with, even marry, some younger woman who has firmer breasts, a smaller waist, who is as sexy as a civet, who worships me and wants to have an intense and meaningful relationship with me, who would attend to my every word, and think I was the Messiah or at least worthy of the Nobel Prize. Many of my colleagues have done that. I could never see—except when I was most exasperated with my wife and fed up with being a father—why these friends of mine, otherwise sensible, wished to play the same record over again. I find someone whose perspective is smaller than mine, or who wants me to be their father, or who is but an echo of my own perspective, rather boring. Flattering, but boring. And I don't want to father anybody because I've been a father. I find a grown person of the opposite sex incites me much less to rape or riot than a young girl but more interesting by and large, at least to listen to.

It takes a long time to give up manipulative and mystifying ways of relating to others in order to trust oneself in dialogue. My training and experience as a psychotherapist have influenced my conception and experience of marriage, or perhaps it's the other way around. My colleagues in the American Academy of Psychotherapists are indeed a rather eccentric lot with many backgrounds and theoretical orientations. All were trained in some way of acting with a patient which was believed to influence, heal, or otherwise impose magical power upon the sufferer. All learned through experience that whatever else they did, they helped people grow by entering into dialogue with them, by being fully present, struggling through impasses, and growing through those struggles. Impasses were not to be avoided, they were to be sought out and celebrated, as painful as they were. They helped their patients grow by staying in relationship with them. The growth that is crucial in this conception of therapy is increased awareness of one's own worth as a person and a realization that one is vastly stronger than anyone had ever imagined. This sense of worth and of strength protects one from entering into and staying in a way of relating to another that is devitalizing and sickening.

A book on marriage which I have read—and I have read many including the O'Neills' (O'Neill & O'Neill, 1972)—which addresses this mystery of growth with some of the respect that it deserves is a small volume written by Israel Charny called *Marital Love and Hate* (Charny, 1972). Compared to his vision, many of the other books fail to acknowledge, I think, the depths of misery and destructiveness which are the other side of personal growth. Charny sees the family not strictly as haven or a place for fun and games, although it can be that, or as a place for sexual delights, but as a place where that most savage of all creatures, man, can learn to share time and space nonviolently and nondestructively. Armed by his vision, as well as by my own, I can see that many so-called successful marriages and happy families are that way because someone is repressing his perspective or is colluding with others in the destruction of his own perspective.

According to this view, marriage is not for happiness, I have concluded after 26½ years. It's a many-splendored thing, a place to learn how to live with human beings who differ from oneself in age, sex, values, and perspectives. It's a place to learn how to hate and to control hate. It's a place to learn laughter and love and dialogue. I'm not entirely persuaded that marriage and family counseling is a profession with any particular contribution to make to the quality of life. There is so far as I now know no way for people to live alone or with others that God endorsed as *the way* that She intended. (Laughter) Why is that funny? Certainly She intended that we cohabit to conceive and then to rear children, but the exact way we should live with one another was never specified. We have to grope and search, according to this view. As near as I can see, such groping for viable, non-destructive ways proceeds best within a context of dialogue.

Dialogue takes courage and commitment to honesty. When people find they can no longer live with their partner, it is not divorce or separation that is indicated. This is in some ways like suicide. The person who tries to kill himself is being unduly literal. By his act he is saying that he no longer wishes to live in the way he has been, and he is also saying that he can imagine no other way to live. He doesn't necessarily wish to stop living, just to stop living in that way. His failure is a failure of imagination as much as it is a failure of nerve.

Divorce too frequently means that one partner or the other refuses to continue living married in that way. The divorcee then finds someone with whom some other dimension of himself can be expressed. This looks like change or growth. I have wondered whether hitherto unexpressed dimensions of self could not have emerged in relation to the spouse because with the new partner an impasse will arrive and there will be the necessity to struggle with it.

If there is growth in serial marriage—and there is—one wonders why there could not be growth in the first. I know of many marriages in which one partner or the other refused to acknowledge or value the change in the other. The unchanged one ordered the changed one to revert to the way he or she was earlier, on pain of divorce.

The failure of marriage is the failure of our culture to provide models and reasonable expectations about human relationships. Because we lie so much about our relationships, especially to our children, and because the breadth and depth of authentic experience is not presented in movies, comics, books, or TV, nobody knows what is expectable or what is healthy or lifegiving or potentially lifegiving in marriage. People think that if they get angry or bore one another or fail to respond sexually that the marriage is finished, that they are out of love. Perhaps the overestimation of romantic love is one of the more pernicious patterns in our society.

When spouses deceive one another for the first time that is the time the potentially life and growth-promoting aspects of marriage can begin. When the couple finds themselves in rage, that is the time not for divorce but for celebration. Whimsically, I thought that the first betrayal of marriage should come on the honeymoon, so that it can be gotten over and the dialogue resumed.

Marriage is not an answer, but a search, a process, a search for life, just as dialogue is a search for truth. Yesterday's marriage or way of being married is today's trap. The way out of the trap is to resume the dialogue, not to end it, unless someone is pledged not to grow and change. One of my colleagues is being divorced after 22 or 23 years of marriage. He is a Southern fellow, his wife an extremely pious member of the Methodist Church, a "lousy lay" he assures everyone, and he explored another young woman. And the way he put it, "You know, when I went to bed with her she liked it." He carried on, "It was great and I discovered there was another way, but then my wife found out about it and she made me confess to our children and then made me give her up" and so on. And, sadly, he is divorcing her, or she is divorcing him, they are divorcing each other, because she wants to remain exactly as she was when she was 14 or 15. He's growing and searching. Yesterday's way of being married is today's trap. The way out of the trap is to resume the dialogue, not to end it.

If marriage counseling is not training and experience in dialogue, then it falls short in my opinion of its help-giving potential. How does one function as a marriage and family counselor? In the same way two porcupines mate—with difficulty and great care. I know of no techniques for counseling individuals, or couples, or entire family units. There *is* something about the experience of having struggled to retain one's self-respect and joie de vivre in the face of marital disaster, one's own marital disasters, that helps one to listen with empathy and humor to others' difficulties. I think that inventiveness and a profound faith in every individual's capacity to overcome all disasters and to find his own strength is helpful. I am always astonished at how couples convince themselves that they cannot live more than five minutes if their partner changes in one way or if they are incommunicado from their partner for five minutes. That is astonishing when you think about it, two reasonably adequate human beings live together and then if one of them changes in one jot or tittle, the other person is either to commit murder, suicide, or divorce. Or if they split for a day, or a week, or a month to recenter themselves, the one who did not choose to be apart for a while will very frequently do everything in his or her power to punish the one who is seeking to recenter herself or himself.

In various earlier papers I have explored the importance of modeling, of being an exemplar of viable ways to live, or of the possibility of overcoming difficulties in living. Theory and technique are valuable in counseling, as they are in any other enterprise, but they can be the refuge of scoundrels and fools, like patriotism. If he or she is not a spokesman for and an exemplar of dialogue, integrity, and a relentless commitment to a search for viable ways to live and grow, then he or she will be found out. There is no way to impersonate integrity for very long. As in all realms where human beings deal with one another, there is no place in family counseling for dissembling and technical manipulation by the professional person. Marriage and family counseling to enhance or to terminate marriages proceeds best, perhaps only, through dialogue.

ALTERNATIVE LIFESTYLES

Robert N. Whitehurst

ARE THEY A THREAT TO CONVENTIONAL FAMILY LIFE?

Most of the social forces that we presume made past marriages and family life solid, if not happy, seem to be evaporating in front of our eyes. At the same time, a great variety of alternatives to conventional marriage and family have suddenly loomed on the horizon. Recent changes seem to favor more divorce and family disorganization; dissatisfactions with marriage tend to create an atmosphere of distrust of this basic institution.

It may be that marriage and family forms will become even more diverse in the future; but this will probably be contingent upon economic and political conditions. In any case, it is unlikely that the nuclear family will fade out as a dominant form, unless the whole human race goes with it—a distinct possibility as human behavior is now going! In the exploration that follows, it will be suggested that marriage is not a healthy institution for many people today, but it is not about to die; further, the future of alternatives is simply not predictable, given the status of current political winds and economic uncertainties. Given certain conditions, however, some probable options might come to fruition. In the following pages, these options will be speculated upon.

MAKING MARRIAGE WORK

One of the first items in the discussion of the functioning of future family life is inevitably the Western institution known as marriage. Traditionally, marriage as we know it has emerged from a particular ethos. When people have experienced a strong sense of community, a strong set of principles adhered to rigidly as life guidelines, complete with strong sanctions and a tight supportive group, a customarily rigid family form has emerged. Since we have in this century weakened the basis of most of the previously effective social controllers, such as religion, the community, and the family, we should not be surprised that marriages fail more frequently. During the present period, no one knows if marriage is better,

SOURCE: Robert N. Whitehurst, "Alternative Lifestyles." This article first appeared in *The Humanist,* May/June 1975 and is reprinted by permission.

worse, or simply more of the same in qualitative terms. We only know with some degree of certainty that as a culture we are "hooked" on the notion of finding happiness in marriage but that it doesn't really seem to happen that way very often. It seems likely that the key differences between marriage in the past and contemporary marriage are attributable to our leisure, affluence, higher expectations, and mobility, coupled with an inordinately high opportunity level to meet potential mates. We are probably no more nor less neurotic as a people than those before, but we distinctly have fewer solidifying forces compelling us to obey the still-dominant conventional community norms. *Social structure, not personality, is what must be understood if we want to know why divorce is rampant and why families are not "happy."*

As a society, we have cut loose more people (the young, with their own rooms, TV sets, cars, booze, drugs, money, free time, and, most of all, freedom from responsibility), with more tragic results, than any people in history. Most of our older people are stashed in retirement villas or "nursing" homes and, as Jules Henry and others have shown, are simply the unwanted surplus of a rapidly moving technological society. The high social cost of overspecializing the family and creating children who founder, oldsters who despair, and the rest of us who are uncertain, doubtful, or anxious can be seen not only in divorce rates but in simmering family problems that prevent real living and meaningful relating among people. The rise of alternative forms can be seen in part as a response to conventional family failure to satisfy many of the needs that have been developed recently in a freer kind of society. In contemporary life, custom, religion, and community have come to mean less. The needs for family and marriage, however, have come to mean more. We have reached a hiatus involving a large potential for those who either seek or promote alternatives to traditional marriage.

In a society changing as rapidly as ours, it is impossible to maintain stable marriage forms not aligned with people's real needs. If we free women to go into the marketplace, give people leisure, money, and opportunity to meet others, and take them away from home for long periods, solidarity in the old-fashioned sense cannot be the result. The need for intimacy is probably a constant in humans, but our sense of legitimizing multiple ways of searching for it is subject to radical changes over time. We have expected more intimacy from relationships today, and we have provided more means of searching for it than in former times. It is doubtful that people have ever been able to find much intimacy, but the fact that we *expect* it today and have *expanded means of seeking* it makes the search for alternatives an understandable imperative.

One of the salient factors in understanding the rise of alternatives may lie in comprehending the nature of the need for intimacy, both physical and emotional. Christianity has traditionally placed heavy emphasis on fidelity and monogamy. No one has yet made the case, however, that rigid insistence in such matters is mainly a reflection of a religious institution's need to control people in terms of the biases of its later apostles. The conditions that prompted these demands on humankind may have since vanished. We now have a markedly different situation. In short, as people are freed to live closer to themselves as natural, not churchly, beings, we may expect forms to emerge that reflect the true diversity of human desires and needs instead of a narrow monolithic institutional imperative. This seems to be a part of what is happening now.

It need not be feared that there is an immediate danger of masses of people dropping their marriages and joining communes, swinging clubs, or other such activities. The institutional forces still alive in the culture have enough sanctioning power to prevent total chaos from enveloping families; the institutions that prevail, however, do not have enough power to keep families and marriages on an even keel, as was more true in the past. Thus, the dilemma we now face involves having more freedom than in the past to live as many of us would wish, but not enough to live as many would see fit if we had a truly pluralistic and open society. It is in this cultural limbo, this no-man's-land of vague and shadowy family supports that are more apparent than real, that we find ourselves today. Bereft of old supports to make them operate well, families limp their way along. Alternative-searching goes on in this limbo, in which we are neither enslaved to a past nor freed to a positive future, but caught in an uncomfortable place between. In such a situation, it would be difficult to conclude that family life is endangered by the existence of alternatives to marriage; marriage and family life, if they are threatened at all, are in jeopardy because the entire social structure and set of institutional underpinnings are in jeopardy. It is as rational to see alternative-seekers as trying to save the family as trying to destroy it. In some sense, however, old forms are always dying, so it is probably true that alternative-seekers may in some ways be hastening the demise of the family—at least as it is presently known. It is patently false to assume that the existence of alternatives has created the problem of the family today. The quest for alternatives is only one of many reactions to family strains and problems.

Given a situation as described above, it would be a false conclusion to claim that the family is in trouble today because people are seeking alternative routes to sexual satisfaction and family life; rather, it would be more correct to suggest that the search for alternatives grew out of conventional family failures created by a changing and unstable society that made some new forms both possible and seemingly desirable in a changing social context. Alternatives can thus be perceived less as a threat to the family than as a means of reconstituting it in different forms.

ALTERNATIVES ARE NOT A THREAT

In the following descriptions of alternatives, it will be suggested that *none of these will replace conventional monogamous marriage as a modal form in the foreseeable future.* There is no sign of divorce rates lowering, but this does not necessarily pose a threat to family life as long as we are so enamored of marriage as the only way to live. Indeed, divorce hurts and disrupts both children and adults, but it does not appear to materially affect cultural stability. The same can probably be said for extant alternatives today. This is especially so since most of them occupy so few people in terms of statistical significance. Be this as it may, we are likely to see changing and even expanding rates of alternate life-styles, dependent on future economic and political changes, especially inflation, recession, and depression. Among the rationales for the formation of alternate life-styles are ecological and economic arguments, as well as stressing the needs for intimacy in groups larger than the conventional nuclear-family group. It is assumed that the forms enumerated below will predominate as alternatives, roughly in decreasing order of importance as they are described. These involve modified open marriage, post-marital singlehood, triads, a variety of cooperatives, urban collectives and urban communes, extended intimate networks, rural communes, and finally swinging, cohabitation, and part-time marriage. Rationales will be discussed of why each of these will be more or less successful and why some will persevere into the future.

MODIFIED OPEN MARRIAGE

With changing sex-role socialization, with people's liberation (including men's groups as well as women's), with increasing legal equality for children and women, and with a likely increase in women workers at all levels, it will be imperative that more marriages extend the benefits of greater freedoms to both sexes. This will eventuate in a form of marriage that will not likely be fully open in terms of free sexuality, but will be vastly different from the average marriage of today. It is probable that there will be more sexuality practiced outside of marriage because of these new freedoms for women, but the forms are not distinguishable at this time.

The basic revolution before us lies in sex roles, not in sexuality—at least the equalizing of sex roles should be the first order of business. The middle seventies have brought only the barest beginning of equality for husband and wife in work, household tasks, and child care. Whether this will in its turn bring the incidence of female sexual activity up to or beyond that of the average male is unknown. Given what we know now about female sexuality, it is likely that many females will surpass many of their brothers in this sphere; the impact of this upon marriage and family forms is simply unknown.

POST-MARITAL SINGLEHOOD

Given the high divorce rates and the uncertainties of remarriage, larger numbers of people will probably opt for longer periods of singlehood in the future. In a world where there are more singles than ever before, we are likely to develop some norms that will put them into the "normal" range, which is not generally the case at present. Although pressures are still tremendous for people to marry and remarry, this may change so that a more benign atmosphere will enable people to tolerate singlehood more easily. Many young people today are either wary of marriage or are extremely cautious about getting into second marriages; given the continuance of this trend, social acceptance of this form as a more or less permanent adaptation to adult life will become a reality. Support for nonmarriage is developing in many avant-garde quarters. Although making predictions is risky, it is safe to suggest growing numbers in this category. Since it is likely that freer sexuality will be practiced among nonmarrieds and that our norm of valuing privacy will continue, it is probable that more people will be able to make it without marriage, supported by the apparent success of those already in the group. This will, of course, still constitute a small proportion of most of the adult population; we are still reared to think that marriage is the only right way to live. There are simply not, as yet, that many deviants in this culture, and nonmarriage is surely a form of deviancy from conventional norms. An increase in singlehood of all kinds may be predicted, but it will not become a modal form.

TRIADS

With present urban sex ratios favoring men in the marketplace of sex and partner selection, triads will likely become a more important form of living arrangement as an alternative to conventional marriage. Not only will more people be willing to share a spouse, but as the benefits of this form come to be known, more people are likely to be willing to try this adaptation. Among the more obvious advantages: greater flexibility in child care, more adult models in the family, better and more equitable distribution of household chores, better economic foundation for the family, less social isolation for some now living alone, and the greater ease of three people making accommodative rules and adaptations to each other than in other alternative forms.

To form a triad, there must be three people who like each other and have some tolerance for being alone at times, as well as being left out at times. There have been numerous cases of triads working for long periods of time, and they stand to become more numerous, given present conditions. If we add to this the relative ease with which the extra family member can be explained away to conventional society, we can see how this form might become more prevalent. Although the triad has its drawbacks and is definitely not a panacea, it is more likely to occur than many other forms of living arrangements now being tried.

COOPERATIVES, COLLECTIVES, URBAN COMMUNES, AND EXTENDED INTIMATES

A panoply of cooperatives, communes, and other sharing arrangements is currently being developed with varying results. Churches of moderately liberal persuasion are even attempting to establish forms of community, sharing patterns, and extended intimacy networks. Although such forms at times develop into sexual sharing, this is not a dominant mode as yet and tends to be associated with problems, if not divorces and remarriages, because supports for sexuality outside marriage in the usual urban cooperative or collective have not worked smoothly. Short of large-scale renovation of marital and sexual norms, this will apparently not happen. It is also for this reason that alternatives might best be seen as an adjunct to marriage and not as a replacement for it—at least for a large number of people now participating in so-called alternate life-styles. There is, however, some evidence that people unavoidably get into sexual problems outside their marital relationships once alternatives are entered. The rate of successful integration of extramarital sexuality into the average marriage is apparently low. For all this, there are many attempts to try to extend family conceptions by enlarging the number of people included in economic sharing, social rituals, and a variety of other quasi-family experiences, sometimes even including sexuality. Given economic hard times, these groupings stand to proliferate. In the less likely event of increased leisure and affluence, such arrangements still may expand on some kind of experimental basis as a way to salvage the goodness of family life and the ethic of sharing. These styles will be juxtaposed against what is perceived as the relatively isolated and encapsulated existence currently being experienced by most nuclear families.

SWINGING AND GROUP MARRIAGE

Although the research of Larry and Joan Constantine has shown that there are some stable and lasting forms of group marriage, the complexities and problems of four or more people being married to each other loom so large that this form is impractical for large numbers. Hitherto privatized, nuclear-family cultures do not lend themselves easily to such an adaptation; our sense of possessiveness with spouses and jealousy still bulk in the way of such solutions. Perhaps another generation, reared without sexism and jealousy, will adapt better to such a form, but the numbers are few who can make it work well today. Swinging, although declining as a family sport, can be said to arise basically as a variation of the older clandestine adultery pattern. In no way does most swinging tend to alter family behavior. Most couples do not indoctrinate their young into swinging. With the exception of valuing the variety in swinging, no value changes are apparent in the lives of the swinging population. Although large numbers (but small percentages of the total populace) still continue this pattern, there is no indication that swinging will replace clandestine adultery as the model pattern of extramarital sexual practice. Among the principal ways swinging affects marriage is the creation of tension between partners with unequal commitment to the activity. Divorce, then remarriage to someone with more consonant values, often follows. Swinging does not seem to constitute a genuine alternative; rather, it involves a sorting mechanism to insure value-similar partners for the swingers' activities.

COHABITATION

Increasing interest in the living-together patterns of the unmarried over the past several years has eventuated in some good research on the topic. We still do not know if the practice, in fact, makes for better marriages; it may do so in the short run, but probably has little overall effect on marriage in the long run. Cohabitation does not appear to substantially affect marriage rates or marriage stability, at least as far as we know.

Cohabitation cannot seriously be considered as an alternative to marriage for many people; it is rather a *preliminary* for most who practice it and an occasional habit of people not yet ready to settle down into a second marriage; it is seldom an alternative to marriage. No doubt a more sensible mate-selection device than methods previously used, cohabitation does not seem to deter large numbers from the goal of formal marriage.

PART-TIME MARRIAGE

An increasing number of married partners are engaging in what might be called part-time marriages. These are usually professionals who for career reasons must separate on occasion and for varying periods of time. Some marriages survive these periods of separation and some do not. Some remain as monogamous in absence as in presence, but some do not. There seems to be a wide variation in the patterns possible in part-time marriages. Although the habit is still quite new and obviously a function of high-mobility and dual-career marriages, it may increase as people tend to find separateness an advantage for a period of time. This adaptation does not affect great numbers of people now and probably will not, unless current trends regarding women's employment and liberation proceed at a faster pace than at present.

OTHER POSSIBLIITIES

If we engage in the mental exercise of extending current behavior patterns into the future and extrapolating from them, we may find some interesting potential for alternate life-styles of the future. For example, if the clandestine-adultery pattern becomes a more ubiquitous phenomenon, it seems unlikely that nearly everyone could go on playing the hiding game forever; at some point, it is possible that a consensus will emerge that casual adultery is "okay"—given certain contexts and sets of rules by which the players must abide. Already, there is a set of informal and well-understood rules by which clandestine adultery is played. Firm consensus and more players are probably all that is necessary to create an informally institutionalized code of sexual behavior for large numbers of people. This would not necessarily constitute an alternative to marriage; rather, it would be one more addition to the already complex set of roles that spouses must play today.

For those who want something more than the "game" described above, there may be such a concept as informally sanctioned *binogamy*. Although this term bastardizes two standard terms used in family sociology (*monogamy* and *bigamy*), it seems apropos—although contemporary binogamists cannot be *married* to two wives, they very often, in fact, render loyalty and fealty to two persons, one of whom is the legal spouse. This pattern, a bit unlike triads, does not necessarily involve a common living arrangement. It is rather an extension of the long-lasting affair, which even when it becomes known is still not dropped in favor of monogamy. Caring, some sharing, and continued sexual relations may all be a part of this pattern. This pattern is already practiced by an unknown number of people and, by all signs, the number is increasing. Whether binogamy can be considered a true alternative is moot, since it is distinctly nonmonogamous and in some ways considerably alters nuclear-family interactions. It is, however, functional, in that it appears to ease social isolation, sexual frustration, and, perhaps, economic problems of some who maintain social and sexual needs and are not married.

SUMMARY AND CONCLUSION

A key characteristic of the times is the tendency to open up marriages and to provide more opportunities for expression of life-styles at variance with older patterns. It is true that conventional marriages are floundering because of the failure of supportive institutions and groupings that once worked to keep people on track. At the same time, so-called alternatives—most of which are neither true alternatives to marriage nor threatening to it—are emerging and being practiced in a normative vacuum, which makes most of them problematic in terms of their longevity. What seems to be emerging is an era of pluralism, unlike anything ever before witnessed in the Western world. Homosexuals are "coming out," many people are less prone to keep their sex lives secret, and varieties of living forms, with some exception, are becoming at least tolerated, if not more understood. In an era of economic hardship, however, people are still careful not to jeopardize their jobs by blatantly flouting sexual mores. It is fairly clear by now that neither the supporters of conventional norms nor alternative-seekers have an easy time of adapting in the seventies; relationships are simply difficult, no matter what the variety.

If the economy and the political situation both tighten up and create a repressive environment, alternatives will change form; although there will be less blatant sexuality, there will be more sharing, cooperative ventures, and perhaps a developing sense of community, as people are no longer able to use the wheeled escape. If the economic situation becomes more optimistic, there will probably be more sexual deviation surrounding marriage, more experimentation, and, perhaps, more forms yet to emerge as yet unknown. Both inflation and depression give birth to their own styles of conservation, but perhaps the days of easy affluence, which spawned much of the enhanced interest in sexuality, are gone. We have known the flower child. The earlier modes of a more constrained existence are not likely to return.

Pluralism seems to be the key word of the near future; we have not as yet learned to live easily with it. A democratic-humanistic approach can be more positive than the monolithic and repressive experience of the past. We have only made a beginning at developing enlightened cultural supports for sensuousness, pleasure, and a broader-based sexual practice that does not press all people, regardless of taste and desires, into a common behavioral mold. It is now a moral imperative to develop norms of acceptance for differences. Perhaps the rest of this century will correspond with the last one in the respect that our new laissez-faire policy will extend into our conception of other people's sexuality.

THE SELF-ACTUALIZING PERSON IN THE FULLY FUNCTIONING FAMILY: A HUMANISTIC VIEWPOINT

Ellis G. Olim

Any discussion of the American family today must take place within the context of what many observers regard as a crisis or, at best, a troublesome time of questioning and transition. We have been beset by an unpopular war, social unrest, the repolarization of racial attitudes, the disarray and underfinancing of our public school system and public health services, student revolts, dissent and civil disobedience, the pollution of our air and water supplies, crime in the cities and towns, experimentation with drugs, experimentation with new forms of social structure,[1] and alarm over both birth and abortion rates. This litany of troubles, it seems, adds up to a crisis. The crisis is occurring in the decade we call an "age of affluence." There is a connection between the affluence and the crisis, but not all would agree on what the salient features of that connection are, and even fewer perhaps would agree on the conclusions to be drawn from the connection.

LOOKING BACKWARD

There are some who urge a retreat to an earlier age. They look at the past through gold-colored glasses, forgetting the evils of that past. They have a merciful amnesia about how things really were when they were young. An example of this is the position taken by Dr. Graham B. Blaine, Jr. (1966). He complains that our youth no longer have impulse control; that this comes from the failure of their parents to instill in them clear con-

SOURCE: Ellis G. Olim, "The Self-Actualizing Person in the Fully Functioning Family: A Humanistic Viewpoint," *The Family Coordinator*, July 1968. Copyrighted 1968 by the National Council on Family Relations. Reprinted by permission.

1. This refers not merely to the Hippie groups, but what may prove to be more significant, to experiments in intense group experiences and new social arrangements for the family (see Stroller, 1967, pp. 28-33).

ceptions of what is right and what is wrong. He states that children should have definite limits firmly set by parents upon their impulsive behavior by clear disapproval, spanking, or deprivation. He says that willingness to punish and firmness of conviction about what is right and wrong are essential qualities of the good parent. It may be granted that there are some victims of overindulgent or negligent parents. Some of our youth have shed the old without having found viable new forms, new patterns, new ways of life. But there are far more victims of the affluent society than the victims of overindulgence: the same kinds of victims which we have had in periods of scarcity. Much of the juvenile delinquency and much of the civil disorder occurring today are occurring among the culturally disadvantaged and socially and economically deprived. "Black power" is *not* a response to parental indulgence.

The advice of those who urge a return to the past seems tedious. If anyone could show by any reading of history that man has ever been able to turn back the clock and recreate an earlier age, we should become more receptive to the point of view expressed by Dr. Blaine. Perhaps what the clock turners fail to grasp is that the behavior of individuals at the present time, or indeed at any time in history, is the result of a fantastically complex interaction amongst an incredibly large number of psychosociocultural variables. The recreation of an earlier age is impossible without the most thoroughgoing destruction of the present social structure. Not even those who yearn nostalgically for the past would subscribe to such a program of destruction.

MAN AS BECOMING

The view to which we subscribe, rather, is that man has a rendezvous only with the future. What we need today is a conception of man that is suitable for the world of tomorrow. We cannot accept the conception that parents know what is right and what is wrong, that they know what limits to impose on their children. Parents do not necessarily and automatically know what is good for the child, nor what is the good and what is the bad. And we certainly cannot accept today, in the face of research and clinical observation to the contrary, the idea that punishment and deprivation are good for children. True, if particular types of behavior intrinsically lead to unfortunate consequences for the individual, such punishment probably has some values. However, if punishment or deprivation is perpetrated by an agent, such as a parent or a teacher, there are unfortunate side effects, one of which is resentment and rebelliousness against the punisher. Of course the punishment may work in the short run but the undesirable behavior is merely driven underground, usually ready to reappear when the punisher is absent. If the internalization by the child of his conception of the parents' moral code is *too* effective, so that the child is a life-long victim of a harsh superego (Freud's conscience), the underground, undesirable behavior may never reappear, but in such instances, substitute forms will appear. In such cases, the victim is doomed to live in purgatory all his life, cheating himself of the opportunity to live fully and spontaneously.

We do have a new conception of man. It is a conception that enables us to go forward into the future instead of trying to hold back the course of human development. This new conception is that man is constantly becoming. Man need not be a fixed outcome of environmental influences except in the case of the abnormal man who suffers from being fixated at a level of personality development from which he cannot rise, or in the case of men in those preliterate societies which were static, which remained the same over thousands of years. But it is a truism that our society is an evolving one, constantly changing, an open society. Our society challenges its members to develop a flexible stance, a stance that enables them to adapt to changing conditions. What we want, then, is not to encourage a static type of personality based on traditional notions of right and wrong, but the kind of person who is able to go forward into the uncertain future. The man of the future should be self-actualizing. This means that he should ever be moving toward a greater realization of his human potential and, equally important, that he be constantly transcending himself. The idea of self-transcendence has two meanings. In one sense, it means that man should overcome his egocentricity and enlarge his self to include concern with humankind. Its other, more modern, sense is that man is in a constant process of evolving into higher and higher forms of humanness, that his self is constantly going beyond previous selves. Man's human potential is not finite; it is infinite. There are no limits to the process of becoming.

Thus, Maslow (1955) talks of the "self-actualized" person; Rogers (1959) of the "fully functioning" individual; Allport of man as having a "passion for integrity and for a meaningful relation to the whole of Being in his most distinctive capacity" (1955, p. 98); Sullivan (1940) of the basic direction of the organism as forward; Horney of the powerful incentive "to realize given potentialities," "an incentive to grow" (1942, p. 22).

MENTAL HEALTH AND NORMALITY

The question of what kind of people we should be has been argued extensively by those who are concerned with what is mental health, or by a related question—what is the normal personality? One conception of mental health is that it is completely relative to the particular culture in which it occurs, i.e., each society has its own definition of normality. Usually, this conception also assumes that the normal or healthy personality is the modal personality; that the abnormal personalities are at the extremes (see Singer, 1961, pp. 9-90; Mowrer, 1948, pp. 17-46). Wegrocki (1948) argues against both the statistical-normative and the cultural-relativistic points of view. He holds that it is possible to achieve a pan-human definition of normality. He defines the normal person as one who does not react to an inner conflict by unconscious and symptomatic escape from inner conflict but who faces his problems. Mowrer (1948), also seeking a pan-human definition, asserts that all societies, no matter how diverse in form, have some ethical system, and that those members of the society who "play the game" and subscribe to the ethical system are normal. Neither Wegrocki nor Mowrer has refuted the notion of cultural relativity. One can always find commonality among diverse elements if one is willing to utilize a sufficiently high degree of abstraction to the point of lack of content. If we accept the notion that societies differ in the degree of freedom and openness allowed their members and the view that the personality is formed in interaction with the environment, then members of different societies will differ in their need to escape from conflict and in the amount of conflict experienced. And the conception of a standard of normality as "playing the game" falls apart when we try to apply it to real people in real societies. For example, were both Dean Rusk and Dr. Martin Luther King playing the same game? Are we to assume that Neville Chamberlain and Albert Schweitzer shared a common definition of "normality?" What is left out of Wegrocki's and Mowrer's definitions is attention to what it means to be *human*.

THE HUMANIST'S CONCEPTION OF THE IDEAL PERSONALITY

The conception of man as becoming, as self-actualizing, as moving toward the fully functioning individual, uses a different criterion, the conception of the "ideal" personality. But like the preceding definition, it, too, is a value judgment. It has no support in traditional scientific methods of verification. Its support comes, in the main, from persons who have become self-actualizing or who have observed others become self-actualizing. Though this is not considered good scientific evidence by those who are addicted to a nineteenth century conception of science, it has been sufficient evidence to motivate some to give up the quest for man as a successful achiever, and to think of him as a process of becoming human. Though the humanistically oriented psychologists and psychiatrists believe that this is the road to self-fulfillment, they cannot prove it. But they are willing to take a chance, to encourage people to move from static, fixed, stereotyped personalities to dynamic, ever-changing, variegated personalities.

SELF-ACTUALIZATION AND THE FAMILY

How can we relate this conception of the self-actualizing person to the family? At the strictly sociological level of analysis it is customary nowadays to talk about the functions of the family not in terms of the older kinds of functions, such as that the family provides sustenance for its members, provides clothing and shelter, provides religious or other education and the like, but in terms of the family as an interaction system (Parsons and Bales, 1955). The family is the primary socializing agent in early childhood. Personality development, from a sociological point of view, is a function of this socialization process. In the nuclear family of America, there are two other important functions (Parsons and Bales, 1955)—the instrumental function, which is related to the external aspects of the family, to providing for the maintenance and physical well-being of the family; and the expressive function, which is related to the internal aspects of the family, to providing integrative and socio-emotional support for the family members. But this conception of the functions of the family as system does not demand that the children be socialized to any particular kind of behavior, that they develop any particular kind of personality. Nor does it require that the integrity of the family be maintained and sustained in any particular way.

What needs to be understood about Parsons's approach and that of Wegrocki, and with the approach in general of devising abstract conceptual systems is that these conceptualizations are heuristic devices and not statements about the content that goes into the conceptual system. They do not have the generality of laws in physics, for example, but rather the generality of mathematics. Physical laws can be confirmed by actual instances. However, the statement in mathematics that two plus two equals four cannot be confirmed by actual instances because it is pure abstraction. Although two apples plus two apples equals four apples, the statement that two pieces of white coal plus two pieces of white coal equals four pieces of white coal is not a statement about anything that exists outside the realm of fantasy. The conceptions of man-as-becoming, of man as self-actualizing, are not pure abstractions but deal with demonstrable processes and demonstrable outcomes, processes and outcomes that can be evaluated by some criteria.

What, then, might be some of the implications of the humanist view when applied to the family? What kind of family life would we have if every member of it were on the road to self-actualization? What kind of people would we produce in a fully functioning family? Before undertaking to answer such questions, however, by way of pointing up the contrast, we should like to mention briefly some of the cultural beliefs and values that have contributed to producing persons who are *not* self-actualizing.

It is a truism today that our culture has tended for a long time to promote conformity, triviality, and dehumanization. In the affluent society, things become the measure of man. Unfortunately, the views of Darwin, Weber, and Freud (Maddi, 1967) have been used by many social scientists to reinforce these tendencies.

Because Darwin documented the connection between man and subhuman animals, the characteristics of man that are not present in lower animals have sometimes been dismissed as unimportant or explained in simplistic terms. But man differs markedly from lower animals with respect to those things that make him human. There are internal, psychological processes in man that do not occur in lower animals. Man is aware of himself, he has values, he exercises judgment, he has imagination, he questions his own existence, he sometimes strives to become more human. Actually there is nothing in the concept of a phylogenetic scale that requires that we overlook the importance of characteristics that emerge at higher levels of development (Maddi, 1967). Nor is Darwinism incompatible with the view that man alone among the species undergoes a social evolution so that his personality is ever-evolving into higher forms that are different from those of earlier men.

The sociologist Weber is credited with one so-called sociological view of personality. This view is that the personality is the sum total of the social roles played by a person. We may readily grant that many people have personalities that come close to matching this conception. Nevertheless, persons who are merely the sum of their roles are hollow people. Such people lack an acute sense of personal identity. To them all the world is a stage, and they are actors on it. They are socialized to conformity instead of "creative becoming" (see Allport, 1955, p. 34). Actually though, the sociological role conception of personality can be reconciled with a psychological view of personality (Maddi, 1967). Since man is evolving socially, the social roles that he creates are evolving and changing, too. Social roles can encourage the development of imagination, of aesthetic experience, of creativity, of spontaneity, of the exercise of reason—behavior that leads to growth and self-enhancement. Another type of reconciliation that can be effected is described by Maslow (1967). He points out that in self-actualized individuals their vocational role is not something apart from their identities but that their vocation is an incorporated, inextricable aspect of the self.

The humanist view differs from the orthodox Freudian position. In classical libido theory, Freud gives expression to the belief that life represents a compromise between the necessity of playing social roles—the accomplishment of which is done by sublimation of instinctual drives into socially acceptable channels—and the demands of biological, instinctual drives. In Freud, the ego, that part of the personality that is in contact with reality, is essentially defensive in nature. It serves to defend the individual against his anxiety-provoking instinctual drives on the one hand, and the harsh demands of his superego and of society on the other. To the classical Freudian, the wholesome individual is the well-defended one. Abnormality for Freud consists of extremes—of being defenseless or of being overly defended. The normal individual is optimally defended. But, with the exception of sublimation, all the defenses, according to Freud, distort reality to some degree. When the distortion seriously cripples an individual, the defenses are called pathological. There is no denying Freud's monumental contribution to our understanding of man. However, the Neo-Freudians and the ego psychologists have gone beyond Freud's original conception. Some of the ego psychologists reject the notion that the defenses are even necessary. They assume that defenses are always crippling, they deny that sublimation is a defense at all, and assert that it is a coping or adaptive mechanism, and they hold that the road to mental health consists in liquidating the defenses or preventing their origination, substituting adaptive, coping mechanisms in their place. The ego psychological view is extended further by humanists. Maslow (1967) describes self-actualizing people as "expressing" rather than "coping," as spontaneous, "more easily themselves" instead of playing the roles of other people.

THE FULLY FUNCTIONING PERSON

What is the difference between the fully functioning person (at this stage in history, such a person is more an ideal than a fact) and the kind of person here referred to as a conformist, as defensive, as operating at less than his potential, as not being on the road to self-actualization? One critical difference is that the fully functioning person has an acute sense of his own personal identity. As a consequence, he has also an awareness of his own powers to relate effectively to the world. He changes the world. He exercises mastery over it and over himself. The locus of evaluation of himself rests within himself. On the other hand, the normal personality, according to the classical Freudian description, or according to the view of a stimulus-response psychologist, places man in a reactive role. He reacts to environmental influences. He has little or no subjective awareness of his identity as a unique human being, but tends to see himself only as others see him, to see himself as a commodity (Fromm, 1947). He is molded by others; he is programmed as though he were a machine. For him technological progress becomes the automation of dehumanization, to use Kenneth Clark's apt phrase.

Let us now turn to how the fully functioning person might develop. He is not born fully functioning. The development does come about through environmental influences and, in early childhood, this means notably the parent-child relationship. Later it means also the relationship between the child and significant other persons in his environment. Still later his development will be affected by others through what he reads. The most essential ingredient for starting a child on the road to self-actualization is, according to Rogers (1959), the presence of unconditional positive regard. This means that the growing child is appreciated as a human being. He is not punished for being human. He is not taught to become ashamed and guilty about his humanness. Valuing the child for his humanness means that he must be valued for the development of imagination, symbolization, aesthetic awareness, empathy, and reason. When the child is so valued, the initiative for learning and development comes from within the child, not from external rewards or punishments. Obviously the child must be taught some things. Each child cannot discover the whole history of man and man's thought all by himself. Nevertheless, wide latitude must be given to the child to discover and construct reality for himself, to find his own values, his own beliefs, his own moral code, what he wants to do with his life, his own identity. The roles he takes must be selected by him, not foisted upon him. If, as a parent, you wish to cripple your child, value him only when he does the things you want him to, disvalue him when he differs. Emphasize to him that he must assume certain social roles, and that he may not assume others. Concentrate on his roles; neglect his psychology.

To become a self-actualizing individual requires the courage to face the unknown. Therefore, the fully functioning individual is frightening to a conformist, who seeks the security of the known. It can be demonstrated that this is so because we have today in our midst young people who are on the road to self-actualization: the student activists. During the 1950's university students were called the "quiet" generation. They had "buttoned down" minds (Flacks, 1967). Polls, such as the Purdue poll, showed that students were unconcerned with deep values. They were complacent, status-oriented, committed only to exurbanite conformity. They wanted to wear gray flannel suits, become organization men, live in suburbia, and drive station wagons. Then suddenly in the 1960's, there burst upon us a new generation of young people. These people questioned. They protested. They were indifferent to the opportunity for status and income. These were not youths who were attracted to activism because they were economically deprived, or because their opportunities for upward mobility were blocked (Flacks, 1967). These were highly advantaged youths, whom some call the "victims" of an affluent society. Nor can these young people be explained as a generation in revolt. The youth of the early thirties were, by and large, a generation in revolt. These youths were not. Nor is it entirely a matter of generation gap. The good baby doctor stands shoulder to shoulder with the babies whose rearing he helped to shape. Studies have shown (see Flacks, 1967, p. 20 ff) that the parents of student protestors often share their off-springs' views, that the parents are not conventional conformists. Most activists come from a very special kind of middle or upper-middle class family. Both parents tend to be college educated, the father is a professional, the mother often has a career as well, both parents and children tend to be political liberals. The student activists state that their parents have been permissive and democratic. The parents describe themselves in these terms also. These youths do not want to find meaning in their lives in terms of status and role. Neither are the student activists, by and large, interested in copping out. They are willing to assume some of the dominant values of our culture. They are willing to contribute, but they are not willing to work for things that only have a price tag. They are not willing to make the compromises with their own sense of integrity that the upwardly mobile child from a deprived or non-affluent environment is all too willing to make. To the person willing to compromise and to the conformist, growing up means developing a cynical attitude toward the virtues. Thus, becoming conservative does not often mean desiring to conserve the best in man, but becoming a conformist, a compromiser, a "realist." The student activist rejects this. He has a basic concern with individual development and self-expression, with a spontaneous response to the world. The free expression of emotions and feelings is viewed as essential to the development and integrity of the individual. He is also concerned with self-development and expression in aesthetic and intellectual areas. Moreover, he is concerned with the social condition of others. He has a strong humanitarian outlook. This is what accounts for the popularity of VISTA and the Peace Corps, for the campus revolts, for students joining in civil rights struggles, and for student dissent.

The self-actualizing individual is above all a doubter. Descartes' famous affirmation of his existence, "I think, therefore I am" is well known. What is often overlooked is the context of the statement. It occurs in *Discourse on the Method* and expounded in his *Meditations on First Philosophy*, in which he describes how he arrived at his insight by starting with a profound doubt about the truth of anything (Haldane and Ross, 1931). The self-actualizing person doubts. He questions the meaning of life, of existence. This is a completely different kind of anxiety from the debilitating feeling with which Freud was concerned. Existential anxiety is the anxiety that one feels as one plunges into an ever-changing, unknown world. Doubt is the mark of man.

There is a serious clash in our society today between a "successful" and "affluent" society, which demands that behavior follow relatively fixed rules of conduct as defined by tradition, and the emerging values and doubts of the new humanists. One of the stated purposes of insisting upon rules is to protect the individual against unpredictable, and possibly destructive, impulses. Some fear that we will create monsters if we permit children to actualize themselves. This is an unfounded fear, a myth. There is nothing in our study of evolution or in our study of man that warrants the conclusion that if allowed to become human, man will be other than humane. Man, humane, is not interested in destroying himself. The humanist therefore rejects fixed rules. He is more flexible. He sees the spontaneous flow of feelings and ideas as intrinsically good, indeed essential, for optimal personal growth. To the child who has grown up in a humanistic environment, pursuit of the status goals encouraged in him by society, by the public school, by college means hypocrisy, and the sacrifice of personal integrity.

THE FULLY FUNCTIONING FAMILY

Implicit in the foregoing is the notion that the fully functioning family is one in which all the individuals in it are open to one another, and are open to experience. They do not take stereotypical roles. They do not confuse conservatism with conformity. The fully functioning individual will find his way to traditional values that should be conserved. A person will not find his way to them if they are foisted upon him by moral exhortation, by citation of tradition and authority. The climate in the fully functioning family is thus flexible, highly fluid, in a continuous state of process, of becoming. The members in the family are defenseless before one another. They value one another in toto, not merely for certain aspects of their behavior. Do we not want to create people who are able to work not under coercion, not without any sense of self-fulfillment, but able to work joyously, to work with the thrill and excitement of the artist, the creator? And do we not want to create people who are able to love fully and deeply, to love not only those close to them but to love all mankind?

Humanistic parents raise their children in an environment relatively free of constraints, an environment that is favorable to experimentation, expressiveness, and spontaneity. Humanistic parents stress the significance of autonomous and authentic behavior, freely initiated by the individual and expressing his own true feelings and ideas.

Parents who are afraid of children like this, then, may not have understood the meaning of self-actualization. They have not understood what it means to have a mature mind. If doubt, questioning, and non-conformity seems too high a price to pay for growth, the alternative is likely to be the payment of a much higher price in tribulation, bitterness, and despair.

REFERENCES

Allport, G. W. *Becoming: Basic Considerations for a Psychology of Personality.* New Haven: Yale University Press, 1955.

Blaine, G. B., Jr. *Youth and the Hazards of Affluence.* New York: Harper & Row, 1966.

Flacks, R. Student Activists: Result, Not Revolt. *Psychology Today,* 1967, 1, 18-23, 61.

Fromm, E. *Man for Himself.* New York: Rinehardt and Company, Inc., 1947.

Haldane, E. S. and G. R. T. Ross (Trans.) *The Philosophical Works of Descartes.* Vol. I, New York: Dover Publication, Inc., 1911.

Horney, K. *Self Analysis.* New York: W. W. Norton & Company, Inc., 1942.

Maddi, S. The Existential Neurosis, *Journal of Abnormal Psychology,* 1967, 72, 311-325.

Maslow, A. Deficiency Motivation and Growth Motivation. In M. R. Jones (Ed.), *Nebraska Symposium on Motivation,* 1955.

Maslow, A. A Theory of Metamotivation: The Biological Rooting of the Value-Life. *Journal of Humanistic Psychology,* 1967, 7, 93-127.

Mowrer, O. H. What Is Normal Behavior? In L. A. Pennington and Irwin A. Berg (Eds.), *An Introduction to Clinical Psychology.* New York: The Ronald Press Company, 1948.

Parsons, T. and R. F. Bales. *Family, Socialization and Interaction Process.* Glencoe: The Free Press, 1955.

Rogers, C. R. A Theory of Therapy, Personality, and Interpersonal Relationships, as Developed in the Client-Centered Framework. In S. Koch (Ed.), *Psychology: A Study of a Science.* Vol. 3, New York: McGraw-Hill, 1959.

Singer, M. A Survey of Culture and Personality Theory and Research. In B. Kaplan (Ed.), *Studying Personality Cross-Culturally.* Evanston: Row, Peterson and Company, 1961.

Stroller, F. H. The Long Weekend. *Psychology Today,* 1967, 1, 28-33.

Sullivan, H. S. *Conceptions of Modern Psychiatry.* New York: W. W. Norton & Company, Inc., 1940.

Wegrocki, H. J. A Critique of Cultural and Statistical Concepts of Abnormality. In C. Kluckhohn and H. A. Murray (Eds.), *Personality in Nature, Society, and Culture.* New York: Alfred A. Knopf, 1948.

HUMANISTIC PARENTING

I. David Welch
Ernest W. Flink

We can be certain that the kind of persons our children grow into depends very much upon us. As Earl Kelly once said, "When we begin to complain about the younger generation, we have to remember that there wasn't anything the matter with them when we got them." The question we have to answer is: "What kind of people do we want them to grow up to be?"

Arthur W. Combs makes the point that every good experience given a person is given forever. This means that a sincere effort, no matter how small it may appear to be, to create a climate in which another is freed to grow and become what he can become, is given forever; it may help to decide whether or not a child lives a happy and effective life of his own.

Fritz Redl, talking about juvenile delinquents, once said, "There isn't very much difference between a good child and a naughty child, but there is a world of difference between a naughty child and a real tough delinquent." Here are some guidelines which, hopefully, will help us just keep them naughty.

LOVE

History provides us with an excellent experiment that tells us how important love is in rearing a child. In the thirteenth century, Frederick II conducted an experiment to discover what language children would speak if no one spoke to them. He hired nurses to care merely for the physical needs of the children but did not permit them to cuddle or speak to the children in their care. For Frederick II the experiment was a failure because all the children died and he failed to learn man's innate language! For us the experiment testifies to the fact that children have an innate need for a great deal of love.

Harry Harlow's research with Rhesus monkeys also discloses this need for love. The monkeys were reared by either a dummy covered by

SOURCE: Reprinted by permission of the authors.

soft, cuddlesome terrycloth warmed from within by a light bulb or by a similar sized dummy with an uncovered wire frame. When given a choice the baby monkey ran to the terrycloth mother even when fed by the wire surrogate, thus showing that a baby monkey's attachment to the mother is more than merely a matter of having its physiological needs satisfied. Harlow further found that monkeys reared by the terrycloth surrogates showed much greater emotional security and curiosity. A young monkey reared by a terrycloth mother would bolt to her, embrace her, and cling passionately, even after a year's separation. Unfortunately, the love and security experienced in relationship with the terrycloth mother were not sufficient for normal monkey development and Harlow's animals grew up neurotic and sexually inadequate.

How do Harlow's findings relate to human infants? We need look no further than the work of Rene Spitz. Spitz studied the effects of institutionalization on young children. He found them to be retarded in each of the four worlds of normal development: the physical, intellectual, emotional, and social. He also found that strong healthy babies placed in orphanages grow weak, listless, joyless, and apathetic when denied a minimum amount of human warmth and attention. However, the same children, it was found, begin to recover and mature normally when cuddled and given some attention and love.

It is clear the infant or child needs more than simply having his physiological needs met. He also needs what we are calling love. Unless children are cuddled, cared for, and given love, they wither and, if the deprivation is severe enough, die. Perhaps even worse than death, such children are sent out into the world psychological cripples unprepared to face the demands and stress of daily life. They are damned to a life of inadequacy and despair. Abraham Maslow points out that if you want to create a dependent child, simply deny him the love he needs and he will cling to you for the rest of your life, always trying to discover some new method, gimmick or trick to pry loose that modicum of attention or love he so desperately needs. But if you want an independent child, a child that will grow into adulthood, well-prepared to face the frustrations of living and capable of fulfilling his love needs, you can begin now by giving him a great deal of genuine love. Adequately loving the child, you help to give to the world the kind of person it needs, one whole, happy and equally able to love others.

Arthur W. Combs (1971, p. 355) says it well:

> With our new understanding of human potential, we now understand that stupidity and maladjustment are not "the will of God" but the lack of will of men. . . . In previous times our production of stupid and depraved people was excusable because we didn't know any better. That excuse no longer exists! We now know that con-

stant deprivation leads to depravity, while *being given* leads to growth. In light of that knowledge, we live in grievous sin if we do not act upon it. If we do not help the next generation to expand its world, we have failed everyone—the child, the parents, our institutions, the nation itself. It is in our own best interest to help expand the world of children. But even if we do not act upon our new understandings for such selfish reasons, we ought to do it anyhow—*just because we LOVE them* (emphasis ours).

LIMITS

We can all remember as teenagers that just before leaving the house we were told when to be home. As that preordained hour approached, things seemed to pick up and we went home certain that we were missing all the fun. Then came the night when we were told to decide for ourselves what time to be home. More often than not, we discovered that there really wasn't a lot to do at one in the morning. Our hours adjusted themselves and we adopted a routine of getting enough sleep to handle our responsibilities. We only stayed out very late on special occasions.

This is not, it is evident, a cry for permissiveness but a plea for instilling responsible freedom in our children. As parents it is our responsibility to facilitate the growth of responsible freedom in our children. By limits, we mean a broad and encompassing way of life that provides a sense of security while allowing the child to exert his freedom and explore the world. One of the great misconceptions attributed to the "permissivists" is that they are said to insist that we should permit the child to do anything he desires to do. This, of course, is nonsense, and so is the belief that children should be allowed to do anything they are capable of doing!

One author has said that when the child discovers a hammer the whole world becomes a nail. If we permit the child, who has discovered a hammer, to do anything he wants to do, we may not only be driven to distraction (as we are anyhow) but be driven literally, perhaps, into our kitchen floor!

What the permissivists argue against are the arbitrary, inane, senseless and stupid regulations we sometimes insist our children follow when we neither believe in nor follow them ourselves. They argue that children are neither chattel nor property owned as some people use to own slaves. They are human beings—admittedly immature human beings—who must be treated as persons if they are to develop as persons.

What we must realize, as well, is that children *are* persons. Of course, they are inexperienced persons, unwise about many things, and positively stupid about some others. Piaget has demonstrated that a child thinks in the concrete until approximately eleven years of age. When setting limits for children who are younger we must tie these limits to something concrete. For example, concerned about the safety of young children, we want to prevent them from playing in the streets. But simply telling a child he may be hit by a car often doesn't work. The child may feel that a car doesn't hurt; on the contrary, to the child a car is something that takes him to get an ice cream cone. The child doesn't head for the street in defiance of our orders. He goes there because it is an exciting part of his world. As an adult it is our job to supply a concrete reminder that he must venture out only so far in his exploration of the world. A fence, of course, is best, but a painted line *might* suffice as a concrete reminder to the child that his world has some boundaries.

The question we have to answer is: "What kind of limits or, more appropriately, what kinds of freedom can our children have?" The answer depends on the amount of freedom for which they can be responsible.

How much freedom can a two-year old have? How much responsibility can he assume? Not much. But he can decide things like which clothing he wants to wear and whether or not he's hungry.

How much freedom can a twelve-year old handle? Certainly, more than a two-year old!

How much freedom can a twenty-two year old handle? As much as he has learned to handle by assuming, throughout his life, a greater and greater degree of responsibility for his own life.

It is important that an individual's limits and responsibilities within the family be defined or chosen democratically. Each member is a vital part of the family unit and should participate in establishing the limits or rules under which he will live. When people play a part in the setting of rules, they have an easier time following them. In the happier, more harmonious home, rules and regulations are not imposed or merely forced on others; they are the results of shared decisions, genuine concern, and mutual trust and respect.

LISTENING

There's a television short which dramatizes the experience of a boy who rushes into his home to tell his mother about some great happening in his life. The mother, who is preparing the evening meal, is too busy to listen and sends him on to his father. The father ignores him and continues to read the evening paper. So the little body leaves the house, his story untold, to find his dog who listens gladly.

Listening means sitting down and listening to the child talk. It doesn't mean what many parents mean when they say, "I had a talk with my son today." Too often this means that the kid sat there passively while the parent talked. If we had to describe some parents today, we would describe a head with eyes, nose, mouth and NO EARS! Listening means not telling, not lecturing, but sitting still and hearing (as parents so often admonish their children to do).

Our children have important things to tell us about the world they experience and one they often understand better than we do. One way to be more open to their understanding of their experienced world is to be more receptive to their language and life styles. For our youth it was "cool," "man," and "ducktails." For many it may have been "23 Skidoo" and "ain't that the berries." Today it's "rip off," "snowbird," and "rap." But beside these trivial things (because language is relatively unimportant to people who are really trying to understand each other) we need to recognize our children have important questions to ask because they can learn significant things from us. For example, when a five-year old asks, "Mommy, do some people not want their babies?" his question may be his attempt to find out if such children exist and to establish that he is not one of them.

Listening to our children affords them a chance to grow emotionally. All of us have both short- and long-term emotional feelings that need to be expressed or shared to facilitate our becoming more fully functioning human beings. When a child says, "I hate you, Daddy!" he is probably saying that he is angry and that, at the moment, you are not his favorite person. If as an adult we react to his anger by saying, "Nice boys don't say that!" or "You are not allowed to say such things!" we deny or reject his feelings and give him two problems instead of one. Now he is made to feel guilty for not only what he's said but for what he feels.

We must avoid falling into the trap of denying the child a meaningful place in the family, one in which he is freed to be, to disclose who he is. We must avoid telling the child, "I'm an adult and you are a child; I'm right and you are wrong." If we persist in such an attitude, we will continue to lose our children to the fads, drugs and securities of the counterculture simply because it has more to offer to them than we do.

LETTING-BE

Perhaps this is the hardest of all because it requires that we realize our children's lives essentially belong to them and not to us. Love has often been interpreted as "protection" and, of course, it means this some of the time. But love also means "not protecting" and respecting the right of the child to experience and learn on his own, to face and conquer the challenging situations in his experienced world and, by both failing and succeeding, grow in strength and self-confidence.

Love means, too, a psychological letting-be. We all need privacy, especially as adolescents. Perhaps what we need even more is respect for our need of privacy. A little time to sit quietly and try to confront and resolve one's doubts, fears and frustrations—without parents or brothers or sisters nosing around—is a must as children seek their own identity and their own way of being in the world.

Letting-be also means not controlling children's lives by insisting they always behave accordingly or perform appropriately. It means respecting their decisions as well as their efforts and accomplishments. We can all be proud of our children's accomplishments because they are a vital part of our lives. It is not the accomplishment that necessarily makes us proud but our children. The difference lies in respecting them as persons rather than merely respecting or loving them for their particular achievements.

Letting-be means the freedom to marry whomever they want to marry, to choose the career they want to follow. But most of all it means freeing them to develop as persons in their own right. As Gibran (1964, pp. 17-18) writes in *The Prophet:*

. . . Your children are not your children.

They are the sons and daughters of life's longing for itself.
They come through you but not from you,
And though they are with you yet they belong not to you.
You may give them your love but not your thoughts,
For they have their own thoughts.
You may house their bodies but not their souls,
For their souls dwell in the house of tomorrow, which you cannot visit, not even in your dreams.
You may strive to be like them, but seek not to make them like you.
For life goes not backward nor tarries with yesterday.
You are the bows from which your children as living arrows are sent forth . . . .

CONCLUSION

Love, limits, listening and letting-be characterize the home in which parents view parenthood as a relationship with children rather than a tightly defined role. Instead of controlling their children, such parents seek to guide their children toward responsible freedom. Instead of repeatedly criticizing their actions, such parents accept their children's inexperience and allow them time to grow toward maturity and the increasing capacity to make responsible decisions. Instead of dictating to children *their* needs, goals and desires, such parents create a democratic climate in the home in which both decisions and responsibility are shared. Instead of merely lauding their accomplishments, these parents convey to each child that he is loved, not merely when he performs well but simply because he is a person and worthy of love.

Each person deserves the opportunity to become the best person he can become. Those parents who seek to create a home environment characterized by love, limits, listening and letting-be provide such an opportunity.

REFERENCES

Combs, Arthur W. "New Concepts of Human Potentials: New Challenge for Teachers." *Childhood Education,* Vol. 47, No. 7 (April, 1971), pp. 349-355.

Gibran, Kahlil. *The Prophet.* New York: Alfred A. Knopf, 1964.

RELIGION, VALUES AND MORALITY

RELIGIOUS-TYPE EXPERIENCE IN THE CONTEXT OF HUMANISTIC AND TRANSPERSONAL PSYCHOLOGY

Peter A. Campbell
Edwin M. McMahon

The purpose of this article is to propose: (1) that a basic distinction made by Andras Angyal may serve as a convenient way to distinguish the general areas of experience which interest humanistic and transpersonal psychology; (2) that some humanistic psychologists may have allowed personal prejudices regarding the nature and alleged origins of transcendent or religious-type experiences to inhibit engaging in valid psychological study of such phenomena.

In a thoughtful article titled "A Theoretical Model for Personality Studies," Andras Angyal (1956) noted that the overall pattern of personality functioning may be described from two different vantage points which express two fundamentally diverse tendencies.

> Viewed from one of these vantage points, the human being seems to be striving basically to assert and to expand his self-determination. He is an autonomous being, a self-governing entity that asserts itself actively instead of reacting passively like a physical body to the impacts of the surrounding world. This fundamental tendency expresses itself in a striving of the person to consolidate and increase his self-government, in other words to exercise his freedom and to organize the relevant items of his world out of the autonomous center of government that is his self. This tendency—which I have termed "the trend toward increased autonomy"—expresses itself in spontaneity, self-assertiveness, striving for freedom and for mastery (pp. 44-45).

SOURCE: Peter A. Campbell and Edwin M. McMahon, "Religious-Type Experience in the Context of Humanistic and Transpersonal Psychology," *Journal of Transpersonal Psychology*, No. 1, 1974. Reprinted by permission.

It appears to us that facilitation of this first tendency toward increased autonomy or self-determination has been a major goal and concern of humanistic psychology. This does not seem to be the case, however, with the second tendency.

> Seen from another vantage point, human life reveals a very different basic pattern from the one described above. From this point of view the person appears to seek a place for himself in a larger unit of which he strives to become a part. In the first tendency we see him struggling for centrality in his world, trying to mold, to organize, the objects and events of his world, to bring them under his own jurisdiction and government. In the second tendency he seems rather to surrender himself willingly to seek a home for himself in and *to become an organic part of something that he conceives as greater than himself.* The super-individual unit of which one feels oneself a part, or wishes to become a part, may be variously formulated according to one's cultural background and personal understanding. The superordinate whole may be represented for a person by a social unit—family, clan, nation—by a cause, by an ideology, or by a meaningfully ordered universe. In the realm of aesthetic, social, and moral attitudes this basic human tendency has a central significance. Its clearest manifestation, however, is in the religious attitude and religious experience (pp. 45-46).

It seems to us that the recent development of a transpersonal effort is primarily directed toward an understanding and encouragement of this second tendency.

Angyal focused attention on the religious attitude and experience as the clearest example of the second tendency. This was probably because the experience of unity and unification, of "becoming an organic part of something conceived as greater than self" lies at the heart of mystical consciousness. Most authors qualified to discuss these matters bear out such a conclusion. As William James (1958) noted,

> One may say truly, I think, that personal religious experience has its root and centre in mystical states of consciousness. . . . This overcoming of all the usual barriers between the individual and the Absolute is the great mystic achievement. In mystic states we become one with the Absolute and we become aware of our oneness. This is the everlasting and triumphant mystical tradition hardly altered by differences of clime or creed. In Hinduism, in Neo-Platonism, in Sufism, in Christian mysticism, in Whitmanism, we find the same recurring note, so that there is about mystical ut-

terances an eternal unanimity which ought to make the critic stop and think (p. 292).

W. T. Stace (1961) succinctly summarized the tendency toward union and religious-type experience: "The sense of the unity of all things, the 'unifying vision' . . . is not only *a* characteristic of all mystical experience but is the nuclear and essential characteristic." It is this serious investigation of the unitary viewpoint—perhaps most clearly manifested within religious experience but by no means restricted to it—that has caught the attention of transpersonal psychology as a legitimate area of study. This brings us to the second point we wish to make.

When considered from the vantage point of therapeutic process, a higher level of self-determination is regarded as a goal to be attained and hence as a kind of end state to the actual process of therapy. Moreover, in the practical order, before a person can *maturely* "surrender himself willingly to seek a home for himself in and to become an organic part of something that he conceives as greater than himself," it would seem that he must first enjoy a degree of self-possession, autonomy and self-determination. Yet, these are some of the precise qualities generally lacking in the person who comes for therapy. It seems to us that humanistic psychology has evolved practical, effective means for achieving a quality of self-determination consistent with its open-ended, developmental view of man and human potential. The principal focus of humanistic effort has been to foster that type of self-possession and capacity for self-determination which is a necessary first practical step along the path toward fuller human functioning.

However, a rather serious question must also be asked regarding some psychologists' attitudes toward what may well prove to be a more extensive process of personal development. It appears today that some psychologists are still influenced by preconceived notions and prejudices concerning what have been called transcendent or religious-type experiences—most often because of the traditional religious connotations associated with such phenomena. Unfortunately, such prejudicial attitudes can diminish openness and lead them to repress, deny, or in some other way block their personal development of "second tendency" or transpersonal experiences. In this way, they run the risk of cutting themselves off from both investigating and experiencing what may be an important and integral element of fuller human functioning. Moreover, such cutting off is frequently extraneous to the human value inherent in a development of this kind of experience. Rejection seems to be based upon the historical fact that such experience has often been associated with religion and anti-scientific or anti-humanistic thinking.

Such an attitude then tends to make an ultimate or final goal out of self-determination itself. But this is inconsistent with the basic concept of man as a becoming—an open-ended process, a continual-going-beyond his present level of self-actualization. A personal investment in holding to an admittedly important but, nonetheless, limited tendency toward self-determination as the ultimate value and goal in the growth process may close one off to the more extensive implications of "a growth-centered attitude" (Sutich, 1967).

Abraham Maslow realized the problems involved in any serious psychological investigation of the "second tendency" described by Angyal. Becoming an organic part of something conceived as greater than oneself inevitably tends toward the generally murky domain of mysticism with the myriad over-beliefs and dogmatic systems which have developed to explain the "ultimate cause" for this type of human experience.

There is a crucial language problem associated with studies in the transpersonal realm. While psychologists may have evolved certain concepts and explanations to describe the process and experience of self-determination, they still have extremely vague terms for the experience of "becoming an organic part of something that we conceive as greater than ourselves." Usually, this latter type experience has been left in the hands of theologians and religious leaders. Unfortunately, their quite different and sometimes highly elaborate over-beliefs about the essential nature of that ultimate "superordinate whole" with which/whom we become one, often tend to cloud the issue when attempts are made to scientifically discuss the actual human experience of transcendence and union.

Maslow (1964) found the identification of transpersonal experience with religion and the language difficulties it raised to be extremely problematic when he attempted serious study in this area.

> As a matter of fact, this identity is so profoundly built into the English language that it is almost impossible to speak of the "spiritual life" (a distasteful phrase to a scientist, and especially to a psychologist) without using the vocabulary of traditional religion. There just isn't any other satisfactory language yet. A trip to the thesaurus will demonstrate this very quickly. This makes an almost insoluble problem for the writer who is intent on demonstrating that the common base for all religions is human, natural, empirical, and that so-called spiritual values are also naturally derivable. But I have available only a theistic language for this "scientific" job.

One of Maslow's chief concerns was, as he put it:

> . . . to demonstrate that spiritual values have naturalistic meaning, that they are not the exclusive possession of organized churches,

that they do not need supernatural concepts to validate them, that they are well within the jurisdiction of a suitably enlarged science, and that, therefore, they are the general responsibility of *all* mankind.

Study and research carried out under the broad umbrella of transpersonal psychology, with its more positive image of the nature of man, would seem to provide just such a "suitably enlarged science."

Some humanistic psychologists, obviously, have chosen to focus their attention primarily on augmenting self-determination as the next *practical* step in implementing the process of self-actualization. This is a praiseworthy and legitimate goal. However, given the open-ended view of the nature of man espoused by humanistic psychology, others within the humanistic orientation are beginning to explore the "second tendency" described by Angyal. If such a move is distasteful for some because of implied religious overtones or past historical associations, it must be remembered that this is hardly sufficient reason to hinder psychological research by diverting time and energy into intramural bickering and name-calling.

The issue for transpersonal psychology is not whether the God of various religions exists or does not exist. It is, rather, the empirical fact that man acts and believes *as if* a God or "the One," "the All," "the superordinate whole" somehow exists and that man feels called, impelled, destined or meant by his very nature to extend himself into and in some way to become one with this larger reality.

People actively seek degrees of unitive experience which are not reducible to their self-assertive, autonomous tendencies. This is a fact which cannot be overlooked by psychology. Angyal stated the perspective clearly when reflecting on the meaning of love—which also cannot be reduced to man's self-assertive tendency.

> When two persons love one another they clearly or dimly have the feeling that something greater is involved therein than their limited individualities, that they are one in something greater than themselves or, as the religious person says, they are "one in God." . . . This statement does not have to be understood in a theological sense. In this context it is not our concern, e.g., whether or not the "superordinate whole" is reality or not; we state only that man appears to function *as if* he were or would experience himself as a part of a superordinate whole (p. 48).

No doubt, for some the phrase *as if* might seem to constitute a rather shaky foundation upon which to build an *empirically* based science. However, we would stress once again that the proper concern of transpersonal psychology is not to validate the existence or non-existence of the ultimate superordinate whole in itself. Rather, the starting point for psychological research is the fact "that man appears to function *as if* he were or would experience himself as a part of a superordinate whole." Such a powerful source of human motivation cannot be disregarded by psychology or disdainfully relegated to the dustbin of pathology.

Furthermore, we must not confuse empirical evidence for unitive experience which appears to go beyond man's self-assertive tendency, with validation of what may be postulated or believed in as the "Ultimate Cause" of such experience. The latter may truly be called a *belief* as far as psychology is concerned and one may, for personal reasons, label such an attitude anti-humanistic. Investigation of unitive-type experience may be confused with an effort to establish the existence of that which is sometimes interpreted to be the "Ultimate Cause" of such experience. Obviously, this need not be the case. Such experience and the motivation which it produces is not merely an unverifiable belief but an observable fact open to empirical investigation.

When transpersonal psychology seeks to better understand the universal human tendency to become an organic part of something conceived as greater than oneself, there is no conflict between pursuit of this purely secular, empirical goal and the fact that what is often interpreted as "religious" experience may be involved.

In conclusion, we have attempted to show that Andras Angyal's distinction of two tendencies in the overall pattern of personality functioning may point to the need for serious study of religious-type experience by humanistic and transpersonal psychologists. Despite the problems arising from only having available at present a "theistic language" for such a "scientific job," we feel, as did Abraham Maslow, that the issues involved are too important either to neglect them or leave them in the hands of those lacking scientific expertise for an adequate investigation.

Humanistic and transpersonal psychology appear to be well on the way toward becoming the kind of "suitably enlarged science" that can handle such a delicate scientific task. It would, indeed, be a great tragedy if we bypassed the opportunity to work together in accepting the responsibilities and challenges of such a new venture.

REFERENCES

Angyal, A. A theoretical model for personality studies. In C. Moustakas (Ed.), *The self: Exploration in personal growth.* New York: Harper, 1956.

James, W. *The varieties of religious experience.* New York: Mentor, 1958.

Maslow, A. H. *Religions, values, and peak-experiences.* Columbus: Ohio State University Press, 1964.

Maslow, A. H. *Motivation and personality.* (2nd ed.) New York: Harper & Row, 1970.

Stace, W. T. *Mysticism and philosophy.* London: Macmillan, 1961.

Sutich, A. J. The growth-experience and the growth-centered attitude. *J. Humanistic Psychol.,* 1967, 7, 2, 155-162.

HUMANISM IN A TIME OF RELIGIOUS REVIVAL

Morris B. Storer

Why today, in an age of science and universal education, are increasing numbers of Americans turning from the firm ground of sense and reason to the promises of faith, from questing naturalism to the unquestioning embrace of supernaturalism?

The American experience from the beginning prepared the minds of the settlers for the revivalist's appeal. All of them—men *and* women—were absorbed in demanding practical affairs as they moved in to open up a virgin continent. There was little time for philosophy, for taking thought about the first and last questions. People largely relied on answers provided by the religions they brought with them. The French Enlightenment was a great awakening and far-reaching education for western Europe; but it was only a distant rumble for most Americans, whose ears were tuned to a different kind of rumble—of gunfire at Lexington and Concord and Saratoga and Yorktown.

Nor was there more time or interest or respect for such total truth concern later on as the industrial revolution and the free-enterprise economy unfolded. People were busy with more important things—trying to "get ahead." And in our own time, the disillusionments of Vietnam and Watergate and the sufferings and fears and anxieties resulting from unemployment, inflation, and mounting crime rates have all been contributing factors in preparing the spirits of men and women for the revivalists' messages of hope and salvation through a force from a world beyond the unsavory natural world, a supernatural force of redeeming grace.

Conspicuous among the first-hand causes is the exploitation of television and radio by revivalists, appealing to a national audience with voices of evangelical authority, supported by bright stars of stage and playing field, and reporting and promising miracles of faith-healing and instant success in business.

SOURCE: Morris B. Storer, "Humanism in a Time of Religious Revival." This article first appeared in *The Humanist,* January/February 1977, and is reprinted by permission.

Another factor in recent years has been the frustration of the general-education movement in American colleges and universities, designed to broaden the horizon and deepen the understanding of the students. The success of the program was distinguished in many schools. But the priorities of the system we live in—the emphasis on technical advance, the drive for private profit, the concentration of power in conscienceless corporations, and the dominance of these forces in university administrative boards and offices—have blocked advance in this broadly humanistic enterprise and have cut it off at the roots in many cases. If, then, our campuses are alive today with fanatic Crusaders for Christ and Jesus freaks and Hare Krishna chanters, it is in part a commentary on this eclipse of general education. A month's study of the Bible, its authorship and development and substance, if responsible literature is available, is enough to provide most students with an entirely new perspective on the issues of revelation and scriptural infallibility; and philosophically oriented comprehensive courses in the humanities and in physical and biological and social and behavioral science produce students with eyes opened to new ranges of reality and equipped to face the serious problems of the years ahead on a more realistic basis. Such programs must be sustained and strengthened and recognized everywhere as the backbone of the system of higher education.

Do people *need* the supernatural the way they need food and clothing? Do they need a belief in God; in a personal Savior; in the immortality of the soul? There is strong evidence to the contrary in the history of Confucianism. Five hundred years before Christ, Confucius taught his followers a way of life and a moral standpoint that made no reference to the supernatural and was, in fact, agnostic about it. "The history of China might be written in terms of Confucius' influence," writes Will Durant in *Our Oriental Heritage.* "With the help of this philosophy China developed a harmonious community life, a zealous admiration for learning and wisdom, and a quiet and stable culture which made Chinese civilization strong enough to survive every invasion, and to remould every invader in its own image." The *New York Times Encyclopedic Almanac, 1970* lists the devotees of Confucianism, basically naturalistic in their orientation, as numbering over 371 million.

Yet there is obviously a *sense* of need in large numbers of people who have been reared in the environment of Christian fundamentalism and whose education has offered no alternative and no conception that there might be an honorable alternative. They hunger for what their background religion has to offer—association with people committed to the same creed, united in familiar song and ritual observance. They "need" the strength that comes from assurance of priest or preacher or rabbi that here is God's truth. No relative truth. The *absolute.* They "need" help in the torment of indecision about right course—"need" to be told;

they "need" an ear to listen to confession of sin and a voice to give assurances of forgiveness. They "need" comfort in loss, right guidance for children, and an atmosphere of mystery to relieve them of concern about the seeming contradictions of the facts.

But the sense of need springs not from the underlying human constitution but from the limitations and prejudices of the education that is provided and its failure to furnish students with an introduction to the humanist alternative. The successful funding of "The Humanist Alternative" television series for more massive programming in the coming year should be a potent corrective force.

Contemplating the wave of religious revival in all its aspects, what stance and program are appropriate for humanism? We have models that are richly suggestive:

Confucius, a source figure in world humanism, simply declined to discuss the supernatural. He turned attention from other worlds to this world, concentrating on questions of morality and wisdom in the individual and the state.

Voltaire, after devoting the greater part of his life to relentless attack on the "infamous evils" of superstition in the Church and the persecution of unbelievers, came in the end to acknowledge the virtue of tolerance, surrendered the masses to superstition and mythology, and hoped to win some "forty thousand sages" from the educated strata of the middle class—a challenge to *The Humanist* today.

Thomas Jefferson, essentially a humanist and, like Voltaire, a deist before the new light from Darwin, kept his humanism sub rosa out of political discretion and, like Confucius, devoted himself to building an enlightened idealism into the constitution of a new nation.

George Santayana, a "materialist" by his own account and a basic humanist, stood fast for a lifetime in the Catholic Church of his rearing, interpreting religion as poetry, an allegory of the truth, protesting that "there is no God and Mary is his mother," according to the tarnished epigram.

Will Durant, a humanist and prophet, in an inspiring address in Los Angeles when he and his wife, Ariel, were presented with the Humanist Pioneer Award, invoked no arming for battle, but a gentle tolerance of difference, combined with an affirmative emphasis on the examined truth in every area.

Modern humanism needs to hold before itself and the world its ancient history and its priceless heritage. And Will and Ariel Durant, in their sublime eleven-volume *Story of Civilization,* provide us a glorious textbook of that history and that heritage that every humanist should read.

The models that I have cited are largely at one in recommending that we face other beliefs with generous respect and a recognition of our own fallibility, acknowledging "need" as an understandable human basis of belief, although ultimately untenable. Consistent with this, we should devote ourselves to affirmations of our own beliefs and to spelling out the evidence and reasoning on which they rest. But nothing less than direct attack is in order when dogmatic institutional beliefs precipitate "holy wars," violation of human rights, interference with liberal education, or conspiracies against progress toward a world society of justice and freedom.

What seems called for then is a coordinated program of publication, television and radio broadcasting, and discussion in humanist-sponsored meetings and conferences in the following areas, in every case examining the implications of humanist belief for specific concrete problems: (1) the authorship and development of the Bible; (2) the meaning of truth and the avenues of knowledge; (3) the humanist moral standpoint; (4) the basis of individual freedom and responsibility; (5) the nature of purpose and the evidence of purpose in the universe; and (6) the essentials of humanist belief overall.

To such a program, organized humanism seems called upon, in this time of mass revivalism, to turn the tide and serve human advancement by calling people to the firm ground of confirmable reality.

EDUCATION

HUMANISTIC GOALS OF EDUCATION

Arthur W. Combs

Modern education must produce far more than persons with cognitive skills. It must produce *humane* individuals, persons who can be relied upon to pull their own weight in our society, who can be counted upon to behave responsibly and cooperatively. We need good citizens, free of prejudice, concerned about their fellow citizens, loving, caring fathers and mothers, persons of goodwill whose values and purposes are positive, feeling persons with wants and desires likely to motivate them toward positive interactions. These are the things that make us human. Without them we are automatons, fair game for whatever crowd-swaying demagogue comes down the pike. The humane qualities are absolutely essential to our way of life—far more important, even, than the learning of reading, for example. . . .

SELF-ACTUALIZATION—PRIMARY GOAL OF EDUCATION

Social scientists in recent years have given increasing thought to the problem of self-actualization. "What," they ask, "does it mean for a person to be truly operating at the fullest extent of his possibilities?" The answers they find to these questions are helping us to understand what self-actualizing persons are like and how it is possible to produce them. These studies are in many ways among the most exciting currently occurring on the psychological scene. To this point, four basic qualities seem to be central to the dynamics of such personalities. Self-actualizing persons are:

1. Well informed
2. Possessed of positive self-concepts
3. Open to their experience, and
4. Possessed of deep feelings of identification with others.

SOURCE: Arthur W. Combs, *Educational Accountability: Beyond Behavioral Objectives*. Washington, D.C.: Association for Supervision and Curriculum Development, 1973, pp. 23-40. Reprinted with permission of the Association for Supervision and Curriculum Development and Arthur W. Combs. Copyright © 1972 by the Association for Supervision and Curriculum Development.

Informed educators have taken their cues from this work.

Self-actualization is not just a nice idea—whatever we decide is the nature of the fully-functioning, self-actualizing person must also be the goal of education, as of every other institution for human welfare. The production of such persons is, after all, what it is all about. In 1962 one group of educators tackled the problem of trying to define what the basic principles of self-actualization might mean for education. This work has been published in the ASCD 1962 Yearbook entitled *Perceiving, Behaving, Becoming*,[1] a volume which is among the most popular in educational history and which, though it is now ten years old, continues to be an educational best seller.

The authors of this book began with a series of papers by four outstanding psychologists who defined the nature of self-actualization. From that beginning the educators asked, "If these things are so, what does this mean for education?"

In the course of their examination they found innumerable aspects in the current educational scene which actually prevent the development of healthy personalities. They were also led in their discussions to point the way toward new objectives for education more likely to achieve the production of self-actualizing persons than those to which we have been accustomed.

Many people believe that there is no place in our educational structure for "affective" concerns. They ask, "Do you want education for intellect or adjustment?" As though it were necessary for us to make a choice between the production of smart psychotics and well-adjusted dopes! Affective, healing aspects of behavior are not something separate and apart from cognition. Modern psychologists tell us that affect or feeling is simply an artifact of the degree of personal relevance of the event perceived. We have no feeling about that which is of no concern to us. The greater the degree of personal relevance, the greater is the degree of feeling or affect or emotion which is likely to be experienced by the behaver. The attempt to rule out the humane aspects of life from the classroom is thus to make the classroom sterile. If affect has to do with relevance, then we are either going to have affective education or none at all. If the human qualities we expect of education are important, they must be given their proper place in the perspective we take on accountability. We cannot afford to be so preoccupied with the cognitive, behavioral aspects that we later find we have "thrown out the baby with the bath water."

Unfortunately, humane qualities are already relegated in our public schools to "general" objectives—which means they are generally ignored—while teachers concentrate their efforts on what they are going to be evaluated on. English teachers concentrate on English, coaches concentrate on winning football games, science teachers concentrate on getting students into national science competition, and elementary teachers are evaluated on how well children learn to read, write, and figure. But no one evaluates teachers on whether their students are becoming good citizens, learning to care for each other, work together, etc. Everyone knows that people tend to do those things they are being evaluated for. Indeed, it is an understanding of this fact that has brought about the pressures for accountability. If humane qualities are to be achieved, such qualities must be given front rank in importance and schools must be held accountable for their nurture.

If the four qualities of self-actualization previously mentioned are accurate, we need much more than behavioral objectives as criteria for their achievement. Such questions as a positive self-concept, openness to experience, and identification do not lend themselves to behavioral measurement. Aspects of self-actualization can be assessed, but rarely in precise behavioral terms. Indeed, the attempt to do so may even impede their effectual development. The humane qualities we seek in education, such as positive self-concepts, feelings of identification, responsibility, openness to experience, adaptability, creativity, effective human relationships are, like any other behavior, outcomes of *personal meaning;* and it is here that we need to look for answers to our problems of accountability.

THE ASSESSMENT OF PERSONAL MEANING

To deal effectively with the internal qualities of personal meaning and the humane objectives of education, a new approach is needed. Called for is a psychology that differs from the limited concepts available to us in the various forms of S-R psychology with which we traditionally have lived. What is needed is a humanistic psychology expressly designed to deal with the human aspects of personality and behavior, a psychology which does not ignore the student's belief systems but makes them central to its concerns. Fortunately, such a psychology is already with us.

The past 30 years have seen the appearance of "humanistic" psychology on the American scene. This approach has a holistic character capable of dealing quite directly with many of the more general objectives of education.[2] Psychologists attached to this new frame of reference call themselves by many names: self psychologists, transactionalists, existentialists, phenomenologists, perceptualists, and the like. By whatever name, however, these psychologists are concerned with more than the specific, precisely designed behaviors of individuals. They are deeply concerned with questions of values, human goals and aspirations, feelings, attitudes, hopes, meaning, and perceptions of self and the world. These are the qualities which make us human, and it is because of these concerns that this point of view has come to be known as the humanistic approach. Humanistic approaches to psychology, it should be clearly understood, do not deny the tenets of behavioral approaches. Quite the contrary, they include such approaches, but extend beyond them to deal with more holistic matters not readily treated in the older behavioral system. This is precisely what is needed in modern approaches to educational accountability.

Behavioral objectives provide too narrow a basis for proper assessment of educational outcomes, and our concepts of accountability must be expanded if they are properly to match the broadest goals and requirements for our educational system. Humanistic approaches to psychological thought provide us with theoretical guidelines to effective practice consistent with these broader goals. It is high time that these new conceptions be made an integral part of the training of educators and given wide dissemination throughout the profession. Interested readers may find an introduction to this position in the work of such writers[3] as Carl R. Rogers, Abraham Maslow, Arthur W. Combs, Earl Kelley, Gordon Allport, and William Purkey.

What is needed now is a systematic attempt to give principles and contributions of humanistic psychology wider understanding at every level of our educational structure. This is a point of view specifically designed to deal with the problems of personal meaning. As a consequence it is able to provide important guidelines for thinking about our broader objectives, for finding better ways to achieve them, and for assessing whether or not our educational processes have truly achieved their objectives.

If behavior is symptom and meaning is cause, then if we could somehow assess meaning we would not need to be so concerned about measurement of behavior. Meanings, however, lie inside persons and, at first glance, it would seem impossible to assess them. It is true that meanings cannot be observed directly, but neither can electricity, and we have managed to measure that pretty effectively by inference. The same thing works for personal meaning. While meanings cannot be read directly, they can be inferred by a process of "reading behavior backward." If it is true that behavior is the product of perception, then it should be possible to observe a person's behavior and infer the nature of the perceptions which produced it.

Actually, this is what all of us do in interpreting the behavior of those who are important to us. In our research at the University of Florida on the helping professions, we find it also the approach to students, patients, and clients which distinguishes effective counselors, teachers, nurses, professors, and Episcopal priests from ineffective ones.[4] Such inferences are not made by seeking one-to-one concomitants. The process calls for a holistic rather than an atomistic approach to understanding human behavior. Instead of cataloging specific behaviors, the observer uses himself as an observation instrument and observes all he can by immersing himself in the situation. By a continuous process of observing, inferring, and testing his inferences over and over, he is able in time to arrive at accurate understandings of the peculiar meanings producing the behavior in the persons he is observing. Meanings can be assessed.

The problem is not one of learning to do something entirely new. It is a matter of learning to do what all of us already do occasionally with persons who are important to us. We have little trouble being sensitive to and interpretive of meanings existing for those above us in the heirarchy, such as principals, supervisors, and superintendents. What is needed now is to learn to do these things more often, more precisely, and in more disciplined fashion with persons in positions subservient to us, such as students. These are skills that can be learned. Indeed, many fine teachers already have them.

The assessment of meaning has an additional advantage. It focuses the attention of educators on the causes of behavior directly. The attempt to catalog behaviors with too great specificity may actually take us further and further away from the basic meanings producing them. Assessing outcomes through global behavior is likely to be somewhat closer to the basic causes of behavior but may still be far less exact than we might desire. As a matter of fact, too much attention to the observation of specific behavior can seriously interfere with understanding the causes of behavior, by concentrating attention on symptoms rather than causes. Like hundreds of other teachers of "Human Growth and Development," I used to send my young teachers-in-training to observe the behavior of a child in the classroom, insisting that they should record precisely what the child did from moment to moment. These instructions were intended to discipline the student into being a careful observer.

This is still standard practice in many colleges of education. Unfortunately, what it does is to concentrate the student's attention on the behavior of the child instead of on the causes of that behavior. In recent years I have found it more helpful to send students into a classroom, not to observe it, but to participate in it. They are instructed to "get the feel" of the classroom. "See if you can figure out how the child is thinking and feeling about himself, his classmates, his teachers, the work of the school. See if you can figure out his purposes, what he is trying to do, then tell me what you saw that made you think your inference was accurate." This procedure concentrates the student's attention on making and supporting inferences about the causes of children's behavior rather than on simply observing the symptoms. I find that since we have adopted this system my students have become far more effective than previously.

If such procedures for assessing meaning seem imprecise and vague as we have described them here, they need not be. It is quite possible to make inferences with high degrees of accuracy and reliability by application of the usual tests for scientific [validity: 1) feelings of subjective certainty, 2) conformity with known facts, 3) mental manipulation, 4) predictive power, 5) social agreement, and 6) internal consistency.] . . .[5] Inferential techniques are already widely used in psychological research, especially in the study of such personal meanings as attitudes, beliefs, self-concept, and purposes. The assessment of meaning outcomes of education can be made with whatever degree of precision is desired, from informal observation to highly controlled and systematized procedures.

The exploration of highly personal meaning, of course, does not lend itself well to study by standardized techniques. There are, however, procedures in fairly wide use for the assessment of meanings of a more general sort. With a comparatively small diversion of funds and human talent currently assigned to behavioral approaches to the problem, many more could be developed within a comparatively short time. If the heart of learning is the personal discovery of meaning, the proper assessment of educational outcomes should be the most accurate possible understanding of the personal meanings being produced by the system. Use of behavioral objectives is a highly inaccurate approach to that problem. If the goals of accountability are to be achieved, we are going to have to find ways of assessing personal meaning more accurately and simply.

Traditional psychologists of S-R, behavioristic persuasion are often aghast at inferential procedures which seem to them to be grossly unscientific and subjective. Their commitment to the behavioristic approach to psychology makes it impossible for them to accept inferential techniques, even though these have long since been adopted in many of the physical sciences for solution to some of their knottiest problems. The formulation of inferences *can* be made highly accurate by use of the very same techniques as those used in any of the other sciences.

The attempt to approach accountability through assessment of personal meaning is not only likely to be more effective, it has additional advantages of great practical value in the classroom. This approach is far simpler for teachers to manage than are highly specific lists of behavioral objectives, because with such an approach there are fewer concepts to master. Attention can be given to basic principles rather than to limitless details. The teacher preoccupied with manipulating behavior is likely to find himself dealing with classroom problems through various forms of reward and punishment, or such controlling devices as force, coercion, exhortation, or bribery. Such approaches are very likely to produce their own resistance in the students whose behavior he is attempting to change. It is a part of our American heritage to resist being managed, and it should not surprise us if such techniques call forth in students ingenious and creative devices for sabotaging the system.

The teacher who is concerned about personal meanings of students is much more likely to find that his relationships with students are warmer and more human. Human aspects are not rejected but actively sought and appreciated. Empathic teachers, honestly concerned with understanding how students think, feel, and perceive are far more likely than other teachers to be liked by their students, have less problems with motivation and discipline, find themselves more successful in carrying out their assigned tasks—to say nothing of being more relaxed and happy on the job.

A major objection to inferential approaches to the study of behavior proposed by behavior modification-performance criterion advocates is that inferences can only be made from behavior, and thus this approach is no different from the goals they seek. "We are willing," they say, "that you should make inferences about behavior if you wish, but what is the point? Why not simply observe behavior?" Of course it is true that humanists must begin their studies of student behavior from careful observation of it. Every psychologist, no matter what his allegiance, must begin from that base. A major point of this discussion, however, is that sole reliance on observation of behavior is but a symptomatic approach to assessing outcomes of teaching. Approaching accountability in that fashion thus concentrates attention on the wrong dynamic, and the attempt endlessly to catalog specific desired behaviors creates an unnecessary and complicating detour for understanding.

The holistic-inferential approach to assessment offers a much more direct and efficient approach to the causes of behavior. It does not attempt to itemize all behavior or gather it up in great masses. Instead, it uses the observer himself as an effective screen for observing those aspects of behavior providing the most efficient clues to the causes he is seeking to understand. . . .

Precise answers to the assessment of personal meaning extend considerably beyond the scope of this essay. Many techniques have already been worked out, either informally over the years by persons engaging in the various helping professions or, more recently, in the work of humanistically oriented psychologists. Since a great many persons today believe the problem is important, almost certainly we should be able to make tremendous strides in this form of assessment in the future. The immediate need is to go to work on a three-pronged effort directed toward:

1. *Making meaning important.* Since people only do what seems important to them, the first step in improving our capabilities for the assessment of meaning is to regard it as an important question. This calls for encouraging teachers, principals, supervisors, administrators, and everyone else engaged in the educational effort to understand that their

inferences are important and helping them at every level to sharpen their skills in this regard. This will not be an easy task in view of the current preoccupation with strictly behavioral approaches to educational problems. The extraordinary pressures being placed on educators everywhere to emphasize such objectives leave little room for much concern with the development of skill in the assessment of personal meaning. A major first step in the encouragement of attention to personal meaning will, therefore, need to be the development of a more adequate perspective on assessment problems and deceleration of the current tallyho for behavioral objectives, behavioral modification, and performance-based criteria.

Beyond that, educators at every level of operation need to be encouraged to experiment with the assessment of personal meaning and to sharpen their own skills toward these ends. As we have previously stated, the process of inference is a matter of reading behavior backwards, and this is a process that all of us naturally use in dealing with people who are important to us. The problem for people on the firing line is to learn to do this more often, more systematically, and more effectively in their professional roles.

2. *Collection and evaluation of already existing techniques.* People have been making inferences about other people since time immemorial. As a consequence, we already have in existence ways of assessing personal meaning of an informal character accumulated through the experience of persons in helping professions over generations. A serious attempt should be mounted to gather these, assess their effectiveness, and make them more readily available to others throughout the profession.

In addition to such informal techniques, psychologists, sociologists, anthropologists, and others in the social sciences have developed an ever increasing number of more formal techniques over the past 30 or 40 years for assessing human attitudes, values, beliefs, and perceptions of self and the world. There is, for example, a very large literature on projective techniques and the use of personal documents for assessing personal meaning. Such studies need to be exhumed from wherever they are buried in the literature, examined and assessed, and made more widely available to persons who are interested in measuring personal meaning in more formal terms.

3. *The development of new techniques.* Vast sums of money are currently being poured into the effort to improve America's schools by the application of behavioral objectives approaches to assessment and by the injection of industrial techniques into every aspect of our educational effort. These tremendous capital outlays are matched by vast expenditures of human energies focused on behavioral approaches to educational accountability. We have already mentioned how this preoccupation can

actually inhibit or destroy the search for viable alternatives to educational assessment.

Most of our financial and human resources are currently focused on doing more of what we already know very well how to do. What is badly needed now is the diversion of very large chunks of these financial and human resources to the exploration of problems we have so far sorely neglected. A redistribution to concentrate efforts on the study of personal meanings and their assessment in educational settings would provide education with enormous dividends within a comparatively short time.

WHO IS RESPONSIBLE FOR WHAT?

In the final analysis, whatever success or failure education achieves will be dependent upon how effectively teachers carry out their professional responsibilities. Teachers surely must be accountable, but what can they truly be held accountable for? Current attempts at accountability recognize this principle and seek to make teachers accountable for the behavior of their students. Is this a tenable position? To answer that question we need to answer a prior one, namely, to what extent can *any* person, teacher or not, be held accountable for another person's behavior?

Since behavior is never the exclusive product of any one stimulus or set of stimuli provided by another person, it follows that no human being can ever be held responsible for the behavior of another except under three possible conditions:

1. *If the other person is too weak or too sick to be responsible for himself.* Adults have to be responsible for some aspects of children's behavior, especially acts which might prove harmful to the child or to others. The same rule applies to persons who are too sick to be able to care for themselves and who need the help of others. Acceptance of the responsibility to aid them has long been a basic tenet of our Judeo-Christian philosophy. Such conditions of responsibility are comparatively short-lived, however, existing only until the individual can care for himself. Generally speaking, the older a child becomes, the more it is necessary for him to assume responsibility for himself. The principle is clearly recognized in our courts. It is also the goal of human development as the organism strives for freedom, autonomy, and self-actualization. It ought to be the goal of education as well.

2. *If one person makes another person dependent upon him.* Whoever takes upon himself the responsibility for making decisions for another person has also assumed responsibility for his behavior. A person who, for whatever reason, has induced or seduced another to surrender his autonomy has at the same time assumed responsibility for his actions. This may occur in the case of some physicians who accept the

principle of "total responsibility for the patient." It may also occur in the case of the psychotherapist who permits his client to develop a deep transference, or in the case of a teacher who seeks to assume the role of a child's mother. Such dependent relationships may sometimes be desirable in the doctor-patient relationships.

In most of the other helping professions, not dependent on the helper *doing* something to his client, the development of such dependency is generally regarded as unfortunate and undesirable. Most modern approaches to psychotherapy, for example, carefully eschew the development of dependent relationships because they believe strong dependence of the client on the therapist saps the client's capacities to solve his own problems and unduly prolongs the therapeutic relationship. Certainly the development of dependency can have little place in education, an institution whose basic objective is the production of intelligent persons, capable of acting autonomously and freely with full responsibility for themselves.

3. *If responsibility is demanded by role definition.* Sometimes responsibility for another may be imposed on an individual by virtue of his peculiarly assigned role. An example might be the responsibility of the prison guard to make certain that prisoners do not escape. Such role-defined responsibilities for the behavior of others, however, are ordinarily extremely limited and generally restricted to preventive kinds of activities. So a teacher, by reason of his role, might be held responsible for keeping children from fighting with each other. Holding him responsible for whether or not a child does his homework is another question. One cannot, after all, be held responsible for events not truly within his control, since few of us have much direct control over even the simplest behaviors of other persons.

The basic democratic philosophy on which our society rests holds that "when men are free they can find their own best ways." Citizens are regarded as free and responsible agents. Each is held accountable for his own behavior, very rarely for the behavior of others. Educators share these common responsibilities.

But what of professional responsibility? For what can teachers be held accountable simply because they are teachers? Surely not for the behavior of students five years from now; too many others have had their fingers in that pie. The teacher's influence on all but the simplest, most primitive forms of student behavior even in his own classroom cannot be clearly established. As children get older, the less can even those few items of behavior be laid at the teacher's door. The attempt to hold teachers responsible for what students do is, for all practical purposes, well nigh impossible.

Even if this were not so, modern conceptions of the teacher's role would make such an attempt undesirable. Increasingly, teaching is understood not as a matter of control and direction, but of help and facilitation. Teachers are asked to be facilitators rather than controllers, helpers rather than directors. They are asked to be assisters, encouragers, enrichers, inspirers. The concept of teachers as makers, forcers, molders, or coercers is no longer regarded as the ideal role for teachers, a position firmly buttressed by evidence from research. Such shifts in our thinking make the act of teaching a process of ministering to student growth rather than a process of control and management of student behavior.

We are accustomed to thinking of the proper model for teaching in medical terms, of the doctor, who *knows,* telling the patient, who does *not* know, what the problem is and what must be done. Such an approach to dealing with human beings works fine when dealing with their bodies, which can be manipulated by some outside force. Applied to teaching, learning in this sense is seen as the interaction of a teacher who knows and a student who does not know.

Actually, when dealing with human affairs the reverse of the medical model is far more often required. When changes to be produced must be made inside the individual where they cannot be directly manipulated, it is the student who knows and the teacher who does not know. Counselors and psychotherapists have come to understand this relationship, and almost all new concepts of psychotherapy are based in one form or another upon an open system of operation. In my own experience as a psychotherapist I have long since given up trying to guess how my clients will solve their problems. They always find much better solutions than anything I ever thought of, and with good reason. After all, it is their problem, they are living with it, and all I know about it is what they tell me in an hour or two a week. Since they are possessed of far more data than I, it is small wonder they find better solutions than the ones I might have thought of. I find the same principle is true in working with students in the classroom, and my teaching has immensely improved since I gave up deciding in advance the precise outcomes in terms of which my students should behave.

Teachers can and should be held accountable for behaving professionally. A profession is a vocation requiring some special knowledge or skill; but the thing which distinguishes it from more mechanical occupations is its dependence upon the professional worker as a thinking, problem-solving human being.[6] The effective professional worker is one who has learned how to use himself, his knowledge, and skills effectively and efficiently to carry out his own and society's purposes. Professional teachers, therefore, can properly be held accountable for at least five things:

1. Teachers can be held accountable for being informed in subject matter. This is so self-evident as to need no further discussion.

2. They can also be held responsible for being concerned about the welfare of students and knowledgeable about their behavior. It cannot be demanded of teachers that they love children. Love is a human feeling and cannot be turned on and off at will. Besides, some children are sometimes not very lovable. Professional responsibility, however, requires

concern for the persons involved in the process, and such concern can and should be demanded of teachers and made an important aspect of assessment procedures.

3. Educators, whatever their titles, can also be held professionally responsible for their understanding of human behavior. Since people behave in terms of their beliefs, the beliefs teachers hold about what children are like and how and why they behave as they do play a crucial role in their influence upon students placed in their charge. Professional educators need the most accurate, sensitive, effective understandings about children and their behavior that it is possible to acquire in our generation. This also seems self-evident but is all too often violated in practice.

The beliefs many teachers hold about what students are like and why they behave as they do are sometimes little short of mythology. False and inadequate concepts abound throughout the profession and find expression in practices that are not only hindering, but are often downright destructive. One reason for this may be the inadequate behavioristic psychology which has served as the basic foundation for American education for more than 50 years. Whatever the reason, the beliefs teachers hold about the nature of behavior are crucial for their behavior toward students; and the character of these beliefs can and should be explored in any comprehensive attempt at assessing professional accountability.

4. Teachers may be held professionally responsible for the purposes they seek to carry out. Human behavior is purposive. Each teacher behaves in terms of what he believes is the purpose of society, of its institutions, of the schoolroom, of learning a subject, and, most especially, in terms of his own personal needs and goals. . . . So many things are done with no clear understanding of the purposes behind them. Too often the question "why" is not even asked.

The purposes held by educators play a vital role in determining what happens to students everywhere. They provide the basic dynamics from which practices are evolved. They are basic causes of teacher and administrator behavior and determine the nature of what goes on in classrooms and the schools and systems in which they exist. Yet purposes can also be explored, evaluated, and, when necessary, changed. As a consequence, any system of accountability must give the exploration, assessment, and continuous review of educators' purposes an important place in its attempt to help education achieve its fundamental objectives.

5. Professional educators can be held responsible for the methods they use in carrying out their own and society's purposes. This does not mean that educators must be required to utilize some previously determined "right" kinds of methods. So far as anyone can determine, there are no such things. Methods, in themselves, are neither good nor bad. They can only be judged in terms of the purposes they were used to advance and the impact they had on the persons subject to them.

The methods teachers use, we are beginning to understand, must be highly personal. They must fit the teacher, the students, the subject, the school, and the circumstances in which they are employed. This is likely to be a highly unique and individual matter, difficult or impossible to measure in terms of any previously concocted criteria. The essence of good professional work calls for thinking practitioners able to confront problems and find effective solutions. Often these solutions may be highly unique and incapable of measurement by standard techniques.

Professional responsibility does not demand a prescribed way of behaving. What it does require is that whatever methods are used have the presumption of being good for the client. The emphasis is not upon guaranteed outcomes but on the defensible character of what is done. Doctors, for example, are not held responsible for the death of the patient. What they are held responsible for is being able to defend in the eyes of their peers that whatever they did had the presumption of being helpful when applied. Teachers, too, must be prepared to stand this kind of professional scrutiny of their information, beliefs, purposes, and the adequacy of the techniques which they use. Whatever they do should be for some good and sufficient reason, defensible in terms of rational thought, or as a consequence of informal or empirical research. This is an area of accountability sadly overlooked in most educational thinking.

In research on good and poor teachers at the University of Florida, good teachers stand up very well under these five criteria. The good ones seem to have developed positive perceptions of their subject matter, themselves, children, purposes, and methods in the course of their growth and experience without anyone consciously attempting to instill such perceptions. One wonders what might be done to improve the quality of teaching by a systematic process of helping teachers explore and discover more adequate conceptions in each of these areas. A program of accountability focused on such goals might prove to be far more significant for the production of positive change.

In the preoccupation with behavioral objectives and performance-based criteria as approaches to the problems of accountability, the factors involved in professional competence which we have mentioned have been given little attention. If one could be assured, however, of high levels of professional responsibility in school personnel many of the problems of accountability would solve themselves. Speaking as a parent, I would be quite content to entrust the education of my children to professionally responsible teachers who understood behavior, were concerned about youngsters, knew their subjects, ascribed to positive purposes, and were willing and able to discuss and defend the practices they engaged in. If I had that I would feel little need to assess their productivity. I could rest content that in the process of responsibly carrying out their own professional goals they were also contributing to mine, my children's, and society's, too.

I have made a strong plea for broader perspectives on the problem of educational accountability. I have pointed out what seems to me to be an unfortunate and dangerous distortion of our educational effort brought about by the current preoccupation with behavioristic and industrial approaches to educational problems. In doing so I have called for greater attention to the humanistic aspects of education. Whenever humanists make such pleas they are often accused of being anti-intellectual, or of approaching difficult problems with nicey-nice unwillingness to confront hard issues.

The humanist does not ask the substitution of humanistic concerns for intellectual ones. As I have pointed out, learning always consists of two aspects: the gaining of new information on the one hand and the discovery of its personal meaning on the other. The humanist's complaint is that this balance is now badly out of kilter and education is in serious trouble, not so much for lack of providing information, but from failure to deal effectively with the meaning half of the learning equation.

What the humanist asks is redress of a balance overloaded on one half of the problem. Donald Snygg, a former colleague of mine, used to tell the story of an aboriginal tribe which believed that the worst thing that could happen to a man was that his spirit should escape from his body. Accordingly, when a man got sick people began to worry that his spirit might escape and, if local medicines and the witch doctor's charms did not prove enough, the family would gather about the patient's cot and stuff all of his body openings with a mixture of grass, leaves, and mud to keep his spirit from escaping from his body. Under this treatment, of course, the patient always died—but everyone felt better for having done something about it! Many a wrong in human history has been carried out by men of good intentions without proper perspective. The plea of the humanist for education is not that we give up behavioral approaches, but that we realistically recognize their assets and liabilities, and thereafter use them in proper balance with the humanistic aspects of the problem.

I am not opposed to accountability or even to behavioral objectives. I am opposed to oversimplification of the problem. Unfortunately, the behavioral objectives approach sounds infallible to the lay public, to industrialists, businessmen, and legislators. To them, the behavioral objectives, performance-based criteria approach seems like the perfect solution to education's problems. Professional educators should know better. If they permit this distorted view to prevail unchallenged as the primary approach to educational accountability, they will have failed everyone: themselves, the schools, society, but most of all a generation of students who will have to live out the consequences of such unquestioning capitulation to a partly right idea. At least four steps seem necessary to prevent such a tragedy from occurring:

1. Since people do only what seems important to them, *humanistic goals* for education must be rescued from oblivion and raised to front rank. There seems little hope of counteracting the iron grip of behavioristic approaches in which we currently find ourselves without much deeper understanding and appreciation of viable alternatives to accountability. These alternatives must be clearly stated, and stoutly debated in every possible arena.

2. Humanistic aspects of education and the kind of alternatives advocated here clearly must be valued. Humanistic thinking and objectives expressed in practice must be systematically recognized and rewarded wherever they are found throughout the system.

3. A moratorium on the current press for behavioral objectives should be called in order to give time for careful study of the consequences of this approach on students and teachers. Whatever is done in the name of accountability must, itself, be carefully assessed to assure that its ultimate outcomes do not interfere with the larger objectives of education. Special attention should therefore be given to the distorting effect behavioral approaches impose by almost exclusive preoccupation upon skills and the simplest, most primitive aspects of education. Whatever is done in the name of accountability must be used appropriately, and the accounters themselves must be held accountable for the effect of the practices they impose on the system.

4. A major effort designed to explore the nature of humanist thought and its implications for educational practice is called for. The effort might begin with the issues outlined here but, almost certainly, would soon find itself moving far beyond these questions to new and exciting possibilities as yet undreamed of. A place to begin might be with the deflection to more humanistic concerns of a lion's share of the funds and human energies currently devoted to championing behavioral objectives. Such a diversion would provide the means and the manpower. It would also contribute to the moratorium called for. It might even result in saving the taxpayers a great deal of money.

REFERENCES

1. A. W. Combs, editor. *Perceiving, Behaving, Becoming: A New Focus for Education.* ASCD 1962 Yearbook. Washington, D.C.: Association for Supervision and Curriculum Development, 1962.
2. A. W. Combs, D. L. Avila, and W. W. Purkey. *Helping Relationships:*

Basic Concepts for the Helping Professions. Boston: Allyn and Bacon, Inc., 1971.

3. Some sample titles are: C. R. Rogers. *Freedom to Learn.* Columbus, Ohio: Charles E. Merrill Publishing Company, 1969; A. H. Maslow. *Motivation and Personality.* New York: Harper & Row, Publishers, 1954; A. W. Combs and D. Snygg. *Individual Behavior: A Perceptual Approach to Behavior.* New York: Harper & Row, Publishers, 1959; E. C. Kelley. *Education for What is Real.* New York: Harper & Row, Publishers, 1947; G. W. Allport. *Personality and Social Encounter.* Boston: Beacon Press, 1964; W. W. Purkey. *Self Concept and School Achievement.* Englewood Cliffs, New Jersey: Prentice-Hall, Inc., 1970.

4. Combs, *Florida Studies in the Helping Professions,* University of Florida Social Science Monograph No. 37, University of Florida, Gainesville, Florida, 1969.

5. G. W. Allport, *The Use of Personal Documents in Psychological Science,* Bulletin No. 49, New York: Social Science Research Council, 1942.

6. A. W. Combs. *The Professional Education of Teachers: A Perceptual View of Teacher Preparation.* Boston: Allyn and Bacon, Inc., 1965.

SOME EDUCATIONAL IMPLICATIONS OF THE HUMANISTIC PSYCHOLOGIES

Abraham H. Maslow

The upshot of the past decade or two of turmoil and change within the field of psychology can be viewed as a local manifestation of a great change taking place in all fields of knowledge. We are witnessing a great revolution in thought, in the Zeitgeist itself: the creation of a new image of man and society and of religion and science (1, 16). It is the kind of change that happens, as Whitehead said, once or twice in a century. This is not an *improvement* of something; it is a real change in direction altogether. It is as if we had been going north and are now going south instead.

Recent developments in psychological theory and research are closely related to the changes in the new image of man which lie at the center of the larger revolution. There are, to oversimplify the situation, two comprehensive theories of human nature which dominate psychology today. The first is the behavioristic, associationistic, experimental, mechanomorphic psychology; the psychology which can be called "classical" because it is in a direct line with the classical conception of science which comes out of astronomy, mechanics, physics, chemistry, and geology; the psychology which can be called "academic" because it has tended to emanate from and flourish in the undergraduate and graduate departments of psychology in our universities. Since its first detailed and testable formulation by Watson (24), Hull (5), and Skinner (21), "classical," "academic" psychological theory has been widely applied beyond its original limited focus in such diverse areas as acquisi-

SOURCE: A. H. Maslow, "Some Educational Implications of the Humanistic Psychologies," *Harvard Educational Review*, Fall 1968. Copyright © 1968 by the President and Fellows of Harvard College. Reprinted by permission. Based on a talk given to Superintendents of member schools in the New England School Development Council, July 12, 1967. I would like to acknowledge the assistance of David Napior, Barbara Powell, and Gail Zivin of the *Harvard Educational Review* in preparing this article.

tion of motor skills, behavior disorders and therapy, and social psychology. It has answers of a kind to any questions that you may have about human nature. In that sense, it is a philosophy, a philosophy of psychology.

The second philosophy of psychology, the one which dominates the whole field of clinical psychology and social work, emerged essentially from the work of Freud and his disciples and antagonists. In light of its emphasis upon the interplay between unconscious emotional forces and the conscious organization of behavior, I refer to this school of thought as "psychodynamic" or "depth" psychology. It, too, tries to be a comprehensive philosophy of man. It has generated a theory of art, of religion, of society, of education, of almost every major human endeavor.

What is developing today is a third, more inclusive, image of man, which is now already in the process of generating great changes in all intellectual fields and in all social and human institutions (2, 6, 8, 20, 25). Let me try to summarize this development very briefly and succinctly because I want to turn as soon as I can to its meaning for learning and education.

Third Force psychology, as some are calling it, is in large part a reaction to the gross inadequacies of behavioristic and Freudian psychologies in their treatment of the higher nature of man. Classical academic psychology has no systematic place for higher-order elements of the personality such as altruism and dignity, or the search for truth and beauty. You simply do not ask questions about ultimate human values if you are working in an animal lab.

Of course, it is true that the Freudian psychology has confronted these problems of the higher nature of man. But until very recently these have been handled by being very cynical about them, that is to say, by analyzing them away in a pessimistic, reductive manner. Generosity is interpreted as a reaction formation against stinginess, which is deep down and unconscious, and therefore somehow more real. Kindliness tends to be seen as a defense mechanism against violence, rage, and the tendency to murder. It is as if we cannot take at face value any of the decencies that we value in ourselves, certainly what I value in myself, what I try to be. It is perfectly true that we do have anger and hate, and yet there are other impulses that we are beginning to learn about which might be called the higher needs of man: "needs" for the intrinsic and ultimate values of goodness and truth and beauty and perfection and justice and order. They are there, they exist, and any attempt to explain them *away* seems to me to be very foolish. I once searched through the Freudian literature on the feeling of love, of wanting love, but especially of giving love. Freud has been called the philosopher of love, yet the Freudian literature contains nothing but the pathology of love, and also a kind of derogatory explaining-away of the finding that people do love each other, as if it could be only an illusion. Something similar is true of mystical or oceanic experiences: Freud analyzes them *away*.

This belief in the reality of higher human needs, motives and capacities, that is, the belief that human nature has been sold short by the dominant psychological theories, is the primary force binding together a dozen or so "splinter groups" into this comprehensive Third Force psychology.[1] All of these groups reject entirely the whole conception of science as being value-free. Sometimes they do this consciously and explicitly, sometimes by implication only. This is a real revolution because traditionally science has been defined in terms of objectivity, detachment, and procedures which never tell you how to find human ends. The discovery of ends and values are turned over to non-scientific, non-empirical sources. The Third Force psychology totally rejects this view of science as merely instrumental and unable to help mankind to discover its ultimate ends and values (11, 18).

Among the many educational consequences generated by this philosophy, to come closer to our topic now, is a different conception of the self. This is a very complex conception, difficult to describe briefly, because it talks for the first time in centuries of an *essence*, of an *intrinsic* nature, of specieshood, of a kind of animal nature (9, 14). This is in sharp contrast with the European existentialists, most especially with Sartre, for whom man is *entirely* his own project, *entirely* and merely a product of his own arbitrary, unaided will. For Sartre and all those whom he has influenced, one's self becomes an arbitrary choice, a willing by fiat to be something or do something without any guidelines about which is better, which is worse, what's good and what's bad. In essentially denying the existence of biology, Sartre has given up altogether any absolute or at least any species-wide conception of values. This comes very close to making a life-philosophy of the obsessive-compulsive neurosis in which one finds what I have called "experiential emptiness," the absence of impulse-voices from within (12, 14).

The American humanistic psychologists and existential psychiatrists are mostly closer to the psychodynamicists than they are to Sartre. Their clinical experiences have led them to conceive of the human being as having an essence, a biological nature, membership in a species. It is very easy to interpret the "uncovering" therapies as helping the person to *discover* his Identity, his Real Self, in a word, his own subjective biology, which he can *then* proceed to actualize, to "make himself," to "choose." The Freudian conception of instincts has been generally discarded by the humanistic psychologists in favor of the conception of "basic needs," or in some cases, in favor of the conception of a single over-arching need for actualization or growth (19). In any case, it is implied, if not made explicit, by most of these writers that the organism, in the strictest sense, has *needs* which must be gratified in order to become fully human, to grow well, and to avoid sicknesses (9, 14). This doctrine of a Real Self to be uncovered and actualized is also a total rejection of the *tabula rasa* notions of the behaviorists and associationists who often talk as if *anything* can be learned, *anything* can be taught, as if the human being is a sort of a passive clay to be shaped, controlled, reinforced, modified in any way that somebody arbitrarily decides.

We speak then of a self, a kind of intrinsic nature which is very subtle, which is not necessarily conscious, which has to be sought for, and which has to be uncovered and then built upon, actualized, taught, educated (13). The notion is that something is there but it's hidden, swamped, distorted, twisted, overlayed. The job of the psychotherapist (or the teacher) is to help a person find out what's already in him rather than to reinforce him or shape or teach him into a prearranged form, which someone else has decided upon in advance, *a priori*.

Let me explore what I call "introspective biology" and its relation to new ideas for education. If we accept the notion of the human essence or the core-self, i.e., the constitutional, temperamental, biological, chemical, endocrinological, given raw material, if we do accept the fact that babies come into the world very different from each other (anyone of you who has more than one child knows that), then the job of any helper, and furthermore the first job of each of us for ourselves, is to uncover and discover what we ourselves are. A good example for pedagogical purposes is our maleness and femaleness, which is the most obvious biological, constitutional given, and one which involves all the problems of conflicts, of self-discovery, and of actualization. Practically every youngster, not to mention a good proportion of the older population also, is mixed up about what it means to be a female and what it means to be a male. A lot of time has to be spent on the questions: How do I get to be a good female, or how do I get to be a good male? This involves self-discovery, self-acceptance, and self-making; discoveries about both one's commonness and one's uniqueness, rather than a Sartre-type decision on whether to be a male or a female.

One constitutional difference that I have discovered is that there are differences in triggers to peak-experiences between the sexes. The mystical and peak-experiences, the ultimate, esthetic, poetic experiences of the male, can come from a football game, for example. One subject reported that once when he broke free of the line and got into the open and then ran—that this was a true moment of ecstasy. But Dr. Deborah Tanzer has found women who use the same kinds of words, the same kind of poetry, to describe their feelings during natural childbirth. Under the right circumstances these women have ecstasies which sound just the same as the St. Theresa or Meister Eckhardt kind of ecstasy. I call them peak-experiences to secularize them, to naturalize them, to make them more empirical and researchable.

Individual constitutional differences, then, are an important variable. It continually impresses me that the same peak-experiences come from different kinds of activities for different kinds of people.[2] Mothers will report peak-experiences not only from natural childbirth but also from putting the baby to the breast. (Of course this doesn't happen all the time. These peak-experiences are rare rather than common.) But I've never heard of any man getting a peak-experience from putting his baby to *his* breast. It just doesn't happen. He wasn't constructed right for this purpose. We are confronting the fact that people are biologically different, but have species-wide emotional experiences. Thus I think we should examine individual differences in all of our given biochemical, endocrine, neurological, anatomical systems to see to just what extent they carry along with them psychological and spiritual differences and to what extent there remains a common substratum (14).

The trouble is that the human species is the only species which finds it hard to be a species. For a cat there seems to be no problem about being a cat. It's easy; cats seem to have no complexes or ambivalences or conflicts, and show no signs of yearning to be dogs instead. Their instincts are very clear. But we have no such unequivocal animal instincts. Our biological essence, our instinct-remnants, are weak and subtle, and they are hard to get at. Learnings of the extrinsic sort *are more powerful than our deepest impulses*. These deepest impulses in the human species, at the points where the instincts have been lost almost entirely, where they are extremely weak, extremely subtle and delicate, where you have to dig to find them, *this* is where I speak of introspective biology, of biological phenomenology, implying that one of the necessary methods in the search for identity, the search for self, the search for spontaneity and for naturalness is a matter of closing your eyes, cutting down the noise, turning off the thoughts, putting away all busyness, just relaxing in a kind of Taoistic and receptive fashion (in much the same way that you do on the psychoanalyst's couch). The technique here is to just wait to see what happens, what comes to mind. This is what Freud called free association, free-floating attention rather than task-orientation, and if you are successful in this effort and learn how to do it, you can forget about the outside world and its noises and begin to hear these small, delicate impulse-voices from within, the hints from your animal nature, not only from your common species-nature, but also from your own uniqueness.

There's a very interesting paradox here, however, On the one hand I've talked about uncovering or discovering your idiosyncrasy, the way in which you are different from everybody else in the whole world. Then on the other hand I've spoken about discovering your specieshood, your humanness. As Carl Rogers has phrased it: "How does it happen that the deeper we go into ourselves as particular and unique, seeking for our own individual identity, the more we find the whole human species?" Doesn't that remind you of Ralph Waldo Emerson and the New England Transcendentalists? Discovering your specieshood, at a deep enough level, merges with discovering your selfhood (13, 14). Becoming (learning how to be) fully human means *both* enterprises carried on simultaneously. You are learning (subjectively experiencing) what you peculiarly are, how you are you, what your potentialities are, what your style is, what your pace is, what your tastes are, what your values are, what direction your body is going, where your personal biology is taking you, i.e., how you are *different* from others. And at the same time it means learning what it means to be a human animal like other human animals, i.e., how you are *similar* to others.

It is such considerations as these that convince me that we are now being confronted with a choice between two extremely different, almost mutually exclusive conceptions of learning. What we have in practically all the elementary and advanced textbooks of psychology, and in most of the brands of "learning theory" which all graduate students are required to learn, is what I want to call for the sake of contrast and confrontation, *extrinsic learning*, i.e., learning of the outside, learning of the impersonal, of arbitrary associations, of arbitrary conditioning, that is, of arbitrary (or at best, culturally-determined) meanings and responses. In this kind of learning, most often it is not the person himself who decides, but rather a teacher or an experimenter who says, "I will use a buzzer," "I will use a bell," "I will use a red light," and most important, "I will reinforce this but not that." In this sense the learning is extrinsic to the learner, extrinsic to the personality, and is extrinsic also in the sense of *collecting* associations, conditionings, habits, or modes of action. It is as if these were *possessions* which the learner accumulates in the same way that he accumulates keys or coins and puts them in his pocket. They have little or nothing to do with the actualization or growth of the peculiar, idiosyncratic kind of person he is.

I believe this is the model of education which we all have tucked away in the back of our heads and which we don't often make explicit. In this model the teacher is the active one who teaches a passive person who gets shaped and taught and who is *given* something which he then accumulates and which he may then lose or retain, depending upon the efficiency of the initial indoctrination process, and of his own accumulation-of-fact process. I would maintain that a good 90% of "learning theory" deals with learnings that have nothing to do with the intrinsic self that I've been talking about, nothing to do with its specieshood and biological idiosyncrasy. This kind of learning too easily reflects the goals of the teacher and ignores the values and ends of the learner himself (22). It is also fair, therefore, to call such learning amoral.

Now I'd like to contrast this with another kind of learning, which is actually going on, but is usually unconscious and unfortunately happens more outside the classroom than inside. It often comes in the great personal learning experiences of our lives.

For instance, if I were to list the most important learning experiences in my life, there come to mind getting married, discovering my life work, having children, getting psychoanalyzed, the death of my best friend, confronting death myself, and the like. I think I would say that these were more important learning experiences for me than my Ph.D. or any 15 or 150 credits or courses that I've ever had. I certainly learned more about *myself* from such experiences. I learned, if I may put it so, to throw aside many of my "learnings," that is, to push aside the habits and traditions and reinforced associations which had been imposed upon me. Sometimes this was at a very trivial, and yet meaningful, level. I particularly remember when I learned that I really hated lettuce. My father was a "nature boy," and I had lettuce two meals a day for the whole of my early life. But one day in analysis after I had learned that I carried my father inside me, it dawned on me that it was my father, through *my* larynx, who was ordering salad with every meal. I can remember sitting there, realizing that *I* hated lettuce and then saying, "My God, take the damn stuff away!" I was emancipated, becoming in this small way me, rather than my father. I didn't eat any more lettuce for months, until it finally settled back to what my body calls for. I have lettuce two or three times each week, which I now enjoy. But *not* twice a day.

Now observe, this experience which I mentioned occurred just once and I could give many other similar examples. It seems to me that we must call into question the generality of repetition, of learning by drilling (4). The experiences in which we uncover our intrinsic selves are apt to be unique moments, not slow accumulations of reinforced bits. (How do you repeat the death of your father?) These are the experiences in which we discover identity (16). These are the experiences in which we learn who we are, what we love, what we hate, what we value, what we are committed to, what makes us feel anxious, what makes us feel depressed, what makes us feel happy, what makes us feel great joy.

It must be obvious by now that you can generate consequences of this second picture of learning by the hundred. (And again I would stress that these hypotheses can be stated in testable, disconfirmable, confirmable form.) One such implication of the point of view is a change in the whole picture of the teacher. If you are willing to accept this conception of two kinds of learning, with the learning-to-be-a-person being more central and more basic than the impersonal learning of skills or the acquisition of habits; and if you are willing to concede that even the more extrinsic learnings are far more useful, and far more effective if based upon a sound identity, that is, if done by a person who knows what he wants, knows what he is, and where he's going and what his ends are; then you *must* have a different picture of the good teacher and of his functions.

In the first place, unlike the current model of teacher as lecturer, conditioner, reinforcer, and boss, the Taoist helper or teacher is receptive rather than intrusive. I was told once that in the world of boxers, a youngster who feels himself to be good and who wants to be a boxer will go to a gym, look up one of the managers and say, "I'd like to be a pro, and I'd like to be in your stable. I'd like you to manage me." In this world, what is then done characteristically is to try him out. The good manager will select one of his professionals and say, "Take him on in the ring. Stretch him. Strain him. Let's see what he can do. Just let him show his very best. Draw him out." If it turns out that the boxer has promise, if he's a "natural," then what the good manager does is to take that boy and train him to be, if this is Joe Dokes, a *better Joe Dokes*. That is, he takes his style as given and builds upon that. He does not start all over again, and say, "Forget all you've learned, and do it this new way," which is like saying, "Forget what kind of body you have," or "Forget what you are good for." He takes him and builds upon his *own* talents and builds him up into the very best Joe Dokes-type boxer that he possibly can.

It is my strong impression that this is the way in which much of the world of education could function. If we want to be helpers, counselors, teachers, guiders, or psychotherapists, what we must do is to accept the person and help him learn what kind of person he is already. What is his style, what are his aptitudes, what is he good for, not good for, what can we build upon, what are his good raw materials, his good potentialities? We would be non-threatening and would supply an atmosphere of acceptance of the child's nature which reduces fear, anxiety and defense to the minimum possible. Above all, we would care for the child, that is, enjoy him and his growth and self-actualization (17). So far this sounds much like the Rogerian therapist, his "unconditional positive regard," his congruence, his openness and his caring. And indeed there is evidence by now that this "brings the child out," permits him to express and to act, to experiment, and even to make mistakes; to let himself be seen. Suitable feedback at this point, as in T-groups or basic encounter groups, or non-directive counseling, then helps the child to discover what and who he is.

In closing, I would like to discuss briefly the role that peak-experiences can play in the education of the child. We have no systematic data on peak-experiences in children but we certainly have enough anecdotes and introspections and memories to be quite confident that young children have them, perhaps more frequently than adults do. However, they seem at least in the beginning to come more from sensory experiences, color, rhythm, or sounds, and perhaps are better characterized by the words wonder, awe, fascination, absorption, and the like.

In any case, I have discussed the role of these experiences in education in (15), and would refer the reader to that paper for more detail. Using peak-experiences or fascination or wonder experiences as an intrinsic reward or goal at *many* points in education is a very real possibility, and is congruent with the whole philosophy of the humanistic educator. At the very least, this new knowledge can help wean teachers away from their frequent uneasiness with and even disapproval and persecution of these experiences. If they learn to value them as great moments in the learning process, moments in which both cognitive and personal growth take place simultaneously, then this valuing can be transmitted to the child. He in turn is then taught to value rather than to suppress his greatest moments of illumination, moments which can validate and make worthwhile the more usual trudging and slogging and "working through" of education.

There is a very useful parallel here with the newer humanistic paradigm for science (11, 18) in which the more everyday cautious and patient work of checking, validating and replicating is seen, not as *all* there is to science but rather as follow-up work, *subsequent* to the great intuitions, intimations, and illuminations of the creative and daring, innovative, breakthrough scientist. Caution is then seen to *follow* upon boldness and proving comes *after* intuition. The creative scientist then looks more like a gambler than a banker, one who is willing to work hard for seven years because of a dazzling hunch, one who feels certain in the *absence* of evidence, *before* the evidence, and only *then* proceeds to the hard work of proving or disproving his precious revelation. First comes the emotion, the fascination, the falling in love with a possibility, and *then* comes the hard work, the chores, the stubborn persistence in the face of disappointment and failure.

As a supplement to this conception in which a noetic illumination plays such an important role, we can add the harsh patience of the psychotherapist who has learned from many bitter disappointments that the breakthrough insight doesn't do the therapeutic job all by itself, as Freud originally thought. It needs consolidation, repetition, rediscovery, application to one situation after another. It needs patience, time and hard work—what the psychoanalysts call "working through." Not only for science but also for psychotherapy may we say that the process *begins* with an emotional-cognitive flash but *does not end there!* It is this model of science and therapy that I believe we may now fairly consider for the process of education, if not as an exclusive model, at least as an additional one.

We must learn to treasure the "jags" of the child in school, his fascination, absorptions, his persistent wide-eyed wonderings, his Dionysian enthusiasms. At the very least, we can value his more diluted raptures, his "interests" and hobbies, etc. They can lead to much. Especially can they lead to hard work, persistent, absorbed, fruitful, educative.

And conversely I think it is possible to think of the peak-experience, the experience of awe, mystery, wonder, or of perfect completion, as the goal and reward of learning as well, its end as well as its beginning (7). If this is true for the *great* historians, mathematicians, scientists, musicians, philosophers and all the rest, why should we not try to maximize these studies as sources of peak-experiences for the child as well?

I must say that whatever little knowledge and experience I have to support these suggestions comes from intelligent and creative children rather than from retarded or underprivileged or sick ones. However, I must also say that my experience with such unpromising adults in Synanon, in T-groups (23), in Theory Y industry (10), in Esalen-type educative centers (3), in Grof-type work with psychedelic chemicals, not to mention Laing-type work with psychotics and other such experiences, has taught me never to write *anybody* off in advance.

NOTES

1. See (16), Appendix, for list.
2. For some ways in which educators can use peak-experiences, see (15).

REFERENCES

1. Braden, W. *The private sea: LSD and the search for God.* Chicago: Quadrangle, 1967.
2. Bugental, J. (ed.). *Challenges of humanistic psychology.* New York: McGraw-Hill, 1967.
3. Esalen Institute. *Residential program brochure.* Big Sur, California, 1966 and subsequent years.
4. Holt, J. *How children fail.* New York: Pitman, 1964.
5. Hull, C. L. *Principles of behavior.* New York: Appleton Century-Crofts, 1943.
6. *Journal of Humanistic Psychology.* (Periodical.) American Association of Humanistic Psychology, Palo Alto, California.
7. Leonard, G. *Education and ecstasy.* New York: Delacorte Press, 1968.
8. *Manas.* (Periodical.) Cunningham Press, South Pasadena, California.
9. Maslow, A. Criteria for judging needs to be instinctoid. In M. R. Jones (ed.), *Human motivation: A symposium.* Lincoln, Neb.: University of Nebraska Press, 1965.
10. Maslow, A. *Eupsychian management: A journal.* New York: Irwin-Dorsey, 1965.

11. Maslow, A. *The psychology of science: A reconaissance.* New York: Harper and Row, 1966.
12. Maslow, A. Neurosis as a failure of personal growth. *Humanitas,* III (1967), 153-169.
13. Maslow, A. Self-actualization and beyond. In J. Bugental (ed.), *Challenges of humanistic psychology.* New York: McGraw-Hill, 1967.
14. Maslow, A. A theory of metamotivation: The biological rooting of the value-life. *Journal of Humanistic Psychology,* I (1967), 93-127.
15. Maslow, A. Music education and peak-experiences. *Music Educators Journal,* LIV (1968), 72-75, 163-171.
16. Maslow, A. *Toward a psychology of being.* (Revised edition) Princeton, N.J.: D. Van Nostrand, 1968.
17. Moustakas, C. *The authentic teacher.* Cambridge, Mass.: Howard A. Doyle Publishing Co., 1966.
18. Polanyi, M. *Personal knowledge.* Chicago: University of Chicago Press, 1958.
19. Rogers, C. *On becoming a person.* Boston: Houghton Mifflin, 1961.
20. Severin, F. (ed.). *Humanistic viewpoints in psychology.* New York: McGraw-Hill, 1965.
21. Skinner, B. F. *Science and human behavior.* New York: Macmillan, 1938.
22. Skinner, B. F. *Walden two.* New York: Macmillan, 1948.
23. Sohl, J. *The lemon eaters.* New York: Simon and Schuster, 1967.
24. Watson, J. B. *Behaviorism.* New York: Norton, 1924 (rev. ed., 1930). Also *Psychology from the standpoint of a behaviorist.* Philadelphia: Lippincott, 1924.
25. Wilson, C. *Introduction to the new existentialism.* Boston: Houghton Mifflin, 1967.

SECTION IV
PHYSICAL
ENVIRONMENT

The Physical Environment. We have stretched the meaning of physical environment in this section to mean not only the physical world but our bodies as well. What an image it is to conceive of nature as a woman. Mother Earth. We owe our lives to her. She provides us with all we need to survive, live and grow. We grew in her womb and she bore us as mighty creatures able to manipulate our world. We are able to do more than endure our environment. We are able to change it. We have repaid her, of course, by behaving as spoiled and ungrateful children. We have raped Mother Earth in the name of profit. Some would have us scar America from one coast to another, and the fear is that, if they had a bulldozer large enough, they would plow us under and create a concrete America with neon and plastic signs lining our highways to the virtual exclusion of all else. When devoid of beauty we would lose touch with our own humanity and become merely mechanics servicing some technological horror.

While our future is surely not dependent on so frightening a future, we are confronted daily with some new ecological disaster. Humanists look with some alarm at the assumption that bigness and progress are one in the same and that any suggestion of reconsidering our attacks on the environment attacks progress or represents some foolish wish to return to the past. Rather, the humanistic position is one that asks us to consider the effects of more and more development and to figure into our equation the future costs to human beings.

Our planet has suffered the indignities of profit-motivated ecological disasters, but our people have allowed another disaster to take place as well. It might be called a disaster of the mind. Science has served as western humankind's primary tool for understanding our world. The scientific model has served us long and well. Many feel, however, that our conception of science has become too limited to continue to serve us as we come to understand more and more of what it means to be a human being. That is nowhere more apparent than in the social sciences where outdated and ineffective models of science may actually hinder further understandings of humanity and our life in the world. The humanistic position asks us to look afresh at our conception of science.

Another way of looking at the physical environment is to consider ourselves a part of it. Our own bodies can be a part of the physical world. We have tended to treat our own bodies in much the way we have treated the rest of the physical world. We have assumed that it is a machine and have acted toward it in mechanistic ways. If it is true that revolutionary thought is being used to try to save the physical environment and science, then there appears to be another humanistic revolution going on in medicine as well. No longer does everyone accept the mechanistic model that demands the impersonal treatment of patients as objects with a part or two that needs to be removed or replaced. The increasing awareness of the patient as person and the effects of the psychology of illness are causing many physicians and other medical personnel to view their clients with a new appreciation for their humanity. A part of that new concern is a new look at patients' rights and the right to die. It is the belief of many that the extraordinary means that are applied to keep patients alive may be more harmful to the patient and family than they are helpful. For some, the fear that such measures may be applied to keep them alive beyond any hope for the continuation of a meaningful life contributes to the anxiety of death.

ECOLOGY

"WE MUST MAKE THINGS SMALLER AND SIMPLER"

Sam Love

THE FUTURIST: In your writings you state that you think one of the most erroneous views underlying present economics is the idea that the problem of production has been solved. Would you elaborate on this?

SCHUMACHER: Virtually all production, including industrial production, depends on energy, and the energy is derived not from production but from nature's storehouse. We have "solved" the problem of production by turning oil into wealth. But the oil is finite in quantity, so the problem isn't really solved: The oil will run out. Look at it this way: Here is oil that is a once-and-for-all endowment of the earth. We take this oil and use it by turning it into all sorts of products which can be used to turn other materials into products. To say that we have solved the problem of production by using oil is to a large extent like saying that someone who's inherited a fortune from a rich aunt has solved the problem of earning his keep.

One of the most basic facts about our industrial system is that fossil fuels are not income, but capital. They are what we have inherited and we're just using them—and using them at a steadily accelerating rate. If I've inherited 10,000 pounds, I can have a spree for five or six months and that's the end of it: I haven't solved the problem of my livelihood by having the spree. In business we distinguish between using income that we earn and using the capital that we started with. We provide for depreciation, so that we have enough money in the kitty to restore the situation as before. But we don't do that in our economies as a whole: we just use up our capital—our fossil fuels—and we count as cost only what it costs us to fetch our inheritance out of the ground.

Take the American oil or natural gas situation. The oil production has been going on at a greatly accelerating rate for about 100 years and not only is oil more and more difficult to find but in fact it's not been pos-

SOURCE: Sam Love, "We Must Make Things Smaller and Simpler." Reprinted from *The Futurist: A Journal of Forecasts, Trends, and Ideas about the Future.* Published by World Future Society, an Association for the Study of Alternative Futures: Washington D.C., December, 1974.

sible to expand its production in the U.S. any more. Oil production reached its peak about 1970 and the projections are now that it will go down, not because people will not make more effort but because the oil just isn't there—at any rate, it's not there accessibly. It's a fool's paradise to imagine that cheap and plentiful oil will continue forever and ever, and that an economy built on cheap and plentiful oil can continue unchanged.

THE FUTURIST: Are there directions in which we can move to begin to rethink this problem of production? What is it that we should be doing now?

SCHUMACHER: We should look very calmly at what's happened over the last 100 years, and of course, most importantly in the last 30 years, since the second world war. We find that man has created a technology, a style of production, a style of consumption, and a style of settlement that are all dependent on cheap and plentiful fossil fuels. Now if these fossil fuels are no longer cheap and plentiful, what are the consequences? The technology that we have developed is extremely dependent on oil and is what you might call oil-intensive. This is illustrated in agriculture, but also in building styles, transportation, and the distribution of production units.

Our society has an immensity of transport: If I travel from London to Glasgow on one of the big motorways, I find myself surrounded by huge lorries carrying biscuits from London to Glasgow and I look across to the other lane and I find an equal number of lorries carrying biscuits from Glasgow to London. Any impartial observer from another planet would come to the conclusion that biscuits, in order to achieve proper quality, must be transported at least 500 miles. Now this criss-crossing of transport can be explained in economic terms only because transport is cheap, and it is cheap because oil is cheap and plentiful. If oil becomes expensive we can't carry on like this. We'll price ourselves out of the market with this transport.

THE FUTURIST: Could you elaborate further on the changes that we might expect in society as fossil fuels become more expensive?

SCHUMACHER: To understand them it is necessary to realize that a basic characteristic of technological development has been its creation of ever bigger units in order to increase its efficiency. For example, in the brick industry a hundred years ago a brickworks would produce 10,000 bricks a week. Fifty years later the standard was about 100,000 bricks a week. Now it's about a million bricks a week and they're talking about two, three, four, or five million in the future. If you produce ever more bricks in one place you must cart into that place all sorts of materials and more importantly you have to disperse the product over a very wide radius. The bigger the production unit, the more transport it entails. So this big unit is made possible through cheap transport, and now we have big units.

But if oil ceases to be cheap and plentiful, the most viable units will be small. We will then have local production from local resources for local use. For this mode of operating we have no technology now. Of course, I'm not talking about spices and other things that you cannot produce locally, and I'm not talking about total self-sufficiency; I'm talking about a particular development of non-self-sufficiency and geographical specialization in large units which has been made possible primarily by the cheapness and plenty of fossil fuels, particularly oil and natural gas.

THE FUTURIST: Some people feel—and in some of your presentations you have alluded to it—that we're approaching a very critical point in history and that there is a major crisis emerging in our society that will necessitate large scale social reorganization. Could you elaborate on what you see as the reasons that the crisis is emerging?

SCHUMACHER: I talk in my book about a three-fold crisis. First, at the level of man, there is a sociological crisis, with people and societies becoming more and more ungovernable. The symptoms of sickness are seen in steeply rising crime rates which have risen to a height that was not known before the second world war. In addition, we have drug addiction, truculence, discontent, and so on. You name it and we've got it. Somehow, sociologically we have an inability to solve problems. As a European I look at the United States economy and I read the statistics that the income per head is twice that of western Europe. Now if more income and more production can solve the problems, then surely the problems should have been solved in the United States. But they're every bit as big in the U.S. as they are in Europe, and in many cases bigger. Poverty has not been eliminated in America. So that is what's happening to human beings.

As for non-human living nature, you have all the environmental scares. Nature is telling us, "I can't take it any more. I'm breaking down. The burden you're placing on me is greater than I can bear." And beside the sociological crisis and the environmental crisis, we also have a resources crisis. Suddenly you find people alarmed, and they are often the same people who for decades have been saying there is nothing to worry about. Many years ago, in the early 1950s, President Truman established the Paley Commission to find out about U.S. resources, and the Commission reported that the resources were finite, but nobody took the slightest notice. All sorts of clever people said science would invent solutions, but now these same people are not so sure.

If you want a diagnosis, I come to the conclusion that our problems have a lot to do with technology which, although it is a human creation, moves somehow by its own laws without any kind of limits. While man may shape technology, technology becomes a very powerful force and starts developing by its own laws. And then technology starts shaping man, just as when a man builds a house and then lives in it, the house does a great deal to shape his personality and character. In the last 30 years, technology has been moving ahead at an accelerated rate in four directions:

First, ever increasing size of units. Things are mass-produced by ever bigger machines. That's what I call giantism. We are now far beyond the normal human scale and have reached a point where a factory spews out articles at such a rate that they have to travel around the whole globe.

Second, a tendency to let things become ever more complex. This complexity is very often created for the most trivial reasons, such as eye appeal. This applies even to fruit. There's a tremendous deployment of human science and ingenuity for pest controls so that apples should come out completely unblemished and all the same size—solely for the sake of eye appeal. The finest apples that we have in Britain—Cox's orange pippin—look quite shabby and have some blemishes, but, my goodness, they taste like paradise. Most apples from Australia and California don't. The unblemished apples require a tremendous expenditure of ingenuity and technology. People say that there are more scientists and technologists alive today than in all previous history put together, so you can see how complex society must have become to find employment for those chaps.

Third, the immense amount of capital that you have to have under your control to do almost anything. (This point is interconnected with points one and two.) In his book, *The New Industrial State*, John Kenneth Galbraith relates how the Ford Motor Company got started with a capital of $30,000. Who can start a motor car company today with $30,000? It's got nothing to do with inflation: If you double or treble this amount to allow for inflation, the question changes little: Who can start a motor car company with $100,000? A motor car company has become so complex and the scale that is necessary is so great that you have to be immensely rich or powerful to start one.

Now these three points—giantism, complexity, and high capital intensity—serve to exclude more and more people. The days are gone when a little chap who lives frugally for a few years and accumulates a little capital can set himself up and become productive and perhaps even rich—unless the chap stumbles on a unique invention. The ordinary chap can't personally do anything, so he just becomes a job seeker. Some people never desire anything more than becoming job seekers, but not all of them. The really energetic people would like to do their own thing, but technological development has made this virtually impossible, not totally but virtually.

A fourth point is that technology is becoming too violent, especially with regard to the environment. In modern agriculture, for example, we don't work with the rhythms of nature. We don't use a piece of land in accordance with the condition of the soil, and we don't save certain strains of plants when they don't produce high yields. We've got agri-business and agri-industry, or what some people call hydroponics. The soil is simply the mechanical support for the plant, which is then fed by chemical fertilizers. The health of the plant and the quality of its food are not much of a consideration, because if there should be any infestation or disease, it is killed off by insecticides, fungicides, or herbicides. This I call a violent technology.

After all, the globe has only an extremely thin film of living soil and we are bombarding it with a vast array of poisons. Mind you, we are finding again and again that poisons which have been used for many years and have been hailed as wonderful achievements are suddenly prohibited because people have discovered—after using them for decades—that they are not harmless. So we are really playing poker with the very existence of biological life. Human beings with judgment are no longer able to do things; it's now machines churning away.

THE FUTURIST: Given that we've come to this crisis point, what directions can we move in to begin to create a more positive future?

SCHUMACHER: Recognizing the four trends—giantism, complexity, capital intensity, and violence—suggests the direction in which we should be looking. The questions we must raise are: Can't we make things smaller, so that they're not so oppressive? Aren't there simpler solutions? Do things have to be so complicated and complex? Can't modern knowledge produce equipment that's not so expensive? Finally we must deliberately say, "No, this technology is too violent. We want a non-violent, soft technology."

I'm not suggesting that we redirect 100% of our research and development in this opposite direction, but that we should do some research on these questions. If 5% of the research and development expenditures of American industry were devoted to looking in the opposite direction, you would discover (as we are discovering in our own work) that you can make things small, so that small people can make themselves productive. You can make things far simpler. You can devise technological methods so that people can start with very little capital and you can achieve a much greater degree of non-violence—and that's really worth going for. And then if a cataclysm or other real difficulties come, you have a chance of survival.

THE FUTURIST: Can you give us some practical examples of where these ideas are being implemented?

SCHUMACHER: Let's take farming: It's no longer a matter of debate among knowledgeable people that you can achieve just as high yields with organic methods. Organic farming is possible and productive, although it's not easy to make a living at it in a society supported by chemical farmers. There are many organic farmers who make a very good living and have very high productivity per acre without all the backing of official research which helps the chemical farmers. In Britain the government expenditure per annum for agricultural research is about 35 million pounds per year and none of it supports organic farming. All the research is for the benefit of chemical farmers, with the exception of plant breeding, which helps organic farmers also.

Nothing is done specifically to solve the problems of organic farming, and yet we have organic farmers in Britain, in the United States, in Australia and in many countries making a good living and achieving good yields. The inputs which they require from industry are minimal. They are not bothered now—except for certain mechanical equipment—by the petroleum crisis. So let's put some effort behind this. Let's learn from these people. Let's spend some of the immense amounts spent on research and development to find out about compost piling and so on. We can develop more suitable equipment. You know a combine harvester used to have a little appliance that collected the weed seed, but not any more. Why? Because we have herbicides that just kill the weeds, so we don't mind where the seed falls. This is a brutal way of going about farming. The organic farmer needs a harvester which will have an appliance to collect the weed seeds.

In fact, I know of many farmers who tinker about and design such appliances by themselves. But you don't get a good job done with pure amateurs. We have lists and lists of problems that the organic farmers are crying out to get attention paid to, but no one takes any notice. These problems should be attended to, and it wouldn't cost 35 million pounds a year to do this research. A small percentage of the current expenditure for agricultural development would take care of the proper requirements of this alternative system.

A similar approach can be applied in other areas: If we develop a more decentralized mode of production we will find that carrying biscuits from Glasgow to London and simultaneously from London to Glasgow is not very clever. We would also find that we must consider more than new transport technology, because an intelligent person doesn't try to solve transport problems merely by using new gadgets and streamlining (as we do inside a factory); instead he would solve the problem by minimizing the *need* for transport, that is, by arranging things so that goods from the factory don't have to be shipped criss-cross all over the place.

Now let's consider industry: I think that a non-violent technology, based on small units, that lends itself to use by people who are not very sophisticated or very rich and powerful would be a blessing in every respect. The moment you have smaller communities which the mind can encompass, people realize that they *are* somebody and they *do* count. That creates a feeling of responsibility and then if they are responsible citizens instead of just masses, they will also behave responsibly.

I admit that is a bit speculative, but through intermediate technology and small scale operations we coud achieve a social structure that is far more ecologically sound, soft on resources, and sociologically satisfying than what we have now. For example, in an industry where production units of a thousand tons a day are considered normal, we have had design studies made which show that one 150th of that scale—6½ tons a day—is also economical. We have developed a machine for the production of packaging material for eggs where we reduced the scale to 2% and also cut the capital cost to 2%, and it was fantastically economical, because instead of having one unit we could have fifty.

A large and complex unit requires top-level management and all sorts of systems, whereas a unit 2% of that size can be managed without any bureaucracy. It can be managed in your head, as it were. The ideal is to have a minimum of administration, not a maximum, because administration is very difficult. If it's badly done, it ruins the whole thing. And people who can do this very difficult job well are not very common, and those very able people really want to do the actual job. If you drag them up to the top of the large organization, then you're missing them down below. And if you have people at the top who are not masters of the art of administration, then the first-class brains you have down below get frustrated. Transport, size, administration—one should look upon them as things to be minimized, not maximized.

THE FUTURIST: Could you distinguish between appropriate and intermediate technology? Do you see a difference between them?

SCHUMACHER: I started both these terms. In development economics, everyone took technology for granted. But I said that the rich man's technology is not necessarily appropriate for poor countries and that it cannot be appropriate for rural areas. What would be an *appropriate* technology? Something intermediate—intermediate between the very low level of technology that exists in the rural areas of the third world and the very highly sophisticated technology that the rich countries deploy. If you ask me how I define intermediate, that's just what I've been doing when I state these four criteria: Intermediate technology will tend towards *smallness* and *simplicity*. It won't be very capital intensive, and it will tend in the direction of non-violence. It will fit into the rural areas and will be within the reach of poor people.

THE FUTURIST: Do you see this as the technology of the future or do you see nuclear fission or nuclear fusion as tomorrow's technology?

SCHUMACHER: I'm not prepared to really talk about fusion because I know that the time to develop that technology is going to be very long. You will not see any measurable contribution to world energy supplies through fusion in your lifetime, and I certainly won't see it in my lifetime. The lead time is far too long. We have an energy problem now!

We have no experience on earth of the sun-like temperatures necessary for the fusion reaction. And if you imagine that this degree of violence can occur on this earth without ecological and other consequences that nobody even dreams of, then I think you are just dreaming. So fusion is out for any sensible discussion. Now nuclear energy is already a reality and to me the most terrifying, the most depraved, and the most irresponsible technology that exists because of its radioactive byproducts.

THE FUTURIST: There is almost a wave breaking in the publishing industry of dystopian or very pessimistic literature. Probably the most popular one in this country is Robert Heilbroner's book, *An Inquiry into the Human Prospect.* Others, like Roberto Vacca's *The Coming Dark Age,* have received some attention in Europe. What do you view as the real prospect for the future?

SCHUMACHER: I once reviewed Heilbroner's book *The Great Ascent* and I said that this man is a dreamer. He's gone in his psyche on this great ascent, and after the great ascent comes the fall into despondency. I think it's an inevitable reaction of any man against his earlier totally unjustified, fantastic optimism. I think we should take a very sober view, and the sober view is the view of people who are prepared to do some work. I mean that if somebody tells me that the oil supplies to Great Britain will be cut in half, that reduction would mean a reduction of about 30% in total supplies. Well, only 30 years ago we used about 60% of what we're using now and we had a decent society and nothing to be afraid of.

The only thing to be afraid of is fear and despondency and the paralytic reaction to changes which prevents people from doing anything. Let's get down to work. Let's look at agriculture, at transport, at industry, at the distribution of population, at all our arrangements, and let's get busy. There are lots of people who are already in tune to the problems and we can do something. Sitting around moaning doesn't help. I have no sympathy with two classes of people—the doom-watching pessimists, because they just spread paralysis, and the Herman Kahn-type optimists, who are the blind leading the blind.

What we need are what I would call optimistic pessimists who can see clearly that we can't continue as before, but who have enough vigor and joyfulness to say, all right, so we change course. I know it can be done and it will be done if people are not paralyzed by either the optimists or the pessimists.

VOLUNTARY SIMPLICITY AND THE UNFOLDING OF MAN

Duane S. Elgin

THE ECOLOGICAL FLOW OF THE UNIVERSE

Many persons who have explored the further reaches of human awareness agree on an essential perception: behind the apparent disarray of random events there is a deeper harmony, a moving point of equilibrium and balance, a patterned unfolding of reality as a symphonic whole. In China, this patterned flow of the universe is called the Tao. Although it may be given a name, it is a process and experience beyond dogma, ideology, philosophy, or religion. It is "the way of the universe, the norm, the rhythm, the driving power in all nature, the ordering principle behind all life" (Smith, 1958). Although a concept traditionally identified with Eastern perspectives, it is nonetheless becoming an increasingly common notion in the West. This is reflected, for example, in the writing of the mathematician, Norbert Weiner (1954): "We are not stuff that abides, but patterns that perpetuate themselves; whirlpools of water in an ever-flowing river."

Congruent with this view of reality, the essence of wisdom is to act in harmony with the Tao, or natural rhythm of the universe. Smith also characterizes the basic quality of life in tune with the universe as "creative quietude"—a process that combines within a single individual two seemingly incompatible conditions: supreme activity and supreme relaxation. Creative quietude *(Wu Wei)* is "the supreme action, the precious suppleness, simplicity, and freedom that flows from us, or rather through us, when our private egos and conscious efforts yield to a power not their own" (p. 181). Other forms of life act this way spontaneously and unconsciously. But man, being conscious of his acts, occupies a unique role as a knowing participant in evolutionary processes. Thus, man bears an awesome responsibility for acting in ways that do

---

SOURCE: Reprinted by permission.

not disrupt the flowing equilibrium of the universe. LeGuin (1972) poetically describes Taoistic action in man and nature:

> . . . an act is not, as young men think, like a rock that one picks up and throws, and it hits or misses, and that's the end of it. When that rock is lifted, the earth is lighter; the hand that bears it heavier. When it is thrown, the circuits of the stars respond, and where it strikes or falls the universe is changed. On every act the balance of the whole depends. The winds and the seas, the powers of water and earth and light, all that these do, and all that the beasts and green things do, is well done, and rightly done. All these act within the Equilibrium. From the hurricane and the great whale's sounding to the fall of a dry leaf and the gnat's flight, all they do is done within the balance of the whole. But we, insofar as we have power over the world and over one another, we must *learn* to do what the leaf and the whale and the wind do of their own nature. We must learn to keep the balance. Having intelligence we must not act in ignorance. Having choice, we must not act without responsibility (p. 74).

Thus, actions that abuse our conscious, co-creative role in the evolutionary flow will rebound and, directly or indirectly, obtain their ecological retribution from persons and societies that have disrupted the equilibrium. If this is true, then it is important to examine the flow of industrialization in the West and the extent to which this flow has been resonant or discordant with the Tao.

THE DISRUPTIVE FLOW OF THE INDUSTRIAL PERIOD

The industrial revolution began with its own Taoistic-like premises—limited as they were. Adam Smith, in 1776, postulated the "Tao of socioeconomic processes":

> Every individual endeavors to employ his capital so that its produce may be of greatest value. He generally neither intends to promote the public interest, nor knows how much he is promoting it. He intends only his own security, only his own gain. And he is in this led by an *invisible hand* to promote an end which was not part of his intention. By pursuing his own interest he frequently promotes that of society more effectually than when he really intends to promote it (p. 423).

Western man's image of self during the industrial period was far different from the perennial wisdom associated with a deeper understanding of the Tao. Man perceived himself as rationalistic (able to calculate what was in his own self-interest), mechanistic (a part of the larger productive system), individualistic (responsible for taking care of himself), materialistic (with material ends as the primary, if not exclusive, reward and control mechanisms), and master of his own fate (man is uniquely apart from nature, so that it was his destiny to master the natural environment) (Elgin, 1974). Although these value premises did not specify the form of society that would evolve, they did articulate the ground rules from which it would emerge.

Where has the socioeconomic Taoism of the industrial period led? Judged on its own terms, the industrial transformation has been an enormous success in achieving what its internal dynamic premised as its major objective: the realization of an unparalleled level of material abundance for a majority of people. Nonetheless, it no longer seems proper to judge the industrial era on its own terms. The value premises of the industrial era, and the social form they support, fit neither the prevailing physical reality nor our growing appreciation of what it means to be human. Our powerful technologies coupled with an expressed belief in our right—indeed, obligation—to subjugate nature to our own ends have allowed us to achieve, at best, only a temporary stalemate in our struggle against nature. However, in struggling against nature we are gradually discovering that we have been struggling against ourselves. Only now are we finding that the mind of man—though powerful enough to create technologies for the manipulation and destruction of nature on a vast scale—is not powerful enough to comprehend or assume responsibility for that which has been manipulated and destroyed. We mistake our power for wisdom. Indeed, our mastery of nature is a deception, for it presumes that we are apart from nature. Because we have acted with only partial awareness—without taking the time to learn "what the leaf and the whale and the wind do of their own nature"—we have upset the equilibrium and have torn the fabric of the universe, which now returns to exact its ecological reparation.

Our outer world reflects our inner conditions; environmental degradation, alienation, urban decay, and social unrest are mirrors of the shortness of our vision of man and the universe. The arrogance of an anthropocentric perspective that places the Tao of man above that of the universe has brought us to the edge of disaster as we confront the possibilities of nuclear holocaust, world famine, population out-stripping our resources, and global environmental poisoning.

RESTORING THE BALANCE (I)—THE EMERGENT TAO OF SOCIETY

The idealistic vision of Taoistic action has become a pressing and realistic need. We cannot afford a lesser vision as we cope with enormously difficult and complex problems that reach global proportions. To realize this vision we must pause and, with stillness of mind, attempt to discern more clearly the overall pattern of social change that is emerging about us. With a clearer understanding of the emergent order and rhythm of social form, we may be able to act with greater insight and wisdom. But what is the Tao of social form—that is, the social currents, forces, pushes, pulls, depletions, and newly forming streams of human activity that merge into one continuous stream of social evolution? Presented below, in an austere simplicity that cannot begin to reflect the rich, organic complexity of reality, are personal perceptions of the natural flows of social form that seem to be emerging. Three dominant flows are considered: the failing impetus of the industrial paradigm, the pushes by natural and political ecology that are deflecting us from the social trajectory defined by the industrial paradigm, and the gathering strength of pull from an emerging image of humankind—predicated on the voluntary simplification of material aspects of life, coupled with exploration of non-material/inner aspects of life. These flows are considered, in turn, below.

The Diminishing Impetus of the Industrial Paradigm

"Paradigm" refers here to the total pattern of values, beliefs, perceptions, and ways of acting that are characteristic of a culture. Thus, to say that the industrial paradigm is losing momentum is to say that the interdependent constellations of values, beliefs, and behaviors of the industrial era are collectively faltering. In short, the powerful engine of technological advance and economic growth, predicated on the seemingly unstoppable drive of our "economic will to power," now appears to be running out of steam. A number of factors may account for this.

Our cultural learning (through schools, work, and family) is supposed to mold and shape the rough outlines of personality and behavior and thereby provide a shared cultural context for existing in our society. Yet, the enculturation process seems to be breaking down; the cultural "glue" that makes our social system a cohesive whole seems increasingly ineffectual. The rapid pace of social change, the enormity and complexity of our social institutions, the demise of the extended family, the high rates of geographic mobility that further loosen once secure ties and bonds—all have converged to create an anarchic and confusing enculturation process. By organizing for economic efficiency, we have inadvertently disorganized our traditional enculturation mechanisms; it is no wonder then that we are set adrift and lost from any firm cultural moorings.

We confront a massive tangle of complexity in our social, political, and economic systems. We have aggregated comprehensible systems (small towns, and small transportation and communications networks) into supersystems of incomprehensible complexity. Our capacity to create powerful supersystems does not automatically confer a commensurate capacity to comprehend that which we have created. Consequently, we are increasingly dependent upon those supersystems but are incapable of understanding them, thus becoming the victims of a technological society that we created to serve us.

In our present form of social organization, we seem to be reaching the threshold of efficient organization and intruding upon a region of "diminishing social returns." In other words, we must expend enormous energy—physical, social, political—simply to maintain our complex socioeconomic system. Further growth of that system, in its present form, requires inordinate amounts of additional energy to yield increasingly smaller increments of real improvement in the overall quality of life.

People are beginning to question that which we do best; namely, the creation of unparalleled levels of material affluence for masses of people. We have extended a rational concern for material well-being into an obsessive concern for unconscionable levels of material consumption. However, while many yet live in material poverty, many more have experienced the affluent life and have come to know an inner poverty and alienation. Poverty can indeed make us unhappy, and there is no shortage of that in America; however, the overriding reality is that of wasteful and extravagant levels of material consumption, which inhibits the realization of our larger human potentials. We are possessed by our possessions, consumed by that which we consume.

In sum, we are compelled to rethink what life means and where we wish to go. We are obliged to sort out the trivial from the significant, the ephemeral from the durable, and to find an alternative image of human and social possibility that captures our collective imagination and provides a renewed sense of direction as we proceed into the future.

Deflecting Pushes from Natural and Political Ecology

Even if the momentum of the industrial paradigm were not abating, there are strong forces that are deflecting our society from the historical trajectory of increasing material growth. The success of our industrial era has been predicated, to a substantial degree, on the existence of an inexpensive and abundant supply of energy and raw materials. Now, however, we confront a "new scarcity," which is inexorably invalidating the crucial premise of energy and material abundance.

For example, the costs of nuclear energy, in both money and potential hazard, are escalating and will probably inhibit the introduction of a critically needed energy source at a time when we are stretching traditional sources to their limits (Armstrong and Harman, 1975). Further, we have overestimated the existing reserves of natural gas and oil, which in turn will make the day of reckoning even sooner (Science, 1975). Despite the rhetorically ambitious program (Project Independence) to attain energy self-sufficiency, it seems most plausible that we will become increasingly dependent on energy controlled by international cartels such as the Organization of Petroleum Exporting Countries.

Industrialized nations are becoming increasingly dependent on developing countries to supply them with raw materials. U.S. reliance on imports of major industrial raw materials has grown steadily since 1950, and by the end of this century the United States is expected to be dependent on foreign sources for virtually all of its principal raw materials (Brown, 1975). Many of these raw materials are localized within small groups of developing nations that will probably form cartels much like OPEC. Thus, both natural and political ecology may combine to raise the price of important raw materials and to further inhibit industrial production.

The problems of energy and materials scarcity are exacerbated by a growing world food crisis, which is compounded by an apparent adverse shift in world climate patterns and by continued high rates of world population growth (Elgin, MacMichael, and Schwartz, 1975). Thus, it seems unlikely, in a world fast becoming a global village, that the United States will be able to maintain grossly inequitable levels of consumption. The new scarcity is not a transient phenomenon; it is a real and enduring feature of the global environment and will inexorably push us toward a level and form of consumption much more consistent with the pressing reality of global shortages and vast inequities in material well-being.

If we were to look no further than this, the future would seem bleak indeed. An industrial apparatus faltering under its own weight and pressed to alter its trajectory by natural and man-made "limits to growth" presents a desperate picture. Without a sense of alternative possibility to pull us into a desirable future, the social prospect is analogous to that of pushing on a string—with the string of our social fabric merely bunching up in front of us the harder we push. Our constructive evolution requires an additional element—an individual and social vision equivalent to that of pulling on the string—a coherent and practical image of the future that respects and integrates the diminishing and deflecting pushes considered above.

The Pull of Voluntary Simplicity

As the pace and confidence of industrialism slows and as its direction is turned by the new scarcity, hard necessity dictates that we forge a new relationship with the material aspects of existence. A river overflowing its banks and finding its new level and channel is an uncertain process unless there is at least a partial new channel ready to redirect its flow. Likewise, how awkward and difficult the rechanneling of social form will be will depend on the clarity and rapidity with which a new image of individual and social possibility becomes manifest. The skeletal outlines of this new relationship are gradually emerging, although we cannot specify in detail what its exact form will be. We face a situation much like the advent of the industrial era when societies were undergoing the upheaval of defining the ground rules, or value premises, from which a new social order would grow. Even an approximate awareness of the unmanifest flow of social form is critically needed to lend direction and perspective to present actions. Explored below is one emerging dimension of social flow that may give greater coherence and Taoistic balance to current social actions—namely, the movement towards voluntary simplicity.

Historically, in the West in general and in America in particular, consumption has been viewed as a primary end of human activity. This view is reflected in the customary measure of man's happiness—his "standard of living"—which is calculated almost exclusively in material terms. We have attempted to maximize consumption, implicitly assuming that the level of consumption is directly related to the level of human well-being and happiness. This seems an ill-founded and excessively limiting assumption for approaching the totality of human satisfactions. There is growing evidence that, beyond the level of material "sufficiency," money does not buy happiness. After a survey of this topic, Easterlin (1973) concludes:

> When everyone acts on [the assumption that more money will bring more happiness] and incomes generally increase, no one, on the average, feels better off. Yet each person goes on, generation after generation, unaware of the self-defeating process in which he is caught up (p. 10).

Thus, the attempt to buy happiness is an illusory phenomenon, "a distant, urgently sought, but never attained goal" (Easterlin, p. 10).

In visceral response to this knowledge, a growing number of people appear to be adopting an alternative life-style, which, though materially more modest, is overall more satisfying and enriching. Voluntarily simplifying the external/material aspects of one's life may significantly contribute to the enrichment of internal/nonmaterial aspects. The late Richard Gregg, in a prescient article written in 1936, eloquently states the rationale for voluntary simplicity.

> Voluntary simplicity involves both inner and outer conditions. It means singleness of purpose, sincerity and honesty within, as well as avoidance of exterior clutter, of many possessions irrelevant to the chief purpose of life. It means an ordering and guiding of our energy and our desires, a partial restraint in some direction in order to secure greater abundance of life in other directions. It involves a deliberate organization of life for a purpose. Of course, as different people have different purposes in life, what is relevant to the purpose of one person might not be relevant to the purpose of another. Yet it is easy to see that our individual lives and community life would be much changed if every one organized and graded and simplified his purposes so that one purpose would easily dom-

inate all the others, and if each person then reorganized his outer life in accordance with this new arrangement of purposes—discarding possessions and activities irrelevant to the main purpose. The degree of simplification is a matter for each individual to settle for himself.

Though perhaps appealing, it is yet unclear what voluntary simplicity may mean when translated into daily life-worlds. An initial attempt to define how voluntary simplicity may become manifest is explored in Table 1.

Although voluntary simplicity may be a practical response to the new scarcity that we confront, there is little reason to think that such "frugality" would be voluntarily adopted without a compelling purpose to motivate its acceptance. What, then, is the pull to frugality/simplicity? First, whatever the purpose or magnetic pull, it needs to be strong enough to elicit a willing frugality from people. Second, it needs to be consistent with traditional values that respect individual freedoms. Third, it must be both idealistic (thereby offering a compelling image of future possibility to give direction) and pragmatic (showing respect for the real material problems that we confront). A purpose that fulfills the above needs is that of exploring, in community with others, the internal/nonmaterial frontier of man himself, coupled with voluntary simplification of the external/material aspects of life. Material necessity seems to coincide with evolutionary possibility, so that we might restrain the material aspect of life to explore more fully the nonmaterial dimensions of human existence. Rather than a passing fad or an escapist retreat from the real world, this seems a rational response to a pressing situation.

RESTORING THE BALANCE (II)—THE TAO OF MAN UNFOLDING

Simone de Beauvoir has written, "Life is occupied both in perpetuating itself and in surpassing itself; if all it does is maintain itself, then living is only not dying." At present, it is not clear whether we can either maintain ourselves or surpass ourselves. There seem to be two fundamental reasons for this evolutionary crisis: first, a lack of "internal" evolution commensurate with our external/material evolution and, second, a failure to recognize that "internal" growth is central to human evolutionary processes. These problems are discussed in turn below.

Our present civilizational crisis emerges, in part, out of a gross disparity between the relatively underdeveloped internal faculties of man and the extremely powerful external technologies at our disposal. When we had limited mastery of our environment, we could not do much harm. Today, with our power enormously magnified, we can do irreparable damage. Unless we expand our inner learning to match our technological learning, we are likely to exercise our magnified power unwisely, to the detriment of both man and nature. We must right the imbalance of our present era by fostering a degree of interior human growth and maturation that is at least commensurate with the enormous exterior technological growth that has occurred in the last several hundred years. If we are to assume a co-creative role in evolutionary processes then we must do, with consciousness, care, and intention, what nature does in nonconscious and instinctual ways. Aurobindo states: "Man occupies the crest of the evolutionary wave. With him occurs the passage from an unconscious to a conscious evolution." In Julian Huxley's phrase, man must assume the position of "a trustee of evolution on this earth." In assuming that role we are obliged to act with a level of awareness or consciousness that is equal to the power and responsibility inherent in that role. LeGuin (1971) describes the character of evolutionary trusteeship:

> Everything dreams. The play of form, of being, is the dreaming of substance. Rocks have their dreams, and the earth changes. But when the mind becomes conscious, when the rate of evolution speeds up, then you have to be careful. Careful of the world. You must learn the way. You must learn the skills, the art, the limits. A conscious mind must be part of the whole, intentionally and carefully—as the rock is part of the whole unconsciously (p. 161).

Metaphorically, our present social predicament may be akin to standing amid the flow of rushing water in a stream. We feel the pressures, changing currents, resistances of the water no matter which way we turn; with greater awareness we might feel secure enough to "let go" and find that we can float almost effortlessly on the surface of the water. Likewise, our consciousness must evolve if we are to become aware enough to flow with, rather than against, the gentle imperative of the Tao. Thus, the evolution of our consciousness (and supportive social forms) is not a peripheral concern; rather, it is of central importance to the successful realization of our human agenda.

Evolutionary growth is more than purely physical evolution. To be sure, the primary manifestation of evolutionary growth is physical, the material world being the medium of most overt expression of change. However, the world of physical appearance is not the sum total of the world of reality. There is another and oftentimes unacknowledged aspect of evolutionary growth: the growth of consciousness in all living things. Krippner and Meacham (1968) state:

> Throughout time, the whole universe has been moving toward greater intensity and range of consciousness. 'Evolution is an ascent towards consciousness,' wrote Teilhard de Chardin, and man is at the frontal edge of this process (p. 154).

Table 1
Changes in Values and Life-styles
Congruent with Voluntary Simplicity

• *Human Growth: Transfer of growth potential from a substantially material dimension to an increasingly nonmaterial dimension*—Arnold Toynbee, in his Study of History considers what constitutes growth of civilization; he comes to the conclusion that real growth of a civilization does not consist of increasing command over the physical environment, nor of increasing command over the human environment (power over other people). Rather, civilizational growth lies in what he calls "etherealization" or the development of intangible relationships (Gregg, 1936). As Gregg further notes, "this process involves both a simplification of the apparatus of life and also a transfer of interest and energy from material things to a higher sphere." The trend toward voluntary frugality in the material aspects of life and increasing richness in the ethereal/ephemeral dimensions of man's relationship to the universe, nature, society, and self are logical evolutionary extensions of our civilizational growth.

• *Material Growth: From a goal of material abundance to a goal of material sufficiency*—Rather than seek the maximum level of consumption, the goal may become that of ensuring material sufficiency consistent with a prevailing ethic of voluntary simplicity. What level of material sufficiency is appropriate may largely be decided by individual choice constrained by resource availability and the prevailing cultural norms. Clearly, this presumes a strong cultural context with widely shared beliefs as to approximate levels of material adequacy/sufficiency. Finally, although material growth may tend toward a steady-state condition of dynamic equilibrium, this need not imply a materially static society. With selective or differentiated growth, some sectors of the economy could grow rapidly while others may contract (for example, rapid growth of "intermediate" technology and greatly slowed growth of items of "conspicuous consumption").

• *Freedom: From believing that there is freedom in affluence to believing that there is freedom in a simplified life-style*—We have traditionally assumed that if people earn "enough" money they then have freedom to exercise choice in their pattern of consumption. However, the very act of earning "enough" money constrains the social, psychological, and material choices that one can make; for example, demands arise for conforming to a particular life-style, level and form of consumption, pattern of behavior and place of residence. Voluntary simplicity implies a life-style more detached from such demands and is predicated on the notion that simplifying one's level and form of consumption allows greater time and freedom (social, psychological, material) to explore largely nonmaterial dimensions of human growth.

• *Life Environment: From living and working in large, complex environments to living and working in smaller, less complex environments*—Smaller and less complex living/working environments seem consistent with a trend toward voluntary frugality because they are more comprehensible, more approachable, and more amenable to direction and control at a grass-roots level. This may imply, for example, the substantial migration of people from larger to smaller urban/rural environments; indeed, within the last several years, an historic reversal of population migration has occurred. The balance of recent migration flows, to the surprise of most experts, is away from large urban areas to small town and rural places (for further discussion, see Elgin et al., 1974). More generally, it seems plausible that the appeal of simplicity and smaller scales will have an effect on urban size and form, our governing processes and the degree of federalization of control, our tolerance for massive multinational corporations as the primary providers of goods and services, our large educational institutions, and so on. Consistent, then, with a trend toward voluntary simplicity would be the reconstitution of many of our social institutions and productive apparatuses at a lower level of aggregation and complexity.

• *Identity: From identity consumption to identity discovery*—For many persons in America, the most effective way to establish identity distinctions is through different styles of consumption. Consumption has become not simply an expression of identity, but is basic to the sense of identity itself. The voluntary "frugal" sector would probably avoid identity creation through the vehicle of American mass consumption—viewing it as a straight jacket into which the vast human potential cannot be compressed. Alternative ways of discovering identity could, for example, include: material frugality as a mode of identity expression; exploring the limits to social honesty and caring in group relationships; and exploring introspective/meditative sources of identity discovery.

• *Technology: From a high technology imperative to the careful application of "intermediate" technology*—The imperative of high technology assumes that virtually any technology that is possible to develop is therefore necessary and desirable (for example, the supersonic transport and the massive antiballistic missile system). An alternative is a simpler technology that is more appropriate for a conserving and frugal life-style (Schumacher, 1973). Such technology will probably be ecologically more sound, energy conserving, functional, low polluting, comprehensible by many, integrated with nature, and efficient when used on a small scale (Clark, 1975). Examples of such technology include solar and wind power generators, smaller and more efficient cars, and the Clivus Multrum toilet.

Metzner (1968) elaborates the conjunction between evolution and consciousness:

> The history of evolution has been a constant increase in awareness, an increase in the meaningful universe encountered by the organism. . . . In the course of evolution, over millions of years, increasing complexity of the brain or nervous system has apparently been accompanied by an increase in perception and consciousness (p. 21).

This persistent theme emerges from many cultural perspectives; Aurobindo (1963) states:

> An evolution of consciousness is the central motive of terrestrial existence. . . . A change of consciousness is the major fact of the next evolutionary transformation (p. 27).

Nonetheless, this is a purpose so far removed from the daily life-worlds of most people in the West that it is almost totally unacknowledged. Nasr (1974) provides an insightful metaphor.

> It is as if an audience of deaf people testified together that they did not hear any music from the performers playing before them, and considered the unanimity of their opinion as proof of its objectivity (p. 87).

Our cultural conditioning has rendered us perceptually deaf to our own higher human possibilities even though Western culture provides a more fertile ground for exploring these potentials than perhaps any in history. Nasr incisively explains how this "ignore-ance" emerged:

> Modern man has simply forgotten who he is. Living on the periphery of his own existence, he has been able to gain a qualitatively superficial but quantitatively staggering knowledge of the world. He has projected the externalized and superficial image of himself upon the world. And then, having come to know the world in such externalized terms, he has sought to reconstruct an image of himself based upon this external knowledge. There has been a series of "falls" by means of which man has oscillated in a descending scale between an evermore externalized image of himself and of the world surrounding him, moving ever further from the center, both of himself and of his cosmic environment (p. 86).

Behind the veil of our cultural hypnosis, through which we can only dimly perceive, lie vast and largely untapped human potentials. William James wrote:

> I have no doubt whatever that most people live, whether physically, intellectually, or morally, in a very restricted circle of their potential

being. They make use of a very small portion of their possible consciousness, and of their soul's resources in general, much like a man who, out of his whole bodily organism, should get into a habit of using and moving only his little finger . . . we all have reservoirs of life to draw upon, of which we do not dream.

An important dimension of the vast spectrum of consciousness into which we may evolve is revealed through so-called mystical experiences. Though called by many names (cosmic consciousness, the absolute Tao, satori, samadhi, peak experiences), they refer to experiences that have been similarly described by persons in virtually all cultures through history. The experience does *not* depend on or refer to an ideology, philosophy, or dogma; it refers to an intense, oftentimes overwhelming and ineffable experience far beyond the reach of words. Edward Carpenter (1905) wrote:

> Of all the hard facts of science, I know of none more solid and fundamental than the fact that if you inhibit thought (and persevere) you come at length to a region of consciousness below or behind thought and different from ordinary thought in its nature and character—a consciousness of quasi-universal quality, and a realization of an altogether vaster self than that to which we are accustomed . . . it is to wake up and find that the I, one's real, most intimate self, pervades the universe and all other beings—that the mountains and the sea and the stars are a part of one's body and that one's soul is in touch with the soul of all creatures.

These expanded states of awareness appear to constitute the *highest* common denominator of human experience. This is a profoundly hopeful discovery in that, before the people of the world can cope with the problems of our global village, there must be some degree of shared agreement as to the nature of "reality" within which we collectively exist. Mystical experiences may provide an important element of that common agreement at a level that transcends cultural differences. Yet, are these experiences so far removed from the daily life-worlds of most people that they are without significance, being essentially unapproachable and unattainable? Apparently not. Results from a recent national poll (Greeley and McCready, 1975) indicate that mystical experiences "are widespread, almost commonplace, in American society today." One may infer from the poll data that at least 40% of the adult American population has had what may be termed mystical experiences. Though perhaps infrequent, spontaneous experiences of expanded perception do exist; nonetheless, they are largely unacknowledged and unintegrated into our contemporary cultural experience.

Throughout history, many persons have spontaneously attained expanded states/processes of awareness. Fewer have had the opportunity and the inclination to "train" themselves to explore the further reaches of human awareness. Further, the conscious, purposeful evolution of consciousness has not been a substantial possibility for most people, and for good reason: A vast proportion of all human history has seen the majority of the world's population engaged in one essential enterprise—that of survival. Only a few people have had enough determination in the face of material adversity to surpass themselves when occupied with the fight to maintain themselves physically. The struggle for subsistence has placed substantial constraints on any pervasive and intentional evolution of man's consciousness. Our era of relative abundance contrasts sharply with the material poverty of the past. Today, with simplicity, equity, and wisdom we can have both substantial freedom *from* want and freedom *to* evolve our consciousness as individuals in community with others. The industrial revolution, then, may be viewed as a major evolutionary breakthrough that provides the material base to support the pervasive, intentional evolution to expanded states/processes of individual and sociocultural awareness.

Returning to an earlier theme, how does this evolutionary advance fit with the notion of voluntary frugality? Human needs, values, and beliefs seem to be hierarchically ordered so that "higher" needs emerge when "lower" needs are relatively satisfied (Maslow, 1954; Graves, 1974). This concept implies that as we become relatively satiated materially, other needs arise to assume a place of primary importance. In the scheme of Western humanistic psychologists such as Maslow and Graves, these higher needs include those of friendship, love, and "self-actualization" (realizing higher states of awareness). Emergence of a new scarcity corresponds to a time when many persons (with important exceptions, given inequitable material distribution) have become relatively satiated at the material needs level. Consequently, increasing numbers of people now appear to be seeking satisfaction at higher levels. An effective way to do this is by reducing material needs (by voluntarily simplifying one's life-style), which in turn allows a transfer of interest and energy to the exploration of nonmaterial dimensions of life.

Thus, economic necessity (which dictates either enforced or voluntarily assumed simplicity), Taoistic "necessity" (which impels us to evolve our awareness to assume evolutionary trusteeship), and human possibility (to evolve to higher levels of awareness/consciousness) all combine to create what seems to be a gentle but increasingly insistent evolutionary imperative toward individual and societal transcendence.

If we are to realize this "new frontier" of social and human possibility, it seems likely that something akin to the following "ethics" must emerge. First is a Self-Realization Ethic, which asserts that each person's proper goal is the evolutionary development of his fullest human potential. Accordingly, this ethic insists that social institutions provide an environment supportive of self-realization. Second, we must develop an Ecological Ethic, which accepts our earth as limited, recognizes the underlying unity of the human race, and perceives man as an integral part of the natural environment. These two ethics—the Self-Realization Ethic and the Ecological Ethic—are two sides of a single coin. Orchestrated with one another, they leave room for both cooperation and for wholesome competition, for sociality and individuality. Indeed, each serves as a corrective for possible excesses or misapplications of the other (Elgin, 1975).

Accepting the challenge of this new frontier neither denies nor turns away from our earlier, largely external/material frontier. Both necessity and opportunity require a change in proportion and balance—a shift in the center of social gravity—toward the nonmaterial dimension of an evolving human consciousness. This is not to deny our technological and economic achievements; rather, we must build on them if we are to progress into the next frontier. Yet, for some, the inward turning implied by this new frontier could be seen as an escapist retreat from the hard problems of the "real world." A growing interest in enhanced human awareness could be dismissed as a return to the superstitions and irrationalities of an earlier, more gullible age. Some may insist that we stand at the violent conclusion of all history, while others reassure that we now stand amid a changing stream of social evolution that reflects the first glimmerings of a profound change in human awareness. This frontier, like all new frontiers, generates both hope and despair as different people look upon its possibilities.

CONCLUSION

A number of themes have been explored in the preceding pages, and it may be useful to summarize the major ones here:

- There is a dynamic, flowing equilibrium in the universe; nature keeps that balance unconsciously, instinctively; man must keep the balance by learning to do so consciously; he is the trustee of conscious evolution on this earth.
- The restrictive "economic Taoism" of the industrial period no longer seems appropriate to prevailing physical realities or human possibilities; though a path that yields seeming power over nature, it is one that lacks the wisdom and heart to allow us to maintain the delicate balance with the larger Tao.
- Our industrial society is currently experiencing a loss of momentum and drive—largely because of the self-limiting properties of our large complex systems—and a deflection from the societal trajectory of extrapolated industrialism because of the emergence of new scarcity.
- Our industrial society is now beginning to experience the gentle

tuggings of a practical and hopeful alternative life-style/values constellation called voluntary simplicity, which implies the voluntary simplification of the material aspects of life and the transfer of a greater proportion of our drive for growth to exploring, in community with others, inner human potentials.

• Exploring those inner potentials is central to the human agenda; individual and civilizational growth are both manifest in the degree to which we evolve our consciousness in ecological harmony with others.

• Without the compelling process/goal of exploring our inner potentials, it seems unlikely that there will be sufficient motivation to adopt voluntarily a life-style of greater material simplicity. Without greater simplicity, it seems unlikely that we will be able to cope successfully with the problems of the new scarcity.

• Finally, unless we explore our inner potentials, it seems unlikely that we will develop the degree of internal maturation necessary to act as wise trustees of conscious evolution on this earth.

The foregoing themes stand in marked contrast to prevailing social realities. How, then, do we get from our present societal circumstances to those implied by voluntary simplicity and the unfolding of man—if indeed that is where we want to go? On the one hand, incremental change is typically seen as being inadequate to overcome the resistances of institutions that must somehow be fundamentally changed. On the other hand, revolution might cause so much social disruption that the cure could be worse than the disease. Perhaps we first need a *conceptual revolution* that allows us to view the process of social change as being different from any change allowed by either of these two perspectives. If we could view individual and social evolution as a dynamic process that is an integral part of our daily human lives, then it might be less difficult to pursue the creative, experimental, and open-ended process of social and individual transformation. The goal becomes not a static end state, but rather a continuous process of human and social growth. This concept was expressed by Dunn (1971) in his phrase, "process teleology," in which human beings

> . . . establish the process of human development as the goal of the process of social evolution. Both the process and the goal are understood to be open to further transformation as we advance with the practice and understanding of them (p. 244).

A conceptual revolution, then, could allow us to transcend the conflict inherent in the tension between a revolutionary and an incrementalist perspective of social change. Revolutionary changes at the conceptual level in the short run (accompanied by substantial incremental changes at the operational level) could lead eventually to a thoroughgoing transformation of our society.

In conclusion, hard material necessity and human evolutionary possibility now seem to converge to create a situation where, in the long run, we will be obliged to do no less than realize our greatest possibilities. We are engaged in a race between self-discovery and self-destruction. The forces that may converge to destroy us are the same forces that may foster self and societal discovery. The path of discovery requires us to first learn the way of the universe—the gentle imperative of the way of the Tao.

REFERENCES

Armstrong, J., and W. Harman, *Plausibility of a Restricted Energy Use Scenario*, Center for the Study of Social Policy, Stanford Research Institute, Menlo Park, California (January 1975).

Aurobindo, S., *The Future Evolution of Man* (All India Press, India, 1963).

Brown, L. R., "The Discontinuities Before Us," *The Futurist* (June 1975).

Carpenter, E., *Towards Democracy* (G. Allen and Unwin, London, 1905).

Clark, R., "Characteristics of 'Soft' Technology," *The Futurist*, (December 1974).

Dunn, E. S., Jr., *Economic and Social Development: A Process of Social Learning* (Johns Hopkins Press, Baltimore, Maryland, 1971).

Easterlin, R., "Does Money Buy Happiness," *The Public Interest*, No. 30 (Winter 1973).

Elgin, D. S., "Economic Man: Servant to Industrial Metaphors," in *Changing Images of Man*, Stanford Research Institute, Menlo Park, California (May 1974).

Elgin, D. S., et al., "City Size and the Quality of Life," Stanford Research Institute, Menlo Park, California (November 1974); also available through the U.S. Government Printing Office, Washington D.C.

Elgin, D. S., "The Third American Frontier: The Evolution of Consciousness and the Transformation of Society," Center for the Study of Social Policy, Stanford Research Institute, Menlo Park, California (1975); also to appear in Association for Humanistic Psychology textbook, 1976.

Elgin, D. S., D. MacMichael, and P. Schwartz, "Alternative Futures for Environmental Policy Planning: 1975-2000," Stanford Research Institute, Menlo Park, California (September 1975).

Graves, C., "Human Nature Prepares for a Momentous Leap," *The Futurist* (April 1974).

Greeley, A. M., and W. C. McCready, "Are We a Nation of Mystics?" *New York Times Magazine* (January 26, 1975).

Gregg, R., "Voluntary Simplicity" (1936); reprinted in *Manas*, Los Angeles, California (September 4 and 11, 1974).

James, W., in "Letter to W. Lutoslawski," *William James on Psychical Research*, G. Murphy, ed. (Viking Press, New York, New York, 1969).

Krippner, S., and W. Meacham, "Consciousness and the Creative Process," *The Gifted Child Quarterly* (Autumn 1968).

LeGuin, U., *The Farthest Shore* (Atheneum Publishers, New York, New York, 1972).

LeGuin, U., *The Lathe of Heaven* (Avon Books, New York, New York, 1971).

Maslow, A., *Motivation and Personality* (Harper, New York, New York, 1954).

Metzner, R., "On the Evolutionary Significance of Psychedelics," *Main Currents* (September-October 1968).

Nasr, S. H., "Between the Rim and the Axis," *Main Currents* (January-February 1974).

Schumacher, E. F., *Small is Beautiful* (Harper Torchbooks, New York, New York, 1973).

Science, "Geological Survey Lowers Its Sights," Vol. 189 (July 18, 1975).

Smith, A., *The Wealth of Nations* (The Modern Library, New York, New York, 1937).

Smith, H., *The Religions of Man* (Harper & Row, New York, New York, 1958).

Weiner, N., *The Human Use of Human Beings* (Avon Books, New York, New York, 1954).

SCIENCE

TOWARD A SCIENCE OF
THE PERSON

Carl R. Rogers

I share with Maslow and others the view that there are three broad emphases in American psychology. These resemble three ocean currents flowing side-by-side, mingling, with no clear line of demarcation, yet definitely different none the less. Like the flotsam and jetsam which floats on each ocean current, certain words and phrases identify, even though they do not define, these separate flowing trends. Associated with the first trend are terms such as *behaviorism, objective, experimental, impersonal, logical-positivistic, operational, laboratory.* Associated with the second current are terms such as *Freudian, Neo-Freudian, psychoanalytic, psychology of the unconscious, instinctual, ego-psychology, id-psychology, dynamic psychology.* Associated with the third are terms such as *phenomenological, existential, self-theory, self-actualization, health-and-growth psychology, being and becoming, science of inner experience.*

What I wish to do in this paper is to consider the question: What are the consequences, for psychological theory and research, of the third stream of thought—the phenomenological, existential, self-theory stream? In considering this question there will doubtless be occasional comparative glances at each of the other currents of thought, yet the primary emphasis will be upon the third.

I would like to make it clear at the outset that I am speaking only for myself, from the perspective which my own experience has given me. I am certainly not attempting to speak for psychology as a whole. And though I consider myself a part of this third trend, I am not attempting to speak for it. It is too diversified, its boundaries too vague, for me to endeavor to be a spokesman. Rather, as a member of this group, I shall be concerned with the meaning that this current has in modern psychological life as I perceive it. Toward what shores, what islands, what vast-

SOURCE: Carl R. Rogers, "Toward a Science of the Person," *Journal of Humanistic Psychology,* Fall 1963. Reprinted by permission. Paper prepared for a symposium on "Behaviorism and Phenomenology: Contrasting Bases for Modern Psychology" at Rice University, Houston, Texas, March 20-22, 1963. The author would like to acknowledge his indebtedness to Allen Bergin and Eugene Gendlin for very helpful suggestions and criticisms of the manuscript.

nesses of the deep is its compelling current carrying us? What will it mean for psychology as a science that this current has become a part of our profession?

THREE WAYS OF KNOWING

In order to lay a ground work for what I wish to say, I should like to comment upon our process of "knowing." All knowing consists essentially of hypotheses, which we check in different ways. These hypotheses may be regarded as proven beyond question, or they may be held very tentatively. They may be concerned with any content whatsover, from "2 plus 2 equals 4," to "I am beginning to love her"; from "She hates her mother," to "I am six feet tall"; from "He is an untrustworthy person," to "e equals mc^2."

Sometimes we endeavor to divide such hypotheses as I have given, such examples of knowing, into objective and subjective knowledge. Perhaps this is not a helpful dichotomy, since every instance of knowing involves coming to terms in some way with the subjective and phenomenological. To me it has been helpful to think of three ways of knowing, ways which differ primarily in the manner in which we check our hypotheses. Let me describe these three approaches, though I would stress the fact that there are also other ways in which we may view this process of knowing. The threefold perspective I shall describe seems to me especially relevant to psychology and other behavioral sciences.

SUBJECTIVE KNOWING

Within myself—from within my own internal frame of reference—I may "know" that I love or hate, sense, perceive, comprehend. I may believe or disbelieve, enjoy or dislike, be interested in or bored by. These are all hypotheses, which we often check, as Gendlin (9) has shown, by using the ongoing flow of our preconceptual experiencing as a referent. So I may check my hypothesis by asking, "Do I really hate him?" As I refer to my experiencing, I realize that it is envy rather than hate which I feel. Or I may wonder, "Do I love her?" It is only by reference to the flow of feelings in me that I can begin to conceptualize an answer. In respect to another situation, I am placed by a psychologist in a dark room in which there is a pinpoint of light. I am asked if the light moves, or if it is stationary. I consult my experiencing of the situation and I say that it is moving. (The fact that "objectively" it is stationary will be dealt with later.) I form an inner hypothesis from the experiencing going on in me.

I hope these fragmentary subjective examples will give some sense of the fashion in which a person tests, within his own skin, the inner hypotheses which he forms. These hypotheses are corrected by being more sharply differentiated, by becoming more precise and accurate. Anyone who has experienced psychotherapy will have lived through this way of sharpening or of contradicting previously held inner hypotheses. Often an example of it in psychotherapy is the way in which the client searches and searches for the word that will more accurately describe what he is experiencing, feeling, or perceiving. There is a sense of real relief when he discovers a term which "matches" his experiencing, which provides a more sharply differentiated meaning for the vague knowing which has been present, which permits him to be more congruent within himself (9, chaps. 1, 7).

The person who has tackled a complex new job, or who is faced with complicated data in a research, has also experienced this same process within himself. At first his "knowledge" of the task is global, imprecise, undifferentiated. Then he begins to sense pattern—that these events or these facts seem to go together, that these other events or facts, while they loom large on the surface, are probably not important. He act tentatively to test these inner hypotheses, moving forward when the pattern is sensed as becoming stronger, or correcting his direction when his sense of the pattern fades. Polanyi (21, chap. 3) has given an excellent description of the compelling pull which an inner sense of the significance of pattern has upon the scientist.

Thus one important way of knowing is through the formation of inner hypotheses which are checked by referring to our inward flow of experiencing as we live in our subjective interaction with inner or outer events. This type of knowing is fundamental to everyday living. Note that though external cues and stimuli may be involved in this type of hypothesis formation, it is not the external situation against which we test our hypotheses. It is our inner experiencing to which we refer to check and sharpen and further differentiate the conceptual hypotheses we are forming from the implicit meanings.

Since this mode of knowing is not infallible, does not lead to publicly validated knowledge, little attention is given to it today. Yet this seems to me our most basic way of knowing, a deeply rooted organismic sensing, from which we form and differentiate our conscious symbolizations and conceptions.

I would voice the opinion that even the most rigorous science has its origin in this mode of knowing. Without the creative inner hypothesis, all the machinery of outward verification would be sterile. As Einstein said in regard to his search for the principle of relativity: "During all those years there was a feeling of direction, of going straight toward something concrete. It is, of course, very hard to express that feeling in words; but it was decidedly the case, and clearly to be distinguished from later considerations about the rational form of the solution" (32, pp. 183-184).

This aspect of science—the creative inner hypothesis which is checked and rechecked against the relevant aspects of one's experiencing, and which may then eventuate as the formal hypothesis to be operationally tested—has been greatly ignored in American science. Especially has it been ignored in American psychology, where it has been considered slightly obscene to admit that psychologists feel, have hunches, or passionately pursue unformulated directions. Curiously enough, we are indebted to a strict behaviorist for a case history of his research development which freely describes this all-important subjective phase (26, pp. 76-99). Here the account of the development of his investigative directions is studded with such phrases as "This was, of course, the kind of thing I was looking for," "I was bothered by," "I can easily recall the excitement of," "Of course, I was working on a basic assumption." Such phrases point up a sorely needed emphasis—that science always has its *beginning* as an inner subjective hypothesis, highly valued by the investigator because it makes patterned sense out of his experiencing.

It may be mentioned in passing that if I try to test these inner hypotheses by checking with others or with the external environment then we have passed to the "objective" way of knowing. If I ask you, *"Am* I falling in love?" or *"Is* this light moving?" then I am using intersubjective verification, and this is part of another way of knowing.

OBJECTIVE KNOWING

Let us turn to this way of knowing which has been so highly regarded as "objectivity." In this type of knowing, the hypotheses are based upon an external frame of reference, and the hypotheses are checked both by externally observable operations, and by making empathic inferences regarding the reactions of a trusted reference group, usually of one's colleagues. Thus, if a physicist says that he "knows" that the speed of a freely falling object is expressed by the formula $v = 32t$ (where $v =$ velocity in feet per second, and $t =$ time in seconds), what he means is that various individuals whom he trusts have each gone through similar operations, which can be precisely described, and have observed similar results, and each has arrived at a similar subjective conviction, which is expressed in the formula, which is understood in a similar manner by all. The physicist believes the convictions *are* similar because he has exercised his own empathic ability in understanding the communications of, and the internal frame of reference of, these others. This psychological process is the basis of all logical positivism, operationalism, and the vast structure of science as we know it. Its achievements have been most impressive.

There are certain characteristics of this approach which have not been sufficiently understood. It deals only with observable objects and, in order to study any problem, must view its elements only as publicly observable objects. Thus, if I wish to study the effect upon myself of a

fever-inducing drug, I observe myself as an object. The rise of temperature in degrees upon the thermometer, the observable flush which
ensues—these are the kinds of qualities which can be a part of this objective knowing, since these are observable by others, and my observations can be checked by another. Objectivity can only be concerned with
objects, whether these are animate or inanimate. Conversely, this way of
knowing transforms everything it studies into an object, or perceives it
only in its object aspects.

There is another characteristic of this approach, which is concerned
with the direction of the empathy of the knower. In the first mode of
knowing, the subjective mode, it would be accurate to say that the
knower is directing his capacity for empathy toward himself, trying to
understand more deeply the implicit meanings of his own experiencing
and to make those meanings more explicit. In the objective mode of
knowing, empathic understanding is directed solely toward the reference
group. Perhaps an illustration will help here.

Suppose a psychologist wishes to introduce an event into his experiment which will be a stimulus to his experimental animal. What is a
stimulus? If he is to be objective, there are, I believe, only two possible
and related criteria. The event must be one which is understood to be and
accepted as a stimulus by his psychological colleagues. Or if he wishes to
be even more precise, then others, as well as himself, must see the later
behavior of the animal as a response to this event, which therefore
defines it for each observer as a stimulus, and this conclusion is known to
the experimenter through his capacity for understanding the internal
frame of reference of these others. This matter is well discussed by Jessor
(12, 13). It should be clear that a stimulus is not a simple objective event,
but a mutually understood, and mutually agreed upon, subjective perception by qualified colleagues. The same reasoning applies to such terms as
"response" and "reinforcer" as well.

It must be evident that the choice of a reference group is extremely
important in this type of knowing. Polanyi (21, pp. 216-222) has pointed
out the intricate web of overlapping appraisals which functions for the
scientist in choosing, more or less consciously, a respected group who in
some sense confirm each other as careful observers, and whose communications, properly understood, are the mechanism of intersubjective
verification.

The importance of the reference group is perhaps best shown by
mentioning some reference groups which are too narrow. In any closed
system, intersubjective verification can be obtained by admitting to the
group only those who have agreed in advance to a series of observations
or beliefs which will *not* be questioned. Thus, many religions, the Communist party, orthodox psychoanalysis—to mention a few—obtain intersubjective verification of knowledge by admitting to their groups only

those who have agreed in advance not to question core elements of the structure. Most of us regard the knowledge which emerges in these systems as having a pseudo objectivity rather than a true objectivity. In general, the broader the range of individuals who are regarded as a competent reference group, the surer is the basis of knowledge obtained through this way of knowing.

There is still another point to be made about this objective way of knowing. Since it has had such vast importance, and since it has led to such incredible technological advances, it is often forgotten that it is not necessarily superior to the first, subjective way of knowing, and that in crucial instances, it bows to it. For example, the evidence for extrasensory perception is better than, or certainly as good as, the evidence for many of the principles which psychologists believe. Yet, with very few exceptions, psychologists reject this evidence with vehemence. It is not easy to impugn the methods which have been used in studying ESP, for they are the same as those used in any field of psychology. But the psychologist falls back on this subjective knowing. The evidence does not fit with the pattern of knowledge as he expects to find it, does not fit with his experiencing of the world. Therefore he rejects it.

There have been many instances of this sort in the history of science. Sometimes the intuitive and subjective knowing of scientists in general has been upheld, and seemingly firm evidence has crumbled under some new experimental approach. But probably just as often the rejected evidence has come, in the long run, to be accepted as true (21, pp. 150-160). The reason for pointing out these crucial uncertainties is to indicate the error of the widespread notion that objective knowledge is "out there," firm, impersonal, and secure. Quite the contrary, it is a very human invention—one of enormous value, to be sure, and containing some of the best safeguards man has devised against deceiving himself—but it is none the less a fallible and human way of knowing, depending basically upon an intelligently intuitive personal selection of the hypothesis, adequate operations for testing it, the wise selection of a reference group, and the empathic understanding of the experiences of that reference group when they actually (or more often in imagination) repeat the operations of the experimenter.

INTERPERSONAL KNOWING, OR PHENOMENOLOGICAL KNOWLEDGE

Logically somewhere in between the two types of knowing I have discussed is a third mode which applies primarily to knowledge of human beings and the higher organisms, and which, for lack of a better term, I have called interpersonal knowing. Here I "know" that you feel hurt by my remark, or that you despise yourself, or that you have a strong desire to get "to the top of the heap," or that you believe the Republican party to be an excellent organization, or that you are concerned about thermonuclear war. These knowings, like those described before, are all hypotheses. But in these instances the way of checking these hypotheses is to use whatever skill and empathic understanding is at my command to get at the relevant aspect of your phenomenological field, to get inside your private world of meanings, and see whether my understanding is correct. I may simply bluntly ask you if my hypothesis is correct, but this is often a very inadequate method of inferring your private world. I may observe your gestures, words, inflections, and base my inferences on these. Or I may—and here is the essence of my experience in psychotherapy—create a climate which makes it psychologically safe and rewarding for you to reveal your internal frame of reference. Then you find that you can share with me your unsatisfied ambition, the disgust you feel with yourself, your pattern of beliefs, or any other aspect of your world of personal meanings. In psychotherapy we have found this way of knowing to be most fruitful. Utilizing empathic inference to the fullest, checking our hypotheses against the phenomenal world of the client, we have gained knowledge which has led to the formulation of psychological principles related to personality change.

In this interpersonal or phenomenological way of knowing, then, the direction of the empathy is toward the other individual. Our hypotheses are tested by relating them to the most accurate picture we can obtain of the internal frame of reference of this individual. The knowledge it gives is of a particular individual, but from this knowledge generalizations can be formed which can be tested in the same manner. It provides us scientific leverage in getting at the nonobservable events which go on within the individual.

It may have seemed surprising that I did not limit this way of knowing to knowledge of other human beings. I believe that this way of knowing is limited only by the limits of our capacity for empathy, and the degree of our ingenuity in getting at the internal frame of reference of the organism. Classic studies by Snygg (27) and Krechevsky (15) indicate that it is possible to check a hypothesis against the inferred internal frame of reference of the rat. I am sure that such studies could be extended. Nevertheless, this mode of knowing is obviously of most significance in promoting our knowledge of the human being.

What are the criteria for this type of knowing? When am I justified in feeling that I "know" something in this interpersonal sense? I believe the criteria are twofold; either my hypothesis about the internal frame of reference of this individual is confirmed by the individual himself, or the inferences made about his internal frame of reference are confirmed by a consensual validation. For example, I sense that you are feeling unhappy this morning. If I say, "Looks as though your world is pretty dark this morning," and you by word or nod show your agreement, then I have checked my hypothesis and found that it has some validity. Another method of checking would be that if I kept to myself my empathic sensing of your unhappiness, but during the morning three other individuals came to me independently to speak of their concern over what seemed to them your sadness, your depression, and the like, then the probability of the correctness of the inference as to your internal state would be greatly increased. In some instances, as in the animal experiments cited, the inference as to the phenomenological field is supported by the fact that it is the most reasonable and most parsimonious explanation of the behavior.

THE RELATEDNESS OF WAYS OF KNOWING

Here then are three ways by which we extend knowledge, by which we confirm or disconfirm the hypotheses which we are continuously forming, both as a part of our everyday living and as a part of our psychological science. I would advance the view that any mature psychological science uses *each* of these ways of knowing in appropriate relationship to the other two, that it is only as these three modes of knowing are adequately and appropriately interwoven that a satisfactory behavioral science can emerge.

If I may be permitted a slight digression into analogy, I would point out that the psychologically mature person, like the mature science, uses these three modes of knowing in an integrated fashion. The mature person trusts his experiencing, and the meanings and hypotheses which he formulates from his inner flow. He forms and tests extremely significant hypotheses for living in his empathic relationships to the significant others in his life. He recognizes that all hypotheses are put to their most severe test in the objective world, and he, like the good scientist, remains open and receptive to the experiences which confirm or disconfirm his tentatively held hypotheses. Thus the psychologically healthy person is open to the finer differentiations of meaning in his inner experience which check and sharpen his hypotheses, to the rich sources of hypothesis formation and testing which exist in the other person, and to the testing of his hypotheses in real actions in a real world.

But this is a digression, and I should like to return to certain limitations which apply to these three ways of knowing.

I trust that I have made it plain that no method of knowing is infallible, that there is no royal road to scientific certitude. As Dr. Polanyi has remarked to me, "Every way of acquiring knowledge is risky." Whatever approximations to the truth we are able to achieve in the behavioral sciences will not come automatically through following one approach to knowledge. There is no such thing as a "scientific methodology" which will see us safely through.

I believe that recent history shows us that we make a serious mistake when we attempt to use one of these channels of knowing in isolation, without reference to the others. Thus the behaviorist frequently regards himself as using *only* the objective mode of knowing, and sees the other modes as objects of scorn or, at least, as completely unnecessary to a developing science. Some current existentialist thinkers, on the other hand, seem equally passionate in rejecting the objective way of knowing, relying entirely on the subjective and phenomenological way of knowing.

Another type of mistake is made when we confuse or equate these very different modes of knowing. It is of the utmost importance to be entirely clear as to the mode we are using at any particular moment or in any particular enterprise. When we become confused as to which avenue to knowledge is being utilized, or attempt to equate the knowledge from these three modes, serious trouble arises. Much psychoanalytic writing exhibits this latter error to a painful degree.

The new third force in psychology seems hopeful in that it shows signs of being willing to use, with confidence and clarity, all three of these channels to knowing, in such ways as to advance and enrich and deepen our science. Individuals in this group do not seem to be afraid of using their subjectivity, their "indwelling" in their professional experience, as an explicit basis for their hypotheses. They build heavily on interpersonal knowing as a far richer mode of arriving at insights about nature and human nature than any purely external approach could possibly be. This is perhaps one of their most significant contributions. They recognize, too, the full importance of the objective mode in its proper place as one of the later phases of scientific endeavor. Thus I believe that their entrance into the psychological field will have important effects, and these I should like to try to spell out.

A MORE INCLUSIVE SCIENCE

One of the major consequences of this phenomenological-existential trend is that psychology will become a more inclusive and more profound science. There are, without doubt, some individuals in this current of thought who maintain the hope that this new point of view will supplant the behaviorist trend, but to me this is both highly undesirable and highly unlikely. Rather it will mean, I believe, that psychology will preserve the advances and contributions which have come from the behavioristic development, but will go beyond this. Psychology will now be capable of focusing on a broader reality, which will include not only behavior, but the person and perspective of the observer, and the person and perspective of the observed. It will recognize, as physical scientists have been forced to recognize, that "as human beings, we must inevitably see the universe from a centre lying within ourselves and speak about it in terms of a human language shaped by the exigencies of human intercourse. Any attempt rigorously to eliminate our human perspective from our picture of the world must lead to absurdity" (21, p. 3). It is from this absurdity that the new trend will rescue the science of man.

It is quite unfortunate that we have permitted the world of psychological science to be narrowed to behaviors observed, sounds emitted, marks scratched on paper, and the like. In an attempt to be ultra-scientific, psychology has endeavored to walk in the footsteps of a Newtonian physics. Oppenheimer has expressed himself strongly on this, saying that "the worst of all possible misunderstandings would be that psychology be influenced to model itself after a physics which is not there any more, which has been quite outdated" (18, p. 134). I think there is quite general agreement that this is the path into which our logical-positivist behaviorism led us.

As I read the history and philosophy of science, there seems to me no alternative to the view that science in every field has advanced by discovering new perspectives, by theorizing in new ways, by utilizing new methods, quite without regard to the question of whether they fitted into the then current tradition in science. While, of course, it is obvious that the newness of a method or a theory or a perspective is no guarantee of its heuristic value, it is nevertheless true that science should resolutely set its face against anything which would limit its own scope, or which would arbitrarily narrow the methods or perspectives of its own pursuit of knowledge.

Valuable as have been the contributions of behaviorism, I believe that time will indicate the unfortunate effects of the bounds it has tended to impose. To limit oneself to consideration of externally observable behaviors, to rule out consideration of the whole universe of inner meanings, of purposes, of the inner flow of experiencing, seems to me to be closing our eyes to great areas which confront us when we look at the human world. Furthermore, to hold to the beliefs, which seem to me to characterize many behaviorists, that science is impersonal, that knowledge is an entity, that science somehow carries itself forward without the subjective person of the scientist being involved, is, I think, completely illusory.

In contrast, the trend of which I am speaking will attempt to face up to *all* of the realities in the psychological realm. Instead of being restrictive and inhibiting, it will throw open the whole range of human experiencing to scientific study. It will explore the private worlds of inner

personal meanings, in an effort to discover lawful and orderly relationships there. In this world of inner meanings it can investigate all the
issues which are meaningless for the behaviorist—purposes, goals,
values, choice, perceptions of self, perceptions of others, the personal
constructs with which we build our world, the responsibilities we accept
or reject, the whole phenomenal world of the individual with its connective tissue of meaning. Not one aspect of this world is open to the
strict behaviorist. Yet that these elements have significance for man's
behavior seems certainly true.

It is clear to me as it is to the behaviorist that to enter these areas,
which have always been thought of as the realm of the subjective, could
lead to a morass of speculation and introspectionism. But the vital hope
for the future is the fact that this does not necessarily follow, as I hope I
can show. If this trend should lead only to a pseudo science, as I am
afraid the Freudian insights have done, then it would be tragic indeed.
But there is increasing evidence that this need not and probably will not
be so.

Let me sharpen the point I have been making. We need no longer live
in an inhibited science of psychology. The trend toward a phenomenological, existential, self-theory emphasis in the field means that we
can, with fresh vigor, open our minds and our thinking, our theories and
our empirical research, to all the significant problems of psychology. We
can utilize all channels of knowing, not simply certain prescribed
channels. We can permit the full creativity of thought of the psychologist
to be exercised, not simply a narrowly inhibited and traditional type of
thought. In this respect I believe that the psychologist will experience a
new burst of creative freedom, such as has occurred in other sciences
when old bonds and boundaries have been broken. No problem, no
method, no perspective, will be out of bounds. Men can work freely and
creatively toward discovering the significant relationships between
humanly important variables in the psychological realm.

NEW CLASSES OF VARIABLES EXPLORED

I have stressed the greater scope which this new trend will bring to psychology as a science. One of the consequences of this broadened scope is
that there will be whole new areas of problems explored, of variables measured. I should like to give several examples of work which I believe
heralds the future direction. In each of these examples we find that the
measures used have many of the qualities valued by the behaviorist.
These are thoroughly objective measures, whose results are publicly
replicable. Yet they are used without some of the philosophical assumptions of the behaviorist group. And they are used to measure

variables which could only come from a profound concern with the phenomenological world of the individual, from a concern with the human
being as a process of valuing and choosing, of being and becoming.

Meaning

Consider first some problems connected with meaning. We may wish to
investigate the possibility that when the structure of meanings within
our phenomenal world changes, then our behavior changes. As an
example, it seems probable that the meaning of the word "China" underwent a striking change of meaning in the minds of the Indian people when
Chinese troops crossed the mountains into territory held by India, and
that a change in the whole patterning of behavior then ensued. It is an
exciting thing to realize that, thanks to the ingenuity of Osgood and his
co-workers (20), we have a precise means of measuring such a change in
meaning, the so-called semantic differential. We could chart the course in
"semantic space" of the meaning of the concept "China." We could determine its changing relationship to other concepts such as "friend,"
"strong," "black," "honest," "democracy," and the like. We can also
study the relationship between its changing meaning and various
external behaviors. Or, to comment on another and perhaps more basic
use of the tool of the semantic differential, we can determine whether
semantic space has essentially the same fundamental dimensions in
different cultures, speaking different languages (19). We can determine
whether divergent cultures have, in spite of their differences, an underlying generality in the way in which they perceive meanings. Here we see
an impressive example of studies of functional relationships, using
methods which are strictly operational, but dealing with problems of
inner phenomenological meanings as they exist in the private world of
each individual, and discovering orderly relationships between those
meanings. What more intangible problem could be dreamed up than to
measure the figurative space which exists between two or more meanings
in a person's experience, and the way in which these spatial relationships
change over time? Yet this important existential area has been convincingly dealt with in a thoroughly objective manner, giving results
which are replicable by any qualified scientist.

The Self and Related Variables

I should like to turn to another example, or rather to a cluster of related
examples. An object of vast importance in the phenomenal world of each
individual is his self. Many years ago the significance of this in psychotherapy was driven home to me, in spite of an initial prejudice against
anything so vague, so unobservable, so tainted with introspectionism.
Clients persisted in expressing themselves in terms such as these: "I feel
I'm not being my real self," "I wouldn't want anyone to know the real

me," "It feels good to let go and just *be myself* here," "I think if I chip off all the plaster façade I've got a pretty solid self underneath." Gradually I became aware that change in therapy was very vitally concerned with the self—yet how could this ever become a part of psychological science?

I can well remember the mounting excitement I felt when a graduate student told me of the new *Q* technique which William Stephenson (28) was presenting, and the possibility that it might be used for tapping or measuring the individual's conception of, or perception of, himself. Since that time there has been a burgeoning of self-measurements. One can develop an adequate objective representation of "myself as an adolescent," "myself as I see myself now," "the self I would like to be," "myself as my mother perceives me," and so on. It has given us a tool often inadequately understood and, without doubt, sometimes improperly used, but none the less a tool for the objective representation of one of the most important aspects of the inner phenomenal world. Instead of measuring all sorts of peripheral behaviors, we can go straight to what is often hypothesized as the dynamic core of the personality and a most significant influence upon behavior. Indices derived from such measures, such as the correlation between the perceived self and the valued self, have proven to be a satisfactory measure of maladjustment and one of the most satisfactory measures of change in psychotherapy (23). Most important of all, the possibility of giving objective representation to this meaningful phenomenal object has opened up various aspects of self-theory for empirical test (5, for example). The extent to which the self has become an acceptable object of study to psychologists is indicated by Hebb in his presidential address to the A.P.A., where he says: "The self is neither mythical nor mystical, but a complex mental process. . . . It is not really remote and inaccessible in the laboratory, any more than it is in the clinic." (11, p. 743)

Closely related to studies of the self is the study of self-esteem, the degree of similarity between "the self you are and the self you would like to be." Shlien (25), in an ingenious and thought-provoking paper, compares a number of ways of measuring this completely phenomenological variable. Among other things he constructed a physical device, completely abstract in its nature. It consists of two plexiglas squares which may be placed edge to edge, or overlapping to varying degrees, or exactly superimposed one upon the other. The individual is instructed to regard one of these as the self that he is, the other as the self he would like to be, and to place them in their proper relationship to one another. Shlien produces evidence to indicate that this completely abstract, nonverbal, behavioral measure provided by the placement of the squares is closer to the unique personal perception of the self-ideal relationship than is the subject's sortings of a structured, *Q* sort. It shows that when we begin to focus on the problem of measuring phenomenological constructs, we can find all sorts of ingenious methods. One would, a priori, regard it as quite impossible to construct an instrument which would measure a certain abstract subjective value-feeling in different persons, taking into account that in each person such a value-feeling is based on a consideration of elements mostly unique to that person, and where even these elements are differently weighted by each person. Yet this is precisely what Shlien has achieved in a very simple fashion.

Further Variables from the Psychotherapeutic Interaction

I should like to stress still further the point that an investigation based upon a phenomenological approach permits us to test significant variables much more directly. Gendlin (8) cites the example of a research in psychotherapy in which a rating of the degree to which the client focused on his relationship with the therapist—in other words, the degree to which he verbalized about it—was not found to be associated with outcome measures. But, when the scale was reformulated in terms of the specific phenomenological experience it was intended to capture, the result was different. This time, cases were rated as to the degree to which the relationship was a source of new experience for the client, indicated by such client statements as, "I've never been able to let go and feel dependent as I do now." Such ratings were definitely associated with the outcome measures.

I should like to draw in some further examples, again from the field of psychotherapy. Attempts to study therapist behavior in any meaningful way have not in the past met with much success. Recently, much more positive results have been emerging. On the basis of naturalistic clinical observation, it has been hypothesized that the degree of sensitively accurate empathic understanding experienced and communicated by the therapist in the relationship may have something to do with personality change in the client. Working directly with this highly existential-phenomenological concept, three different investigators (2, 10, 29) have developed different measures for the therapist's empathic quality in the relationship, and have applied such measures to different groups of therapists, working with very divergent kinds of clients. In all three instances, a significant association has been found between the measure of therapist's empathy and measures of personality change.

The most recent and carefully controlled study involved therapists working with a group of hospitalized schizophrenic individuals (29). Here the average empathy score in the case, based on ratings of recorded interview segments made by naive raters, correlated very significantly with an independent measure of the degree and direction of personality change over therapy. Here is evidence of a significant and lawful relationship between two inner variables, both essentially phenomenological in nature.

This same research investigated a still more subjective feeling in the therapist (30). Ratings were made of the degree of his unconditional positive regard for his client—the extent to which he exhibited a non-evaluative, nonpossessive warmth and liking. The measures of this elusive phenomenological quality also correlate very significantly with the independent measure of personality change over therapy.

Let me bring in two other illustrations. Clinically it has been felt that the way the client relates to himself and to his problems tends to predict the probability that he will or will not be able to change in therapy. One such hypothesis is that a willingness to discover new feelings and new aspects of himself is a predictor of personality change. Another hypothesis has to do with the immediacy of the client's experiencing, whether he is remote from and unaware of his feeling life, or is able to experience his feelings with immediacy as they occur. Instruments have been developed to assess the indicators of these highly subjective inner variables. Although the instruments are decidedly imperfect, some exciting findings are emerging. For example, in the group of schizophrenics mentioned above, a measure of the depth of self-exploration in the *second interview* correlates significantly (at the 1 per cent level) with the independent measure of personality change at the end of therapy one, two, or three *years* later. Even the assessment of the closeness of the client to his own experiencing shows a similar though somewhat less significant correlation (at the 5 per cent level) with the final measure of change. The client's manner of relating to his own problems at the time of the second interview is similarly related (again at the 5 per cent level) to the degree of change he shows throughout the whole period of therapy (31).

What is suggested by findings such as these is that when we proceed directly to discover and measure objective indices of subjective inner phenomenological events judged to be significant, we may more readily find lawfulness and order and predictive power than when we limit our conceptualization to external behaviors.

A NEW MODE IN PSYCHOLOGICAL THEORIES

In the realm of theory construction I believe this third current in psychology will have an invigorating effect—in fact, elements of such vigor are already emerging (Reference 3, for example). There will be more of a tendency to build theories which have connection with the fundamental problems of human existence. There are likely to be more developments of truly psychological theories, to supplement some of the essentially physiological theories of the past. It is likely that there will be more freedom and freshness in theory construction, once thinking has burst out of the bounds prescribed by a strict behaviorism.

I think that there are evidences that in the theoretical formulations which grow from this field there will be more concern with process, or, as Bridgman says, with "doings or happenings" rather than with "static elements" and abstractions. I believe that this is one of the important functions of theory. Some years ago I attempted to state this view, saying that:

> Objective research slices through the frozen moment to provide us with an exact picture of the inter-relationships which exist at that moment. But our understanding of the ongoing movement— whether it be the process of fermentation, or the circulation of the blood, or the process of atomic fission—is generally provided by a theoretical formulation. . . . (24, p. 127)

An illustration of the kind of theoretical concept likely to emerge is provided by Gendlin (9) in his careful delineation of the preconceptual process of experiencing and the manner in which it functions in the creation of personal meaning. Here is a concept rooted in naturalistic observation, purely phenomenological in origin, of a process nature, which helps to bridge the gap between the subjective and objective in the way in which it lends itself to objective research.

At the risk of oversimplification, let me endeavor to give some of the main features of Gendlin's concept, and the reasons he regards it as significant for the development of new theories and a more adequate science.

Experiencing refers to the ongoing feeling of *having* experience, "that partly unformed stream of feeling that we have at every moment." It is preconceptual, containing implicit meanings. It is something that is basically prior to symbolization or conceptualization. It may be known to the individual by direct reference—that is, one can attend inwardly to this flow of experiencing. Such direct reference is differentiation based upon a subjective pointing to, or attending to, the experiencing. The experiencing which is going on may be symbolized and this symbolization may be based upon direct reference, or more complex symbolizations may develop out of it, such as those we term conceptualization. Meaning is formed in the interaction between experiencing and symbols. Thus, as the individual refers to his experiencing, the implicit meaning becomes symbolized into "I am angry," or "I am in tune with what he is saying," or "I am uncomfortable with what is going on." Thus our personal meanings are formed in this interaction. Furthermore, any datum of experiencing—any aspect of it—can be symbolized further and further on the basis of continuing inward attention to it. Increasingly refined and differentiated meanings can be drawn by symbolization from any experiencing. Thus in the last example the individual who feels uncomfortable with what is going on may continue to refer to his experiencing and form further meanings from it. "I'm uncomfortable because I don't like to see another person hurt." "No, it is more than that. I resent his power, too." "Well, I guess another aspect of it is that I am afraid that he may hurt me." Thus a continuing stream of more and more refined meanings may come from a single moment of experiencing.

I have described this concept at some length, to indicate the extent to which this is an existentially oriented, phenomenologically based concept. Yet, as Gendlin points out, reliance upon this concept of experiencing can assist us to select and create scientific variables which are significant to the existential predicament of man, and which can then be operationally defined and empirically tested. His thinking constitutes one step in transcending the subject-object dichotomy which plagues our thinking today.

I will do no more than mention other examples of theorizing which have their base in an existential-phenomenological orientation. The burgeoning of self-theory is an example (1, 16, 17). The redefinition of motivation, of stimulus and response, of learning, of the whole field of human psychology from a perceptual point of view, is well-illustrated by the work of Combs and Snygg (7). The title of a recent volume of several contributors, *Perceiving, Behaving, Becoming* (6), is suggestive of a whole range of theorizing going on.

SCIENCE AND THE "UNREAL"

I should like to turn for a moment to the uneasiness which such thinking creates in the minds of many psychologists, and perhaps in the minds of other scientists as well. The uneasiness stems from what they regard as the "unreal" nature of the referents in much of this thinking. What is to become of psychology if it turns its attention to such ephemeral, vague wisps of fog as experiencing, the self, becoming? What has happened to the solidity of a science which was built on a tangible stimulus, an observable response, or a visible reward? To such uneasy ones, I would like to point out the course of the physical sciences.

I am fully aware of the pitfalls involved in reasoning by analogy, yet I think we may learn something, and perhaps be reassured, by considering some of the developments in physics and mathematics, insofar as they are understood by this outsider. It seems quite clear that most of the recent striking advances in these sciences have come about, not through following the channel of logical positivism—though its continuing contributions cannot be denied—but through the fantastic imaginings of experienced, insightful, thoughtful men. Such men have raised strange questions regarding the meaning of infinity, for example, and have developed strange hypotheses regarding it—infinity, which no one has seen or measured, or even comprehended. These odd theoretical developments have resolved some long-standing mathematical problems. Or they have developed strange new constructions of space, formulations of types of space never seen, and never really imagined, but existing only in mathematical symbols. They have developed hypotheses about these new types of non-Euclidean space. Or, the most famous of them all harbored revolutionary thoughts that perhaps neither weight nor the force of gravity existed, and that time and space are one—thus robbing our universe of almost all of the solidity which it had for us. So far have these developments gone that a competent mathematician writes:

> We should regard any theory about physical space, then, as a purely subjective construction and not impute to it objective reality. Man constructs a geometry, Euclidean or non-Euclidean, and decides to view space in those terms. The advantage in doing so, even though he cannot be sure space possesses any of the characteristics of the structure he has built up in his own mind, are that he can then think about space and use his theory in scientific work. This view of space and nature generally does not deny that there is such a thing as an objective physical world. It merely recognizes that man's judgments and conclusions about space are purely of his own making. (14, p. 429)

Yet we need to recognize that it is these subjective creations which have made possible the theory of relativity, the release of atomic energy, explorations in space, and many other advances in knowledge and technology.

If I may draw a cautious conclusion from this for the field of psychology it would be this: There is no special virtue attached to the policy of limiting our theories to observable behaviors. Neither, I would add, is there any *inherent* virtue in basing our theorizing on phenomenological variables. The fundamental question will be settled by the future. What theories will prove to be genuinely heuristic, leading to the discovery of significant functional relationships having to do with human life? There is at least as much reason to believe that theories based upon existential-phenomenological constructs will be successful, as to believe that theories based upon observable behaviors will be successful. A theory which postulates relationships between inner subjective phenomena not directly measurable, may, like theories regarding non-Euclidean space, prove to be more valuable in advancing our knowledge than theories regarding observable behavior.

THE PHILOSOPHICAL VIEW OF MAN

There is one other consequence of this phenomenological-existential view in psychology. It carries with it a new philosophical underpinning for psychological science which is, I believe, more fruitful and more human than the presently held philosophies.

Each current in psychology has its own implicit philosophy of man. Though not often stated explicitly, these philosophies exert their influence in many significant and subtle ways. For the behaviorist, man is a machine, a complicated but none the less understandable machine, which we can learn to manipulate with greater and greater skill, until he thinks the thoughts, moves in the directions, and behaves in the ways which are selected for him. For the Freudian, man is an irrational being, irrevocably in the grip of his past and of the product of that past, his unconscious.

It is not necessary to deny that there is truth in each of these formulations, in order to recognize that there is another perspective. From the existential perspective, from within the phenomenological internal frame of reference, man does not simply have the characteristics of a machine, he is not simply a being in the grip of unconscious motives, he is a person in the process of creating himself, a person who creates meaning in life, a person who embodies a dimension of subjective freedom. He is a figure who, though he may be alone in a vastly complex universe, and though he may be part and parcel of that universe and its destiny, is also able in his inner life to transcend the material universe, who is able to live dimensions of his life which are not fully or adequately contained in a description of his conditionings, or of his unconscious.

It is not my purpose to go deeply into the philosophical issues. I believe, however, that we are leaving behind the narrowly mechanistic philosophy which has tended to accompany behaviorism. I believe an increasing number of people would agree with the physicist, P. W. Bridgman, when he says, "It is evident that ... the operational approach cannot be completely general and that it can by no means provide the basis for a complete philosophy." (4, p. 2)

It is my judgment, as I try to understand the vigorous thrust of this phenomenological-existential movement in a variety of other fields, as well as in psychology, that it represents a new philosophical emphasis. Here is the voice of subjective man speaking up loudly for himself. Man has long felt himself to be but a puppet in life—molded by economic forces, by unconscious forces, by environmental forces. He has been enslaved by persons, by institutions, by the theories of psychological science. But he is firmly setting forth a new declaration of independence. He is discarding the alibis of *un*freedom. He is *choosing* himself, endeavoring, in a most difficult and often tragic world, to *become* himself—not a puppet, not a slave, not a machine, but his own unique individual self. The view I have been describing in psychology has room for this philosophy of man.

CONCLUSION

Let me try to state very briefly, and in somewhat different terms, the consequences in psychology of this fresh new current in modern culture, which is so incompletely described by terms like existential, phenomenological, self-oriented.

It will make confident use of subjective, intuitive hypotheses formulated by the scientist who has immersed himself in his field of study, and who senses a pattern, an order, which he can perhaps only partially articulate.

It leads, I believe, to a naturalistic, empathic, sensitive observation of the world of inner meanings as they exist in the individual. The whole range and scope of the human situation as it exists in each individual is thus opened for consideration.

It leads to the formulation of heuristic concepts based upon such observation. In my judgment, these concepts will tend to have more of a process quality than do the psychological concepts of the past.

It requires careful definition of observable behaviors which are indices of these subjective variables. It is recognized that variables of inner experience cannot be measured directly, but it is also realized that the fact that they *are* inner variables does not preclude their scientific study.

It is leading, and will, I believe, increasingly lead, to the imaginative development of clearly operational steps and operational tools for the measurement of the behaviors which represent these inner variables.

It seems quite evident that it will lead to a diminishing of the dichotomy between subject and object as it studies the relationships between the internal variables and such external variables as environmental stimuli, outward behavior, and the like. A study, for example, which relates the changes in the self-perceived behavior of an individual to the maturity of that individual's behavior as it is observed by his friends (23, chaps. 13, 15) brings more closely together the subjective and the objective world.

It will lead to theoretical formulations which will be as shocking to conventional psychologists as theories of non-Euclidean space were for conventional physicists. We will be attempting to discover the functional process relationships which hold for the inner world of personal meanings, and to formulate these with sufficient precision that they may be put to empirical test.

It contains within it the seeds of a newer philosophy of science which will not be fearful of finding room for the person—both the observer and the observed—in his subjective as well as his objective mode. It will carry within it a view of man as a subjectively free, choosing, responsible architect of self.

REFERENCES

1. Allport, G. W. *Becoming: Basic Considerations for a Psychology of Personality.* New Haven, Conn.: Yale University Press, 1955.

2. Barrett-Leonard, G. T. Dimensions of Therapist Response as Causal Factors in Therapeutic Change, *Psychological Monographs* (in press).
3. Bergin, A. E. Worknotes toward a Science of Inner Experience (paper presented at the meeting of the New Jersey Psychological Association, December, 1961).
4. Bridgman, P. W. *The Way Things Are*. Cambridge, Mass.: Harvard University Press, 1959.
5. Chodorkoff, B. Self-Perception, Perceptual Defense, and Adjustment, *Journal of Abnormal and Social Psychology*, Vol. 49 (1954), pp. 508-512.
6. Combs, A. W. (ed.). *Perceiving, Behaving, Becoming*. Washington, D.C.: Association for Supervision and Curriculum Development, 1962.
7. Combs, A. W., and Snygg, D. *Individual Behavior: A Perceptual Approach to Behavior*. New York: Harper, 1959.
8. Gendlin, E. T. Operational Variables from the Practice of Psychotherapy (unpublished paper given at American Psychological Association convention, 1962).
9. _____. *Experiencing and the Creation of Meaning*. New York: Free Press of Glencoe, Macmillan, 1962.
10. Halkides, G. An Experimental Study of Four Conditions Necessary for the Therapeutic Change (unpublished doctoral dissertation, University of Chicago, 1958).
11. Hebb, D. O. The American Revolution, *American Psychologist*, Vol. 15 (1960), pp. 735-745.
12. Jessor, R. Phenomenological Personality Theories and the Data Language of Psychology, in A. E. Kuenzli (ed.), *The Phenomenological Problem*. New York: Harper, 1959; pp. 280-293.
13. _____. Issues in the Phenomenological Approach to Personality, *Journal of Individual Psychology*, Vol. 17 (1961), pp. 27-38.
14. Kline M. *Mathematics in Western Culture*. New York: Oxford University Press, 1953.
15. Krechevsky, I. "Hypothesis" in Rats, *Psychological Review*, Vol. 32 (1939), pp. 516-522.
16. Maslow, A. H. *Toward a Psychology of Being*. Princeton, N.J.: Van Nostrand, 1962.
17. Moustakas, C. E. (ed.). *The Self*. New York: Harper, 1956.
18. Oppenheimer, R. Analogy in Science, *American Psychologist*, Vol. 11 (1956), pp. 127-135.
19. Osgood, C. E. Cross-Cultural Generality of Visual-Verbal Synesthetic Tendencies, *Behavioral Science*, Vol. 5 (1960), pp. 146-169.
20. _____, Suci, G. J., and Tannenbaum, P. *The Measurement of Meaning*. Urbana: University of Illinois Press, 1957.

21. Polanyi, M. *Personal Knowledge.* Chicago: University of Chicago Press, 1958.
22. Rogers, C. R., Kell, W. L., and McNeil, H. The Role of Self-Understanding in the Prediction of Behavior, *Journal of Consulting Psychology,* Vol. 12 (1948), pp. 174-186.
23. _____, and Dymond, R. (eds.). *Psychotherapy and Personality Change.* Chicago: University of Chicago Press, 1954.
24. _____. *On Becoming a Person.* Boston: Houghton Mifflin, 1961.
25. Shlien, J. M. Toward What Level of Abstraction in Criteria? in *Research in Psychotherapy,* Vol. 11. Washington, D.C.: American Psychological Association.
26. Skinner, B. F. *Cumulative Record.* New York: Appleton-Century-Crofts, 1961.
27. Snygg, D. Mazes in Which Rats Take the Longer Path to Food, *Journal of Psychology,* Vol 1 (1936), pp. 153-166.
28. Stephenson, W. *The Study of Behavior: Q-Technique and Its Methodology.* Chicago: University of Chicago Press, 1953.
29. Truax, C. B. The Relationship between the Level of Accurate Empathy Offered in Psychotherapy and Case Outcome (unpublished research report, Psychotherapy Research Group, Wisconsin Psychiatric Institute, 1962).
30. _____. The Relationship between the Amount of Unconditional Positive Regard Offered in Psychotherapy and Case Outcome *(ibid.).*
31. _____. The Relationship between the Extent to Which the Patient Engages in Depth of Intrapersonal Exploration and the Case Outcome of Constructive Personality Change *(ibid.).*
32. Wertheimer, M. *Productive Thinking.* New York: Harper, 1945.

COMMUNICATING THE SCIENCES: A HUMANISTIC VIEWPOINT

I. David Welch
John R. Rodwick

WHAT IS THE PURPOSE OF SCIENCE?

A psychological interpretation of science begins with the acute realization that science is a human creation, rather than an autonomous, nonhuman, or *per se* "thing" with intrinsic rules of its own. Its origins are in human motives, its goals are human goals, and it is created, renewed and maintained by human beings. Its laws, organization, and articulations rest not only on the nature of the reality that it discovers, but also on the nature of the human nature that does the discovering (Maslow, 1970, p. 1).

We believe the purpose of science is to help man understand. For the "natural" sciences, that means understanding the natural world, and for the behavioral sciences it means understanding ourselves. As one man has said, "to illumine the dark corners of human knowledge is the goal of science, but not all those dark corners are in the icy reaches of interstellar space or among the vagrant particles of the atom. Some of them are in ourselves. It is fitting that in this day when science reaches out to probe the farthest stars it has not lost contact with man himself."[1] The misguided effort to make believe science is imbued with some intrinsic, autonomous, arbitrary and chesslike rules apart from man, we consider unrealistic, false and even anti-empirical. Such a view ignores the man in the process and that is our concern.

SOURCE: Reprinted by permission of the authors.

1. Charles Collingwood, from the CBS television program, *Conquest,* "Mother Love."

COMMUNICATING RESEARCH

The function of the natural and behavioral scientists, as researchers and citizens, is to communicate their findings and ideas to their colleagues and laymen alike. Curiously enough, it may be even more important that scientists communicate their findings to laymen than it is for them to communicate their findings to other scientists! This is true because, ultimately, laymen are the beneficiaries of the scientists' work. If their work is not known, then ignorance can continue to take its awful toll of human life and happiness. If their work is misunderstood or only partially understood, then science can become a weapon more harmful than ignorance. When scientists fail to communicate, they thwart the purpose and function of science. When science confounds us (or better, when scientists confound us), it not only fails us but may possibly lead to misuse or disaster. In other words, when scientists fail to communicate, that is, fail to help laymen and other scientists understand their research and findings, we can only expect confusion and misunderstanding.

The failure of behavioral scientists to communicate their understandings to laymen has led to serious errors of judgment in education, industry and interpersonal, as well as international, relations. Laymen need to be allowed inroads into the "mysterious" world of scientists because, ultimately, it is they who hold the reins of government and they who must make the decisions about how science and its discoveries will be used. To the degree that laymen understand the function, values, and findings of science is the degree to which science, itself, will be used for good and evil in our world.

Perhaps, one of the basic misunderstandings of science, and one of the reasons for our failure to communicate our findings widely, is the belief science is "something objective" with rules that supersede the imprecise emotions of men. In our rush to glorify reason, the intellect and objectivity, we forget that scientists are men themselves, motivated, like other men, by species-wide needs for affection, respect, status and self-respect. We forgot the separation between intellect and emotion is an arbitrary separation useful only for study and not a reality. We forgot man's need for love, or respect, is quite as real as his need for the truth. Maslow (1970, p. 3) says it well when he writes that " 'Pure' science has no more intrinsic worth than 'humanistic' science, nor has it any less . . . The Greek respect for reason was not wrong but only too exclusive. Aristotle did not see that love is quite as human as reason."

Of course, our reasons for insisting on objectivity were in the hope that, "unhampered" by values and human emotion, we could see more clearly the "truth," but it may happen that the pure, objective, disinterested curiosity of the pure scientist could prove as dangerous to human beings as the most malevolent dictator. After all, the limits of pure science are not Einstein and Newton, but rather the Nazi "sci-

entists" of the concentration camps or the "mad" scientists of Holly-
wood. Science for science's sake can be just as sick as art for art's sake.
We too often forget the original theorizers of science often thought
science was primarily a means to help the human race.

When we lose sight of this purpose, it becomes easy to isolate ourselves into elite groups. Sidney Jourard (Jourard, 1968, p. 40) has suggested "that there is growing reason to believe that psychologists and
psychiatrists, through default, have truly become agents for the ruling
class." From this it isn't very difficult to believe science could become a
political force against the populace, unless laymen have easy inroads into
the discoveries of science.

INADEQUATE MEN

Our central thesis is: The failure of science is usually the failure of men.
Scientists function as men; therefore, if they function inadequately as
men it may be they function inadequately as scientists as well. If we are
to understand the failure of science to communicate, especially the behavioral sciences, it is probably wise we understand the nature of the inadequate or disorganized personality. This is a difficult case to make, but
perhaps we can make it.

Combs and Snygg (1959, p. 267) describe the inadequate personality
in the following way:

> Inadequate people see themselves in generally negative ways. As
> a result of their past experiences, they have come to define them-
> selves, for example, as unworthy, unwanted, unacceptable, and
> unable . . . a self defined in negative terms is a poor instrument for
> dealing with the vicissitudes of life. It leaves one helpless and fear-
> ful before the demands of living. It provides but a shaky and
> tenuous foundation for effective existence.

Such a personality is a poor instrument for observing and accurately reporting on his fellow human beings; such a personality provides a shaky
and tenuous foundation for "sciencing" as well. Interestingly, psychiatrists have been known to become specialists in particular disorders (pho-
bias, Oedipal complexes and the like) because that happened to be their
particular "hang up" and they came to see it in all of their clients. If it is
true the primary tool of science is observation, then it is certainly true
the disorganized personality makes a poor scientist, because the perception of disorganized personalities is distorted to the degree that they do
not see "reality" but project upon it their own inadequacies. And that is
another characteristic of the inadequate personality. Their perceptions of
reality are restricted; the picture of reality becomes incomplete in the
same way the total view of scenery is restricted when driving through a

tunnel. Just as the tunnel physically prevents us from seeing what is going on around us, personal inadequacy psychologically prevents us from seeing what is going on around us. As Combs and Snygg (1959, p. 268) write: "It is not surprising, therefore, to find that inadequate personalities are often characterized by rigid, inflexible patterns of behavior or that they are quite likely to be inaccurate in their assessment of themselves and the world about them."

Rigid, inflexible thought hampers one in daily living, but it is a disaster for a scientist! A rigid, inflexible scientist does not so much advance knowledge as he restricts it. If the restriction is based on his own inadequacy, it is because the new produces fear and doubt. Both are based on ignorance and both disappear in the light of understanding. The "scientist" knows this and attacks fear and doubt systematically in order to destroy them, but the inadequate scientist, or man, runs from them. The inadequate scientist, characterized by rigid, inflexible thought, goes even further. He actually enlists in the ranks of his enemies by seeking to maintain the very fear and doubt that so threatens and confuses him. To change is even more frightening and confusing.

Inadequate personalities are unable to accept new or conflicting perceptions of themselves, of others, or of their environment. Such characteristics can be disastrous to the behavioral scientist. Again Combs and Snygg (1959, p. 268) write:

> He is forced to behave on the basis of restricted or partial evidence. Behavior originating from only part of the data must necessarily be less precise and effective . . . Like trying to build a house with but part of the necessary lumber, the product is unsatisfactory to everyone concerned.

Even when they have sufficient lumber, inadequate personalities make bad carpenters because what they lack is the ability to organize the lumber into a house.

ADEQUATE MEN

If we accept the thesis that inadequate personalities make poor scientists, especially behavioral scientists, then perhaps it is even more important we demonstrate that the characteristics of the adequate personality actually lead to success in communicating science and that one of the primary goals in producing young scientists would be to assure their movement toward personal adequacy.

Perhaps the most important contributions toward understanding personal adequacy have been made by Combs and Snygg, Rogers, and Maslow. Combs and Snygg describe adequate personalities as those who

(1) perceive themselves in essentially positive ways, (2) are capable of acceptance of others (widely identified with his fellow man), (3) are open to their experiences and (4) are well informed. We can hardly think of a better description of a scientist than that!

Rogers' "fully functioning self" expands on Combs and Snygg. Rogers' description of the fully functioning person is summarized by Hamachek (1971, p. 55) as follows:

1. He tends to move away from facades.
2. He tends to move away from "oughts". In other words, he ceases to guide his conduct in terms of what he ought to do, ought to be or ought to become.
3. He tends to move away from meeting other's expectations and moves more toward meeting his own expectations.
4. He tends to move away from pleasing others and begins to be more self-directing.
5. He tends to be more accepting of himself and able to view himself as a person in the process of becoming.
6. He tends to move toward being more open to his experiences in the sense of not having to always blot out thoughts, feelings, perceptions, and memories which might be unpleasant.
7. He tends to move in the direction of greater acceptance of others.

Abraham Maslow, like Combs and Snygg and Rogers, was very much interested in determining what conditions contributed to the development of the adequate or fully functioning person. Maslow hypothesized man had certain needs and these needs were arranged in a hierarchy: basic physiological needs, safety needs, love and belongingness needs, esteem needs, and self-actualization needs or the need for personal fulfillment.

Maslow used the term self-actualizing to describe people who seek to satisfy needs he defined as essentially idiosyncratic, who seek to fulfill their own personal abilities to the fullest after the other needs have been fulfilled. To test these ideas, Maslow sought out and interviewed people whom he thought might be self-actualizing people. The descriptive list (Hamachek, 1971, pp. 56-58) is probably the most extensive and most complete yet devised.

1. They are realistically oriented.
2. They accept themselves, other people, and the natural world for what they are.
3. They are spontaneous in thinking, emotions, and behavior.
4. They are problem-centered rather than self-centered in the sense of being able to devote their attention to a task, duty, or mission that seemed peculiarly cut out for them.

5. They have a need for privacy and even seek it out on occasion, needing it for periods of intense concentration on subjects of interest to them.
6. They are autonomous, independent, and able to remain true to themselves in the face of rejection or unpopularity.
7. They have a continuous freshness of appreciation and capacity to stand in awe again and again of the basic goods of life: a sunset, a flower, a baby, a melody, a person.
8. They have frequent "mystic" or "oceanic" experiences, although not necessarily religious in character.
9. They feel a sense of identification with mankind as a whole in the sense of being concerned not only with their immediate families, but with the welfare of the world as a whole.
10. Their intimate relationships with a few specifically loved people tend to be profound and deeply emotional rather than superficial.
11. They have democratic character structures in the sense of judging people and being friendly not on the basis of race, status, religion, but rather on the basis of who other people are as individuals.
12. They have a highly developed sense of ethics and are inclined to choose their behavior with reference to its ethical implications.
13. They have unhostile senses of humor, which are expressed in their capacity to make common human foibles, pretensions and foolishness, the subject of laughter, rather than sadism, smut, or hatred of authority.
14. They have a great fund of creativeness.
15. They resist total conformity to culture.

Maslow's self-actualizing person can be viewed as an extension of Combs' and Snygg's adequate personality or Rogers' fully functioning person. Each of the three concepts are interrelated; they are not mutually exclusive.

EFFECTIVE SCIENTISTS

From this review of what constitutes optimally effective people, we can now turn to the examination of how such knowledge can facilitate the communications process for us as scientists. We have already noted success in communicating the sciences is related to the personal adequacy of the scientist, that is, his feelings of openness and acceptance. In the final analysis, science depends on the honesty of its scientists. Method can never protect us because method is only as good as the men who use it. Frank Goble (1970, p. 18), in his book on the psychology of Abraham Maslow, writes:

The scientist needs to be secure, confident, and mentally healthy in order to have a good perception of the reality he is studying. The scientist needs to approach problems with an open mind; he needs to be problem-centered rather than ego-centered. The behavioral scientist needs a broad general background since over-specialization is not productive.

Maslow indicates our most successful scientists are ones who have broad interests (examples: Aristotle, Einstein, Leonardo da Vinci and Thomas Jefferson). They must be men of courage who are willing to study the difficult, not men who are terribly proficient in technique but have no vision and who study less and less important things with more and more skill. They must be men who realize the scientific method as more than five steps, but a systematic, honest and creative frame of mind sometimes allowing the method to be created by the demands of the study instead of allowing the study to become ineffective by use of a particular method. B. F. Skinner (Evans, 1968, p. 89) makes the point:

> In general, scientific methodology is not an accurate reflection of what the scientist really does. It's a mistake to teach students to "begin with a problem, work it out to a hypothesis, deduce a theorem, design an experiment to test the theorem and confirm or disprove the hypothesis." This is a posteriori reconstruction of what happens, and it doesn't reflect the actual behavior of the scientist. Fortunately for science, scientific method and statistics weren't formulated until the middle of the 19th century. Science had gotten a good start before scientists were told what they ought to be doing. I certainly don't feel that my own scientific activities are adequately described by statistics or scientific method or model building.

Carl Rogers (1969, p. 181), in his critical statement on graduate education in psychology, writes: "We attach enormous importance to turning out hard headed scientists, and strongly punish any of the sensitive, speculative, sportive openness which is the essence of the real scientist."

Rogers points out that while descriptions of outstanding young men in science and other professions emphasize intuition, the search for the philosophic and esthetic meaning in experience, openness to feelings and emotions, and a deep awareness of self and others, these qualities are precisely those which too many psychologists fear in themselves and ignore or reject in their students. Rogers convincingly writes that these are the very qualities which should be sought and nurtured in students by those graduate programs committed to preparing persons to make important contributions in their field.

The kind of men described above are the scientists we want to produce, the kind of men our world needs. We believe the best scientists, especially the best behavioral scientists, will come from the self-actualizing, fully functioning, and adequate men we produce. Authentic men will produce authentic research and report it in authentic ways. And perhaps, after all, that is truly the goal of science.

REFERENCES

Combs, A. W. and Snygg, Donald. *Individual Behavior.* New York: Harper and Row, Publishers, 1959.

Evans, R. I. *B. F. Skinner: The Man and His Ideas.* New York: E. P. Dutton and Company, Inc., 1968.

Goble, F. G. *The Third Force: The Psychology of Abraham Maslow.* New York: Grossman Publishers, 1970.

Hamachek, D. E. *Encounters with the Self.* New York: Holt, Rinehart and Winston, Inc., 1971.

Jourard, S. M. *Disclosing Man to Himself.* Princeton, New Jersey: D. Van Nostrand and Company, Inc., 1968.

Maslow, A. H. *Motivation and Personality.* New York: Harper and Row, Publishers, 1970.

Rogers, C. R. *Freedom to Learn.* Columbus, Ohio: Merrill Publishing Company, 1969.

PSYCHOLOGY: CONTROL OR LIBERATION?

Sidney M. Jourard

Sartre (1956) described a scene in which a voyeur peeps through the keyhole into a bedroom.[1] Suddenly, he is discovered by another, and becomes, thereby, an object for the other, and for himself. His experience of his freedom oozes away. Whenever a person is caught in the act, when someone hitherto concealed is seen, then the looker turns the one looked at into stone. Psychologists have been inviting the subjects of their research to become as natural objects, like stones. The surprising thing is that the subjects have cooperated. For the life of me, I cannot fathom why, because I do not know of *any* good that has accrued to the subject as a consequence of *being a subject*, that is, an *object*. This is a strong statement for me to make, because I am a psychologist, with 25 years of my adult life dedicated to this discipline. I really do not believe that the humans we have studied, in the ways that we have studied them, have benefited from our research! I do not believe that the quality of personal life has been improved by the results of 80 years of the scientific investigation of human consciousness and action. In fact, there is more basis for me to believe that the knowledge of man that we have acquired has been used to control and limit him rather than to enlarge his awareness, his dignity, or his freedom.

In research, as most psychologists have practiced it, subjects are recruited and asked to make themselves available to the psychologist for observation, interviewing and testing. He records their speech, actions, and reactions with various kinds of equipment. He analyzes his findings, and publicizes them. Typically, the psychologist defines psychology as a scientific discipline which seeks to *understand* the behavior of man and other organisms. Proof of understanding is evident when the psychologist can *predict* the action or reactions under study, by pointing to signs,

SOURCE: Sidney M. Jourard, "Psychology: Control or Liberation?" *Interpersonal Development*, 2, 1971-1972. Reprinted by permission. Presented at the meetings of the British Psychology Society, Nottingham, 1972. Copyright © 1972 by the author.

or by bringing them under some kind of deliberate *control.* Great pains are taken to insure that the observer does not influence the behavior he is studying,[2] so that the persons or animals under study will show themselves 'as they really are'. Ideally the subjects of study would not know that they were being watched,[3] because the experience of being observed affects action.

It is clear from this description that scientific psychology has been patterned, since its inception by *Wundt,* after the natural sciences. While we now draw distinctions among natural, social and behavioral sciences, in each of these, similar assumptions are held by the respective scientists, for example, that determinism prevails, and that the 'laws' which govern the phenomena under study can be discerned if the right questions are asked of the subject-matter in the right way.

Science, so understood, embodies two ambitions which enchanted me as a youngster. One was the wish to read the mind of others. It was fascinating to try to discern what was going on behind my friend's, or some stranger's opaque exterior. Did they like me? Were they going to harm me? If I could see into or through them, I would have fair warning about their intentions, and I could govern myself accordingly. In fact, if I could read minds in this way, it would give me a certain power over others.

Such power over others was the second childhood wish. I imagined what it would be like to be able to get other people, and animals, to do exactly what I wanted them to do. Snake charmers and hypnotists provided a kind of model of the type of control I sought, in entertaining these fantasies. To this day, I am intrigued and mystified by the ways in which trainers can get animals to perform intricate tricks.

Let us look at psychology, as a natural science, in the light of these childhood quests for omniscience and omnipotence. It seems fair to say that psychologists aim to read their subjects' minds, and to gain increments of power over their experience and action.

In the dawn of history, man was probably victimized by nature; animals, plants, seas and soil all acted with 'minds' of their own, indifferent to his needs and wishes. When nature was seen animistically, or deistically, early men could seek some measure of prediction and control by talking to the souls, spirits and gods which moved natural happenings. They would try to propitiate or bribe those animated beings, in order to get them to tell their intentions, and to help a man get power over hostile nature and untrustworthy, unpredictable strangers. Presumably, those men who could best foretell the future and influence the outcome of events were seen by their fellows as having either more powerful gods, or a closer relationship with the gods. In any case, nature was seen as capricious and hostile; man could improve his lot if he could read her mind (predict what was going to happen) and get her to act in ways that would serve his needs and interests. Natural science was developed to tame and demystify hostile Nature.

The modern scientific psychologist faces his subjects, his subject-matter in a posture similar to that of the natural scientist. The other man's action is not always friendly to *someone's* interests. *Someone* can gain if a man's action can be predicted (i.e., if his mind can be read, if his face becomes a transparent mask through which his stream of consciousness can be read), and if he can be induced to act in ways that serve someone's interests. The subjects of research in scientific psychology are deliberately seen as Other, as one of Them, *as a part of nature different from the scientist and those other persons whom the scientist designates as Us.*

Yet we must remember that a psychologist is a human being, living in a time and place, in a society with a class structure, a power structure—and he has economic interests. Typically, he is salaried, and the costs of his research are borne by private or public agencies. We have to assume that these agencies will not willingly countenance research which will undermine their power over people. A pharmaceutical firm is unlikely to spend millions of dollars in the study of placebos, so that drug use in medicine will be diminished. It does not seem farfetched to me to regard the most rigorous, truth-seeking psychologist as a servant, witting or unwitting, of the agencies which pay him and his costs. The agencies that believe it worthwhile financing research into human behavior typically believe that their interests will be furthered if man's behavior becomes less unpredictable. They want men to be transparent to them (while they remain opaque to the others), and they want to learn how to make men's action more amenable to control. Men who can be controlled can serve the controller's interest without knowing it—in which case we could say that they are mystified. If a psychologist studies men, and makes their action predictable, and their experience transparent to some elite—but not to the persons whom he has studied, then he is indeed a functionary, even though he may be a passionate seeker after truth. He may share the class interests of some elite, and he may serve those interests by viewing the subjects of his research as Them, creatures not unlike natural phenomena—floods, earthquakes, animals—which must be understood in order that they be tamed.

My hypothesis is, that unless the behavioral scientist explores the broader social, political and economic implications of his work, then he is a functionary indeed; worse, if he does not realize it, then he is being mystified by those who employ him.

The psychological testing movement likewise can be seen in this light as a quest to read people's minds, and to fathom their talents, strengths and weaknesses, to serve someone's ends, not necessarily the ends of the person being tested. Beginning with *Binet's* contribution, up to and including *Rorschach's,* the ability of one person, the tester, to discover something about the testee is not necessarily good for the latter. I can remember the excitement I felt, as an undergraduate, when I first heard about tests of intelligence, and of personality, by means of which one person could literally make another transparent. But now, the blacks and other so-called culturally deprived people are less than sanguine in their appreciation of what psychometrics are good for. In fact, quite properly, many blacks see the testing movement as one of the many means by which their subordinate status in the education establishment, and hence the professional world, is maintained. And as we come to take a fresh look at psychiatry, for which profession the projective and many 'objective' (like the MMPI) tests of personality were developed, we see that psychiatric classification is less an analogue of differential medical diagnosis, and more a subtle way to invalidate a human being.[4] Projective techniques can be seen as violations of the fifth amendment in the USA—sneaky means by which a person might reveal himself to another. 'Unobtrusive measures' which have come to be seen as an answer to uncooperative research subjects, or to experimenter bias, likewise are ways to get a person to reveal himself unwittingly, thereby giving information which may not help him *(Webb et al.,* 1966; *Westin,* 1967).

Am I saying any more than that knowledge of man, like knowledge of nature, gives power, and power corrupts? Perhaps not, but saying that is still to say something which we in psychology must take into account. Are we seeking the truth about man that sets all men free? Or are the truths we discover (which our subjects let us learn about them—because men are part of Nature, but they are men who can cooperate with, or block our efforts to study them) only making some men more free and powerful, while others become more vulnerable to manipulation?

It seems clear to me that the image of man entertained or assumed by a psychologist researcher or practitioner will affect his research strategies, his theories, and his ways and areas of consulting. If he views man as a natural object, rather than as a being not unlike himself, his science and its applications will be as I have described.

I will now look at the fields of psychotherapy and counseling, as well as at the behavior-modification movement which also serves as an area for the application of truth learned by scientists—in and out of the laboratory—about man.

Once again, economics rears its head. Psychological practitioners, who apply scientific knowledge of man artfully, do not sell their services cheaply. If in private practice, they charge substantial fees to the individuals and agencies which engage their services. Otherwise, they are retained or salaried by government or private agencies, to utilize their know-how in order that the agency might fulfill its aims more fully. For example, psychologists are employed by advertising agencies, business concerns of many kinds, in order that the public being 'served' will more readily buy the company's products or in order that workers will produce more, and more cheaply. Sometimes the service sold by the psychologist is knowledge about how masses of people will respond to symbols; some-times, they train people in the art of seeming sincere, friendly and authentic.

The arts of counseling and psychotherapy, seen from the perspective of a natural science of psychology, become arenas for the practice of *techniques,* ways to influence the experience and hence the action of the client or patient. Psychoanalysts, behavior-modification experts, even client-centered counseling technicians are all encouraged to believe that if they master a repertoire of laboratory-tested or clinic-tested techniques, they will 'get the patient to change.' Of course, the techniques of behavior modification by environmental control, as in token economies in mental hospitals, represent a subtle exercise of power. Hypnosis, 'shaping,' and aversive conditioning all represent ways to alter someone's action. The *person* who employs these techniques can remain invisible behind a pro-fessional manner. If he practices his techniques well, he will earn a fine salary from a grateful agency, or many fees from those rich enough to afford his services. Those individuals who are rich enough to afford his services are seldom spokesmen for liberal change in the political and economic system within which they earn the money to pay for their 'treatments.' Moreover, some of the more radical psychiatrists are be-ginning to assert that psychiatric intervention, of whatever sort, is a kind of social control aiming to invalidate and perhaps avert dissent.

If the basic and applied behavior science we have developed thus far has primarily been a quest for knowledge which makes men predictable and controllable, then clearly what is called for is a complementary science, one which uses scientific discipline and knowledge to liberate a man from being the victim, not only of the forces of nature, *but also of the concealed efforts of other men to influence him* for weal or woe.

Man's action and experience are indeed affected by mass media, by leaders, by genes, by his past experience, by reinforcement contin-gencies, by his biology and physiology, and by the social and interper-sonal setting within which he lives his life. Any way of discerning how these realms affect experience and action can be of some use to the person himself, and to others. I think that we psychologists have not served that person. Perhaps this is what Humanistic Psychology, or what psy-chology as a *human* science, can do.[5]

In 1957, I began to study self-disclosure. This was before I had ever heard of anything called humanistic psychology. I was trained in experi-mental as well as in clinical psychology, and a program of research has always been part of my view of the practice of my profession. I defined self-disclosure as a subject for scientific study because I began to wonder what we knew, or could find out about the conditions under which people would reveal personal information to others. *Freud* amply pointed out that psychoanalysis entailed overcoming a patient's reluctance to let his analyst know him, and psychotherapeutic practice called for being an encourager and listener to another's intimate disclosure. And so, using what I regarded (and still do) as appropriate techniques for research, I began collecting self-report data from thousands of people about their past disclosure to parents, friends and other target persons. I wanted a 'scientific' understanding of self-disclosure in order to predict and control this kind of behavior. Certainly, that is what my scientific training in Toronto and Buffalo encouraged me to do and think. Ironically, I soon discovered that *one of the most powerful correlates, if not 'determiners' of one person's self-disclosure was self-disclosure from the other person in the dyad.* Several questionnaire studies pointed to this hypothesis and we confirmed it in numerous experimental interviews conducted under laboratory conditions. We found that we could maximize a person's disclosure of personal data by offering such disclosure first, as a kind of invitation, suggestion, or example of what action was appropriate to the situation. My students and I, in conducting these experiments, did not *pretend* to disclose personal subject-matter. We *really did*, and it was sometimes risky and embarrassing; but we functioned in the spirit of adventurous inquiry, and found the outcomes we have mentioned.[6]

I had begun to experiment with my ways of being a psychotherapist, beginning soon after I discovered that my training did not prepare me to be helpful to Southerners with difficulties in living. I had begun as far back as 1952 to break my professional anonymity, by sharing with a client any experience of mine with problems comparable to those he was exploring with me. I found that such authentic sharing—within bounds of relevance and common sense—encouraged my patients to explore and reveal their experience more fully and freely than was hitherto the case for me. It was as if I had bungled into a new kind of technique, but one which entailed some risk, indeed, some inclusion of my patient into the world of Us, rather than seeing him as one of Them—the neurotics, the psychotics, etc. This experience in conducting psychotherapy appeared to support or confirm my survey and laboratory findings in the study of self-disclosure. But my experience as a psychotherapist influenced my view of research more profoundly. I was motivated to be helpful to the person who sought my professional help, and I found, increasingly, that one way to be helpful was to demystify the patient insofar as it was possible. The patient suffered from difficulties in living because he did not know what was going on. People lied to him, and he to them. Some patients were mystified by nature, others by social structures. It was difficult to know oneself, others, and the world. Our therapy sessions could be seen as an effort at authentic communication between two persons, so both would know what was going on. I found myself sharing *my* understanding of how people not only mystified one another, but invited others to be diminished creatures. I would show, and role-play the way people attributed imaginary traits to one another, which they would then embody and act out—like *Genet* becoming the thief he was defined to be early in life. Gradually, my understanding of what a psychologist's task might be underwent a change. I came to see that, if hitherto, research and practice grew out of a view of man as a natural phenomenon to be studied by an elite in order that he be better mind-read and controlled, it would be elegant to strive to do psychology for man. This, I came to see, must be what a Humanistic Psychology would be, and be for.

Humanistic Psychology could be defined, I saw, as an effort to disclose man and his situation *to himself,* to make him more aware by any and all means, of what forces were influencing his experience and hence his action. I could see that human subjects would not really disclose themselves, would not really let themselves be known to researchers or anyone else whom they had reason to distrust, and so we commenced a program of research within which the researcher was as much to be interviewed by the subject as vice versa. Though we have made only a token beginning at this, the results confirm that different perspectives on man will emerge when more such research is done.

If various institutions aim to control man's action and experience in order to serve the institution's aims, then a task for a humanistic psychology could be to study the means by which the propaganda, rules, and environment produced conformity, so that a person could better choose to conform or not to conform. I discovered in the process of this inquiry that for one person to lie to another is an effort to control this experience and action, so that he will indeed be mystified, and 'determined,' so long as he believes the lies. This is exactly equivalent to the situation of man facing a hostile nature which he does not understand. Not to understand is to be vulnerable to prediction and control—victimization, whether by mystifying nature, or by one's lying and self-concealing fellow man. To be understood, and not to understand the one who understands you, is indeed to be vulnerable—to be a transcendence transcended, as *Sartre* (1956) puts it.

I suppose that the project is to give it away—as fast as man is studied by natural-science psychologists (to learn about the determiners of his experience and action), humanistic psychologists (who can be natural-science psychologists too) can make apparent to all the ways in which their freedom is being eroded by hostile nature or hostile people.

Psychological research, from this perspective, becomes an enterprise wherein the subject becomes privy to the aims of the researcher, and wherein he is free to learn about the researcher as the researcher learns about him.

Counseling and psychotherapy, from the standpoint of humanistic psychology, become enterprises wherein patient and therapist, counselor and client share relevant experience so that the latter can become more enlightened, more liberated from influences that constrain his growth and self-actualization. Indeed, I find myself using the word therapy less and less, seeking some metaphor more aptly descriptive of what goes on in such helping transactions. Terms like teacher, guide, guru, liberator suggest themselves, though all sound fairly pretentious. But in all these cases, one thinks not of a person manipulating another, reading his mind in order to gain power over him; rather one thinks increasingly of a dialogue between I and You.

NOTES

1. Research psychologists would do well to read *Sartre's* sensitive account of the experience of being looked at.
2. *Rosenthal* (1966), of course, has produced much evidence that the experimenter is an important source of variance in the outcome of psychological research. Efforts to make allowance for this influence are discussed in *Miller* (1972).
3. For a review of methods to study man without his awareness, see *Webb et al,* (1966). A more detailed overview of methods for 'peeping' at man is given in *Westin* (1967).
4. *Szasz, T.:* Ideology and insanity (Doubleday, Garden City, N.Y. 1970).
5. An introduction to psychology, seen as a human rather than natural science, is given in *Giorgi* (1971).
6. See *Jourard* (1968, 1971a, b). These three volumes summarize my research and the theory that has grown out of research in self-disclosure, to the present.

REFERENCES

Giorgi, A. *Psychology as a human science* (Harper, New York 1971).

Jourard, S. M. *Disclosing man to himself* (Van Nostrand Reinhold, New York 1968).

Jourard, S. M. *The transparent self;* 2nd ed. (Van Nostrand Reinhold, New York 1971a).

Jourard, S. M. *Self-disclosure.* An experimental analysis of the transparent self (Wiley-Interscience, New York 1971b).

Miller, A. G. (ed.). *The social psychology of psychological research* (Free Press, New York 1972).

Rosenthal, R. *Experimenter effects in behavioral research* (Appleton-Century-Crofts, New York 1966).

Sartre, J. P. *Being and nothingness,* p. 259 (Methuen, London 1956).

Webb, E. J., Campbell, D. T., Schwartz, R. D., and Sechrest, L. *Unobtrusive measures: non-reactive research in the social sciences* (Rand McNally, Chicago 1966).

Westin, A. F. *Privacy and freedom* (Atheneum, New York 1967).

MEDICINE, DYING AND DEATH

A NEW HUMANISM IN MEDICINE

Stuart Miller

THE SEARCH FOR A HUMANISTIC MEDICINE

Among American health professionals and patients there is a widespread malaise. Despite enormous successes, a feeling of uneasiness pervades many of the men and women who work to provide care for the health of Americans, and despite better medical treatment than ever before patients too are dissatisfied.

From without, professionals are being attacked: for their impersonality, their apparent inability to spend time with patients, for the frequent lack of coordination among their services, for the chilling increase in their use of machines and specialized techniques. From within the professions themselves, arises an ill-defined resentment. Many physicians work harder and harder to serve, and die younger and younger. Treating only specialized diseases as many health professionals increasingly do, performing the same routines daily, weekly and monthly, is not satisfying to the human spirit. And yet the benefits of specialization seem to demand such costs. It has been suggested that, in reaction, some physicians develop a consuming interest in making money. No one expects an assembly line worker to be excited by his job, and for many professionals medicine has begun to resemble an assembly line. Untold thousands resist such tendencies but potent forces weigh against them. Government, concerned about inequitable distribution of health resources, proliferates proposals for reforms. But these frequently call for spreading a thinner assembly line, or for training more workers and sending them to assembly lines where they are desperately needed—in Watts, Harlem, Appalachia, all the inner cities and many remote rural areas.

As if these pressures were not enough, from among many of the young entering medicine come calls for a "relevant medicine," for investigating folk medicine, for reaching the people. And in the Harris polls, while the physician still stands as the most trusted of all professionals, in the last ten years his prestige and authority have plummeted more percentage points than any other.[1]

SOURCE: Stuart Miller, "A New Humanism in Medicine." Reprinted from *Synthesis, The Realization of the Self.* © 1974 Synthesis Press, Redwood City, California.

Such a complex set of dissatisfactions and complaints,[2] both within and without the field of health care, is bound to shake the self-confidence of practitioners and the confidence of patients. While no single solution or point of view can claim to cope with this distressing situation, it is apparent that the root cause of this malaise is very deep. One knows that even when health care considered "adequate" by current standards is guaranteed, and indeed delivered, to every American, the malaise will not have disappeared. Perhaps the single fact that best focuses this awareness is this: despite the enormous advances of medical biology a whole host of diseases are *increasing* in every corner of the industrialized world. Professor Luigi Speciani has called them the "diseases of civilization": heart disease, cancer, stomach ulcers, high blood pressure, and the like. The infectious diseases have virtually disappeared in the developed countries, and in their place have appeared these other diseases, diseases that seem to challenge the assumption of the 1940's and 50's that there would be a linear extension of the life span.

There would appear to be some mocking genie in the bottle of scientific progress, one that gives and also takes away. It is the haunting image of this genie beneath all of our medical technology that leads one to believe that the solution to our medical ills will not come from simple quantitative or even technical improvements—no number of new machines, no number of new physicians or nurses or health educators, no number of specialists or sophisticated procedures or plastic tubes will quite satisfy. The malaise underlying medicine parallels the malaise that more broadly underlies our time. And it would appear that an answer cannot be sought merely from outside; it must be sought in a more inward direction.

As in medicine, so elsewhere: the advance of materialistic science and technology has failed to bring all the blessings it promised. Therefore, our task now is to keep the genuine advances of science and technology and to combine them with a health giving way of life.

In medical terms, this means that groups of investigators must begin to concern themselves with the person: not only with the patient, but with his underlying humanness. Not just with his or her disease, but with his body as a whole, and with the feelings, the mind, and the spirit—even the spirit—of the patient. An old answer to the mocking genie is that image of whole humanness, that whole creature symbolized in the great statues and paintings of Greece and Rome and the Renaissance. Those older artists knew that when the inner man's harmony is achieved, the outer form of the body will reflect its radiance. This is, of course, for us, speculation. A hypothesis to be tested. Yet, it may be that many of the health professionals' problems can be solved—as well as many of the problems of patients afflicted with civilized diseases—when we know how whole people can create themselves in the contemporary world.

The study of how human wholeness can create itself in our time is the special province of humanistic and transpersonal psychology. One thinks of the work of such men as Maslow, Assagioli, Rogers, Fromm, Frankl and May, among many others. Drawing on the hundred year old traditions of behavioral science and the ancient traditions of Eastern and Western humanism and religion, the new fields of humanistic and transpersonal psychology have attempted to specify the ways and means by which wholeness can be achieved. At the very least, they have brought important but recently neglected human aspects back into focus: the will, the necessity of the emotional life, the strong relation between mind and body, the overriding importance of values and of the individual spirit. Our attention has been recalled to the evolutionary thrust in mankind and in each individual for higher realizations. The new psychologies have also collected or created hundreds of methods for developing these rediscovered aspects of man.

There have been two main problems, however, in applying the knowledge of the new psychologies to social institutions. The first is the current Western resistance to the experiential education of the whole person. Like the maladies one hopes to cure, this resistance drives in part from a mechanistic view of human beings that has dominated our century—the man as machine. The resistance is buttressed by the parallel concerns with production, external results, and with what can be touched and tasted and weighed. The second problem in bringing a humanistic view back to society and its institutions has been the lack of an overarching theory and a model for professional training and discovery. Fortunately, however, recent years have seen the development of comprehensive theories that unify all the experiential humanistic techniques. In addition, a number of practical attempts to bring the vision of the new psychology and its practical methods into troubled institutions have been successful. My wife, Sara Unobskey Miller, and I have been associated with one such overarching theory—psychosynthesis—and with the design of a practical training model for bringing new humanistic insights into professional situations. It is from this background that the Program in Humanistic Medicine has been developed as a comprehensive attempt to find practical ways of enhancing the full humanness of health care.

THE PROGRAM IN HUMANISTIC MEDICINE

If the task is to create a more humanistic health care, the only people who can do it are experienced health professionals.[3] Who else really knows the problems and has sufficient expertise and expert prestige within the existing health care system? Accordingly, and following the model of earlier work with school teachers and superintendents of schools,[4] we interviewed two hundred health professional applicants for admission to the new program of study we called the Program in Humanistic Medicine. Of these, we selected fourteen. For four years, beginning in September 1972, this group would devote itself to the exploration of the problems of humanness in medicine. Their main new resources would be the theories and techniques of the new psychologies. Their guinea pigs would be themselves. Taking an approach different from the simple extroversion of what frequently passes for human science, they would also look inward. And by looking at themselves, singly and collectively, they would prepare themselves to discover the fuller humanness of their patients. They would work together to test the relevance of the new psychologies to themselves and to others, and finally to the institution of medicine as a whole. They would be careful, slow and thorough. They would see what practical models they could develop to help with the problem of the malaise in medicine.

In the nearly two years since that process began, this group has participated in two dozen weekend workshops, each member has written more than a thousand pages in psychological and professional logs, they have made innovations in their practices, they have written papers about some of their discoveries, and now they are working in teams to write the first preliminary syntheses of some of their experience and learning. Four monographs will be published in September 1974 as the *Second Report* of the Program in Humanistic Medicine. The subjects are deliberately diverse: "The Feminine Principle in Humanistic Health Care," "A Humanistic View of Psychosomatic Medicine," "Humanistic and Transpersonal Psychology in Medicine," and "A First Curriculum for Humanistic Medicine and Health Care."

These are only beginning efforts. The problem of finding humanistic alternatives to today's health care is exceedingly complex, the lives of real people are involved. The Program Staff is inclined to be cautious. It includes seven physicians (six men and one woman), ranging in age from 29 to 56, in specialties ranging from internal medicine to pediatrics and public health administration, in nature of practice from the relative sanctuary of universities to the overworked routine of the downtown physician. Two lay counselors, a Director of Nursing and Vice President of a hospital, a general nurse, and a health educator complete the Program Staff. They were selected by the Directors for their strength, their skepticism, their openness and their good will. They are seasoned, practicing, respected professionals, and most of them hold full- or part-time appointments in health professions schools.

The Directors, however, are not health care people. We are psychologists and humanists. We arrange for consultants from the new psychologies to lead monthly weekend workshops. We attend the workshops and assist the participants to integrate new material. We deal with resistances to the new and threatening, we point out opportunities for growth, we try to help each Staff member find his own way toward a fuller humanness. In addition, we nag. To make sure that logs are submitted every three weeks, that experiential learning does not become an end in itself, and that what has been learned personally and found useful is applied professionally. But we do not determine what forms these applications will take—that is not our job or province.

It has been a healing process, a privilege to work with such people. In the work, we have had what Abraham Maslow would call a "supernormal" window on medicine. What we have observed is encouraging. We observe the tremendous force of latent caring and good will in the medical profession. An enormous idealism, aspiration and desire to serve human beings exists among health care people. But frequently these qualities are squashed by an authoritarian system of training, an overemphasis on the perfection of partial and merely technical skills, by a medical orthodoxy which has slipped, willy-nilly, into seeing people as if they were simply patients and patients as if they were simply collections of organ systems. In the triumph of science and technology over the material, there has come a natural tendency to see all of life as mere matter. To paraphrase one philosopher, "If the only tool you've got is a hammer, everything begins to look like a nail." How moving to see and feel the contrast between the high human aspirations of practitioners and the hammers they are given.

We have learned other interesting things about the health professions. Though the authority of the physician who takes care of physical complaints is plummeting, it is still very high. A mental health professional might work for six months to bring a patient to the point where a professional suggestion might bring about symptom relief. There will be probing on both sides, the slow establishment of trust by the patient for the doctor to meddle with his inner life. But an ordinary physician, by virtue of his concern with life and death matters like the body's care, can frequently carry more immediate weight. If he tells a patient to go and scream at the ocean (catharsis) to partially relieve chronic headaches, the patient often simply goes and does it.

Unfortunately, the sundering of body from mind and spirit is often extreme in conventional medicine. One observer summarized the situation by saying, "the psychiatrists have been given the mind, the clergymen the spirit, and the regular health professionals are left with only the body." But we see in our work that such divisions are not only theoretically indefensible, they are practically inefficient. Because the body is frequently the expression of emotional, mental and spiritual conditions, the health professional must be concerned with all. Just as everyone must be concerned with all. And no objection of the need for specialized "psychiatric" knowledge can obviate the necessity for such holistic concern in all health professionals and, in fact, in everyone.

Such concepts as these and the practical methods to implement them are developed in the annual reports of the Program. To summarize those lengthy documents in such a short space is impossible. The range of this second year's monographs I have already described. The *First Report* contained shorter papers with this range of titles:[5]

"Humanistic Training of Physicians in Care of Dying Patients"
    Kathryn Jean Enot, R.N.
"Biofeedback, Pain and the Patient's Power"
    Morrie Mink, M.D.
"Effect of Physician's World View on Achieving Humanistic Medicine"
    Robert Belknap, M.D.
"Humanistic Curriculum in Sex Education for Health Professionals"
    Mary Morgan, M.P.H.

These titles reflect the range of the problem, that is to say, they reflect the actual complexity of medicine. One can only be humble in confronting such a complicated institution. Gradually, as we think we know more, we are offering it to the health professions—in training workshops, in papers, in monographs, in university courses, lectures, curricula and by other means. This work requires evaluation, refinement and testing by ourselves and others. It is a work in progress.

The Program Staff have, so far, established a few major themes which will be elaborated in the future. Among the themes are these: when the patient is seen as a person, even in the standard medical setting, time is actually saved. This orientation includes searching for the underlying human causes of many physical diseases, rather than repetitively treating symptoms. Many patients seen as persons can be helped, fairly quickly, to take more responsibility for their own health, not just physical health, but the ways of living that help determine their health or disease. Therefore, the physician and nurse can be more than simple authorities, they can become educators and partners with the patient. They can empower the patient.

Finally, illness can frequently be seen as a creative opportunity, a chance for the patient to learn more about himself, about his life direction, about his meaning. The confrontation with pain, disease, and death can be profoundly useful. Sages of all civilizations have said that pain is a great teacher. It underlines the disharmonies. The ulcer may tell us we are working or worrying too much. Pain in general tells us that we must change our lives, we must grow. If necessary, we must achieve that elevation of mind that can accept chronic pain and transcend it. Many have done this. Many health professionals can help others to do this, or to otherwise use pain creatively for growth. But generally, the thrust of contemporary medicine is toward the destruction, obliteration, annihilation and denial of pain, disease and death. That route is not sufficiently broad to be called human.

NOTES

1. I use the word "medicine" in its lay usage, to indicate the larger part of all health care services and organizations.
2. There are many more pressures on medicine than the ones I have summarized, but this brief outline may be enough to evoke the strain which the health care system is suffering.
3. The Program in Humanistic Medicine is only one attempt to address the crises in medicine. Many efforts to discover the human potentialities of medicine are in progress: The Society for Health and Human Values in Philadelphia; Human Dimensions in Medical Education in La Jolla, California; The Intern and Resident Program in Social Medicine, Montefiore Hospital, New York City; The Hastings Center in Hastings-on-Hudson in New York State; Towards a Humanistic Medicine Program at the University of Utah, Salt Lake City are only some of the institutions seeking different ways to create a more humanistic medicine.
4. Two separate study task forces, one of elementary school teachers and one of school district administrators have used a training and discovery process, similar to the Program in Humanistic Medicine, for the purpose of making humanistic innovations in the teaching of elementary reading and in the administration of school districts. The projects were funded by the Ford Foundation, sponsored by the University of California, Santa Barbara, and directed by Sara Miller.
5. Some readers may be interested in the complete set of titles of the *First Report's* papers. These include, in addition to those already mentioned:

> "Developing Criteria for Evaluating Humanistic Aspects of Medical Care," Bernard Schatz, M.D., M.P.H.
> "Detoxification of the Chronic Disease Process in the Adolescent Patient," Naomi Remen, M.D.
> "Evoking Humanistic Communication Between Non-Medical Personnel and Patients," Marguerite Abell, R.N.
> "Checklist for the Evaluation and Treatment of Psychosomatic Disease," Allen Barbour, M.D.
> "Redefining the Limits of Internal Medicine," Robert Blau, M.D.
> "High School Students and Medical Careers," Pamela Antoncich
> "Use of Inner Dialogue in Non-Organic Illness," Anita Astrom
> "Objective and Subjective Dimensions of Emergency Room Care," Ray Hively, M.D.
> "Toward a Cooperative Medicine," Elmer Grossman, M.D.

HUMANISTIC HEALTH CARE: THE EVOLUTION OF THE MEDICAL SYSTEM

Rick Carlson
Dale Garell

Today, virtually no one is sure what our public policy on health should be. A few years ago, secure in the knowledge that the road to health was paved with providers and hospitals, it seemed that the only frontier left was a national health insurance program. However, as we increasingly recognize the limits of the present medical system in the promotion of health, we are puzzled about what to do. Should we enact a national health insurance plan confirming our belief in its fundamental equity, even though we know that it will fail to be the definitive answer to health? Or, given that a national health insurance program is unlikely to have impact on the general level of health in our population, should we decline to pass such legislation? And even if we do pass a national health insurance bill, will its enormous expected costs make it impossible to undertake other programs which show more promise in the effective promotion of health than the simple financing of the current medical system?

Against the backdrop of these questions, let's examine the current state of the art.

There is a lot of evidence to indicate that medicine today is undergoing a profound change. Increasing disenchantment with spiraling medical costs without a significant corresponding improvement in the quality or efficacy of care, and the dehumanizing effects of high technology medical care delivery are the frustrations that many patients and providers feel about the current system. These mutual frustrations are causing us to re-examine our medical models, practices, and goals.

The system of medicine which is practiced at any time is an amalgam of the historical and philosophical understanding a culture has about human health and disease and the technological structure available to

SOURCE: Rick Carlson and Dale Garell, "Humanistic Health Care: The Evolution of the Medical System," *Self-Determination Quarterly Journal*, Vol. 1, No. 2, June 1977.

support health. When cultural conceptions shift, society demands a response to whatever is newly perceived as threatening to health, and slowly medicine changes its focus to accommodate the new thinking.

HISTORICAL OVERVIEW

In order to understand what's going on in medicine today—and many of the new trends will be discussed below—it is important to see these changes in the context of medicine's continuing process of evolution.

Historically, there have been two different strategies in dealing with disease and health in modern medicine. Eric Cassel, in his book, *The Healer's Art: A New Approach to Doctor-Patient Relationships,* characterized these as the "analytic" and the "valuational." The analytic seeks to describe and isolate constituent parts of the individual. The valuational, on the other hand, is that way of thinking which attempts to integrate all the parts of the individual based on a set of values and conceptions about sickness and health. A part of the history of medicine is the history of a dialectic between the analytic and the valuational. How medicine is practiced may be a function of the dominance of one way of thinking over the other.

The analytic, by any measure, has been in the ascendancy for the last fifty years. At present, there seems to be a tendency to return to a more basic relationship between the health professional and patient, and a more human, caring approach to both the patient and the solution of the critical issues presently facing medicine may be emerging. If this is so, medicine may be evolving toward the valuational. Its ultimate evolution may lie in a synthesis of the two—a blending of the power of science with the integrated personal approach of the humanistic movement.

The history of contemporary health care can be divided into four parts: the era of public health and epidemiology; the rise of science and technology the delivery of technological health services; and the transition characteristic of the present post-technological society. These periods are arbitrary and their boundaries are not firm; each new period retains certain elements of the previous ones.

ERA OF PUBLIC HEALTH

The era of public health was marked by the introduction of sanitation coupled with a greatly improved understanding and practice of nutrition. These public health measures of the 1800's were designed to deal with the problems of an industrial era: waste matter; unpotable water; poor diet; harsh labor practices; and unsanitary, debilitating living and working conditions. Improvement of these toxic conditions has accounted for the major progress in health over the last two hundred years.

During this period, the physician practiced without the benefit of modern science and technology—often alone as a cottage industry. With a few known remedies and limited surgical interventions, he offered whatever support and general care that he could to his patients. Though individual patients were helped in this way, the major changes in the standard of health during this period were derived from the public health approach to larger populations: immunizations, waste disposal, dietary advances, and improved housing.

RISE OF SCIENCE AND TECHNOLOGY

Inevitably, medicine began to focus attention on those specific disorders not amenable to public health interventions. Such areas as infectious diseases and organ-specific conditions such as neoplastic, metabolic, endocrine, and congenital disorders became the subject of study and improved technology. Major advances were made in a number of areas, among them: the treatment of bacterial infections; sophisticated surgical interventions; extension of the life span of patients with chronic disease and various malignancies; understanding of the immune system, genetic intervention, physicochemical metabolism of the cell; and pharmacological interventions. This is an impressive list, and most of it has been achieved in the last fifty years.

During this period, health care as an analytical science came of age. Care became increasingly hospital-based, technologically grounded, specialized and responsive to complex organic conditions. Historic esteem for the physician coupled with exaggerated estimations of what could be expected from science led to the belief that no matter what the ill, medicine could correct it, replace it, alter it, cure it.

Despite notable advances in some areas, the problems facing twentieth century medicine expanded; new diseases emerged. "Diseases of civilization" such as smoking, hypertension, obesity, coronary artery disease, alcoholism, drug abuse, suicide, delinquency, automobile and other accidents became the major threats to the public well-being. Medicine was again called upon to respond.

By the mid-sixties, medicine was believed to be a society's major method for improving health, and the "delivery system" of medical care became its chosen tool. The delivery system conceptualized health as a commodity—a product that could be delivered over and over again if only enough variables could be controlled. A system was devised to facilitate smooth delivery of the product: medical care services. Distribution was handled through hospital and physicians' offices, which could be linked together by the physician gaining the privilege of hospital practice. And finally, marketing and promotion were entrusted to insurance companies and increasingly guaranteed by governmental underwriting.

Medical care itself had become extremely sophisticated and depersonalized through the creation and development of specialty and subspecialty practices, by the introduction of new diagnostic aids and therapeutic treatments using computerization and miniaturization, by the regionalization of certain highly specialized and technical services such as renal dialysis, neurosurgery, and cancer therapy, and by specialized service units such as coronary care facilities and neonatal intensive care units.

DELIVERY SYSTEM APPROACH

The concept of the delivery system fit the depersonalized care of the technological period: disease was a malfunction in the human machine, caused either by an internal disorder or by the activity of an external agent. To resolve disease, all that was needed was to accurately analyze it, classify it, and then apply a set of techniques designed to produce like cures in like patients. Health care paradoxically had become predominantly disease-oriented. The professional, too, had become a part of the system. The days of cottage industry had given way to a task force of specialists, technicians, assistants, administrators; the health care industry consumed nearly 8% of the G.N.P.

Despite this burgeoning task force, and even because of it, the professional became even more remote, more distanced from the patient. Both patient and health professional were increasingly dehumanized and became part of the automated delivery of medical care. The delivery system approach began to develop a series of systematic aches and pains. Something had gone wrong.

BROADENING THE EXISTING SYSTEM

In response to this awareness, over the last five years there has been a series of movements which do not fit into the technological/delivery system form of modern health care. These approaches can be characterized as attempts to remedy some of the problems of current health care practices by broadening and enriching the existing medical paradigm and by introducing into care the key concept that the individual can take increased responsibility for his/her own health. Collectively, these movements have tended to increase both public and professional consciousness of the larger issues of dehumanization and lack of power and to suggest a response that may well be the beginning of a humanly relevant health care.

Such a medical paradigm has been described by the Institute for the Study of Humanistic Medicine as follows: "A health care that would acknowledge that the impulse for health lies within the individual and not the health care system, that human health reflects the interdependent nature of body, emotions, mind, and spirit, and that health is a human ability and increasingly a matter of personal choice; a health care that would recognize the possible unique meanings of illness within the perspective of the total life of an individual and see the potential in every illness to be an opportunity for positive change in lifestyle, values, and life goals. Such a medicine is based on the collaborative relationship of the patient and the health professional."

EMERGING ALTERNATIVES

What are some of the current trends which comprise this new medicine? They are many: movements to address the ethical-philosophical dilemmas inherent in scientific medicine such as the redefinition of death, the ethics of distribution of limited health resources, etc.; movements such as those of LeBoyer (birth) and Kubler-Ross (death) to reinfuse critical life situations with recognition of their unique personal meaning, a meaning which high-technology care has tended to de-emphasize if not obliterate; efforts to introduce the study of humanities and arts into medical school curricula, and to encourage health professionals to acquire or improve their interpersonal and communications skills. In addition, there has been an upsurge of interest in alternative therapies: new, nontechnological methodologies including those borrowed from other countries (i.e., acupuncture), or from other cultures or disciplines (meditation), from older medical approaches (nutrition); or varying combinations of technological and person-centered therapies (biofeedback). The focus of all of these movements has been on the healing resources of the individual's body which, when mobilized, may prove as potent as technology in promoting health. The prevailing medical model, being both disease-oriented and predominantly provider rather than consumer empowering, has neglected this human potential.

These movements have also emphasized that the person-patient is a whole being—emotional, physical, mental, spiritual, environmental, and social—and must be treated as a whole, rather than reduced to a "disease entity."

MEDICINE OF THE PERSON

What's fundamentally new and different about this kind of medicine? Haven't generations of physicians been exhorted to "care for the whole patient"? This is indeed true. However, the view of the person implicit in a medicine of the person differs from that of traditional medical practice in at least three ways.

First, since the person is perceived as a dynamic relationship of body, mind, feelings and spirit, he or she can best be healed when all four human dimensions are considered. For the health professional, this view requires a recognition that an intervention at a single level (body, feelings, etc.) of the person's existence not only has effects at the other levels, but may be incomplete and therefore unsatisfactory because of the failure to anticipate those effects. A single level intervention may neglect those variables deriving from other levels which may form part of the etiology of the episode of illness and which, unless addressed, will cause the episode to persist despite therapy.

The second difference lies in the recognition that when people seek medical care, they do not leave their environment at the hospital or clinic door. To "cure" a disease in the hospital is not the same as effecting a cure that continues to be practical in a home or work environment. A medicine of the person demands a consideration of the context within which each human being lives.

And third, the ability of each patient to choose and be self-determining would underlie all health care interventions. Health is seen as a matter of choice of each individual person who is the patient and not with the person who is the professional. The ideal role of the professional and the medical system is not to manipulate the individual to a greater health, but rather to inform individuals of their options and collaborate with them in achieving the options of their choice.

PUBLIC POLICY CHANGES

Public policy is beginning to reflect the impact of these currents of change. A Senate Subcommittee report on a recent National Health Manpower Bill, SB 3239, has called for the development of Centers of Humanistic Medicine to begin the task of integration and synthesis of these widely varied contributions. These centers and others will be charged with the task of developing a systems-wide approach to humanizing health care as well as exploring basic research which furthers our understanding of man as a unique species—an understanding which can form the basis of human health itself.

As never before, the times seem to be ones of opportunity for both medicine and society to redefine critical health issues and to begin a continuing process of reassessment of priorities and policies. Such an endeavor must lead to establishment of the individual as the primary responsible agent for health, an agent to be assisted by the health care system, but not controlled. To do more would be to hinder the continuing evolution of the individual; to do less would be to retreat from the responsibility of providing needed medical services and care. It is a great challenge.

BIOFEEDBACK, HUMANISTIC PSYCHOLOGY AND PSYCHOSOMATICS IN FAMILY PRACTICE

R. T. James, LRCP, MRCS
Terry Burrows, MD

SUMMARY

An innovative educational approach to psychosomatic illness in family practice has been developed. It is a synthesis of experiential methods of non-verbal communication and creativity training developed from psychotronic applications of biofeedback, humanistic psychology and eidetics. The methodology, called eidetic biofeedback, operates on nontraditional models of human potential and involves a holistic approach to the mind/body/environment relationship. The methods work by transferring the responsibility for health back to the awareness of the individual.

Of 200 office practice patients, 60 percent achieved major changes in personality integration and vitality. This was reflected in cessation of the presenting complaint, without symptom substitution and diminished demand for clinical services.

Is there a new approach to the stress-related psychosomatic disorders which constitute the major portion of every family physician's practice—the endless stream of headaches, ulcers, anxieties, depressions, hypertensions, asthmas, rashes, etc.? Is there a new approach to these 'life spoiling' and potentially life threatening complaints which avoids the need for constant conditioning by drugs or hypnosis, or the complicated reinforcement regimes of behavior modification, or prolonged psychoanalysis? Is there a new approach which is widely applicable to a variety of psychosomatic disorders? Which is essentially educational and based on natural processes? With a high degree of carry over from the

SOURCE: R. T. James and Terry Burrows, "Biofeedback, Humanistic Psychology and Psychosomatics in Family Practice," *Canadian Family Physician*, 22: 1449-1459, 1976. Reprinted by permission of the publisher.

doctor's office to 'real life' and which is thus both therapeutic and pre-ventive? Something easily understood and acceptable to both the family physician and the patient?

There is. It is a group of self-awareness and creativity training methods known by the general term 'biofeedback', developed over the past decade in the fields of electronics, behavioral and humanistic psychology, and psychotronics. This group of methods fills not only the criteria mentioned above, but effectively and realistically transfers the responsibility for the maintenance of psychosomatic health back to the patient. Using these methods, the patient is involved in a meaningful and decisive way in his own health care. This is done by giving him the means to learn, quickly and easily, skills of voluntary self-regulation that are based on self discovery and self awareness. He can use these learned skills to restore his psycho-physiological balance if he is sick and to maintain it by continued practice when he is well.

We have used biofeedback methods to enhance self awareness and creativity in the successful management of psychosomatic illness in family practice for 30 months. The methods we use now were for the most part developed independently in our own practical research. They are a synthesis of techniques in non-verbal communication developed in humanistic psychology and Canadian psychotronics. We call our methodology 'self-image feedback' or 'eidetic biofeedback'. The eidetic biofeedback communication process was originally developed in the late 1960s as a method of creativity development and a framework for environmental design, by Evering Consultants, Toronto, Canada. We have added to it a therapeutic application.

The methods we have developed and their underlying rationale were only partly derived from the available professional literature on biofeedback. This literature is largely still being written in a frame of reference which limits the application of biofeedback in everyday practical situations. Up to now most contributions in the field have been written from the viewpoint of mechanistic, behavioristic, hypnotic or psychoanalytic models of the human being. Because of these models themselves, the authors have been led to ambivalent statements about the value of biofeedback.[1] We did not share this ambivalence; this paper reports some of the background and results of our own use of this method in family practice.

BACKGROUND

Humanistic Psychology

The writings of such authors as Maslow[2] gave rise to an approach to psychology which was intended to balance the overemphasis on external control in behaviorism and on psychopathology in psychoanalysis. Humanistic psychology, as this development became known, really expressed a new paradigm of human nature and led to the formation of the Association for Humanistic Psychology in 1962.

Humanistic psychology recognizes the importance of the person as a whole, the uniqueness of each individual and the role of his interactions with his environment. It recognizes that each individual is innately creative and is in a constant state of growth and development; that each person has the innate capacity for self-determination and the ability to move from dependence on external conditioning influences to self-understanding and self-reliance. It also emphasizes mental and physical health rather than illness.

In stressing healthy growth, development, will and creativity as the most universal human characteristics,[2] humanistic psychology naturally leads to new methods of learning the resources of the inner self and the importance of interpersonal interaction. These methods de-emphasize the learning of external facts in favor of internal awareness and non-verbal communication for integration and self-actualization.[3] Eidetic biofeedback is thus a further elaboration and practical application of the human potential paradigm, which is common to both humanistic psychology and psychotronics.

Eidetics and Creativity

The term 'eidetic' refers to the language of the right cerebral hemisphere—its creative, perceptive and expressive functions—just as the term 'verbal' refers to the language of the left cerebral hemisphere.

Recent research following surgical separation of the two cerebral hemispheres across the corpus callosum has revealed that each 'brain', left and right, has its own sphere of consciousness. Each operates its own modes of thinking, information processing and expression, the one being complementary to the other.[4]

The left brain coordinates the individual's relations with his external environment. Its operating mode is logical, analytic and linear. It handles the functions of verbal language and the decisive coordination of musculoskeletal activity. The right brain coordinates the individual's relations with his internal environment. Its operating mode is holistic and it handles information in a gestalt or multiple association pattern. It handles the non-verbal image and symbolic functions of language, the eidetic (or structural) patterns of color, form and texture in imagery. It expresses its experience in action patterns in the visceral nervous system. The left brain is the linear thinking, word brain; the right brain is the gestalt thinking, image/feeling brain.[5]

The cooperative working together of both brains is the operational basis of creativity, spontaneity and personal integration.[6] We have found that most of the psychosomatic disturbances with which we have dealt have been characterized by functional overuse of the left brain. The key to our approach is to bring forward the individual's recognition and use of his own creative right hemisphere. We use biofeedback instruments for the first stage of this reintegration, and the feedback of externally expressed inner eidetic imagery for the succeeding stages.

Biofeedback

The principle of biofeedback is as simple as the principle of the mirror. When you are shaving or combing your hair in the morning, the reflection you get by monitoring your own purposeful, self-directed activities is essential to the successful accomplishment of your task. To do it properly you need to see your own face. Similarly, physiological biofeedback describes the process in which the continuous moment to moment function of a physiological variable (e.g., GSR—galvanic skin response) is monitored and fed back to the attention of the person being monitored. The feedback is in the form of a visual or auditory signal. An electronic monitoring system is used to 'mirror' the physiological function back to the subject so that he can recognize variations in this activity. This recognition is then correlated in his self awareness with his internal psychological states of feeling and attitude, expanding his usual range of self awareness. This self awareness expansion allows the voluntary control of the 'mirrored' physiological variable through the exercise of the individual's own will.

Changes then made are functions of the individual's consciousness and volition. They are not simply conditioned physical reflexes. They are psychophysiological responses (i.e., mind/body responses), which direct the person's energy economy in a new way. However, the individual's ability to express this recognition verbally depends on how well his right and left brains are working together at this level.

The earliest biofeedback experiments with animals demonstrated that rats could be trained to blush alternately in each ear.[7] It was then shown that human beings, "being at least as smart as rats", could learn voluntary control of such specificity that individual motor units could be made to produce "drum beat patterns" on oscilloscopes.[8] Further workers[9,10] observed something more: that not only could individuals learn to control voluntarily the activity of specific body functions such as muscle tension and skin temperature through biofeedback, but that a further change occurred at the same time—in the individuals' self awareness and integration. Over a period of time this change led to a more integrated response to life, a more healthy response to stress and a rebalancing of their psychosomatic 'posture'. This occurred along with the alleviation of pre-existing psychosomatic symptoms, for the most part without symptom substitution.

This additional phenomenon has been the primary interest in our approach to psychosomatics with biofeedback and its occurrence has been strongly confirmed by our experience. We were primarily interested in dealing with the whole person, since it is the whole person that has the psychosomatic problem. We used biofeedback instruments as experiential stepping stones to engage the person with more of his whole self. It is important to note that although biofeedback can be added as a valuable new tool to the family physician's resources for the educational treatment and prevention of psychosomatic illness, it was not primarily developed as a medical tool nor is it considered primarily to be so.

Biofeedback instruments themselves do nothing at all 'to' a person. They are simply monitors, like thermometers or mirrors, whose job is to facilitate the mind's awareness of the body, i.e., how the body is. Their sensing electrodes simply sit on the skin surface, and the instruments have no intrinsic powers in themselves to affect the body or the mind. They can be voluntarily used to assist the intrinsic capacity of a person's own mind to operate his body and to observe himself doing so.

However, our efficiency in operating ourselves can be greatly improved through augmented and integrated feedback, be it from a biofeedback instrument, from a mirror, from other people, etc. This opportunity to discover how to improve our efficiency of self operation should not be restricted to ill health; it is precisely the lack of this experiential knowledge which leads to so many health problems. Accordingly, biofeedback is being used for the training of creativity in education,[11] the business world,[12] as well as psychology,[13] etc.

A Basic Demonstration

It is essential for your own understanding and skill in using biofeedback as an effective, adjunctive, clinical modality, to experiment first with it yourself. A typical battery operated GSR biofeedback instrument gives audible feedback of the arousal level of the sympathetic nervous system by monitoring the electrical changes in conductivity of the skin, due to the sweat gland activity of the finger pads. This glandular activity, and thus the feedback tone, fluctuates in response to the inner mental imagery and thought processes.

When you try this yourself, you will observe that as you visualize a calming image or scene in your mind's eye, the feedback tone subsides in pitch. When you visualize an anxiety-provoking image or situation, the tone will rise in pitch. Explore a variety of images or situations which have personal meaning to you and which cause the pitch to go up and down. When you have localized some, you can now raise or lower the tone of the instrument voluntarily. You do this by focusing your will and attention on the appropriate mental images you discovered (i.e., 'up' images or 'down' images) while at the same time focusing on the fluctuations of the feedback tone. With this dual focus maneuver you can mentally cause the tone pitch to go up or down at will.

At this point, it is important to note one of the many fundamental distinctions of biofeedback from hypnosis. In the biofeedback process, you focus your attention simultaneously inward on your own thought and imagery processes *and* outward on their environmental feedback. This feedback 'mirrors' back to you your body's physiological response to your own thoughts and your own attitude to them. This is a psycho-energetically very active and de-automatizing process. It is a de-hypnotic process.

If you continue your concentration on this focusing task for a period of time (five or ten minutes) to try to relax or lower the tone, for example, your physiological system will manifest biochemical and bioelectric changes which constitute the opposite of the stressful 'fight or flight' reaction.[14] You will then find that you soon feel refreshed, re-energized and rested—without having slept. If your attention wanders from your dual focus, or someone intrudes upon you from the environment, the tone pitch rapidly rises. Thus the feedback tone functions like 'wobble wheels' on a bicycle for the guidance of the new learner trying to find his psychophysiological balance.

Most people can quickly visualize in their mind's eye, eidetic imagery which directs the fluctuation of the feedback tone. The symbolism and meaning of this imagery is uniquely personal, since it arises from their own experience.[15] This eidetic imagery is active in the operation of the individual's psychophysiological energy systems, since it is a message, in symbolic language, from the intuitive and creative aspects of his consciousness, i.e., from his right brain. Such internal communication, when brought to awareness, can give us new ideas about how to transcend and resolve our current problems and to overcome the mind/body energy blocks which cause psychosomatic symptoms.[16] We have found this to be a natural and integrating process subject to learning and practice, and which happens spontaneously in the biofeedback process, even though the individual or others working with him may not notice the experience or choose to take full opportunity of the insight available from it. Thus we see biofeedback as a voluntary skill in self regulation through the mobilization of inner creativity,[17] rather than the conditioning referred to in the behavioristic, hypnotic or psychoanalytic literature on biofeedback.

The Mind/Body/Environment Link—Psychotronics

Like placebo effects and spontaneous remissions of illness, the GSR effect has been known for many years. Each of these phenomena are clues to the mind/body/environment linkage which is at the core of the psychosomatic phenomenon. The quick changes in the so-called autonomic nervous system and other body control systems which can be voluntarily learned with biofeedback demand explanation. In our view, they can only be explained by an expanded frame of reference such as has been necessary in modern physics, where the observer is no longer separable from the observed, and matter has lost its substance in a field of energy.

The physicist's concept of people as interacting electromagnetic fields fundamental to their underlying chemical and physiological structures, and the idea of life forms being complex energy exchange systems, has yet to be absorbed within traditional medicine and psychology.[18, 19] Attempts are still being made to fit biofeedback and indeed, the psychosomatic phenomenon itself, into the older models of conditioning, hypnosis and psychoanalysis. This appears to us to lie in the way of a fuller and more effective use of biofeedback and the practical everyday use of the energies of consciousness.[20]

Central to the issue of psychosomatic health and illness is the fact that cause and effect changes are mediated by some energy exchange process associated with human consciousness, and can be directed voluntarily by human awareness, closely associated with human creativity.[21] A serious search for the nature and relationships of this energy is being made in the science of psychotronics.

METHOD

In the office, the family physician first introduces his patient to the GSR biofeedback instrument, which the physician demonstrates on himself to allay any fears. The person then spends one or two 20-30 minute sessions by himself, making contact with his own mind/body system and exploring how it works. Thus he discovers the all-important fact that he can operate his own system himself, with no help of any kind from anyone. We have found continuous home practice with the instruments speeds up the whole process.

The next step is to encourage the individual to notice his own mental imagery and then externalize it, so that he can have a look at it—to use it like a mirror.[22] The simplest and most effective method requires only a piece of paper and a set of colored felt pens. The person draws a picture of something he has visualized during the GSR biofeedback sessions or something entirely spontaneous. The instruction is "draw anything".

As facilitators of this process, we found that we had to avoid as much as possible projecting our own imagery and attitudes into the person's interaction with his own feedback, either from his biofeedback instrument or from his drawings. Such projections defeat and devitalize the person's encounter with his own creative imagery and energy. The fear of self encounter with feelings is thus rapidly overcome, because the person quickly realizes that he is in complete control and that the world doesn't fall apart when he allows himself to experience dialogue with his own right brain.

Having drawn a picture, the person is then asked to describe in descriptive phrases or adjectives what he sees in his drawing. He is then asked to search for the relationship of what he sees there to his attitude towards himself and his life experience. This very act of verbalizing aspects of an image causes activity between the two cerebral hemispheres, freeing up creative interchange between them. It has been reported that a specific EEG wave form occurs across the corpus callosum at the time of personal insight.[23] This process is very rapid, safe and is based on a model of intrinsic health, rather than intrinsic illness.

The eidetic biofeedback process is non-traumatic because the person does all the work he wants to do *on himself*, with a mandatory minimum of guidance from the physician. The main function of the physician is to make available an empathic environment in which the person feels supported enough to allow himself to change his own patterns. The physician must then keep out of his way while he does so.

RESULTS

We realized very early that the approach which works in family practice is a humanistic approach to the whole person with a marked de-emphasis on drugs. It was also clear to us that focusing attention on the pathological details of the individual symptoms does not help this approach. Therefore, we realized there was little point in presenting our results in terms of the changes in these pathological details, e.g., a statistical analysis of specific organ or system diagnoses, lab and X-ray results, etc. The really important changes take place within the whole person. For this reason, we decided to use pattern recognition and to select operational parameters as indicators for assessing the effectiveness of the method. Thus we watched what patients did and how they changed as people.

Since we know in psychotronics that the observer is always part of the circuit, our assessment was both objective and subjective. We also changed in tandem with our patients. We are aware that this approach to evaluation differs from the traditional emphasis on scientific objectivity. However, modern quantum physicists tell us that there is in fact no such thing as pure scientific objectivity.[24] Even if there were, its exclusive use would be inappropriate to what really goes on in interpersonal interaction in family practice, where assessment is a daily blend of objectivity and subjectivity.

We selected the following parameters:

1. Cessation of presenting complaint.
2. Lack of substituted complaint for periods of five to ten months.

3. Decrease in demand for medication, medical attention and investigation.
4. Changes in personality integration and vitality, and personal growth.

The people we worked with were approximately 100 of Dr. James' own patients, with well-established diagnoses of psychosomatic illness, who had been attending his office for reassurance, counseling and/or tranquilizers for between one and ten years.

In addition to these 100 patients, whose preceding patterns had been observed long enough that they could be used as a form of control in comparing their follow-up course after starting the eidetic biofeedback program, there was a second group of another 100 more recent patients whose previous condition was not so well known. However, their improvement followed the same pattern as the first group.

The changes in the general patterns listed above took place with individuals in both groups to a degree that we judged to be very marked in 60 percent, fair in 32 percent and absent in the remaining 8 percent.

In introducing people to the program, we found that with a simple explanation, there was no resistance to 'working with little radios' or to 'drawing pictures'. In fact, our growing enthusiasm was matched by the patients', and our project very quickly became a team effort. They soon saw that we really thought they could do it themselves. Most importantly, they saw that we were giving them 'permission' and encouraging them to do so. Most of them wanted to help us prove that we were right. The 8 percent who got no benefit wanted to prove that we were wrong.

The average visit length for each patient was 20-30 minutes for two to six visits (some longer) over a one to six week period. We billed the patient's OHIP number for an office call when they came in for a GSR biofeedback practice session only (for those who did not have an instrument at home) and a half-hour visit at the psychotherapy rate for the eidetic feedback work.

Over this period of participation we observed a pattern of self awareness and life experience change in the majority of the participants as follows:

1. An improved sense of independence and self-esteem; improved self-image.
2. Improved ability to cope with ongoing crises.
3. Increased self-control of attitude and somatic reaction.
4. Acceptance of a greater degree of responsibility for their own personal health and well-being.
5. Increased energy for living and lasting personal happiness.

Judging by our observations of those people who benefited the most and the least, we formed the opinion that success depended on the enhancement of a latent sufficiency of certain personality factors:

1. Ability to live in the 'here and now'.
2. Flexibility of attitude; acceptance of self and others.
3. Perseverance.
4. Freedom from over-intellectualization.
5. Growth of awareness of creativity.
6. Ability to experience and voluntarily balance a range of emotions.
7. 'The courage to be'.

Since the belief system of the patient and his family, the belief system of the physician and the belief system of the culture of which they are all a part are essential ingredients in any therapeutic interaction, no matter what therapeutic tools are being used, we consider the necessity for the possession of the above qualities applies equally to the doctor as well as to his patients.[25] The essential elements of such belief systems are: imagery of self and the world, awareness of self and the world, and attitude towards self and the world.

A marked feature of each person's recovery and resultant personal growth was the degree of belief system deconditioning experienced. We call this de-hypnotisation. In fact, the degree of relief from conditioning towards the release of spontaneous self-generated creativity paralleled the degree and rate of resolution of psychosomatic symptomatology and eventual recovery. The common pattern in our experience has been a marked diminution of symptoms and number of visits following the program sessions, plus a marked increase in personal integration and 'aliveness' which has persisted over follow-up visits.

DISCUSSION

In our view, the methods described above offer a new alternative to the sole reliance on chemical or mental conditioning for the treatment of psychosomatic disorders. They are based on each person discovering the unity of his own mind and body and voluntarily resetting his own psychophysiological 'thermostat'. This resetting is based on self awareness and on making and sticking to his own decisions for himself. The same methods used in treatment are better used in prevention. They can be used in both because they are basically educational. They are only therapeutic because of the ability for 'self-balancing' that people can bring about in themselves.

There are other instruments in addition to GSR monitors, including skin temperature, EMG and EEG monitors. They all have application in the management of stress, e.g., headache, muscular disorders, etc. They are effective because of the same basic human principle—self awareness leads to the unlocking of innate creativity.

Biofeedback instruments are being used in schools to a degree, but the educational system is already behind the business world, where biofeedback instruments are increasingly being used for relaxation and stimulation of the creativity that our economic system depends upon so much for new ideas.[12]

The opportunity of using biofeedback as a core part of public health promotion and psychosomatic illness prevention programs is truly exciting. This will require the training of facilitators to teach non-patients how to use biofeedback by themselves. These facilitators will need to be trained in the communication methods of humanistic psychology. So also will physicians and nurses and other professionals using biofeedback therapeutically.

In the publication, *A New Perspective on the Health of Canadians*, Health Minister Marc Lalonde stated: "Programs of prevention directed at large population groups are desperately needed". We certainly encourage all levels of government to look at biofeedback as a means of helping to fill that need.[26] As a potential cost saver at the intake end of the health care delivery system, biofeedback and humanistic psychology offer great promise in widespread application.

REFERENCES

1. Blanchard, E. B., Young, L. D. "Clinical Applications of Biofeedback Training." *Arch. Gen. Psychiatry* 30:573-589, May, 1974.
2. Maslow, A. *The Farther Reaches of Human Nature.* New York, Viking, 1971.
3. Perls, F. *Gestalt Therapy Verbatim.* New York, Bantam, 1971.
4. Bogen, J. E., Bogen, G. M. "The Other Side of the Brain, III". *The Corpus Callosum and Creativity.* Bull. Los Angeles Neurol. Soc. 34:191-220, 1969.
5. Ornstein, R. *The Psychology of Consciousness.* San Francisco, Freeman, 1972.
6. Bogen, J. E. "The Other Side of the Brain, II". *An Appositional Mind,* Bull. Los Angeles Neurol. Soc. 34:135-162, 1969.
7. Miller, M. E., Dicara, L. V. "Instrumental Learning of Vaso-Motor Responses by Rats: Learning to Respond Differently in the Two Ears". *Science* 159, 1485-1486, 1968.
8. Basmajian. "Control and Training of Individual Motor Units". *Science* 141:440-441, August 2, 1963.

9. Budzynski, T. H., Stoyva, J. M., Adler, C. S., Mullaney, D. J. "EMG Biofeedback and Tension Headache: A Controlled Outcome Study". *Psychosom. Med.* 35:484-96, 1973.
10. Sargent, J. D., Green, E., Walters, E. D. "Preliminary Report on the Use of Autogenic Feedback Training in the Treatment of Migraine and Tension Headache". *Psychosom. Med.* 35:129-35, 1973.
11. King, M. "Biofeedback in the High School Curriculum". Association for Humanistic Psychology *Newsletter,* June, 1975.
12. Barrett, F. D. "How to Generate New Ideas". *The Business Quarterly,* Vol. 40:33-39, Summer.
13. Green, E. "Biofeedback for Mind/Body Self-Regulation: Healing and Creativity". *Biofeedback and Self-Control* (Ed. Shapiro et. al.) Chicago, Aldine, 1972.
14. Wallace, R. K., Benson, H. "The Physiology of Meditation". *Sci. Am.* 226:2, February, 1972.
15. Ahsen, A. *Concepts in Eidetic Psychotherapy.* New York, Brandon House, 1973.
16. Burrows, T., Evering, H. "Psychotronic Interfaces of the Eidetic General System". Applications; Medicine, Biofeedback, Eidetic Biofeedback. *Digest.* Second International Congress of Psychotronic Research, Monte Carlo, Monaco, 1975, p. 418.
17. Green, E. "The Ins and Outs of Mind/Body Energy". *Science Year,* Chicago, 1974.
18. Burr, H. S. *The Fields of Life.* New York, Ballantine, 1972.
19. Tromp, S. W. *Medical Biometerology.* New York, American Elsevier, 1963.
20. Kuhn, T. *The Structure of Scientific Revolutions.* University of Chicago Press, 1962.
21. Green, E., Green, A. *Psychophysiological Training for Creativity.* Also; *Brainwave Training, Imagery, Creativity and Integrative Experiences.* Research Department, Menninger Foundation, Topeka, Kansas.
22. James, R. T. M. "Eidetic Biofeedback Methodology in General Medical Practice". *Digest,* Second International Congress on Psychotronic Research, Monte Carlo, Monaco, 1975, p. 414.
23. Don, H. "Cortical Activity Changes During a Psychotherapeutic Procedure: Implications for EEG Biofeedback Training", *Digest.* Proceedings of the Sixth Annual Meeting of the Biofeedback Research Society, Monterey, California, February, 1975, p. 68.
24. Capra, F. *The Tao of Physics.* London, Wildwood, 1975.
25. Simonton, C., Simonton, S. "Belief Systems and Management of the Emotional Aspects of Malignancy". *Journal of Transpersonal Psychology,* 1, 1975.
26. Burrows, T. "Psychotronics and a New Perspective on the Health of Canadians". Paper presented at the Annual Meeting of the Ontario Medical Association, May, 1975.

BENEFICENT EUTHANASIA

Marvin Kohl

As long as we respect human dignity and regard kindly acts as being at least virtuous, beneficent euthanasia, or mercy killing, will be practiced and remain a moral activity. For, as Cicero correctly observed, other things being equal, our first duty is to help most where help is most needed.

I shall present my case in three parts. Questions as to the morality of indirect euthanasia will be considered in Part I. A characterization and brief defense of direct noninvoluntary beneficent euthanasia will be presented in Part II. In Part III, I will consider the most formidable objection: that, no matter the intrinsic rightness of euthanasia, the ultimate consequences would be too costly—that is, that the moral or legal approval of any form of direct euthanasia would in fact lead to a state of unrestrained killing and, that even where an act of killing is not intrinsically wrong and has good particular consequences, the general prohibition should be kept, because not to do so has the consequence of weakening the general prohibition against killing, which we feel necessary to maintain.

Euthanasia is usually defined in one of several ways. Narrowly, it refers to the *inducement* of painless quick death. In one of its broader senses, however, the term refers also to the *allowance* of a painless quick death. I shall follow here the broader usage and roughly distinguish between direct (or active) and indirect (or passive) euthanasia. The former designates acts in which one does something directly to end life when it would otherwise go on; the latter designates acts in which one refrains from doing something so that death will come more quickly.

There are two questions: the morality of direct and the morality of indirect euthanasia. Let us consider the latter one first.

Aside from the problem of undesirable consequences, the question of whether or not an act of indirect euthanasia is sinful or immoral is not apt to arise unless it is already believed that the continuance of mere physical life is an absolute and/or intrinsic good. I suggest that this position, a

SOURCE: Marvin Kohl, "Beneficent Euthanasia." This article first appeared in *The Humanist*, July/August 1974, and is reprinted by permission.

position held by most vitalists and some inalienable-right theorists, is open to formidable objections.

It should be noticed, first, that saying life is intrinsically good means that the existence of life would be a good, even if it existed quite alone, without any accompaniments, goals, or meaning—that is, that the mere physical process, in and of itself, is always a good. I am inclined to believe that the motivation behind this position is well intended. For it often does seem that the best way to protect something is to make protection exceptionless. But surely we do not want a principle that seeks to preserve life at the price of protecting suffering, when that suffering can be shown to be needless.

To say that all human life is intrinsically good is to say that each and every life, whether or not the individual is suffering acutely from incurable conditions or disease, is intrinsically good. It is to say that the life of a child like David Patrick Houle—a child who among other things was born with improperly formed vertebrae, a malformed left side and hand, no left eye or ear, and who if he survived would be partly deaf, palsied, blind, and mentally retarded—is intrinsically good. It is to say that when lives are irretrievably blasted by accident or blighted by some ghastly illness, or that even when all dignity, beauty, and meaning have vanished, these lives are intrinsically good. The flaw in this philosophy lies not in its intention but in its entailments. For unless this position is abridged or more carefully qualified, it entails the acceptance of pointless suffering.

Still another difficulty is that the vitalist position runs counter to common moral intuitions or beliefs about killing. For example, it is widely held that killing in self-defense and the defense of others, especially when necessary to save life, is morally justifiable. In addition, the vitalist's high regard for life *qua* life runs counter to the moral approval of the hero or the martyr who lays down his life for the sake of other values, such as honor or conscience. John Huss, the Bohemian religious reformer, was burned at the stake and his ashes thrown into the Rhine River because he refused to stop attacking the worldliness of the clergy and the interference of the Catholic Church in political matters. I do not think we would be prepared to say that Huss' belief that honor and conscience come before one's own personal safety was mistaken, though we might in practice often lack the courage of that conviction.

The main point is this: there is a difference between saying "X is good" and saying "X is an intrinsic and/or an absolute good." Almost all men hold life to be a good, but few would perceive or hold it either to be good in itself or the highest good. To make a case for these claims, it must be shown: (a) that mere physical life is always a good thing; and (b) that it is the highest good. And this has not been done, and I do not believe it can be done.

My only excuse for insisting on the inadequacy of the vitalist position is that it is not consistently recognized by opponents of euthanasia.

There is some sort of odd bifurcation. For many seem to maintain that what I have said is right when applied to problems of indirect (passive) euthanasia but wrong when applied to problems of direct (or active) euthanasia. Plainly, they cannot have it both ways. If these beliefs are inadequate grounds for opposing indirect euthanasia, then they are inadequate for opposing direct euthanasia.

Let us now turn to, and consider, the more difficult problem: When is an act of direct euthanasia right or morally justified? Correctly conceived, for an act to be one of beneficent (active) euthanasia, the dominant motive must be the desire to help the intended recipient, the act must involve the inducement of a painless quick death,[1] and it must result in beneficial treatment for that recipient. In other words, the term beneficent euthanasia is synonymous with the term mercy killing, that is, the inducement of a painless and quick death, the intention and actual consequences of which are the kindest possible treatment in the actual circumstances of an unfortunate individual. An act is noninvoluntary only if it is either the result of the fully informed consent of the intended recipient or, when the recipient is not mentally or physically free to choose (as in the case of permanent coma), the proper legal guardian (or when this is inappropriate, society or its representative), acting on the individual's behalf, gives consent. I advocate the legalization and practice in certain situations of noninvoluntary direct beneficent euthanasia (hereafter referred to simply as beneficent euthanasia).

I have described the nature of kindly acts and argued for the morality of beneficent euthanasia at length in *The Morality of Killing* (Humanities Press, New York, 1974). Here, I shall summarize some of the basic points.

The argument on behalf of beneficent euthanasia is twofold. First of all, since it is kind treatment, and since society and its members each have a prima facie (though not an equal) obligation to treat members kindly, it follows that beneficent euthanasia is a prima facie obligation. This means that in certain circumstances we actually have a moral obligation to induce death. It is not only virtuous to help most where help is most needed, but often it is a duty to do so.

In addition to the argument from kindness, there is an argument from justice. It has two prongs. The first is that, where an individual is not constrained but physically and mentally free to choose, his consent is necessary. This is an essential safeguard, for one of the best defenses against injustice is that of informed consent. The second is that justice further requires that where possible we give to each according to basic needs; and, since human beings have a basic need to live and die with dignity, it is just that we treat them accordingly. This entails the right to live, the right to die, and the right to death with dignity.

---

1. "Painless quick death" is an abbreviated way of saying "as quick and painless as possible." I am indebted to Stephen Nathanson for a similar point.

Many people would say that when an action is a kindly one it is to some extent desirable and that when it is both kindly and just it is a prima facie moral act, if not obligatory. But some would be quick to add that even a kindly and intrinsically just act is not necessarily moral, whatever the consequences. For, like the utilitarians, they hold that the rule not to kill the innocent must be regarded as universally binding for two reasons: first, because the wisdom of past generations has discovered that the consequences of killing the innocent in permissible circumstances is in fact conducive to the killing of the innocent in nonpermissible circumstances; second, because, even in the case of an apparent exception (beneficent euthanasia), where the killing has good consequences, still the rule should be kept, because in general it is right, and one breach of it would weaken the authority of the rule, which we wish to see generally observed.

Of the two reasons, the first (the so-called wedge or slippery-slope argument) may be ruled out. There is simply no evidence that killing per se is contagious, but there is overwhelming evidence to show that it is not. It is true that people who believe that it is right to kill Gypsies, Jews, or anyone else, provided their death may profit the state, will probably continue to kill if they have the power to do so. But this is not evidence of the seductiveness of killing. Rather, it is evidence that, when men have almost unlimited power, their actions will be consistent with their beliefs and, if their beliefs entail needless cruelty, so will their actions.

No doubt much of the resistance to euthanasia is due to fear, the almost abject fear of the Nazi experience. I think Joseph Fletcher is right in holding that the Nazis never engaged in mercy killing; "what they did was merciless killing, either genocidal or for ruthless experimental purposes." ("Ethics and Euthanasia," *To Live and To Die*, Robert H. Williams, ed., Springer-Verlag, New York, 1973). The motivation behind and the nature and consequences of acts of beneficent euthanasia are radically different. In the Nazi example, the motivation (aside perhaps from sadism) was solely that of maximizing "benefit" for the state. In cases of beneficent euthanasia the motivation is essentially and predominantly that of maximizing benefit for the recipient, that of helping most where and when the individual needs it most. The Nazi form was involuntary, while the form advocated here is noninvoluntary.

There still remains the difficult task of being able to distinguish free, informed consent from that of subtly, or otherwise, coerced acts. Yet this problem should not be blown out of proportion. The obsessive fear of abuse should not prevent us from acting kindly. Nor should it blind us to the fact that some acts are not only freely chosen but easily recognized to be so, and that in cases of beneficent euthanasia the individual has the right and power to reject or terminate that action.

Similarly, there are cases where the proposed act of inducing death constitutes a borderline case of kindness. Here, even if it is freely requested by the patient, one should refrain from acting. *If there is reasonable doubt that the purported act is not kind or not the kindest possible actual alternative, one should refrain from acting.* This is not to say that one does not have a right to self-determination and thereby suicide. Nor is it to say that one should refrain from acting in cases that easily and clearly meet the conditions outlined earlier. It is only to suggest that there is an important difference between suicide and proxy suicide and that the consent of a potential recipient does not in itself necessarily incur the obligation of someone else to assist in the act.

This procedural rule, especially when added to our understanding that an act is only beneficent euthanasia if both the intention and actual consequences of the act is the kindest possible treatment for the recipient, radically separates beneficent from the nonbeneficent varieties of euthanasia.

The second major theoretical consequentialist concern seems to be that the so-called inviolate rule prohibiting the killing of the innocent should be kept, and therefore that beneficent euthanasia should be prohibited. In other words, we are being told that we ought to weigh the maximizing of benefit against the maximizing of harm, and that if we did so, we would find that the consequences of breaking the inviolate rule prohibiting the killing of the innocent are in fact conducive to misery rather than happiness or some other ideal. This charge is, indeed, a serious one. For, not only do utilitarians maintain that the rightness of a rule or action is to be judged solely by consequences, but mixed-deontologists maintain that a necessary, though not sufficient, condition for a morally right act is that it promote the greatest balance of good over evil. If, therefore, the consequences of beneficent euthanasia are in fact more conducive to misery than happiness or its like, then utilitarians and mixed-deontologists should have to reject the practice.

But why should we advocate a rule when we know that it will not in cases of merciful treatment be most beneficial to abide by it? As Professor J. J. C. Smart correctly observes, "to refuse to break a generally beneficial rule in those cases in which it is not most beneficial to obey it seems irrational and to be a case of rule worship." ("An Outline of a System of Utilitarian Ethics," *Utilitarianism: For and Against*, J. J. C. Smart and Bernard Williams, Cambridge University Press, London, 1973). Therefore why dogmatically adhere to a principle that protects innocent life *and* needless suffering? Why not simply formulate a better rule?

In *The Morality of Killing* I suggested that the principle prohibiting killing be reformulated so that it would not apply to cases of beneficent euthanasia. If this strategy is workable we obtain a new prohibition, "Do not do K except in circumstances of the sort C," where K stands for the killing of innocent people, and C stands for the noninvoluntary inducement of a painless and quick death, the intention and actual consequences of which are the kindest possible treatment in actual circumstances of the recipient of that act. The merit of this rule is that it both protects the innocent and allows us to help those in dire need. And this is what morality is largely, if not all, about.

THE LIVING WILL

TO MY FAMILY, MY PHYSICIAN, MY CLERGYMAN, MY LAWYER—

If the time comes when I can no longer take part in decisions for my own future, let this statement stand as the testament of my wishes:

If there is no reasonable expectation of my recovery from physical or mental disability,

I, _____, request that I be allowed to die and not be kept alive by artificial means or heroic measures. Death is as much a reality as birth, growth, maturity, and old age—it is the one certainty. I do not fear death as much as I fear the indignity of deterioration, dependence and hopeless pain. I ask that medication be mercifully administered to me for terminal suffering even if it hastens the moment of death.

This request is made after careful consideration. Although this document is not legally binding, you who care for me will, I hope, feel morally bound to follow its mandate. I recognize that it places a heavy burden of responsibility upon you, and it is with the intention of sharing that responsibility and of mitigating any feelings of guilt that this statement is made.

Signed_____Date_____
Witnessed by: _____

SOURCE: Editors, "The Living Will." This appeared in *The Humanist*, September/October 1971, and is reprinted by permission.

DEATH WITH DIGNITY

Model Bill

An act to amend the Public Health law in order to permit an individual to execute a document directing discontinuance of maintenance medical treatment in the event of terminal illness.

The Public Health law is hereby amended by inserting a new Article to read as follows:

Article _____. Termination of Medical Treatment.
1. As used in this Act, unless the context requires otherwise:
   (a) "Maintenance medical treatment" means medical treatment designed solely to sustain the life processes.
   (b) "Physician" means an individual licensed by the Board of Medical Examiners for the State of _____.
   (c) "Terminal illness" means an illness that will result in natural expiration of life, regardless of the use or discontinuance of maintenance medical treatment.
2. (a) An individual of sound mind and 18 years of age or older may execute a document directing that no maintenance medical treatment be utilized for the prolongation of his life at such time as he is suffering from a terminal illness.
   (b) A document described in subsection (a) of this section is not valid unless it has been executed with the same formalities as a will under Article_____.
3. (a) For purpose of this act, certification of a terminal illness may be rendered only by the physician or physicians in charge of the individual who is terminally ill. A copy of any such certification shall be maintained in the records of the medical facility where the patient is being maintained. If the patient is not being maintained in a medical facility, a copy shall be retained by the physician in his own case records.
   (b) A physician who certifies a terminal illness under this section is presumed to be acting in good faith. Unless it is alleged and proved that his action violated that standard of reasonable professional care and judgment under the circumstances, he is immune from civil or criminal liability for such action.

SOURCE: Society for the Right to Die, "Death with Dignity: A Model Bill." This appeared in *The Humanist*, May/June 1976, and is reprinted by permission.

4. An individual who has executed a document under this Act may, at any time thereafter, revoke such document. Revocation may be accomplished by destroying such document, or by contrary indication expressed in the presence of two witnesses 18 years of age or older.

5. (a) A physician who relies on a document executed under this Act, of which he has no actual notice of revocation or contrary indication, is presumed to be acting in good faith in withholding maintenance medical treatment from an individual who executed such document. A physician is immune from civil or criminal liability when, in reliance upon such document, he has withheld medical treatment, unless it is alleged and proved that his actions violated the standard of reasonable professional care and judgment under the circumstances.

   (b) For purposes of this act, a physician may presume that an individual who executed a document under this Act was of sound mind when it was executed, in the absence of actual notice to the contrary.

SECTION V.
POLITICAL/ECONOMIC SYSTEMS

Political/Economic Systems. Business, industry, management, politics and government have in the last few years been viewed with more suspicion than any of our other institutions. The prevalent assumption has been that one cannot succeed in either business or government without losing one's human values and becoming a cruel and corrupt person.

This section provides a challenge to the assumption that business and government must, of necessity, be institutions in which individual human good is lost. It seeks to provide different assumptions about the nature of human nature and provide strategies for effectively working and moving toward the dream of businesses and governments which promote rather than destroy human dignity.

In order to do this, we probably have to continually remind ourselves that both industry and government begin with people, not with goods or services. The reverse of this assumption has led us to a condition in the world in which our very survival as a species is open to question. Certainly, many are questioning the way things are in the present and believe that they cannot long continue. Our present economic system may not be able to suffer the challenges of the developing nations of the world as they demand increasing amounts of financial aid. If they happen to be a nation without some natural resource or some product that is demanded in the world's marketplace, then our present system has condemned them to perpetual poverty and begging at the door of the rich and powerful. We have used such a system to line up strategic military bases and pressure such nations to vote in particular ways at international meetings. All of this results in anger, resentment and political/economic systems which in the end do not serve humanity well.

One example of this system may well be the problems we are having with oil. A recent news article reported that roughly one-half of the money in the world is in the possession of seven Arab nations. There are excellent prospects that the other one-half will end up there as well, if we continue to rely on oil. It is clear that the powerful nations of the world will not allow themselves to get into a position where the world's money is controlled by seven small Arab nations. The alternatives, however, are not attractive. Invasion by one or another of the powerful in the world would lead to a war between giants over the possession of dwarfs. An agreement of two or three powerful nations to take over the Arab nations simply belies any hope for an organization such as the United Nations. The big and militarily powerful cooperate only so long as things are going their way. We don't know what the solution will be, or if there will be one, but we do know that the present situation demands a radical alteration of our economic systems.

It may very well be that as we come to understand that all of our present economic systems have played our their string of effectiveness, we will begin to search for different and more effective systems for the future. It might well be that the humanistic alternatives explored in this section on political/economic systems can provide clues to that undetermined future.

BUSINESS, INDUSTRY
AND MANAGEMENT

ECONOMICS SHOULD BEGIN WITH PEOPLE, NOT GOODS

E. F. Schumacher

The modern world needs a new model of civilization. Such a statement would have seemed either imcomprehensible or incredible a few years ago. The most one could get away with then was to say that the Third World needed a new model because it would get nowhere by imitating the so-called developed countries. Even this message was treated with incredulity.

But the incredulity did not prevent some people from getting on with constructive work. The Intermediate Technology Group in England set out to elaborate not the supertechnology of the West nor a continuance of the non-technology of the poor countries, but something intermediate that would fit.

To understand the need we should consider how our present model has come into being. I don't mean historically, I mean logically. What is the economics of it? What is it about? The modern world's answer is that economics is about goods. And indeed it is. But everything depends on that point of departure; so the first question is how do we get more goods?

The answer seems clear. You get more goods with machines developed through science and technology. The best results are obtained with bigger and bigger machines, particularly ones that are more and more complex, automated and capital-intensive. Such machines are also labor-saving. In fact, if your interest is mainly goods, machines are a much better proposition than people. The philosopher Whitehead, I believe, once said that life is an assault against the repetitive mechanism of the universe. Mechanized production then can be seen as an assault against the waywardness and unpredictability of life.

The world's need today is for a new model—a model based not on goods but on *people*. The question is not "How do we produce more goods?" but rather "How do we make people productive?" Starting with

SOURCE: E. F. Schumacher, "Economics Should Begin with People, Not Goods." Reprinted from *The Futurist: A Journal of Forecasts, Trends, and Ideas About the Future*. Published by World Future Society, An Association for the Study of Alternative Futures: Washington, D.C., December 1974.

people rather than goods, we will build a different sort of technology, a technology on a human scale. The new technology must be based on four fundamental rules:

1. Make things small wherever possible.
2. Reduce the capital-intensity because labor wants to be involved. We don't want to eliminate the human factor.
3. Make the process as simple as you can. (Anyone can complicate things—it takes a touch of genius to keep them simple.)
4. Design the process to be nonviolent. The "advanced nations" depend on an extremely violent system. In talking about violence, I don't just mean hitting another man over the head; I also include man hitting nature over the head, or man raping the world's resources, the once-and-for-all endowment of the earth with its marvelous substances like oil.

WORLD NEEDS CONCERN WITH PEOPLE

Concern with goods requires mass production, but concern with people necessitates production by the masses. This is not my own formulation. Mahatma Gandhi said, "It is not mass production, it is only production by the masses that could do the trick." So we need different machines. They cannot possibly be big machines because the masses are very numerous: the machines must each be very small. The machines cannot be extremely complex because the masses are not very highly educated. Moreover, the masses are not rich; they can't put their fingers on a hundred thousand dollars. So the machines must be inexpensive. Not capital-intensive, but capital saving.

Let me give you an example from my own experience with intermediate technology. To help rural populations in Africa, all sorts of people were showing the Africans wonderful methods of doubling their agricultural output. But when their back was turned, the Africans reverted to their old methods. The technical assistants then gave learned lectures in London on the stupidity of the Africans.

But we found that the Africans had a perfectly good reason. Doubled output was of no use to them: they couldn't get it to market, because women carrying baskets on their heads provided the only transport, and the women had enough to carry as it was. And so we introduced a very simple type of ox-cart which the local carpenters could make. But there was still one problem: wooden wheels wear out very quickly on rough ground. The wheels needed a steel rim. But how do you get the steel rim around the wooden wheel? As a matter of fact, how do you bend metal in general?

We remembered that peasants in France had developed a tool for doing it which was intellectually brilliant, and which could still be found in some villages. Our technicians upgraded this tool in the light of modern knowledge of engineering and materials, but at the same time making it simpler, rather than more complicated. While hitherto the cheapest available metal-bending machine in the world cost 750 pounds, the National College of Agricultural Engineering developed one costing 7 pounds. And it is so simple that the village blacksmith can make the tool himself and it doesn't require electricity for its operation.

To take another example: we have found that countless cooperatives have been set up and have failed. We came to the conclusion that they failed either because they have no proper accounting at all, or because they are using modern accounting systems which are so complex that auditors' fees can be higher than their entire surplus. We therefore spent three years simplifying the accounting system for cooperatives; this has been a big success, and the new simplified accounting system is now being introduced in a number of African countries.

There is no space here to go into all the new models that are needed. But perhaps this reveals the intensive search that begins when you start with people and not with goods.

INTERMEDIATE TECHNOLOGY
A MINIGUIDE TO INFORMATION RESOURCES

There are now hundreds of resources in this field. The following are only a few examples.

SOME INSTITUTIONS

Brace Research Institute, MacDonald College of McGill University, St. Anne de Bellevue 800, Quebec, Canada. Funded initially under the Canadian engineer James H. Brace, who died in 1956, this group emphasizes research on methods to desalinate sea water and make desert or arid lands available for agricultural purposes. The Institute has done considerable work with solar stills and windmills.

Biotechnic Research and Development (BRAD), Eithin-y-Gaer, Churchstroke, Montgomery, Wales, United Kingdom. Initiated by Robin Clarke, former editor of *Science Journal* (London) and author of *The Science of War and Peace,* this group emphasizes "soft" technology that will not harm the environment.

The Farallones Institute, P.O. Box 700, Point Reyes Stations, California 94956, U.S.A. Farallones designs, constructs and evaluates innovative, inexpensive ways of building; components for self-renewing energy supply and resource recycling; improved means of food and fiber production, including field crops, aquaculture, and wildlife management.

Intermediate Technology Development Group, Parnell House, 25 Wilton Road, London SW1V 1JS, England. The Group compiles inventories of existing technologies which can be used within the concept of low-cost, labor-intensive production, and tests and demonstrates in the field the results of its investigation. It publishes a journal, *Intermediate Technology.*

Low Impact Technology, 73 Molesworth Street, Wadebridge, Cornwall, England. This group, made up principally of people associated with the journal *The Ecologist,* carries on experiments in technology that will not harm the environment.

New Alchemy Institute, P.O. Box 432, Woods Hole, Massachusetts 02543, U.S.A. This research and education group seeks solutions that can be used by people trying to create "a greener, kinder world." "Among our major tasks is the creation of ecologically derived forms of energy, agriculture, aquaculture, housing and landscapes that will permit a revitalization and repopulation of the countryside." The Institute has centers existing or planned for a wide range of climates in several countries.

SOME BOOKS

Alternative Technology and the Politics of Social Change by David Dickson. Fontana Paperbacks, 14 St. James's Place, London SW1, England. 1974. 50 pence ($1.50 Canadian). An analysis of the interrelationships of technology and society, with particular emphasis on attempts to overcome the problems posed by technology. The author is the General Secretary of the British Society for Social Responsibility in Science.

Small Is Beautiful by E. F. Schumacher.

SOME PERIODICALS

Appropriate Technology. This quarterly, published by the Intermediate Technology Group (see above), provides a forum for the exchange of practical information between field workers concerned with the implementation of development projects.

Journal of the New Alchemists. Published by the New Alchemy Institute. (See above.)

Alternative Sources of Energy, Route 1, Box 36B, Minong, Wisconsin 54559, U.S.A.

Undercurrents: The Magazine of Radical Science and Peoples' Technology. Published by the Undercurrents Partnership. 275 Finchley Road, London NW3, England.

HUMANISTIC CAPITALISM: ANOTHER ALTERNATIVE

Willis W. Harman

As it has evolved thus far, the high-technology free-enterprise industrial state seems unable to resolve three fundamental inherent dilemmas:

- It fails to meet the basic condition that every citizen have the opportunity to be a full and valued participant, with the feeling of belonging and being useful.
- It fails to achieve a synergism of individual and organizational microdecisions such that the resultant societal macrodecisions are satisfactory even to those who made the component decisions.
- It fails to achieve a satisfactory equitable redistribution of power and wealth.

Perhaps most seriously, it fails to give contemporary man a sense of being a useful and necessary member of a social whole which in turn is geared into a meaningful plan of existence within the totality of a cosmic or divine order. In the long run, that is a potentially fatal flaw.

The crisis which exists at the present time, when a new "post-industrial" society is in the process of being born, may perhaps be seen most clearly in three troubles that seem intrinsic to the free-enterprise state. These are contemporary forms of the classical economic problems of employment, regulation, and distribution.

A dominant theme in contemporary approaches to these three problems has been enlargement of the public sector's role in providing welfare, creating jobs, regulating industry, and redistributing wealth. Yet this strategy amounts to admission of a fundamental failure of the free-enterprise system. Furthermore, it suffers from the known ills of big bureaucracy and monopoly, and conflicts with rising demands from individuals and minority groups for increased opportunity to control their own destinies. On the other hand, if the free-enterprise system were to develop highly decentralized goal-setting and decision-making, it

SOURCE: Willis W. Harman, "Humanistic Capitalism: Another Alternative," *Fields Within Fields . . .*, Winter, 1973-1974. Reprinted by permission.

could be peculiarly compatible with the apparently strengthening values of self-definition and self-actualization.

Recognizing this dilemma, some urge that we abandon the direction of further technological and economic development and return to the self-sufficient individual and the small community. But the Faustian decision cannot be simply reversed. There is no comfortable way back, if for no other reason than that the majority of the world still hungers to taste the technological fruits.

However, a more penetrating analysis of the nature of the crisis discloses that there is indeed a way through to a humane post-industrial society. To assert that is not to predict we will choose the way, nor to delineate a series of steps that will take us there. It is not even to suggest that we can get there by any very direct route, since—like the neurotic who will evade the solution to his problems until psychic pain drives him to desperate self-discovery—the society will probably have to traverse a period of chaos, disruption, and decline before becoming sufficiently convinced of the need for a major change. Even so, I will attempt in this article to set forth a number of requisite conditions—concerning ethics, institutions, and incentive systems—that will have to be met if the humane society is to come into being.

TWO DOMINANT ETHICS

In the first place, the three basic failures of our industrialized society identified above can find eventual resolution only if the dominance of the growth-and-consumption ethic is replaced by (1) an "ecological ethic," and (2) a "self-realization ethic."

Lynton Caldwell defines an "ecological ethic" which, he argues, is essential to the worldwide, fundamental, and pervasive change required to preserve the habitability of the earth.[1] It involves recognition of the limited nature of available resources, including space, and recognition of man as an integral part of the natural world—hence inseparable from it and from its governing processes and laws. It fosters a sense of the total community of man, and responsibility for the fate of the planet, and relates self-interest to interest of fellow man and of future generations. It implies movement toward a homeostatic (yet dynamic) economic-ecological system, in which man acts in partnership with nature in modifying ecological relationships and in establishing satisfactory recycling mechanisms.

As Caldwell notes, this ethic implies behavior advocated in a variety of ethical systems extending through time, from the legendary Lao Tse through St. Francis to Mahatma Gandhi. Its basic assumptions correspond to the pre-scientific assumptions of many so-called "primitive" peoples. Thus the ecological viewpoint can find support not only in modern scientific knowledge of life on earth, but also in most known cultural or religious systems.

The same is true of a "self-realization ethic" which holds that the proper end of all individual experience is the further evolutionary development of the emergent self and of the human species, and that the appropriate function of social institutions is to create an environment which will foster that process. This too is supported not only by the experience of modern psychotherapy and the recent emergence of humanistic psychology, but is also found at the core of almost all the religious philosophies the world has known. In *The Perennial Philosophy*, Huxley speaks of "the ethic that places man's final end in the knowledge of the immanent and transcendent Ground of all being . . . Rudiments of the Perennial Philosophy may be found among the traditionary lore of primitive peoples in every region of the world, and in its fully developed forms it has a place in every one of the higher religions."[2]

The "self-realization ethic" is the most satisfactory answer to the current alienation and anomie that surface in rebellions at industrial and bureaucratic practices which diminish man; in anxiety that we have somehow lost control of the management of our human affairs, of what our ancestors would have called our destiny; and in seeking (e.g., through return to handicrafts and home gardening) the satisfactions of a work life not excessively shaped by economic incentives. Its dominance is required for the restructuring of social institutions to satisfy the individual's basic need for full and valued participation. As corollaries to this ethic, self-determination of individuals and minority groups will be fostered, social decision-making should be highly decentralized, and the mechanism of a strong free-enterprise private sector should be preferred over public bureaucracy for the accomplishment of most social tasks.

The two ethics, the one emphasizing the total community of man-in-nature and the oneness of the human race, and the other placing the highest value on development of selfhood, are not contradictory but complementary—two sides of the same coin. Together they leave room both for cooperation and for wholesome competition, for love, and for individuality. Each is a corrective against excesses or misapplication of the other.

INSTITUTIONAL CHANGE

The two dominant ethics can be operative only if there are corresponding changes in social and economic institutions—otherwise the individual will find himself repeatedly under pressure from institutionalized values and goals to act contrary to his personal sense of rightness. Among the necessary institutional changes are the following:

1. *Operative goals of large private sector organizations need to become aligned with overall societal goals.*

Social responsibility in the private sector is the alternative to continued expansion of the role of the public sector.

Because of the powerful position of the large corporations, the key change must occur here. Growth and maximizing profit are generally accepted as appropriate corporate goals. But as the "new" ethics become operative, the priority of corporate goals must become:

- To provide satisfying and growth-fostering work for management and employees;
- To contribute to the overall social welfare;
- To engage successfully in a specific group of economically profitable activities.

Those who participate in the corporation, as owners, employees, or clients, will do so through a wish to actualize these goals. It is important to note that profit and capital growth will remain important, though less as ends in themselves and more as control signals.

Although this transmutation of corporate goals may seem at first glance hopelessly idealistic, in fact it is wholly practical in the long run. Two recent trends make it so—the emergence of huge multinational corporations with economic powers comparable to those of nations, and the growth of a mass capital market. As the largest corporations begin to have impacts on human lives comparable to the impacts of political governments, the same demands will be made of them that have historically been made of government—that they assume responsibility for the welfare of those over whom they wield power. As the ownership pattern of corporations changes from the situation not so long ago where less than one percent of the population owned stock to one where the vast majority of the population are in an ownership position (indirectly, in most cases, through pension plans, mutual funds, life insurance, etc.),[3] private corporations become essentially public institutions, owned by the public, serving the public, and exposing the public to the consequences of bad corporate behavior. Thus the boundaries between public and private organizations are blurring, particularly in the extent to which they serve and are responsible to the public at large, and hence in their social goals. (This is by no means to ignore the significant difference between the two, nor the crucial importance of a strong and thriving private sector.) If the free-enterprise market system, with all its very real advantages, is to avoid incurring oppressive government control, it will be because the powerful business and labor organizations align their operative goals with humane and farsighted societal goals.

2. *Every citizen must be assured the opportunity to be a full and valued participant in the society.*

Put another way, every member of the society needs to know that he can, by his own efforts, have his economic needs met and make a contribution which will be judged of worth by the society. For the majority this means structured jobs, and hence it implies government as employer of last resort. But there will be a growing fraction of the population who are capable of structuring their own individual or group activities, and it will be to the advantage of the society that they be enabled to carry these out, thus opening up structured jobs to those with less imagination and self-reliance. I discuss some of the possible implementations of this principle below, in connection with the topic of employment.

3. *All organizations, public and private, need to be structured in such a way that they enhance, not diminish, man.*

Some of what this statement implies is apparent from comparing the family with the factory—in fact, it may not be pushing the point too far to argue that the family model of a nurturing community, rather than the factory model with employees viewed as means to ends, needs to be the norm. The most appropriate structure appears to be an organismic one, with local autonomy fostered and what Cleveland terms a "horizontal" decision-making structure.[4]

In such organizations there will be hierarchies, on a functional basis, but these may change with each new "mission" and there will in any case be widespread participation in organizational goal-setting. Decisions will be made at the lowest practicable level. The workplace will be essentially a setting for satisfying and self-actualizing activity. Jobs will be shaped to the human needs of those who perform them, rather than men shaped to jobs whose form is dictated solely by considerations of economic efficiency. There will be economic incentives, but much more attention will be paid to the other incentives that typically induce men to contribute their best efforts—loyalty, sense of responsibility, aesthetic gratification, the search for truth, and identification with the common welfare.

4. *There has to be a more effective mechanism by which individual microdecisions aggregate to more satisfactory macrodecisions.*

Individuals, corporations, government agencies, in the course of their activities make microdecisions (e.g., to buy a certain product, to employ a man for a particular task, to enact a minimum-wage law) which in effect constitute a set of macrodecisions of the overall society (e.g., to deplete natural gas resources rapidly, to create ghettos in cities, to pollute air and water). The crisis in regulation with which our time is afflicted may be described as a chronic failure of microdecisions made "according to the rules" (of individual pursuit, of self-gain, of mass consumption and throwaway, of maximizing profit, etc.) to add up to satisfactory macrodecisions.[5]

Macrodecisions influencing the future state of a society come about as a consequence of individual, institutional, and social behavior. But this behavior is shaped by motivations and incentives, and these in turn by individual and cultural values. Traditional societies regulate behavior directly through custom, ritual, and taboo. The modern totalitarian state, too, tends to regulate by controlling behavior rather directly, ultimately through coercion. On the other hand, certain technocratic forms proposed for the future would emphasize behavior control via the shaping of motivations through operant conditioning and institutional-ized incentives. However, the only form of guiding microdecisions that is compatible with the Western concept of democracy is through education leading to free choice of wholesome values expressed in open political process—these values in turn influencing motivations and thence behavior. But this process presupposes widespread agreement on some set of fundamental beliefs and values from which the behavior ultimately derives. Lacking this consensus, we find strong pressures toward control through the shaping of motivations and behavior.

5. *Widespread citizen participation in "designing the future" needs to be encouraged.*

Global thinking, attention to future consequences, concern for fellow man and future generations, need to enter into local and immediate deci-sion-making. A wide variety of institutional innovations could foster this kind of participation.

There are two compelling reasons for fostering participation in the guidance of social institutions. One is that such participation is one of the most powerful ways of encouraging the choosing of socially responsible behavior, as opposed to the imposition of necessary constraints through governmental regulation. The other is apparent when we ask, in the light of the two guiding ethics mentioned above, what work are persons to be involved in when only some of the people, and only a fraction of their time, are necessary to produce all the goods and services the society can use. Two activities stand out—so much so that one might almost describe this hypothetical state as "the learning-and-planning society." Learning, in the broadest sense which includes what we usually mean by education, research, exploration, and human development, plus plan-ning—participating in the community of concerned citizens to make a better world—are the two main activities that can absorb unlimited numbers of people not required in jobs of other sorts. They contribute to human fulfillment and social betterment; they are humane, non-polluting, and non-stultifying.

6. *Continuance of adult and career education needs to be fostered and institutionalized.*

This follows from the comment immediately above. Again there is a wide variety of ways in which continuing education can be made the norm. Education should be thought of here not just as formal education, but as learning in a much broader sense. Much of it would probably be self-selected and self-appropriated.

CHANGED INCENTIVE STRUCTURES

The system of economic and legal incentives must be redesigned to reduce conflicts with the ecological and self-realization ethics and to en-courage socially desirable behavior.

In describing characteristics of an eventual society which would have resolved the most serious of the dilemmas facing us today, I am not speaking of a system that could be designed into being. The ethics which guide and control the economic system come to it from outside, and depend upon the ambient culture. Changes in moral temper and culture are not amenable to "social engineering" or political control. The values and moral traditions of a society cannot be "designed" by precept; their ultimate sources are the religious or metaphysical conceptions which undergird a society. Institutions, too, are so intimately connected into the culture that they are resistant to deliberate attempts to alter them.

At present, probably the most effectual lever for deliberate modification of individual and organizational behavior is the system of economic incentives. Much of our present dilemma can be traced to the fact that basic economic incentives oppose socially desirable behavior (e.g., many ways of increasing profit bring undesirable ecological or social consequences; short-term economic considerations lead to a discounting of the future that penalizes future generations). On the other hand, the incentive structure, and most particularly the tax structure, can be altered in ways that would drastically alter the operative goals (i.e., those inferrable from actions) of persons and corporations, and which could free the entire society to pursue goals other than economic growth and short-term efficiency.

For instance, behavior more responsive to the energy requirements of future generations could be encouraged through a worldwide energy tax (proceeds of which might go to research on energy sources and energy conservation), and perhaps another tax on synthetics which use fossil fuels as a base. Tax credits for metals reprocessors could encourage recycling. Other changes in the tax, income, and welfare structures could encourage frequent "sabbatical leaves" for those in the work force, thus opening up opportunities for others.

One of the most promising measures is a "forgiven tax" on corporations to facilitate initiation of socially desirable activity. This would be a tax on some appropriate measure of corporate activity (e.g., total payroll, gross income) that would be forgiven provided the money is used by the corporation for such specified purposes as:

- On-the-job educational experience
- Sabbatical or social-service leaves
- Job creation for social benefit (e.g., hard-core unemployed, apprenticeships and youth employment, post-retirement social service)
- Restructuring work to increase job satisfaction
- Loaning managers to community services, or otherwise contributing to the solution of social problems.

The important advantage provided by this mechanism is enlistment of private-sector enterprise in pursuit of societal goals while minimizing the amount of government direction and avoiding the wastage of collecting tax moneys and then dispersing them.

Another measure with interesting possibilities is the selective graduated wage subsidy. It can be best illustrated by an example. Consider an economically and socially desirable task (e.g., recycling of solid waste) that requires a good deal of low-skill labor and is so marginally profitable that it is not attractive to the private sector. There are various ways in which private-sector involvement could be stimulated—government contracts, direct subsidies, partial dependence on volunteer labor, etc. A government subsidy in the form of a graduated contribution to wages (perhaps half to three quarters at the established minimum wage, tapering to zero at, say, twice the minimum-wage rate) has the potential advantage of accomplishing several desirable objectives simultaneously. It could lower corporate costs to the point where the desired activity becomes economically feasible for private enterprise. It could create jobs for that group of citizens who would otherwise be unemployed because their value-additive capacity is less than the minimum-wage level. Combined with a progressive tax structure, it could help redistribute income in a way that avoids some of the undesirable characteristics of the present welfare-workfare approaches.

Possibly new institutional forms will be found useful. One example is a proposed "general-benefit corporation" whose features include the vitality-promoting competitiveness of the profit-making corporation, the social purpose of the non-profit, and the personal-growth aims of the university. Another example is an expanded-ownership corporation that combines the goals and incentive structures of business and labor legislative and policy actions (e.g., changes in antitrust and corporation law, and in credit policies) could be used to legitimate, encourage, and make economically feasible such kinds of social experiment.

It is unlikely that any one (or any combination) of the above measures will prove to be a complete solution for one or more of the array of serious problems faced by contemporary society. Rather, they should be thought of as examples of the tools available for reshaping the economic incentive structure to reduce the present conflict between the behavior that those incentives induce, on the one hand, and humane individual values and socially desirable goals, on the other.

TOWARD A HUMANISTIC CAPITALISM

Is it too idealistic to consider moving toward a society, guided by the ecological and self-realization ethics, in which the institutions serve the human needs of those whose lives they touch, and in which the inherent incentive structure produces a synergism such that in pursuing his own self-interest the individual also promotes the interest of the whole? At this particular moment in history it seems it may be more practical than ever before.

In the first place, several sorts of indications substantiate that the new ecological ethic and self-realization ethic seem to be emerging. Surveys and polls show significant value shifts among certain elite groups, such as students and corporate executives, in the direction of what Yankelovitch terms "the New Naturalism"[6]—increased emphasis on humanistic and spiritual values, oneness with fellow man and nature, community and quality of life, and decreased emphasis on materialistic values, status goals, and unqualified economic growth. Numerous cultural indicators (e.g., books read, voluntary associations, "New Age" subculture) show greatly increased interest in, and tolerance for, the transcendental, religious, mystical, and spiritual views which have traditionally been associated with these two ethics. Environmental and "human-potential" movements are flourishing.

Particularly significant is the developing scientific interest in "altered states of consciousness"—subjective explorations being augmented by correlations with galvanic skin response, EEG components, body electric fields, etc.—which is resulting in a new legitimation of studies of religious beliefs, psychic phenomena, mystical experience, and meditative states. Wherever the nature of man has been probed deeply, the paramount fact emerging is the duality of his experience. He is found to be both physical and spiritual, biologically determined yet in some sense freely choosing, separate yet bound together in a unity such that the ecological ethic and the self-realization ethic follow as a natural consequence of his immediate experience.

Contemporary developments in business also support the new ethic. The tasks undertaken, particularly by the larger and the high-technology corporations, require high value to be placed on self-knowledge, broad perspective, individual responsibility, and on interdependence, cooperative trust, accurate communications (honesty), and openness. A second look is being taken at such concepts as "division of labor" and "efficiency," as it is discovered to be more efficient in the long term to structure jobs to be rewarding and stimulating rather than time-and-motion efficient and stultifying. That is to say, the values required to put together and operate a highly complex social-technological task are very close to those required to support high quality of life and continued habitability of the earth. In addition, as the society moves further toward the situation where its essential tasks do not require more than a small fraction of the full efforts of the population, the distinction between "job" and creative "non-job" activities (learning, playing, civic service) will become less sharp, which will tend further to support humane values.[7]

There are numerous ways in which changing cultural perceptions and values can affect corporate behavior. Contemporary consumer and environmentalist movements exert a force on choice of products purchased and career opportunities accepted. Companies in competition not only for markets but also for top caliber personnel feel a pressure to be socially responsible and to provide worthwhile tasks that can command the commitment of the best talent.

I have already noted how the advent of large multinational corporations and expanding ownership of business are creating pressures toward alignment of corporate with social goals. The worker in a General Motors plant is very likely to be also a consumer of General Motors automobiles, victim of faulty cars, breather of their exhaust, and (possibly without his knowledge) part owner of the corporation. Thus the radical view of Big Business as a bunch of greedy Other Guys who exploit the consuming and the poor simply won't wash. The model in which managers, owners, workers, consumers, and public are different groups of people doesn't fit the facts. A much more ecological view of the business-government-public system is required. If something is seriously wrong with the system, such that "good" business decisions add up to bad social decisions, then it is the overall culture that needs changing, including modifying the institutions to serve the whole system better. And, to some extent, at least, that is what seems to be happening.

There was a time in this nation when corporate charters were issued for a limited duration and a specific purpose, which purpose had to be demonstrated to be in the public good. This will probably never be the case again. However, if the cultural values continue to shift in the directions noted above, it is not hard to imagine a time when a corporation that pursued its own objectives without explicit regard to the overall welfare of the society would not be allowed to survive.

Already important signs are visible that the bases on which legitimacy of business institutions is granted are shifting away from ownership and management expertise toward increased service to various communities—employees, customers, minority groups, and the general public. While it is far from accomplished fact, there are strong indications that we may be moving toward business "deriving its just powers from the consent of those impacted by its activities."

Thus a transition to "humanistic capitalism," could occur. Let us see how the three key problems of employment, regulation, and distribution might be resolved in that case.

THE END OF UNEMPLOYMENT

It is practically impossible to calculate what failure to provide full employment (in the broad sense of meaningful activity) has cost the society. One would have to consider the lost creative efforts of those who are unemployed, underemployed, employed but essentially featherbedding, and so young or so old that they consider it hopeless to seek employment. Then there is that part of the total welfare cost which comes about because work was not available for the support of dependents and that part of the cost of crime and delinquency attributable to lack of suitable alternatives in productive employment. Those are the economic costs—the human costs are even more incalculable.

Employment (including such non-paid roles as student and house-wife) is symbolic of having a place in the social order. There is no very good way to assess statistically what it means in human terms that a large fraction of the nation's adult population—informed estimates run as high as a quarter[8]—fall into the category of "not needed." These people include the elderly, deprived of useful roles by forced early retirement; the young, held out of the labor market by an assortment of barriers; "unemployables" defeated by recurrent failure to get and hold a job; those who are featherbedding or performing useless makework and know it. All of them are deprived of the self-esteem that comes from having a social role that others judge to be useful. Many of them develop, in connection with this wastage of human potential, such characteristics as chronic life disorganization, listlessness, family instability, mental depression, alcoholism, drug abuse, and other forms of anti-self and anti-social behavior.[9]

There are other social costs, also difficult to calculate. The main barrier to successful education of disadvantaged children and youth appears to be absence of a realistic promise of satisfying employment as a motivating goal. Fear of unemployment or disemployment seems to be a root cause of racial and intergroup conflict. Fear of unemployment inhibits actions needed to improve quality of life, preserve the natural environment, conserve scarce resources, attain more equitable distribution of income, create a more workable world economy, and reduce war-spawning tensions between rich and poor nations.

All of this is to say that, not only is considerable investment justified in resolving the employment problem since failure to solve it is so costly, but further, its resolution is in a crucial sense prerequisite to dealing with a number of other social problems.

Furthermore, the private sector must assume responsibility for employment if we are to avoid distortion of market forces, weakening of motivations, disintegration of the market economy, and inflation necessitating strong price and income controls.

The basic condition to be met might be termed a national full-employment policy, had not that phrase been pre-empted in 1946 to describe a measure that falls far short of what we are contemplating. We mean, here, a policy which individual citizens, institutions, and the federal government have every intention of implementing, a policy which assures every citizen who desires it an opportunity for full and valued participation in the society. (While it is apparently true that direct measures to decrease unemployment tend to be costly in terms of inflation, this does not negate the possibility that long-term cultural changes could result in simultaneously lowered unemployment and inflation.) The main burden of achieving this goal is to be carried by the private and voluntary sectors, for reasons advanced earlier and in ways to be described below. Another large portion of the problem can be solved by what might be termed "enhancement income maintenance" programs, also to be described below. A third source of work opportunities will be created by government public works. For example, a national surtax might be used to finance such public works and job creation projects as recycling systems for reclamation of urban waste and return of organic refuse and sewage to the land, reclamation of areas ravaged by strip mining, urban rapid transit, topsoil building and rebuilding, etc. Fourthly, a subsistence income maintenance provision will be needed for the residuum for whom society fails to make available opportunity for full and valued participation—but this, then, should bring no opprobrium to the hopefully very few people receiving it.

A fifth provision seems necessary, namely, a universal unemployment insurance program (against job loss or inability to work) which would reduce the dread of job loss. It would need to provide not only base-level income maintenance but also some sort of tapering-down supplement—depending on annual income at the time of interruption—to reduce the shock of sudden unemployment. Unless the threat of work interruption is reduced, there is no way of eliminating the pathological psychology of regarding work opportunity as a scarce commodity.

Broadly speaking, there would appear to be four major ways in which a policy of "full and valued participation" could be implemented:

- Participation through voluntary associations
- Direct creation of work opportunities by government
- Private-sector job creation through government contracts
- Stimulation of private sector initiative (and removal of negative incentives) to create meaningful and satisfying work opportunities.

While no doubt all of these will be used, I will concentrate on the last—because it is the one which must be made to work if the advantages of a free economy are to be retained.

Suppose, now, that the "self-realization ethic" comes to dominate and it is a generally accepted principle that corporations, like other social institutions, exist for the public good and to provide satisfying and useful social roles for managers and other employees. Suppose that, as a consequence of this altered concept of corporate purpose, the workplace becomes recognized as one of the main places where humans find their self-fulfillment, and efficiency in a narrow economic sense becomes less of a dominating value—while such values as actualizing human potential, achieving community, and being socially responsible assume more importance.

Under these assumptions, there would be a redesigning of technology and the workplace to invest work with more meaning. There would be job enlargement and reorganization of the work by the workers themselves, to improve efficiency in a broad human sense—efficiency in developing and using human potential. Appropriate participation opportunities and the therapeutic benefits of work would be provided to those whose value-additive capacity is on the low side—the mentally and physically handicapped, those with a "failure" self-image, the elderly, and inexperienced youth. In somewhat the same way that the extended family used to take care of its own, the sub-units of corporations would take on these sorts of broad community responsibilities.

This sort of corporate behavior is a far cry from the present American situation. But then, the present situation is a far cry from a humanly satisfactory society. At the moment, of course, it would be economic suicide for a corporation to accept this broad responsibility for providing "full humane employment" as I have postulated. Incentive structures would have to be rearranged so that the corporation would not suffer economic disadvantage from taking actions to increase the amount of humane employment—e.g., to structure work to increase worker satisfaction; to provide broadly beneficial educational opportunities on and off the job, and apprenticeships and other youth employment opportunities; to design graduated entry pathways for the hard-core unemployables and "New Careers" type advancement ladders; to release employees for sabbatical periods or social-service activities; to assist in mid-career changes of vocation; and to assist entrepreneurs in starting socially desirable new ventures. The "forgiven tax" mentioned earlier is one of the measures that would make the new corporate behavior more feasible; the graduated wage subsidy and "limited-profit corporations" are others.

One unknown in the situation is the extent to which some of these changes might result in a powerful unleashing of motivation and dedicated energy. It is increasingly clear that human behavior, even in strictly economic institutions, is not governed by economic motivations to anywhere near the extent that is presumed in economic theory. But we do not know how much more effectively business organizations might function if they were to restructure their operations and recast their themes to evoke the kind of identification with an enterprise, concern for its outcome, and sense of significant membership in it that have elicited, in other institutions such as the family and some voluntary associations, extraordinary amounts of conscientious giving of one's best, without thought or concern for differentiated rewards, economic or otherwise.

If new corporate roles in providing humane employment constitute one of the foundation blocks for a full-employment society, a changed concept of income maintenance is another. To explain this, we use the following, admittedly oversimplified, model.

Consider individuals arrayed along a dimension which represents something like degree of self-definition, ability to move toward self-selected goals, or manifest motivation to actualize one's own potentialities. Near the lower end of this scale are clustered the people who, for the time being at least, are relatively unable to obtain and hold satisfactory work. Toward the middle are the large group who rather successfully find and hold work roles as important components of their self-definition. Near the top are individuals who find many options open to them, tend to select their own goals, and seem relatively unconstrained by the organizational roles they choose to play. The direction of human development would appear to be ascending on this scale.

The "old" economic system placed emphasis on production of goods and services through the labors of the broad mid-range of persons, coordinated in organizations put together by entrepreneurs from the upper end of the scale. Many of those at the bottom were taken care of through charity, welfare programs, and in more recent thinking, income maintenance.

In an age when production of sufficient goods and services is a matter the society can handle with ease, an adequate economic system must emphasize a sufficiency of work roles that foster growth of self-esteem and actualization of potentialities, and facilitating movement toward self-definition and self-actualization. *Employment is primarily the activity of self-development,* and only secondarily the production of goods and services.

It follows that instead of the present situation of jobs for the major portion of the self-definition scale, and income maintenance for those at the very bottom who are unemployed, the reverse is what makes sense. Those who want and need jobs should have jobs. Those farther up the self-definition scale who are already in structured work situations need some sort of income maintenance to make it easier for them to choose and actualize their own goals—e.g., more education, a different career, a sabbatical year, social service—which will in turn open up job opportunities for those farther down the scale.

The term "enhancement income maintenance" is used for this latter form of aid, to distinguish it from the subsistence income maintenance which will always be required for the group of unfortunates who remain at the bottom of the scale. With enhancement income maintenance, support would be available to those who have demonstrated ability to hold structured jobs but who want to carry out some project of manifest social value. Examples of such activities would be study and research (such as at present provided for an elite few through scholarship and fellowship programs); providing educational opportunities for others; work in the preservation and beautification of the environment; carrying out a social experiment; assisting the handicapped. Funds would be provided for individuals, but also for group projects, as in the recent Canadian experiments with "Local Incentives Programs."

It must be reiterated that the problem of employment as described appears to be intrinsic to the industrial state in its later stages of development. If so, it will be resolved only with a major systemic change. Thus it should not be surprising if some of the individual measures which may accompany that change look, when examined in isolation, to be somewhat impractical. I am arguing that the whole system has, at the present time, approached a point of impracticality, and a profound change in thinking is required.

INTEGRATED PLANNING—"CHOOSING THE FUTURE"

The same changed corporate goals that would free up the private sector to play a leading role in resolving the employment problem are also crucial in regulating the expanding impact of technology and industrialization, and reducing the growing gap between rich and poor nations. The initiative and active participation of the large industrial organizations cannot be brought to bear on these serious issues until the goal of maximizing profits and growth plays a less dominant role than at present.

Perhaps the most perplexing issue is that of growth itself. Clearly the thesis of "limits to growth"[10] has to be taken seriously, at least to the point of recognizing that the planet cannot sustain ever-increasing economic growth in the form in which we have known it. On the other hand, economic expansion has been the safety valve that provided jobs for those whom advancing technology displaced. Furthermore, it has provided the riches to finance the even more rapidly expanding (and apparently necessarily so) public sector. Thus there is well-based apprehension over the consequences of an economic slowdown, at the same time there is recognition of the power of the arguments that seem to show it to be necessary.

However, what is most important is not the amount of economic growth so much as the kind of growth. Changes pointed to earlier in the institutions and incentives of the society could make possible either economic growth without some of its undesirable consequences, or the slackening off of the rate of growth without intolerable unemployment problems.

Achieving profound social change in the face of strong resistance to measures that appear to threaten jobs or income is one of the key challenges in the approaching demise of the industrial era. Another is accomplishing necessary change while avoiding the undesirable aspects of centralized planning and massive public-sector control.

Mentioned earlier as a needed institutional change was a mechanism for obtaining widespread citizen participation in "designing the future" and achieving necessary regulation at the lowest practicable level (which may be the local community for human-welfare issues and the planetary level for oceanic pollution). The complexity and interconnectedness of these tasks demands a well-coordinated network of planning units at local, regional, national, and planetary levels. In general these units have two tasks—the definition and comparison of alternatives, and the selection and actualization of the alternative to be followed. The first task is technical, requiring advanced skills and detailed information. The second task is political, involving citizen participation, stimulation of needed actions, and brokerage of the resources required from concerned organizations and agencies.

One aspect of the technical task is particularly urgent. This is the development of means for equitably inserting public costs (e.g., environmental impact, resource depletion, technological disemployment, overtaxing of public utilities) and benefits (e.g., aesthetic gain, improved services) into the equations governing private decision-making (e.g., regarding application of a new technology), along with the private costs and benefits on which present decision-making is primarily based. This is the next necessary step beyond technology assessment. (Effluent taxes to discourage air and water polluting are an elementary example of such measures. In general they will only be effective to the extent that they are supported by the accepted social ethic.)

At the planetary level, particularly, the large multinational corporations have an important role to play in the planning process. The largest of them have more economic power than most of the members of the United Nations. National boundaries are especially permeable to the corporations. They, more than most other social institutions, have a vested interest in the future well-being of the world economy. Thus they have the technical and financial resources and also the potential motivation to contribute to planning for habitability at the planetary level. If their goals have become aligned with those of the larger society, they will indeed do so.

Of course, planning has been attempted before—for land use, pollution control, easing of disemployment from technological change, altering population distribution, improving urban transportation, and controlling environmental impact of materials production and of industry. Its effectiveness has been limited by insufficient moral force of overarching goals (e.g., quality of the environment, equitability with regard to impacts) coupled with an economic incentive structure that often operated against socially desirable actions. The cultural and institutional changes we have postulated are in the direction of improved planning effectiveness. They appear to be requisite to the control of the growing "Faustian" powers over our environment.

REDISTRIBUTING WEALTH AND POWER

The principle has by now become well-established that some form of re-distribution of income and economic power is appropriate for both individuals and nations. Both problems are difficult, but in vastly differing orders of magnitude.

The means for economic redistribution among individuals within the nation are available, mainly in the form of progressive tax structures for income and various expanded-ownership schemes for capital.[11] The basic fact is that the poor are poor because their labor is worthless and they have no ownership stake in the economy. As cultural values change and the employment problem is resolved in the ways described earlier, satisfactory redistribution among the nation's citizens will become achievable with relative ease.

Redistribution among nations is another matter. The per capita GNP of the richest nations exceeds that of the poorest by nearly a hundredfold, and the gap widens yearly. The developing world is plagued by a monumental problem of unemployment and underemployment, brought about by a labor-replacing technology plus high population growth plus massive rural-urban migrations, which also increase yearly. Meanwhile, awareness of the inequities perpetuated by the present industrial system also grows. Much more assistance from the rich countries, both in the form of direct aid and economic reform, will be necessary for survival of a world economic system and, indeed, of a world civilization.

New forms of world corporations, truly multinational in ownership and management, will play at least as important roles here as national governments and international agencies. They will be the key actors in the resolution of such fateful issues as the real opportunities for advancement available to underdeveloped nations, the distribution of materials among nations (e.g., influencing pressures on less developed nations to sell their reserves preferentially), and resistance of less developed countries to environmental and materials-conserving policies that might slow down their rates of economic growth. Much will depend upon whether these corporations assume an active responsibility for creating a healthy society and a habitable planet—not as a gesture to improve corporate image nor as a moralistically undertaken responsibility, but because it is the only reasonable long-run interpretation of "good business." In the end, good business policy must become one with good social policy.

IMPEDIMENTS TO CHANGE

Very real impediments exist to inhibit such systemic changes as have been postulated here. Perhaps the main ones are:

1. Basic cultural values and premises are not susceptible to direct

manipulation, so the "ecological ethic" and "self-realization ethic" cannot be brought into dominance through any sort of planned government action. However badly needed, they have to come about more or less spontaneously, aided to some slight extent perhaps by educational attempts at inculcation.

2. Institutions have rigidity and inertia, and tend to perpetuate the values and premises that have been built into them. In particular, an economic system constructed on the basis of materialistic values and perceptions of scarcity will tend to resist the very behavioral and institutional changes that now appear to be necessary for the system's survival.

3. Anxiety over change toward an unknown future is reflected in irrational and unconsciously motivated behavior opposing that change. The primary way in which the threat might be lowered is through dissemination of a positive vision of what a reachable and desirable future might be.

4. The world competitive position of the United States will appear to be at risk. When the country is "exporting" manufacturing facilities and jobs, its balance of trade is unfavorable and it has moved far in the direction of pricing itself out of the world market: then how can U.S. business be expected to take on additional burdens? There are short-run problems here, to be sure. A temporary protectionism may be necessary for the transition, although other highly industrialized nations are facing similar problems (and are experiencing similar cultural changes) so that it is not clear they will have much advantage over us. In the end, however, a nation will be strong because it employs its citizens well. It is not using them well to declare a large fraction of them unusable, and to have another large group tied to boring tasks that are stultifying and diminishing in their effect.

In sum, a systemic change to "humanistic capitalism" in which the major contemporary societal problems could find resolution appears to be feasible, providing the necessary supportive cultural change continues to gain force. Whether it happens and whether it is accompanied by relatively violent and disruptive social turmoil, depend to considerable extent on the research, analysis, public debate, and individual and institutional commitment generated within the next few years.

REFERENCES

1. Caldwell, L., *Environment: A Challenge to Modern Society;* Bloomington, Ind.: Indiana U. Press, 1972.
2. Huxley, A., *The Perennial Philosophy;* New York: Harper & Bros., 1945.
3. Drucker, P., "The New Markets and the New Entrepreneurs," *The Public Interest,* Sept. 1970.
4. Cleveland, H., *The Future Executive;* New York: Harper & Row, 1972.
5. Lowe, A., *On Economic Knowledge;* New York: Harper & Row, 1965.
6. Yankelovich, D., *The Changing Values on Campus;* New York: Washington Square Press Pocket Books, 1972. (See also T. Roszak, *Where the Wasteland Ends;* New York: Doubleday & Co., 1972, and W. I. Thompson, *At the Edge of History;* New York: Harper & Row, 1971.)
7. Parker, S., *The Future of Work and Leisure;* New York: Praeger Publishers, 1971.
8. Gross, B., & Moses, S., "Measuring the Real Work Force," *Social Policy,* Sept.-Oct. 1972.
9. O'Toole, J., and others, *Work in America;* Cambridge, Mass.: MIT Press, 1972.
10. Meadows, D., et al., *The Limits to Growth;* New York: Universe Books, 1972.
11. Kelso, L., *Two-Factor Theory: The Economics of Reality;* New York: Vintage Books, 1968.

POLITICS AND GOVERNMENT

POLITICS AND THE NEW HUMANISM

Walt Anderson

In trying to make sense of politics today we lack a fundamental sense of what it is all about, who we are, what we are trying to do, and why. We need new ways of understanding political events and how we as individuals can relate to them.

My aim here is to present humanistic or "third-force" psychology as a perspective from which to consider political events and the way we study them in the social sciences. I do not think there is—or should be—anything remarkable about using a school of psychology as an approach to politics, because I do not think there is any distinction between psychology, sociology, and political science which makes sense anywhere outside of a college catalog. Any psychology is also a political ideology and a scientific methodology.

CONSCIOUSNESS REVOLUTION

It does not do us much good to speculate about whether there might someday be a revolution in America. There is one going on, and the only thing which can prevent us from seeing it is attachment to a concept of revolution more appropriate to 1789 or 1917. Nor can we get far by agonizing about whether we should work inside or outside the system, because the system keeps changing all the time the debate goes on—and anyway there is really no inside or outside if we take a clear look at our evolving political culture. If we find a new perspective, look at political systems in terms of human evolution and at ourselves in terms of human growth, then perhaps we will be better able to understand the changes that are going on around us, and within us, and see new patterns of connection between the two.

Changes of great magnitude are occurring. I have heard the term "cultural revolution" used frequently to describe what's going on, and have found it useful. But a more apt term is "consciousness revolu-

SOURCE: Walt Anderson, "Politics and the New Humanism," *Journal of Humanistic Psychology*, Fall 1974. Reprinted by permission.

tion"—this means that all of us are undergoing a basic transformation of awareness; moving toward a different way of experiencing ourselves; experiencing our relation to history, to other people, and to the world.

We can roughly compare this revolution to the Industrial Revolution, which was equally invisible in its early stages. It started, on a rather small scale, as a way people organized in relation to one another and to the production of goods. It was *not* basically mechanical; the machinery came later. Nor was it basically political, although everything political—and just about everything in the world—changed as a result of it. One specific consequence of the Industrial Revolution was its impact on political philosophy: it made it necessary for people who claimed to understand politics pay attention to economics. Today, the consciousness revolution will require political scientists to pay attention to new factors, especially psychology and biology.

Humanistic psychology—a relatively new intellectual movement—offers us a perspective from which we can look at politics. Underlying this psychology is a view of human life—in fact of all organic life—as moving in the direction of

> an increasing self-government, self-regulation, and autonomy, and away from heteronymous control, or control by external forces. This is true whether we are speaking of entirely unconscious organic processes, such as the regulation of body heat, or such uniquely human and intellectual functions as the choice of life goals [Rogers, 1951, p. 20].

Bugental (1971) has described this perspective as a "humanistic ethic," and lists as its identifying points: (a) centered responsibility for one's own life, (b) mutuality in relationships, (c) here-and-now perspective, (d) acceptance of nonhedonic emotions, and (e) growth-oriented experiences.

All of the above have a good deal more relevance to political change and to the practice of the social sciences than may be readily apparent. Bugental is talking about the idea of psychotherapy as a source of social change, which is considerably different from the "adjustment" goal of more conservative schools of therapy. He is also outlining some of the possible characteristics of a widespread cultural change he calls a "humanistic evolution." This is in sharp contrast to Freud, for example, who said:

> Our mind, that precious instrument by whose means we maintain ourselves alive, is no peacefully self-contained unity. It is rather to be compared with a modern State in which a mob, eager for enjoyment and destruction, has to be held down forcibly by a prudent superior class [Freud, 1932, p. 303].

Psychoanalysis

In a historical sense we can see the emergence of Freudian theory as a recognition of the enormous demands placed upon the human instinctual system by the various forces of nineteenth- and twentieth-century Europe: victorian morality, nationalism, the increasing bureaucratization and organization of life. Such demands, for Freud, were inherent in the process of civilization itself. "It is impossible," he wrote, "to overlook the extent to which civilization is built up upon a renunciation of instinct, how much it presupposes precisely the nonsatisfaction . . . of powerful instincts [Freud, 1930, p. 44]."

He did not believe that a life of gratification of those instincts offered any great promise. Research among primitive peoples, he said, showed that "their instinctual life is by no means to be envied for its freedom [Freud, 1930, p. 62]." The situation of the civilized human being was one of having "exchanged a portion of his possibilities of happiness for a portion of security [Freud, 1930, p. 62]." The task of the therapist was to facilitate this exchange, to aid the civilizing process by teaching people how to accommodate themselves to the demands of society, including those demands they had internalized. His only reply to a patient who wondered what value there could be in a therapy which made no basic change in the circumstances of life was that, "much will be gained if we succeed in transforming your hysterical misery into common unhappiness [Freud, 1893, p. 305]." Freud's life work was in the service of the reality principle. Philip Rieff (1959), who sees him as essentially a moralist, writes:

> Therapy prepares a mixture of detachment and forbearance, a stoic rationality of the kind Epictetus preached. . . . To detach the individual from the most powerful lures in life, while teaching him how to pursue others less powerful and less damaging to the pursuer—these aims appear high enough in an age rightly suspicious of salvations. Freud had the tired wisdom of a universal healer for whom no disease can be wholly cured [p. 327].

In Freud's pessimism and resignation we find the source of his political conservatism. A radical philosophy, a revolutionary program, contains some concept of a possible better future, a resolution of the present misery. Freud's view of society contains no such concept.

Freud's rejection of revolution does not arise from an opinion about its desirability or undesirability, but rather from a conviction that true revolution is simply not possible. External authority is a manifestation of psychological need, an expression of the inner structure of the individual psyche, and therefore no real change can be effected by striking out against institutions. If social authority stands in opposition to some psychological drives—and more primitive ones—it also exists in fulfillment of other, quite powerful, human needs. Thus Roazen (1968) writes:

> Patrick Henry's "Give me liberty or give me death" is, according to Freud, superlatively untrue to human experience. Man wants both liberty and restraint, and the tensions between conflicting needs comprise human tragedy. Freud's description of social restrictions, of the coercions of life, is so intensely real because he sees the extent to which outer authority is linked to our inner needs. Society is coercive precisely because its rules are internalized, are taken into the self; and at the same time society is useful in helping to keep some sort of a balance between various forces. Just as a child needs parental restrictions to handle his aggression, just as he needs to be stopped before the full horror of his murderous impulses becomes evident to him, so social restraints assist man in handling his aggression, both by providing vicarious forms of release, and by reinforcing his inner controls over drives which are alien to his inner security [p. 157].

In contrast to philosophies which view political authority as a result of a conscious and deliberate agreement among members of a society, as a necessary consequence of God's order on earth, or as a reflection of the economic system, Freud sees it as the external manifestation of an internal conflict. This internal conflict is largely unconscious and fundamentally unchangeable.

Although Freud's system is based on notion of evolution, it contains no prescription for future change, certainly no assertion that further progress is inevitable. Human development in his view seems to have reached a painful *detente* beyond which there is little hope of change. This is a great contrast to the view of Marx, whose system was also evolutionary (and who dedicated *Das Kapital* to Charles Darwin) but who offered, in fact, an inexorable dialectic of change and a utopian future of great freedom.

Freud offered no such promises but, instead, worked to devise ways that individuals could learn to live with themselves and with civilization. He gave the world the first system of psychotherapy which contained as an integral part of its intellectual foundation a theory of society and authority. He was the first person who fully recognized the impact of modern society upon the human instincts, and he does not seem to have seriously considered the possibility that modern society could be transformed. He chose to become a teacher of ways of adjusting to things as they are.

The psychoanalytic profession as it has taken form in America is consistent with Freud's view of its social function (i.e., it serves as a means of helping certain individuals adjust to the realities of modern civilization). It offers no program or rationale for fundamental political or social change.

There is no conclusive data on what, if any, changes in political persuasion are likely to result from psychoanalysis, but Arnold Rogow (1970) states that

> The consensus of both psychiatrists and psychoanalysts is that successful psychotherapy, by promoting open-mindedness, relative freedom from intrapsychic conflicts, and a decrease in rigidity of belief, moves patients toward a moderate or middle-road political position if they were not already there at the commencement of treatment [p. 72].

This is a revealing statement of an implicit value assumption about politics and mental health: namely, that the more healthy individual occupies a "middle-of-the-road" political position. This is consistent with a view of therapy as adjustment and with the values which are to be found in applications of Freudian theory to political analysis.

One of the first Americans to take serious note of the implications of Freudian theory for political science was Walter Lippmann, who used some of Freud's concepts in works published prior to 1930 (Lippmann, 1913, 1922). But Lippmann did not attempt to develop a Freudian theory of political behavior; that task was taken up in the 1930s by Harold Lasswell, a political scientist who had made a comprehensive study of Freud's writings and had undergone a training analysis.

In *Psychopathology and Politics* Lasswell (1930) remained faithful to the basic Freudian theory of politics as a manifestation of "internal" personality structure. He dealt with political behavior as a *displacement* of private motives onto political objects.

> The most general formula which expresses the developmental facts about the fully developed political man reads thus:

$$p \} d \} r = P$$

> where p equals private motives; d equals displacement onto a public object; r equals rationalization in terms of public interest; P equals the political man, and } equals transformed into [p. 76].

This formulation is an excellent statement of the Freudian theory of politics. The basic dynamic it describes is present in later psychoanalytically oriented work by Lasswell and others. It asserts that political behavior is in some degree an acting out of internal psychological conflicts which are repressed, unconscious, and irrational: people rationalize—create rational motives for their actions—but the motives they create are not the true sources of behavior.

Revolutionaries and revolutionary movements do not fare very well at the hands of Freudian political analysts. The internal theory of authority as expressed through Lasswell's displacement formula tends inescapably toward a view of any action against constituted authorities as an acting out of repressed hostility. Such an emphasis makes it difficult for the revolutionary to be taken seriously. His or her complaints against the power structure, however valid they may feel subjectively, are all too easily taken to be displacements: "The repressed father-hatred may be turned against kings or capitalists [Lasswell, 1930, p. 76]."

There have been persistent efforts dating back to the early years of the psychoanalytic movement to take Freud's insights in the opposite direction—to make the doctrine of repression the starting point for a program of political revolution and a transformation of human life.

The first of the Freudian revolutionaries was Wilhelm Reich, who in his stormy career managed to be expelled from both the International Psychoanalytic Association and the Communist Party. His troubles within the Freudian and Marxist movements stemmed from his attempts to tie the two together, an attempt which was unwelcome to the orthodox of both camps.

In 1929 Reich argued that psychoanalysis was a materialistic science, based on a description of conflict within the individual and society. Psychoanalysis, he said, was furthermore a revolutionary science: it located the source of sexual repression in bourgeois morality and thereby stated the case for a liberation of human instincts. At the same time, Reich granted that the movement seemed to be losing its sense of mission, and was degenerating into a business and a stylish fad [Robinson, 1969, pp. 41-42]. Later Reich criticized Freud himself for placing his science "at the disposal of a conservative ideology [Reich, 1942, p. 195]."

Reich (1970) felt that the European masses were incapable of acting according to the political and economic logic of their condition. Instead of becoming revolutionary, they had a tendency to become reactionary. He explained the mechanics of it in terms which were quite similar to Freud's theory of the internalization of authority. In Reich's explanation, great importance was attached to sexual suppression:

> The moral inhibition of the child's natural sexuality . . . makes the child afraid, shy, fearful of authority, obedient, "good," and "docile" in the authoritarian sense of the words. It has a crippling effect on man's rebellious forces because every vital life-impulse is now burdened with severe fear; and since sex is a forbidden subject, thought in general and man's critical faculty also become inhibited. In short, morality's aim is to produce acquiescent subjects who, despite distress and humiliation, are adjusted to the authoritarian order. Thus, the family is the authoritarian state in miniature, to

which the child must learn to adapt himself as a preparation for the general social adjustment required of him later [p. 30].

The interference with normal sexuality in the authoritarian family, then, was what maintained the authoritarian state. This is why "the authoritarian state gains an enormous interest in the authoritarian family: *It becomes the factory in which the state's structure and ideology are molded* [Reich, 1970, p. 30]." And it is also the key to understanding the great flaw in the conventional, economically deterministic Marxist ideology: *"Sexual inhibition alters the structure of the economically suppressed individual in such a way that he thinks, feels, and acts against his own material interests* [Reich, 1946, p. 26]."

Since Reich's time there have been other reinterpreters of Freud, most notably Herbert Marcuse and Norman O. Brown. Each of these has found in Freudian theory a promise of human liberation, and both have attained great popular status as the philosophical mentors of rebellious youth. According to Theodore Roszak (1969), "The emergence of Herbert Marcuse and Norman Brown as major social theorists among the disaffiliated young of Western Europe and America must be taken as one of the defining features of the counter culture [p. 84]."

Reich, Marcuse, and Brown share the belief that people are capable of being free and that adjustment to unfreedom is not the same thing as mental health. The approach to political analysis that flows from this perspective is quite different from that of the orthodox Freudians. Reich (1946) sums this up succinctly: *"What is to be explained,"* he said, *"is not why the starving individual steals or why the exploited individual strikes, but why the majority of starving individuals do not steal and the majority of exploited individuals do not strike* [p. 15]."

Behaviorism

Behaviorist psychologists such as Watson and Skinner have been quite willing to extend their theoretical formulations to large-scale architectonic propositions about cultural design, but they have tended to avoid identification with existing ideologies and have maintained that their concepts are above or beyond traditional political issues.

This has not discouraged the critics of behaviorism from drawing conclusions about its political content. For example, Floyd Matson (1964), in a fairly representative summary of the case, writes:

Whether human conduct is conditioned or unconditioned it remains, on the behaviorist account, wholly determinate and predictable; and, in either event, it is open to manipulation by reconditioning .... It seems extraordinary nowadays that such a doctrine could ever have been construed in any sense as democratic: its blindness to personal intention, its scorn of mind, its denial of any freedom of action or capacity for it, its tacit enlistment in the service of a kind of technocratic efficiency and regimentation—these characteristics of classical behaviorism appear rather to confirm the harsh judgment of Mannheim that it bears an unmistakable resemblance to fascism [p. 60].

The judgment of Karl Mannheim to which Matson referred was based on a historical view of behaviorism as a response to the need of modern civilization for a more efficient principle of human organization. Behaviorism, said Mannheim (1940), "is a typical product of thought at that stage of mass society in which it is more important, from the practical point of view, to be able to calculate the average behavior of the mass than to understand the private motives of individuals or to transform the whole personality [p. 213]."

The concern of behaviorism with the needs of society, and the shift of emphasis away from subjectivity, from inner experience, must inevitably produce a social, adjustment-oriented definition of mental health and pathology. For example, to quote Talcott Parsons (1963): "Health may be defined as the state of optimum capacity of an individual for the effective performance of the roles and tasks for which he has been socialized. It is thus defined with reference to the individual's participation in the social system [p. 176]."

Richard Sennett (1971), a sociologist reviewing *Beyond Freedom and Dignity*, analyzed some of Skinner's specific proposals for social improvement and found his political stance to be neither fascistic nor technocratic, but simply, in a bland, middle-American kind of way, conservative.

[Skinner] indicates a few purposes to which he personally would like to see the techniques put.

First, behavior control appears to him a way to get people hard at work again in an age where indolence is rife . . . .

As a corollary to his belief in hard work, Skinner rails against the sexual and other sensual pleasures that he feels have become rampant today, and argues that such behavior needs to be redirected . . . .

Not surprisingly, Skinner also believes that the small group, the town, the village, the little neighborhood circle, is the scale at which behavior conditioning can operate morally . . . .

These beliefs should sound familiar. They are the articles of faith of Nixonian America, of the small-town businessman who feels life has degenerated, has gotten beyond his control, and who thinks things will get better when other people learn how to behave [p. 1].

There is, certainly, a tendency for statements of the possibilities of behaviorist psychology to reflect the existing values of society, and this gives behaviorism a certain middle-of-the-road bias. For all the differences in philosophy and methodology that exist between Freudian and behaviorist psychology, they are rather similar in their tendency to operate as defenders of the social and cultural status quo.

Thomas Szasz (1963) charges that all psychiatry is in fact a form of social control, and that behavior-modification programs, usually imposed from above on institutional inmates, tend to become focal-points for the politicization of therapy.

It is common for behavior therapists to discuss their various techniques as remedial measures undertaken on behalf of, and upon the request of, the patient. In reality, however, consent is a rather more elusive concept; the quality of the consent must be taken into account, for frequently the patient is being influenced strongly by someone else, such as the courts, a prison warden, employer, or family.

Maslow

Let us now begin to look at humanistic psychology. Any science is in part shaped by what its researchers choose to study—by the things that, deliberately or not, they select to be in their line of vision. Abraham Maslow believed that psychologists had allowed themselves to become so preoccupied with mental illness that they had neglected almost entirely to form any meaningful concept of real health, of a fully-functioning human being. "It becomes more and more clear," Maslow (1954) wrote, "that the study of crippled, stunted, immature, and unhealthy specimens can yield only a cripple psychology and a cripple philosophy [p. 180]."

Maslow developed a theory of human *health*, and eventually became convinced that the study of healthy (self-actualizing) people was producing not only a better conceptualization of mental health, but a whole new psychology, a radically different vision of humanity. One of his statements (Maslow, 1968) about self-actualizing individuals is very important to this discussion:

> Such a person, by virtue of what he has become, assumes a new relation to his society and indeed, to society in general. He not only transcends himself in various ways; he also transcends his culture. He resists enculturation. He becomes more detached from his culture and from his society. He becomes a little more a member of his species and a little less a member of his local group [p. 11].

The idea that healthy human growth tends toward deenculturation adds a new dimension to some of the basic concepts of political philosophy, such as obligation and authority. It also opens up new areas for empirical research: behavioral political scientists have done a good deal of research on socialization, but they have made no comparable investigation of any process of *de*socialization. Maslow clearly means that the "transcendence of culture" is a kind of desocialization: self-actualizing people simply outgrow much of what they have been taught about society and their relation to it.

Maslow merely mentioned this particular facet of the character structure of self-actualizing people as one of several points to be considered. Personally, I find it to be a revolutionary idea: it says that there exist within our society a significant number of people—some of our wisest and strongest, in fact—who are "in" the society in a fundamentally different way from the rest of us. The attitude of these people toward some of the things which civilizations traditionally rest upon (cultural norms, laws, etc.) seems to be that they are all right if you keep them in their place.

One important point about Maslow's work is that although he found his self-actualizing subjects to be quite capable of radical social action, such action is not a result of deprivation, which is commonly assumed to be the main source of revolutionary social change, nor is it the acting out of personal pathology according to the Freudian model. Instead, the altruistic, creative behavior of self-actualizing men and women is, in Maslow's view, the natural satisfaction of complex biological needs which emerge when the lower physiological and psychological needs have been satisfied. Maslow (1967) was convinced that the failure to recognize these higher needs (metaneeds) contributed to the "frustrated idealism" experienced by many young people, particularly students:

> This frustrated idealism and occasional hopelessness is partially due to the influence and ubiquity of stupidly limited theories of motivation all over the world. Leaving aside behavioristic and positivistic theories—or rather, non-theories—as simple refusals even to see the problem, i.e., a kind of psychoanalytic denial, then what is available to the idealistic young man and woman?
>
> Not only does the whole of official nineteenth-century science and orthodox academic psychology offer him nothing, but also the major motivation theories by which most men live can lead him only to depression or cynicism. The Freudians, at least in their official writings (though not in good therapeutic practice), are still reductionistic about all higher human values. The deepest and most real motivations are seen to be dangerous and nasty, while the highest human values are essentially fake, being not what they seem to be, but camouflaged versions of the "deep, dark, and dirty." Our social scientists are just as disappointing in the main. A total cultural determinism is still the official, orthodox doctrine of many or most of

the sociologists and anthropologists. This doctrine not only denies intrinsic higher motivations, but comes perilously close sometimes to denying "human nature" itself. The economists, not only in the West but also in the East, are essentially materialistic. We must say harshly of the "science" of economics that it is generally the skilled, exact, technological application of a totally false theory of human needs and values, a theory which recognizes only the existence of lower needs or material needs [p. 110].

Maslow did not go far in the direction of stating the social or political theories which might be derived from his work, but two main propositions come through clearly. These are (a) that, contrary to Freudian theory, the needs of people and the needs of civilization are not *necessarily* antagonistic, and (b) that the possibilities of a society's development are contingent upon the ability of its structures and its members to recognize and encourage higher human needs and the potential for self-actualization. These two propositions are workable guidelines, I believe, toward the development of humanistic politics, and a humanistic political science.

Gestalt

Gestalt therapy talks a great deal about responsibility, but this has a meaning rather different from the traditional moral exhortation to take responsibility for oneself. The gestaltist is convinced that all people already are responsible for most of what is happening to them, but simply unaware of how they manipulate the environment and simultaneously block their own awareness of what they are doing.

The attitude of the passive-suffering projector ... we believe is typical of modern dissociated men. It is imbedded in our language, our world-attitude, our institutions. The prevention of outgoing motion and initiative, the social derogation of aggressive drives, and the epidemic disease of self-control and self-conquest have led to a language in which the self seldom does or expresses anything; instead, "it" happens. These restrictive measures have also led to a view of the world as completely neutral and "objective" and unrelated to our concerns; and to institutions that take over our functions, that are to "blame" because they "control" us, and that wreak on us the hostility which we so carefully refrain from wielding ourselves—as if men did not themselves lend to institutions whatever force they have! [Perls, Hefferline, & Goodman, p. 215.]

The idea of a close relationship between authority and awareness is one of the major contributions of gestalt. It gives us a clinical perspective on a psychological principle that seems to be understood by a growing number of political activists. The principle can be stated this way: *individuals who are under the control of an authority not only surrender their own power to that authority, but to some extent surrender also their awareness of being controlled.* A political corollary to this could be stated: *to become fully aware of being dominated is itself a step toward ending domination.* This principle appears to be influencing a good deal of contemporary radical action. Women's liberation forces especially are aware of the tremendous potential of "consciousness-raising"—bringing the power relationship out into the open—as a technique for social change.

Fritz Perls (1969), a short time before his death, told gestalt therapists that they had a certain kind of historical mission, which was to make a real revolution possible:

> . . . so far we only have a rebellion. We don't have a revolution yet . . . . If there is any chance of interrupting the rise and fall of the United States, it's up to our youth and it's up to you in supporting this youth. To be able to do this, there is only one way through: to become real, to learn to take a stand, to develop one's center . . . [p. 3].

For Perls, then, the work of gestalt was a person-by-person revolution, freeing individuals from their own inner tyranny and fragmentation, paving the way for profound social change.

Hopefully, the psychological foundations of social control are eroding, and the kind of enforced morality we have always known and accepted in America will no longer be possible. To talk of political revolution as we have known it becomes irrelevant to our times. Nobody will have to overthrow the state; we will simply outgrow our need for many of its functions.

Encounter

The encounter movement, too, presents a political challenge. Two of its characteristics are the conviction that alternative styles of interpersonal relationship are truly available and the determination to make personal openness a political issue. It is nothing less than an attempt to transform the whole society's style of interpersonal relating. Like gestalt therapy it aims not at the institutional superstructure but at the person-to-person foundation of society.

Zen

An important source of philosophical influence in humanistic psychology comes from outside Western culture. Many of the concepts and values and techniques of Eastern systems such as Zen, Yoga, and Sufism have found their way into psychological theory, therapy, and encounter-group practice.

Zen, for instance, is hardly a religion in the Western sense; it is primarily a technique for the development of consciousness. And when we deal with Zen as a psychological system we come again to the concept of internalization of social norms. Zen goes much further than Freudian and gestalt theory, however, and asserts that all perceptions of reality, even the very sense of self, are products of social conditioning. This, too, is not entirely alien to Western thought. Fromm (1970), for example, states that:

Every society, by its own practice of living and by the mode of relatedness, of feeling, and perceiving, develops a system of categories which determines the forms of awareness. This system works, as it were, like a *socially conditioned filter;* experience cannot enter awareness unless it can penetrate this filter [p. 99].

Is it possible to become deconditioned, to throw away the social filter, and what are the larger political implications of such a process? Zen is a training process aimed at a specific goal, the *satori* experience. Equivalent terms for *satori* in English are enlightenment, awakening, liberation. Both Fromm and Watts believe that Zen liberation is essentially a release from the psychological conditioning of the society. Fromm (1970) asserts that:

In its historical development each society becomes caught in its own need to survive in the particular form in which it is developed, and it usually accomplishes this survival by ignoring the wider human aims which are common to all men. This contradiction between the social and the universal aim leads also to the fabrication (on a social scale) of all sorts of fictions and illusions which have the function to deny and to rationalize the dichotomy between the goals of humanity and the goals of a given society [p. 98].

If this is true, then obviously an awakening from the socially conditioned consciousness is an experience which profoundly transforms one's relationship to the political order, and the word "liberation" as a synonym for *satori* takes on a political meaning. The individual so liberated is still subject to the laws of the state, of course, but the state's roots in consciousness have virtually disappeared.

Zen also sheds some light on the assertion that the prevailing political order enforces not only certain patterns of economic and social interaction, but also a fundamental definition of reality, a world-view and value system which is the basis for all power, *and which is defined, not simply as patriotism, but as sanity.*

Humanistic psychology can best be understood as a search for some kind of common transcultural meeting ground on which human beings can recognize one another and communicate. In this context, Zen, which teaches that all people contain within themselves a true and unconditioned consciousness which can be trained to break through and make contact with its environment, offers an important contribution.

CONSCIOUSNESS AND POLITICAL ACTION

When we view politics within the Freudian paradigm, we see society as a huge stage for the acting out of internal conflict, a hopeless war between the deep inner needs of individuals and the needs of the system. The behaviorist movement did not offer any such dramatic new paradigm—in part because it was essentially a restatement of what had been a dramatic new paradigm in the seventeenth century: the image of the universe as a smoothly-spinning machine, guided by hard and discoverable natural laws. But although the behaviorist movement produced no single new political theory, it has tended to convey a fairly coherent view of political behavior stressing power and economic motivations, to view society as a kind of vast machine, and to deal with individuals in terms of their social roles and group memberships.

Just as Freud believed that his discoveries about the unconscious brought an entire new world-view into existence, so do humanistic psychologists believe that their discoveries about the growth and integrative possibilities of men and women are not simply additional psychological data but the basis of an entire redefinition of humanity.

All of the humanistic theories that we have discussed seem to indicate that the process of personal growth, especially as it moves into the higher reaches of human potentiality, include some kind of a transformation of the individual's relation to the social order, cultural norms, laws, ideology, and institutions. Third force psychologists have not attempted to work out a systematic theory of consciousness and politics, to devise some kind of an intellectual apparatus to make it clear how the kind of personal development that they are (as theorists) studying and (as therapists) helping to bring about, may affect American society (or how American society may affect it).

Charles Hampden-Turner (1971) holds that the social sciences as they stand conspire to force us to think of humanity in terms that are essentially conservative. This is not the deliberate product of ideological conservatism—in fact most of the social scientists are political liberals—but rather the unexpected yet inevitable result of the use of "scientific" methodology:

> Their social conservatism is *for others*, the object of investigation. Moreover their conservatism is latent in the tools they employ. It comes about less by valuing conservatively than by the "value-free" selection of the less than human . . . . He who is silent assents, and to describe the status quo with detailed and passionless precision is usually to dignify it [pp. 17-18].

Thus academic political science was taken completely off guard by the protest movements of the 1960s and the liberation movements of the 1970s and still has trouble dealing with evidence of idealistic behavior or seriously considering the possibility that any really fundamental change can or will take place in American society. Hampden-Turner argues that the social sciences in general have so successfully directed their attention to men and women as cogs in the power-driven, wealth-manipulating system that they can not see people as capable of any truly creative or idealistic social action.

ON THE STATE AS A STATE OF MIND

"The establishment" or "the power structure" can be viewed as an established consciousness, a psychological power structure. All social institutions rest upon how people think and feel, how they comprehend the *meaning* of being human, how they experience the self, how they perceive their relationship to the environment and to each other. The state, in short, is a state of mind.

In spite of all the efforts of psychiatrists to maintain that their profession is an objective, ideologically neutral science, political issues seem to be turning up in it with increasing frequency. On one hand there are those who agree with Dr. Ewald Busse, 1971-72 president of the American Psychiatric Association, who says:

> It is my opinion that psychiatric services should not be the tool for restructuring society or solving economic problems or for determining new human values. Psychiatric services should be continued as patient oriented activities designed to reduce pain and discomfort and to increase the capacity of the individual to adjust satisfactorily . . . [Halleck, 1971, p. 11].

On the other hand, Dr. Raymond Waggoner, a past president of the same association, says:

> I plead for a psychiatry that is involved with fundamental social goals. I plead for a psychiatry that will eschew isolation altogether and assume its proper leadership role in advancing the total health of our nation. I plead for a psychiatry that is at once concerned with individual liberty and communal responsibility and I ask of psychiatrists that they be not only pragmatists but also dreamers with a vision of the future [Halleck, 1971, p. 12].

This is a fairly mild argument, and yet it represents what I consider to be the basic cleavage between working to maintain the system, and working to clear the way for human growth, wherever that may lead.

The issue becomes clearer as we look at more extreme statements. A behavior-modification psychologist advocating massive use of psychological techniques to deal with crime says:

> ... we'd assume that a felony was clear evidence that the criminal had somehow acquired a full-blown social neurosis and needed to be cured, not punished. We'd send him to a rehabilitation center where he'd undergo positive brainwashing until we were quite sure he had become a law-abiding citizen who would not again commit an antisocial act. We'd probably have to restructure his entire personality [McConnell, 1970, p. 74].

I have described this as an extreme statement, but it would be more accurate to call it a particularly blunt expression of values that is quite widely held. At the other extreme is a new movement calling itself Radical Therapy, which takes the position that the task of therapy must be social change, and that any form of encouragement of adjustment is concealed social control:

> Therapy is change, not adjustment. This *means* change—social, personal, and political. When people are fucked over, people should help them fight it, and then deal with their feelings. A "struggle for mental health" is bullshit unless it involves changing this society which turns us into machines, alienates us from one another and our work, and binds us into racist, sexist and imperialist practices [Glenn, 1971, p. x-xi].

It is characteristic that those who are farthest from the centers of power are most convinced that therapy is inherently political, while those who are in control usually maintain that it is not. Certainly there can be an enormous amount of political power concealed behind the supposedly neutral, objective, or scientific act of defining mental illness. It is a power which can only be effectively exerted by those who already *have* power. Dissenting psychologists can talk about pathology in the acts of leaders, but the leaders are not subsequently subject to the various acts of control—psychiatric diagnosis, behavior therapy, commitment—which are the fate of thousands of people at lower levels of society. Thomas Szasz (1971) goes so far as to assert that, "There is no such 'condition' as 'schizophrenia,' but the label is a social fact and the social fact a political event [p. 84]." In fact, he argues that the existence of such a thing as "mental illness" has never been proven with enough certainty to justify the enormous persecution of all those who happen to get branded with such a designation:

> What we call modern, dynamic psychiatry is neither a glamorous advance over the superstitions and practices of the witch-hunts, as contemporary psychiatric propagandists would have it, nor a retro-

gression from the humanism of the Renaissance and the scientific spirit of the Enlightenment, as romantic traditionalists would have it. In actuality, Institutional Psychiatry is a continuation of the Inquisition. All that has really changed is the vocabulary and the social style. The vocabulary conforms to the intellectual expectations of our age: it is a pseudomedical jargon that parodies the concepts of science. The social style conforms to the political expectations of our age: it is a pseudoliberal social movement that parodies the ideals of freedom and rationality [p. 27].

Most humanistic psychiatrists and psychologists prefer to steer clear of the "medical model," and most humanistic therapies strive to reduce the authoritarian character of the therapist—this is fundamental to Rogerian counseling, to gestalt work in which the patients are expected to take responsibility for themselves, to encounter work in which the leader is also a participant.

POLITICS AS GROWTH

Now, it is undoubtedly true that, so far, the emphasis in humanistic psychology has been upon individual, personal growth, and that when humanistic psychologists have addressed themselves to the possibility of bringing about widespread *social* change, they have often tended to emphasize the incremental results of individual growth (such as the cumulative effect of many people undergoing some kind of personal transformation through therapy or encounter group experience). There has been less of an inclination to consider the possible ways of changing institutions or to understand institutional change as a way of facilitating personal growth for great numbers of people.

Yet humanistic psychology does offer guidelines for looking at institutions—and changing them and creating them—in terms of human needs and human development. These are most highly developed in the works of Maslow and Hampden-Turner: Maslow's hierarchy of needs and Hampden-Turner's model of psychosocial development both address themselves directly to the question of how social arrangements can facilitate (or obstruct) the growth of human beings. They offer propositions which are testable according to the empirical standards of contemporary social science research, and they lead rather easily to ideas about public policy. They also lead toward a different idea of what politics *is*. To get at what I mean let me cite a few general statements about politics by leading political scientists. Robert Dahl (1963) says, "A political system is any persistent pattern of human relationships that involves, to a significant extent, power, rule, or authority [p. 6]." Heinz Eulau (1963) suggests that "what makes man's behavior political is that he rules and obeys, persuades and compromises, promises and bargains, coerces and represents, fights and fears . . . [p. 4-5]." And of course there is Harold Lasswell's (1950) oft-quoted definition of politics as a matter of "who gets what, when, and how."

These definitions all tell us something about politics, and they also tell us something about the range of vision of the definers, what it is that they have chosen to see.

But suppose we try defining politics as the ways people organize themselves in order to attain the greatest satisfaction of human needs possible within the environment. When we look at politics this way we naturally turn our attention to the things which obstruct human development. The most important single limiting factor is the idea which any society has about what the possibilities of human development actually are. A stunted or narrow conception of the human potential, especially when deeply built into cultural norms and reinforced by a society's art and science and philosophy, is as powerful a form of tyranny as any political institution. By stunted or narrow conception I mean any lopsided view which focuses on certain human needs—safety or esteem, for example—to the exclusion of others, or a truncated value system such as our own which sees the acquisition of a great amount of material goods and social prestige as evidence of the upper limits of human growth.

The historical importance of humanistic psychology is that it offers us a new and more expansive vision of human growth at a time when the shortcomings of the old vision have become most evident. Humanistic psychology is a challenge to our commonly held beliefs about what people are, how they grow and change, and what they may become. Humanistic psychology is significant only insofar as it pushes and tugs at fundamental ideas.

It seems to me that if we are guided at all times by some kind of image of the upper reaches of human development, then our way of considering matters of public policy will be fundamentally different. We will not be trying—as in the case of welfare—to remove a potential source of crime, or even to make certain individuals more "socially productive," but rather to release the fullest possibilities of human development. Guided by such a perspective, we would certainly create policies far different from the ones we now have. Our politics, like our psychology, has lost touch with a concept of human health. We think mainly in terms of acute social ailments and first-aid remedies, rarely in terms of the fullest possibilities of human growth and how societies may facilitate it.

I fear that our political science has supported this kind of thinking (take a look again at the above definitions of politics) by making the most outrageous symptoms of political sickness (e.g., the inequitable distribution of goods and services, the conflicts for power and special advantage, the manipulation of the public by office-holders and office-seekers) seem like the norms of civilized life. This "realism" has conspired to banish the search for a more sane and nourishing social order to the realm of "idealism," and thus deprive it of intellectual legitimacy.

But the search—because it, too, expresses a deep and very real human drive—goes on anyway. And we have available to us now a somewhat different conception of human life, which forms the unifying framework of humanistic psychology. It also forms the theoretical basis for the many methods of humanistic therapy and encounter group work. These experiences have touched the lives of thousands of people, and have undoubtedly accounted for some degree of social change. But their application is still fairly limited. We have not—nor has any society in history—made it an effort of high priority to understand the processes and possibilities of human growth and to translate that understanding into social policy.

If we should choose to make the highest development of human beings a deliberate social goal, then the task before us is to think about the growth possibilities of all people, at all social and economic levels, and also to understand fully what it means when a species begins to become responsible for its own evolution. As we consider such questions, the humanistic perspective becomes not merely psychological, but political; we are not talking about principles of research or therapy, but about principles of social action and institutional change. Our new vision of the possibilities of human existence becomes a set of guidelines for building a human community. It is no longer the concern merely of writers and clinicians and social scientists but a *res publica*, a public thing.

REFERENCES

Anderson, W. *Politics and the new humanism.* Pacific Palisades, Calif.: Goodyear, 1973.

Bugental, J. The humanistic ethic—the individual in psychotherapy as a societal change agent. *Journal of Humanistic Psychology,* 1971, 11(1), 11-25.

Dahl, R. *Modern political analysis.* Englewood Cliffs, N.J.: Prentice-Hall, 1963.

Eulau, H. *The behavioral persuasion in politics.* New York: Random House, 1963.

Freud, S. *Civilization and its discontents.* Translated by J. Strachey. New York: W. W. Norton, 1961. (Originally published: 1930)

Freud, S. My contact with Josef Popper-Lynkeus. In *Character and culture* from Collier Books edition of *The collected papers of Sigmund Freud.* Translated by J. Strachey. New York: Crowell-Collier, 1963. (Originally published: 1932)

Freud, S., & Breuer, J. *Studies on hysteria.* Translated by J. Strachey. London: Hogarth Press, 1955. (Originally published: 1893)

Fromm, E., Suzuki, D., & De Martino, R. *Zen Buddhism and psychoanalysis.* New York: Harper Colophon, 1970.

Glenn, M. Introduction to J. Agel (Ed.) *The radical therapist.* New York: Ballantine, 1971, x-xi.

Halleck, S. *The politics of therapy.* New York: Science House, 1971.

Hampden-Turner, C. *Radical man,* Cambridge, Mass.: Schenkman, 1971.

Lasswell, H. *Psychopathology and politics.* Chicago: University of Chicago Press, 1930.

Lasswell, H. *Politics: Who gets what, when, how.* New York: Peter Smith, 1950.

Lippmann, W. *A preface to politics.* New York: Mitchell Kennedy, 1913.

Lippmann, W. *Public opinion.* New York: Harcourt, Brace & World, 1922.

Mannheim, K. *Man and society in an age of reconstruction.* New York: Harcourt, Brace & World, 1940.

Matson, F. *The broken image.* New York: George Braziller, 1964.

Maslow, A. *Motivation and personality.* New York: Harper & Row, 1954.

Maslow, A. A theory of metamotivation: The biological rooting of the value-life. *Journal of Humanistic Psychology,* 1967, **7**(2), 93-127.

Maslow, A. *Toward a psychology of being.* Litton Educational Publishing, 1968.

McConnell, J. Criminals can be brainwashed—now. *Psychology Today,* April 1970.

Parsons, T. Definitions of health and illness in the light of American values and social structure. In E. Jaco (Ed.), *Patients, physicians and illness,* Glencoe, Ill.: Free Press, 1963, 176.

Perls, F. *Gestalt therapy verbatim.* Moab, Utah: Real People Press, 1969.

Perls, F., Hefferline, R., & Goodman, P. *Gestalt therapy.* New York: Delta, 1965.

Reich, W. *The function of the orgasm.* New York: Noonday press, 1942.

Reich, W. *The mass psychology of fascism.* New York: Orgone Institute Press, 1946.

Reich, W. *The mass psychology of fascism.* New York: Farrar, Straus & Giroux, 1970.

Rieff, P. *Freud, the mind of the moralist.* New York: Viking, 1959.

Roazen, P. *Freud: Political and social thought.* New York: Knopf, 1968.

Robinson, P. *The Freudian left.* New York: Harper Colophon, 1969.

Rogers, C. *Client-centered therapy.* Boston: Houghton-Mifflin, 1951.

Rogow, A. *The psychiatrists.* New York: G. P. Putnam's Sons, 1970.

Roszak, T. *The making of a counter culture.* New York: Doubleday Anchor, 1969.

Sennett, R. Review of B. Skinner, *Beyond freedom and dignity. New York Times Book Review,* 24 October 1971.

Szasz, T. *Law, liberty and psychiatry.* New York: Macmillan, 1963.

Szasz, T. *The manufacture of madness.* New York: Delta, 1971.

HUMANISTIC POLITICAL SCIENCE: AND HUMANE POLITICS

Floyd W. Matson

It was George Orwell, I believe, who first made our generation aware of the compelling relationship between political discourse and political behavior. He made his point most dramatically, of course, in the anti-utopian novel *Nineteen Eighty-Four*—in which words became the surgical instruments for mass menticide, a kind of verbal lobotomy practiced upon entire populations by those specialists from the Ministry of Truth whom I cannot help thinking of as the operant conditioners and positive reinforcers.

Orwell also made the same point with equal effectiveness in an essay of nearly twenty years ago entitled "Politics and the English Language," in which he demonstrated how the vocabulary of technical abstraction and official rationalization had already altered our perception of political acts and human crises. Perhaps the classic example of this subliminal modification of perspectives was Stalin's famous "solution" of the Kulak problem, which introduced the term *liquidation* to the language of politics. The very terminology of explanation in effect transformed the brutal slaughter of millions of peasants into an administrative exercise conducted with Stakhanovite precision.

But now I must qualify my earlier remark: that is not quite the classic example. The classic example—may it never be improved upon—was the solution of the Jewish problem by the laboratory technicians and "behavioral engineers" of the Third Reich. In light of the principle of linguistic determinism, it is less difficult to understand how millions of good Germans were able to blind themselves to the mass extermination going on virtually before their eyes. They were, in fact, protected by an armory of perceptual defenses—what Harry Stack Sullivan called the capacity for selective inattention. The events out there in front

SOURCE: Floyd W. Matson, "Humanistic Political Science: and Humane Politics," *Journal of Humanistic Psychology*, Spring 1967. Reprinted by permission. Presented before the Annual Convention of the American Association for Humanistic Psychology, New York City, August 31, 1966.

of them were filtered through the "pictures in their heads," and those stereotyped pictures were painted by the language of objective description and explanation. What the good burghers then perceived was not genocide but eugenics; not extermination but experimentation; not the torture and burning of countless men, women, and children, but the strategic solution of a problem in mathematics.

An instructive illustration of the transforming power of language, cited by Orwell in his essay, is the familiar phrase "pacification of the villages"—which, as I recall, he attributed to the Communists. Somehow I think Orwell would not have been surprised to learn that it is we, the adversaries of Communism and defenders of human dignity, who now invoke the phrase recurrently to account for the burning and bombing of countless men, women, and children in Vietnam.

But I overstate the case, to be sure: the numbers of the victims are not really countless. On the contrary they are quite countable, and statistically even rather unimpressive. (We are assured every now and then, however, that we do have a "favorable kill rate"—surely a comforting thought.) Perhaps we should ask ourselves whether we will respond to the enormity of our actions when the numbers of the slain become enormous—that is, when the nuclear weapons are unleashed. Or will we allow our perceptions, our feelings, our sensibilities, to be overborne by the tranquilizing neologisms of "megadeath," "overkill," "escalation," "floorspace," and the rest of the new strategic-military vocabulary? Do you know, by the way, what "floorspace" is? Let me enlighten you: it is the cleared area of deadly radiation surrounding the point at which a nuclear device (pardon me, a *bomb*) has been exploded.

The style of our discourse, in short, not only reflects the style of our thought and experience; it also shapes it. This was the main thrust of the Whorf-Sapir hypothesis concerning language and culture; it has long been an axiom of the general semanticists; and indeed the concept is possibly as old as the magical veneration of the *Logos*. "In the beginning was the Word." It is noteworthy that whenever the ancients wished to clinch some disputed point with total finality, they had only to say: "It is written . . ." (The modern version of this conversation-stopper is, of course, "If you read it in the *Sun*, it must be true.")

I believe that there are two discernible styles or modes of discourse, two opposed vocabularies, which have contested for supremacy throughout the political tradition of the West. They are variously named; the Greeks knew them as the modes of *dialectic* and *rhetoric*. I prefer to identify them, following Martin Buber, simply as *dialogue* and *monologue*.

The dialogical mode of communication is that which is appropriate to questioning and questing, to learning and yearning, to meeting and understanding. It is the open-ended grammar of discussion and dissent, of contingency and toleration—and the toleration it implies most strongly is that which Else Frenkel-Brunswik used to call "the tolerance of ambiguity." This is the mode which existentialists from Kierkegaard to Jaspers have defined as "authentic communication," in opposition to the mere "talk" which is monologue. It is this connective tissue which permits Abraham Maslow to speak of the "isomorphic interrelationship between the knower and the known" (1966, pp. 195-206), and which has enabled Carl Rogers to develop his participative therapy of mutual respect and unconditional regard. In another but related field it designates that tradition of civility which has been celebrated by Joseph Wood Krutch (1953, Chap. 10), among others, as the heritage of Moral Discourse. And it is what Robert Maynard Hutchins (1956) for some decades has been affirming as the Great Conversation and the Civilization of the Dialogue. I should like to quote Hutchins on this at a little more length:

"The Civilization of the Dialogue," he has written, "is the only civilization worth having and the only civilization in which the whole world can unite. It is, therefore, the only civilization we can hope for, because the world must unite or be blown to bits. The Civilization of the Dialogue requires communication . . . . It assumes that every man has reason and that every man can use it. It preserves to every man his independent judgment and, since it does so, it deprives any man or group of men of the privilege of forcing their judgment upon any other man or group of men. The Civilization of the Dialogue is the negation of force."

Opposed to this open society of the dialogue is the totalitarian system of the monologue. The monological mode of discourse is declined, as a grammarian might put it, in the objective or accusative case. Its purpose is not to commune but to command; its concern not to participate but to persuade. The monologue does not provide an avenue through which one seeks the truth; rather, it is the medium through which the Truth, once revealed and certain, is proclaimed and propagated.

The distinction between the dialogical and monological modes of communication may be personalized as the distinction between Socrates and Callicles (or Thrasymachus). In a later age it was the difference between Marcus Brutus and Mark Antony. In our own time it was the difference, almost exactly, between the two figures who dominated American public address during the 1950's: Adlai Stevenson and Joseph R. McCarthy. If the concept of dialogue embodies what Lippmann has termed "the public philosophy," the concept of monologue reflects what Richard Hofstadter has called (in the title of his latest book) *The Paranoid Style in American Politics*.

But this set of contrasts possibly oversimplifies the issue. For there is also abroad in the land a kind of white-collar paranoia, a soft-sell monologue, which is much more dangerous than the jungle jingoism of the McCarthys and Birchers. This is the discursive style which carries the sound, not of madness, but of purest rationality—the sound not of passion, but of neutrality. And it is this well-bred monologue—the voice of "Science" itself, patient, detached, strategic, operational—which carries, if we attend to it, the message of our doom.

I am reminded, as I write these lines, of a portion of the memorable address delivered by William Faulkner (1949) on the occasion of accepting the Nobel Prize for literature. "It is easy enough," said Faulkner, "to say that man is immortal simply because he will endure; that when the last ding-dong of doom has clanged and faded from the last red and dying sunset, that even then there will be one more sound: that of his puny inexhaustible voice, still talking. I refuse to accept this," he said. "I believe that man will not merely endure, he will prevail. He is immortal, not because he alone among creatures has an inexhaustible voice, but because he has a soul, a spirit, capable of compassion, and sacrifice, and endurance . . ."

Faulkner was talking about the difference between monologue and dialogue—between the inexhaustible voice, just talking, and the compassionate spirit, forever listening and sharing. He knew that we could never be saved by rhetoric, but only by communion. But we have moved no closer to that goal in the seventeen years since he spoke at Stockholm. In the interim the very phrase he uttered as a declaration of faith—"I believe that man . . . will prevail"—has become the desperate question addressed to the world by Erich Fromm (1961): "May Man Prevail?"

The answer may depend upon which voice he hears—which channel he is tuned in to. And in the light of recent developments, both in the tower and the abyss—in political science and in politics—there is very little ground for optimism. The monological mode of discourse indisputably dominates both arenas. This is indeed the contention fiercely argued by Herbert Marcuse (1964, pp. 12, 14) in his recent book bearing the notable title *One-Dimensional Man*. There the political philosopher points to the emergence of "a pattern of one-dimensional thought and behavior in which ideas, aspirations, and objectives that, by their content, transcend the established universe of discourse and action are either repelled or reduced to the terms of this universe." Relating this trend to the rise of operationalism in physical science and behaviorism in social science, Marcuse asserts that "the new mode of thought is today the predominant tendency in philosophy, psychology, sociology, and other fields." Beyond the academy, he maintains, "one-dimensional thought is systematically promoted by the makers of politics and the purveyors of mass information. Their universe of discourse is populated by self-validating hypotheses which, incessantly and monopolistically repeated, become hypnotic definitions or dictations."

This one-dimensional universe of discourse, sanctioned by the categories of its empirical science and formal logic, takes the form of a "technological rationality" which simply rules out of the forum as irrational and irrelevant all that disputes its premises or questions its authority. Our society, says Marcuse, "bars a whole type of oppositional operations and behavior; consequently, the concepts pertaining to them are rendered illusory or meaningless . . . . The operational and behavioral point of view, practiced as a 'habit of thought' at large, becomes the view of the established universe of discourse and action, needs and aspirations . . . . Theoretical and practical Reason, academic and social behaviorism meet on common ground: that of an advanced society which makes scientific and technical progress into an instrument of domination" (pp. 15-16).

The one-dimensional or monological mode of discourse—the language of technical rationality—is also the target of attack in another striking study published at the same time: Anatol Rapoport's *Strategy and Conscience*. The thesis of Rapoport's book is that the cool-headed strategists of game theory, both in the academy and in the government, are leading us down a one-way street of discourse which must terminate, literally, in a dead end for civilization. The only possibility of escape is in reversing course, breaking through the barriers imposed by this mechanistic style of thought, and returning to the mode of moral discourse which reasons not in terms of strategy but in terms of conscience.

What is most remarkable about this argument is that its author, a distinguished mathematician, has been one of the chief expounders of the game-theoretical approach to problems of political and international strategy. Not only has he now had the insight to see the handwriting on the blackboard; he has had the courage to repudiate it and warn against its tyranny. To Rapoport the issue of war and peace, of survival or extinction, is too important to be left to the strategic planners and rational policy-makers. Civilization has become a race between strategy and conscience—between the monological mode of objective calculation and value-neutrality, on the one hand, and the dialogical mode of "conscience-inspired thinking" on the other. Indeed, the central question of the book—concerning which the author is bitterly pessimistic—is whether a meaningful dialogue is possible between these radically opposite ways of thought and discourse.

One of the most hopeful signs of a change for the better in political science—of a breakthrough out of mechanism into humanism—is, I believe, just this shock of moral recognition on the part of more than a few prominent practitioners of hard-core social and physical science. Only a couple of years ago, three sociologists of my acquaintance published a textbook which they dedicated to all the members of the "Humanist Underground" in sociology (Rosenberg, Gerver, & Howton,

1964). I am emboldened to think that more and more of these academic partisans have been surfacing lately, bringing with them into the light of day and of open discussion their revolutionary notes from underground.

What has encouraged and inspirited them, I suspect, is the new mood—not so much of hope as of apprehension—which has been coming over their fellow scientists of behavior and strategy. Rapoport is clearly a case in point; another, still more impressive and indeed remarkable, is that of the late Norbert Wiener, the founding father of cybernetics.

In that brilliant manifesto of the early computer age, *The Human Use of Human Beings,* published in 1950, Wiener revealed the full extent of his genius. He did so by transcending his own scientific categories—by moving beyond cybernetics, and against it. At a time when the awesome power of the new electronic "brains" was just beginning to be recognized, their principal creator had already looked far ahead into the cybernated future and returned with prophetic warnings of the anti-human use of nonhuman machines. "The hour is very late," he announced at the end of a key chapter, "and the choice of good and evil knocks at our door" (1954, p. 186).

Wiener voiced his premonition dramatically through the recitation of three familiar fables: those of the sorcerer's apprentice, the monkey's paw, and the genie in the bottle. Each of these stories tells of a supernatural power capable of granting any wish and carrying out any order; but precisely because the force involved is not of this world, the terror of the tale is in the literal exactness—the relentless rationality—with which the commands are carried out. The very success of the nonhuman agency in executing its tasks carries with it the defeat and doom of its human master.

Wiener (1954, p. 182) went on to point the moral emphatically: beware the temptation to abdicate to the great machine, or to the mechanistic mode of thought, the responsibility for decisions involving human purposes and values. He noted among other things the political extensions of the mathematical theory of games, which had come to exert a hypnotic fascination upon social scientists and decision-makers—rivalling that of the computer itself. "This great game," said Wiener, "is already being carried on mechanistically, and on a colossal scale. . . . A sort of *machine a gouverner* is thus now essentially in operation on both sides of the world conflict, although it does not consist in either case of a single machine which makes policy, but rather of a mechanistic technique which is adapted to the exigencies of a machine-like group of men devoted to the formation of policy."

During the last years of his life, Wiener became increasingly concerned—even obsessed—by the danger of our elevating the Great

Machine, the giant computer, into the status of an oracle. In warning us against this potential inhumanity, he came to appreciate the full significance of the human use of human beings—and to call for a social science and a political wisdom appropriate to that recognition.

Both Wiener, the scientist, and Rapoport, the mathematician, embody to my mind the figure of the new and especially welcome convert to humanism—namely, the reformed mechanist-strategist-behavioralist who has peered deeply into the innermost recesses of the great machine, and there has glimpsed the germinating cell of a malignant possibility. Turning away in fright and remorse, they have joined the ranks of those of us who have long believed, with Hutchins, that the only civilization worth having is the Civilization of the Dialogue—and that the only science worth having is a science, not alone in the cause of operational truth, but in the cause of man.

Permit me a short postscript. There is also a strong degree of hope, from another and different direction, for the advent of humanistic political science. The most constructive event in American higher education in half a century, to my mind, has been the student revolt against the educational monologue: a powerful demand "from below" for the inauguration of a genuine dialogue. This undergraduate declaration of independence carries with it the atmosphere of a humanist activism. For that is what their "radicalism" is: not ideological, not narrowly political, but a *radical humanism* which is making the weight of its concern and commitment felt throughout the whole echoing length of the university corridor. In the face of this new awakening to the values of civil rights and social justice, to the burning issues of poverty and prejudice, political scientists are being forced to re-examine their tired dogmas of value-neutrality and ethical relativism. The politics of abstraction and professional unconcern may at last be giving way, in the academy as well as outside it, to the politics of engagement, responsibility, and care. Let us hope so; for that is humanistic political science—and humane politics.

REFERENCES

Faulkner, W. Nobel Prize acceptance speech. Stockholm, 1949.

Fromm, E. *May Man Prevail?* New York: Doubleday, 1961.

Hutchins, R. M. *Freedom, Education, and the Fund.* New York: World & Meridian, 1956.

Krutch, J. W. *The Measure of Man.* New York: Grosset Universal Library, 1953.

Marcuse, H. *One-Dimensional Man*. Boston: Beacon Press, 1964.

Maslow, A. H. "Isomorphic interrelationships between knower and known." In F. W. Matson & A. Montagu (Eds.), *The Human Dialogue: Perspectives on Communication*. New York: Free Press, 1966.

Rosenberg, B.; Gerver, I.; & Howton, F. W. (Eds.). *Mass Society in Crisis: Social Problems and Social Pathology*. New York: Macmillan, 1964.

Wiener, N. *The Human Use of Human Beings*. Garden City: Doubleday Anchor Books, 1954.